The Morality of

NATIONALISM

The Morality of
NATIONALISM

EDITED BY

Robert McKim & Jeff McMahan

New York   Oxford
OXFORD UNIVERSITY PRESS
1997

Oxford University Press

Oxford   New York

Athens   Auckland   Bangkok   Bogota   Bombay   Buenos Aires
Calcutta   Cape Town   Dar es Salaam   Delhi   Florence   Hong Kong
Istanbul   Karachi   Kuala Lumpur   Madras   Madrid   Melbourne
Mexico City   Nairobi   Paris   Singapore   Taipei   Tokyo   Toronto

and associated companies in
Berlin   Ibadan

Copyright © 1997 by Oxford University Press, Inc.

Published by Oxford University Press, Inc.
198 Madison Avenue, New York, New York 10016

Oxford is a registered trademark of Oxford University Press

Library of Congress Cataloging-in-Publication Data
The morality of nationalism / edited by Robert McKim and Jeff McMahan.
    p.   cm.
Includes bibliographical references and index.
ISBN 0-19-510391-2; ISBN 0-19-510392-0 (pbk.)
1. Nationalism—Moral and ethical aspects.   I. McKim, Robert.
II. McMahan, Jeff.
JC311.M588   1997
320.5'4—dc20   96-21168

9 8 7 6 5 4 3 2 1
Printed in the United States of America
on acid-free paper

To the memory of Gregory Kavka

Contents

Contributors

ALLEN BUCHANAN holds three positions at the University of Wisconsin–Madison: Joel Feinberg Professor of Philosophy, Grainger Professor of Business Ethics, and Professor of the History of Medicine (Program in Medical Ethics). He is the author of over seventy articles and five books in political philosophy, bioethics, ethics, and business ethics. In 1991 his book *Secession: The Morality of Political Divorce*, the first book-length work focusing on the morality of secession, appeared. He is currently working on a book that takes a more institutional approach to the morality of self-determination and will offer a moral foundation for reforming international legal doctrine and practice so that they can deal more effectively and humanely with self-determination crises.

DAVID COPP is Professor of Philosophy at the University of California, Davis. He taught previously at Simon Fraser University and the University of Illinois at Chicago. He has published articles in moral and political philosophy, and he coedited *Morality, Reason, and Truth* and *Pornography and Censorship*. His book, *Morality, Normativity, and Society*, was published in 1995 by Oxford University Press. He is an Associate Editor of *Ethics*.

WALTER FEINBERG is Professor of the Philosophy of Education in the Department of Educational Policy Studies at the University of Illinois. His latest book, *Japan and the Pursuit of a New American Identity: Work and Education in a Multicultural*

Age, was published by Routledge in 1993. In 1996 he was appointed the Benton Scholar at the University of Chicago, where he is writing a book on whether public schools have an obligation to enable subcultural groups to reproduce their cultural identity.

GEORGE FLETCHER is Cardozo Professor of Jurisprudence at the Columbia Law School. His latest books are *Basic Concepts of Legal Thought* (Oxford University Press, 1996) and *With Justice for Some: Protecting Victims' Rights in Criminal Trials* (Addison-Wesley, 1995).

JONATHAN GLOVER teaches philosophy at New College, Oxford.

ROBERT E. GOODIN is Professor of Philosophy, with special reference to social and political philosophy, at the Research School of Social Sciences, Australian National University. He is the founding editor of the *Journal of Political Philosophy*, coeditor of *A New Handbook of Political Science* (Oxford University Press, 1996) and *A Companion to Political Philosophy* (Blackwell, 1993), and author, most recently, of *Utilitarianism as a Public Philosophy* (Cambridge University Press, 1995).

THOMAS HURKA is Professor of Philosophy at the University of Calgary. He is the author of *Perfectionism* (Oxford University Press, 1993) and of numerous articles in moral theory, especially the theory of value.

WILL KYMLICKA is Visiting Professor of Philosophy at the University of Ottawa and at Carleton University. He is the author of *Liberalism, Community, and Culture* (Oxford University Press, 1989) and *Multicultural Citizenship* (Oxford University Press, 1995), the editor of *The Rights of Minority Cultures* (Oxford University Press, 1995), and coeditor (with Ian Shapiro) of *Ethnicity and Group Rights* (New York University Press, forthcoming).

JUDITH LICHTENBERG is Associate Professor of Philosophy at the University of Maryland at College Park and Senior Research Scholar at the university's Institute for Philosophy and Public Policy. She has written on international ethics, immigration, nationalism, and other issues in moral and political philosophy and is the editor of *Democracy and the Mass Media*.

AVISHAI MARGALIT is Professor of Philosophy at the Hebrew University of Jerusalem. He is the author of *The Decent Society* (Harvard University Press, 1996) and coauthor with Moshe Halbertal of *Idolatry* (Harvard University Press, 1992). He writes frequently for the *New York Review of Books*.

ROBERT McKIM is Associate Professor in the Department of Philosophy and in the Program for the Study of Religion at the University of Illinois at Urbana-

Champaign. He has published many articles on the philosophy of religion and applied ethics and on the philosophy of George Berkeley.

JEFF McMAHAN is Associate Professor of Philosophy at the University of Illinois, Urbana-Champaign. He is currently working on *Killing at the Margins of Life* and *The Ethics of Self-Defense and War*, both to be published by Oxford University Press.

STEPHEN NATHANSON is Professor of Philosophy at Northeastern University. He is the author of four books, including *Patriotism, Morality, and Peace* (Rowman and Littlefield, 1993).

ARTHUR RIPSTEIN is Professor of Philosophy and Law at the University of Toronto.

SAMUEL SCHEFFLER is Professor of Philosophy at the University of California at Berkeley. He is the author of *The Rejection of Consequentialism* (Oxford University Press, 1982) and *Human Morality* (Oxford University Press, 1992).

HENRY SHUE is the Wyn and William Y. Hutchinson Professor of Ethics and Public Life and Professor of Philosophy at Cornell University. Before going to Cornell in 1987, he spent eleven years at the University of Maryland's Institute for Philosophy and Public Policy, where he was a founding member and served as Director. He is the author of *Basic Rights* (Princeton University Press, 1980), which in 1996 appeared in a second edition with a new afterword on the institutional implications of right-grounded duties. His most recent articles attempt to bring practical philosophy to bear on global issues, including the development of adequate institutions for handling climate change and the use of military intervention.

YAEL TAMIR is a senior lecturer in the Department of Philosophy at Tel Aviv University. She received a Ph.D. in Political Philosophy from Balliol College, Oxford, working under the supervision of Sir Isaiah Berlin, and has been Visiting Scholar at the Center for Human Values at Princeton University and the Program in Ethics and the Professions at Harvard University. She is the author of *Liberal Nationalism* (Princeton University Press, 1993) and the editor of *Democratic Education in a Multicultural State* (Blackwell, 1995), as well as being author of numerous articles on nationalism, liberal theory, and theories of rights. She is a founding member of Peace Now (the Israeli peace movement) and an active member of the Israeli Civil Rights Association.

CHARLES TAYLOR is Professor of Philosophy and Political Science at McGill University in Montreal. His most recent books include *Sources of the Self* (Harvard University Press, 1989) and *The Ethics of Authenticity* (Harvard University Press, 1992).

MICHAEL WALZER is the UPS Foundation Professor of Social Science at the Institute for Advanced Study in Princeton, New Jersey. He is a coeditor of *Dissent* and a contributing editor of the *New Republic*. His books include *Just and Unjust Wars* (Basic Books, 1977), *Spheres of Justice* (Blackwell, 1983), *Interpretation and Social Criticism* (Harvard University Press, 1987), and *Thick and Thin: Moral Argument at Home and Abroad* (Notre Dame University Press, 1994).

The Morality of
NATIONALISM

1

Introduction

ROBERT McKIM & JEFF McMAHAN

It is incontestable that the resurgence of nationalist sentiment in many areas of the world is one of the most important and least anticipated phenomena of contemporary international politics. People are increasingly conscious of their national identities; they are rediscovering their national histories, pressing for recognition of their distinctness, and making various demands under the banner of national self-determination—for example, demands for the preservation of their cultures and languages, for the right to educate their children in the ways of their ancestors, and often for independent statehood, sometimes with accompanying demands for the expulsion of outsiders from what is regarded as the national homeland. The result, as everyone who can read a newspaper knows, has been a series of struggles—some merely for recognition or enhanced autonomy, others for political dominance, and others still for political separation—that have regularly exploded into violence and atrocious brutality, as, for example, in Bosnia and Chechnya.

To address the problems that contemporary nationalism poses, one must first understand it. There are, however, many dimensions to nationalism and correspondingly many perspectives from which it may be studied. The essays in this volume, all published here for the first time, are intended to illuminate the moral and evaluative dimensions of nationalism. They make no pretense of addressing other issues that are essential to a full understanding. There are, for example, no studies of either past or present instances of nationalism or nationalist conflict, no models for predicting future developments, and no recipes for the prevention or resolution of nationalist conflicts. And although certain chapters do explore the historical and psychological sources of nationalist sentiment, the book as a whole is not a work of social science but remains within the boundaries of moral and political philosophy. It is not, however, a work of moral advocacy. While individual chapters may be broadly pro- or antinationalist in their sympathies, the book as a whole has no agenda but to enhance our understanding of a range of crucial issues.

Some may doubt that specifically moral issues are, in fact, crucial. Practical-minded people are often impatient with what they perceive as the piffling sermonizing of moralists on this and other topics. Our task, they think, is to come to grips with and solve our social and political problems, not to waste time and energy bleating feebly about morality. But at least some moral questions cannot be evaded even by the most resolutely pragmatic person. When they are not explicitly acknowledged, moral and evaluative assumptions lie beneath the surface of every program of action. Even tough-minded realists who are dismissive of the idea that the adjustment of means to ends is constrained by morality must still be guided by some conception of what ends it is desirable to pursue, what changes would be for the better. Thus in every case in which nationalists press for alterations in social structures, political institutions, territorial boundaries, or whatever, it is impossible to have a reasoned response that fails to consider whether the nationalists' inward focus, loyalties and partialities, cultivation of separateness, glorification of their history and customs, claims to self-determination, and so on are defensible and desirable.

It may help to say what we take the central moral and evaluative questions to be, with some indication also of how they are related to one another, why they are relevant to matters of practical concern, and in which essay or essays they are addressed. The essays in part I are primarily concerned with a set of questions about the moral psychology of nationalism that are not strictly normative but nevertheless lie just behind the normative questions that are the main focus of the volume. One such question is whether nationalist sentiments and attachments derive from enduring and unalterable features of human psychology. Is it, for example, inevitable that a sense of tribal belonging will always be central to the sense that individuals have of their own identity? Does identification with one's nation fulfill a need to define oneself in opposition to an enemy, and if so, does this mean that nationalism is necessarily exclusivist, chauvinistic, and at least latently hostile to those outside the nation? Might nationalist attachments arise from a deep human need for shared understandings or perhaps from a need to achieve convergence on certain social conventions, some of which take the form of claims to truth, thereby establishing rival and incompatible systems of thought and practice? These and other related questions are addressed in the essays by Jonathan Glover, Avishai Margalit, and Robert Goodin. The answers to these questions will determine whether nationalism is a phenomenon that in one form or another must be accommodated in our institutions or whether it is a historical accident that may ultimately be reformed beyond recognition or even transcended altogether.

Whether or not the psychological bases of nationalism are a permanent feature of human nature, it is surely true that in periods in the past there were too few people or people were insufficiently territorially concentrated for these elements of human psychology to lead to the development of nations and nationalism. They may have led, for example, to tribalism instead. Indeed, many observers have claimed that nationalism is a response to uniquely modern conditions. It has been argued, for example, that a modern and smoothly functioning economy requires a mobile, flexible, and educated workforce, which in turn requires a common language, a common culture, and a uniform set of educational standards. Modern states therefore have a strong incentive to foster and sustain nationalist sentiments among the citizenry as a whole. These themes are developed in the essay by Charles Taylor, who also contends that nationalism is a distinctively modern phenomenon in that it is a response by traditional elites to pressures toward modernization that tend to disempower them and undermine their dignity. These elites attempt to foster a sense of national unity and identity as a means of asserting their uniqueness and restoring their dignity. These issues receive further discussion in the essays by Walter Feinberg and Will Kymlicka.

It is a defining feature of nationalism that it demands that the members of a nation be loyal both to the nation and to one another, which involves their giving priority to the national interest or each other's interests over the interests of others. The basis for this demand is typically not that the members of the nation are held to be objectively more worthy than others (which, after all, would give outsiders as much reason to favor them as they themselves would have) but that they are related to one another in ways that give them special moral reasons to favor one another. This view raises many difficult questions. What exactly are the relations that bind people together as nations? Are these relations sufficiently morally significant to justify the departures from impartiality that nationalism requires, rather in the way that relations among the members of a family justify loyalty and partiality among them? Or are the relations that are constitutive of conationality more like the relations that define membership in a race, so that national loyalty and partiality may be no more defensible than racism? Even if nationalism is relevantly like racism, the question remains whether it would be possible for people to live decent lives in the absence of those relations that divide people into nations. If not, then must we tolerate the partiality that these relations naturally elicit even though the relations themselves are devoid of intrinsic moral significance? These and related questions are discussed in the essays in part II by Jeff McMahan, Thomas Hurka, Judith Lichtenberg, and Stephen Nathanson.

Nationalism poses particular problems for the liberal theory of the state. Liberals are committed to a belief in the fundamental moral equality of persons. The question whether this belief is compatible with the demands for loyalty and partiality that are integral to nationalism is explored in Samuel Scheffler's contribution in part III. Should liberals repudiate nationalism? Defenders of nationalism often argue that the liberal state is, in fact, critically dependent for its unity and stability on prepolitical bonds that can be provided only by national attachments. Certainly it is true that states typically attempt to forge their populations into nations in an effort to motivate people to make the kinds of sacrifices that modern political organization requires. Yael Tamir, in her essay, explores in detail the ways in which states exploit national sentiment to inspire a willingness among their citizens to make the ultimate sacrifice: risking their lives in defense of the community. Arthur Ripstein's essay disputes the dependence of liberalism on nationalism, noting that the sacrifices required by liberal conceptions of justice and fairness may be quite different from the sacrifices that might be prompted by national solidarity.

The essays by Michael Walzer and Robert McKim in part IV probe the sorts of attitude that members of one nation may have concerning those of another, with particular attention to the sorts of moral attitude that might induce national groups to coexist peacefully with one another. For example, what forms may tolerance among nations take and what sorts of political arrangements are best suited to encouraging each variety of tolerance? And in cases in which nations that are reasonably decent are in competition with each other, is it morally incumbent upon them to move beyond tolerance and to cultivate a sense of pan-national identity and loyalty?

The themes of sovereignty, self-determination, and the value of cultural diversity are the topics of the essays in part V. Is it important for groups, and in particular nations, to be self-determining? If it is, does this mean that each nation has a right to its own state? Is the idea that a nation has a right to self-determination antidemocratic in that it denies minorities who live in the territory over which the nation aspires to have control but who are not part of the nation the right to have a say in the critical decision about independent statehood? Under what conditions should a nation's claim to secession and independent statehood be recognized by others? Must a credible case for secession depend on the need to rectify a wrong, such as an unjust confiscation of land or the violation of human rights? These are among the questions addressed in the essays by David Copp and Allen Buchanan.

Even if we assume that nations have rights to self-determination and that, in some cases at least, the right to self-determination implies a right to independent statehood, there remain further questions about the scope of the sovereign rights that states claim for themselves. We have seen, for example, that nationalists believe that the nation is justified in giving priority to the national interest over the interests of outsiders. But what are the limits to the degree of priority (if any) that is morally justified? Henry Shue, in his essay, considers whether the doctrine of state sovereignty may legitimate a state's pursuit of domestic policies that cause great harm to people beyond their borders (for example, economic policies with global environmental effects).

Further questions that are addressed in various places in the book concern what might be called cultural rather than political self-determination. Do nations have a right to defend their cultures, and given the central role of language in determining the character of a culture, do they (as George Fletcher puts it) have a right of linguistic self-defense? More generally, does it matter whether numerous different cultures flourish, and how important is it to try to preserve particular cultures? The idea that different nations give expression to irreconcilable or incommensurable values—a theme pursued by Margalit—provides the basis for one argument for cultural pluralism and cultural preservation.

This volume consists largely of essays that were presented in earlier drafts at a conference held at the University of Illinois at Urbana-Champaign in April 1994. We would like to thank the following people whose lively participation in the conference helped to shape the ideas and arguments developed in the book, though their own contributions are not directly represented here: Benedict Anderson, Brian Barry, Stephen Douglas, Michael Doyle, Gerald Dworkin, Belden Fields, Liah Greenfeld, Russell Hardin, Carol Leff, David Little, and Thomas Pogge. Arthur Ripstein and Samuel Scheffler generously permitted us to use their papers even though they were not presented at the conference.

We would also like to express our gratitude to the sponsors who made the conference, and hence this volume, possible. We received generous support from the United States Institute of Peace, International Programs and Studies at the University of Illinois at Urbana-Champaign, the Midwest Consortium for International Security Studies, the John D. and Catherine T. MacArthur Foundation, the Carnegie Council on Ethics and International Affairs, the Council for European Studies at Columbia University, and the Program for the Study of Cultural Values and Ethics at the University of Illinois at Urbana-Champaign. We owe special thanks to our colleague Walter Feinberg, who encouraged and contributed to this project from its earliest conception in his capacity as director of the Program for the Study of Cultural Values and Ethics.

Finally, with the enthusiastic approval of all of our authors, we dedicate this volume to the memory of Gregory Kavka, whose early and tragic death prevented him from enlivening it with his own contribution.

I

THE NATURE, SOURCES, AND PSYCHOLOGY OF NATIONALISM

2

Nations, Identity, and Conflict

JONATHAN GLOVER

> We lived happily together for many years and now it has come to killing each
> other's babies. What is happening to us?
>
> —Indira Hadziomerovic, mourning in Sarajevo,
> reported in the London *Independent*, August 8, 1992

There are two histories of nationalism. One history, repeated many times, is of a people rightly struggling to be free. They eventually break away from their large neighbor, a colonial power, or the Soviet Union to attain the dignity of self-governing nationhood. The other history, repeated many times, is of nationalism as tribal conflict. This is the story of the European nations and their quarrels that culminated in war in 1914. More recently it is the story of seemingly endless reciprocal killing: the story of Armenia and Azerbaijan, of Israel and Palestine, of the factions in the Nigerian civil war, of Iran and Iraq, of Greeks and Turks in Cyprus, of nationalists and unionists in Northern Ireland, of the participants in the ethnic conflict in Sri Lanka. It is the story of what was once Yugoslavia.

Are these two histories or one? Is there a good nationalism, linked to freedom and self-government, that can be distinguished from the kind of nationalism whose results can be seen from Belfast to Bosnia? Or is commitment to the idea of a nation-state a dangerous psychological weakness, something to be contained and, if possible, eradicated?

I will approach these questions by exploring three issues. The first is the nature of nationalism. The second is its psychology. Finally, I will put the psychological comments to use in thinking about nationalist conflict and how to contain it.

Nations and Nation-States

Nationalism is the belief that a nation should have self-determination. This is usually thought of in terms of every nation having its own state. There is a universal version: every nation should have self-determination. And there is the particular version: this nation should have self-determination.

Nationalism can function as a solvent, as when it undid the links between Czechs and Slovaks. And it can function as a glue, bringing together people previously separate, as in the Risorgimento. Both aspects can be seen in Giuseppe Mazzini's slogan: "Every nation a state, only one state for the entire nation."[1]

The belief that a nation should have its own state is not clear. The trouble does not come from the phrase "its own state," which refers to a constitution and set of laws and the existence of an independent government. (There is vagueness. How independent is the government of a member state of the European Community or the government of a banana republic? But even these fuzzy edges are relatively unimportant here.) The main obscurity is in the concept of a nation.

The Social Construction of the Nation

Nationality is often thought of as something "natural" or presocial. Swedes are different from Italians in the way the fish of the Baltic are different from those of the Mediterranean. This sense of naturalness is reinforced by stories nations often have about their own antiquity. But some historians and social scientists emphasize the relative modernity of the European nation-states, dating them from around the end of the eighteenth century.[2]

Various influences on the rise of those nation-states are cited. It is suggested that the division of labor created by the transition from an agrarian to an industrial-capitalist economy required large economic units. These in turn may have needed some centralized control of public order and defense, together with a standardized education system. The dominance of national languages may have come partly from the decline of the idea of Christendom and the resulting fading of Latin. The economic need for communication within large units and for national administration is cited to explain why national languages defeated regional dialects. A national base provided a more profitable market than a regional one for the products of print technology.

If these suggestions are correct, European states arose partly for other reasons in addition to being a vehicle for a preexisting national consciousness. In at least some cases, the state may have come into existence before there was much sense of nationhood. Eric Hobsbawm quotes a speaker in the first meeting of the Parliament of the new Kingdom of Italy as saying that "we have made Italy, now we have to make Italians."[3]

In Africa there are more extreme cases of nation-states arising independently of any sense of nationhood. Many state boundaries were lines drawn on maps by colonial governments and administrators, often cutting through the middle of territories inhabited by Africans who felt part of a single community and often putting together groups who had no sense of shared identity.[4]

These accounts by historians and social scientists tend to describe nations as products of nation-states rather than the other way around. And nation-states in turn are explained by citing their usefulness, whether to industrialists and capitalists or to colonial rulers.

No doubt in many cases such factors are part of the explanation of nationhood. But it is hard to believe they are the whole story. I suggest that once we go beyond economic interests or the interests of colonizers, we can see the psychological needs that are met by the sense of nationhood and by the nation-state. A deeper explanation of nationalism requires exploration of these other needs. It is important for this exploration to note that people emotionally committed to nations do not think of them in instrumental terms or as social constructions. They are often thought of in more tribal terms.

The "Tribal" Nation as an Ideal Type

Nationalists often think of their nation in ways influenced by a traditional model of a "pure" or "ideal" case. This ideal version is of a people inhabiting a single, unified territory. All territorial boundaries are clear and undisputed, and there are no minorities over the border. The "people" are a tribe. They are a single ethnic group. They have a common language. They have a shared history, which involves their having a common culture. This culture typically includes shared religious beliefs. The unity of the culture is sustained partly by a common pattern of education and partly by access to such things as the same newspapers and the same television programs.

To talk in this way of a tribal nation is to use a metaphor that may not be very securely grounded in reality. The word "tribe" is typically used by Europeans to describe African groupings, and some are skeptical about its usefulness there. Basil Davidson suggests that the word has no clear meaning and that colonial rulers intent on dividing Africans into tribes sometimes had to invent the tribes.[5] Even if some of the tribes were partly European constructions, the great physical and cultural differences that are sometimes found suggest that not all tribes were merely colonial inventions. But even if originally there had been no tribes in Africa (or anywhere else), the word would still be useful, if only to stand for an ideal type.

The pure case of the tribal nation might seem ideal in another way. Without the conflicts generated by blurred or disputed borders, there might be the hope that tribal nations would live together as good neighbors. Each nation would delight in its own ethnicity, religion, culture, and language, without any hostility to the nation next door.

Why does this seem so unlike most of the real world? One obvious answer is that much of the real world has territorial boundaries only of the messy or disputed kind. And there are other complications. According to one view, the Jewish people before the founding of Israel were a nation without a territory. (This would not mean they had to want their own state. The members of a nation do not have to be, in that way, nationalists.) The United States is only one example of a state with great ethnic variety. Belgium, Switzerland, and Canada are among states without a single unifying language. Between 1945 and 1989, the people of Germany had a divided history. And many states have religious diversity. These departures from the ideal type may lead to a good deal of social construction, such as the efforts to create a shared sense of being American.

Groups, Tribalism, and Identity

If it is true that nationalism arose in Europe only about the time of the industrial revolution, some more general term is needed to include whatever made Englishmen and Frenchmen fight each other at Agincourt. Even without the modern nation-state, it was still the English versus the French and not short versus tall or peasants versus lords. I will use the word "tribalism" to cover the psychological attachments that made the English versus the French the natural conflict even before the nation-state. Tribalism may be the deeper phenomenon, of which nationalism is the currently dominant variant.

In most group conflicts, members of different groups are marked off from each other by some distinguishing characteristics that typically carry an emotional charge, such as religion or ethnicity. One question is whether the psychological core of tribalism is a shared possession of such "charged" characteristics or whether the core has to do with group membership as such.

Minimal Groups

There is some evidence that people can identify with one group and feel hostility toward another even in the case of "minimal groups," those sharing no potentially charged characteristics. The extreme case is where group membership is known to be random. Identification and hostility in such a case came out in a classic social psychological study by Philip Zimbardo.[6] College students who agreed to participate in a "prison" role-playing study were assigned randomly either to the group of "prisoners" or to the group of "prison guards." The participants developed strong identification with their own group and hostility to the other group. After several days, the "prison guards" were treating the "prisoners" so badly that the study had to be called off. This propensity of human beings for identification and hostility even in the case of minimal groups is a puzzling psychological phenomenon.

Group Conflict and the Sociobiological Hypothesis

Biologists sometimes suggest that certain behavior patterns may result from genetically programmed dispositions that had survival value in an earlier environment. Konrad Lorenz cites the example of mobbing a predator, which may once have helped cows and pigs defend themselves against wolves. Modern domestic cows and pigs that have never been threatened by wolves retain the tendency to mob people or animals appearing in their midst.[7]

Some sociobiologists suggest that the disposition toward group identification and rivalry may be a residue of this kind, to be understood as something once conducive to gene survival. W. D. Hamilton's concept of "inclusive fitness" is relevant.[8] Darwin's version of fitness was personal fitness: the individual's capacity to survive and reproduce. But the shift to thinking in terms of gene survival means that the genetic similarity between related individuals is also relevant. The survival of several of someone's relations may do more than his or her own survival for the survival of that person's genes. Hamilton's "inclusive fitness" combines personal fitness with this kinship component.

Inclusive fitness provides the basis of the sociobiological account of the tendency toward group identification and group hostility.[9] A disposition to protect genetically related people from attacks by others could help gene survival. The early development of weapons that allowed killing at a distance would make unrelated individuals more dangerous. This might give added survival value both to fear of other groups and to hostility toward them.

Such a theory needs to explain why the groups that generate identification and hostility are not all kin groups. An explanation can be given by citing the evolutionary advantages of alliances between kin groups to dominate others, together with the advantages of reciprocal altruism within the resulting larger group.

The account suffers from a problem common to much sociobiological explanation. What are the constraints on such an explanation? The danger is that almost anything can be argued to be just what you would have expected to emerge from the evolutionary competition. If there had been a tendency to feel friendly toward other groups and help them, this could no doubt have been explained as coming from the biological advantages of reciprocal altruism. Because these explanations do not predict but explain after the event, they are too easy. This is not to say that such genetically programmed dispositions never exist. Group identification and hostility may well be among such dispositions. But whether this is so will be clearer when the criteria for adequacy have developed beyond intuitions about what sounds like a plausible story.

The idea of a biologically grounded disposition to group conflict has consider-able plausibility. But it is questionable how far this would explain tribalism as a specific form of group identification. A genetically programmed disposition to group identification and group hostility may be the explanation of the Zimbardo phenomenon of identification and hostility even in the case of minimal groups. But even if this is right, we need to supplement the sociobiological account with a psychological account. The explanation of tribalism needs to go beyond account-ing for hostility between minimal groups.

It is at least necessary to explain why some groups and not others generate tribal identification and hostility. Take the case of negotiations within the European Union about economic policy. Sometimes the French government presses for higher food prices to help farmers while the British government presses for lower food prices to help consumers. The result, where it is not an even compromise, is always presented as a victory for France or for Britain rather than as a victory for farmers or for consumers. People do not identify with groups such as farmers and consumers in the way they do with nations. Why, in the modern world, does trib-alism focus on religious, linguistic, ethnic, or territorial groups and in particular on nations?

Identity, Self-Creation, and Tribalism

The hypothesis I want to put forward is a partial explanation of tribalism in terms of our need to create something coherent out of ourselves and our own lives. If there is anything in this, tribalism has roots that go very deep in our psy-chology. Those roots make its elimination impossible or at least dauntingly diffi-cult. Some will welcome this. Others will find it depressing. Those who, like me, find it depressing to accept that tribalism is virtually indestructible will have to think of ways of taming it.

A natural way of thinking of oneself is as a Cartesian ego. My empirical charac-teristics, both physical and mental, are subject to change. Old age may ravage my body, my memory may go, and my personality may change. But behind all of this, I am still fully there.

This Cartesian view has variants in religious beliefs about the soul and in the Kantian "noumenal self." It has fallen on bad times. Lichtenberg argued that Descartes's cogito proves only the occurrence of a perhaps impersonal thought, not the existence of a thinking self. Nietzsche agreed, suggesting that we get used to "getting along without that little 'it' (which is what the honest old 'I' has evapo-rated into)." Hume attacked the ego for its empirical unobservability. William James agreed: "The Ego is simply nothing: as ineffectual and windy an abortion as Philosophy can show." And, in our own time, Derek Parfit has argued that what matters across a lifetime is not the elusive all-or-nothing identity but rather sur-vival, which is a matter of degree.

This reductionist view seems to leave personal unity across a lifetime a more precarious affair than we have usually supposed. Our unity rests on shifting ground: on physical and mental characteristics that may come and go rather than on the persisting ego that was supposed to own them all. The reductionist view is sometimes supported by an analogy with nations. Hume says: "I cannot compare the soul more properly to anything than to a republic, or commonwealth." Parfit agrees: France exists, but it is not an entity distinct from its citizens and its territory. People exist, but a similar reductionist account applies to them. And according to this view, "the fact of personal identity is less deep."[10]

If personal identity is thought of as a "fact," the strong grounds for skepticism about the Cartesian ego do indeed help to undermine its importance. A person's life may consist of a series of stages that are related only contingently and perhaps weakly. In principle, at least, there may be little more coherence between the stages of life than there is between the stones in a pile. Any one stone that happens to be part of this pile could well have been part of another. According to this viewpoint, death becomes less important, as all any individual's death means is that there will be no future experiences related in certain ways to these present ones. There will be similar experiences; it is just that they will be members of series other than this one. There will be other stones; they will just be in piles other than this one.

But the unity of life is perhaps not best seen as a "fact" that is discovered to be there to some degree or other. An alternative view is that this unity is something we, at least in part, create. The analogy with nations holds in more complex ways than Hume and Parfit suggest. Nations and people are not just similar in that there exists neither a national soul nor a metaphysical ego. They are also similar in being to some extent artifacts rather than things whose nature is given.

Many of us care about what sort of people we are, and many of the characteristics we want to have are long-term. The psychoanalyst Carl Jung may have wanted to be someone of integrity, wisdom, and spiritual depth. Perhaps his early life fitted this description. But in 1933 he replaced the editor of a psychiatric journal who resigned because he could not accept its subordination to Nazi ideology. The first issue under Jung's editorship published a Nazi statement saying that *Mein Kampf* was essential reading for psychiatrists. Jung himself wrote in the journal that "the Jewish race as a whole" had an unconscious that could be compared with the Aryan "only with reserve." Saying that Freud and his followers had not understood the German psyche, Jung asked: "Has the formidable phenomenon of National Socialism, on which the whole world gazes with astonished eyes, taught them better?"[11] The conception of Jung as a man of integrity and wisdom is destroyed by these remarks.

It is possible to defend the integrity of a "time slice" of Jung. Jung-before-1933 may have had integrity. But some of us want our central characteristics to be more durable. And this may involve a long-term process of self-creation. This is one reason why an early death can be tragic. To return to the stone metaphor, the thought that it does not matter if there are fewer stones on a particular heap is unconvincing if the stones were being used to create a building that will now remain unfinished.

People care about what their lives add up to. It may seem paradoxical to give this as a reason for the importance of self-creation. Must not the person already be a persisting ego in order to have this kind of concern? Or does the concern belong merely to a momentary time slice? Neither of these need be true. The importance of the concern is bound up with its depth and persistence. But a deep and persistent concern need not presuppose an ego to which this concern belongs. Or, to put it the other way around, the nonexistence of an ego does not entail that all concerns are shallow and brief.

The process of self-creation is partly that of a novelist telling a coherent story about a character. The mixture of freedom and constraint is similar. Various possibilities may be open, but what the character can do depends partly on circumstances and partly on other people in the story. There are also limits on how far acting "out of character" is possible. This story we create about ourselves, partly by what we do and partly by how we edit and narrate the story of our past, is central to our sense of our own identity.

But the story is bound up with the context in which it takes place. This is partly physical context; to be forced into exile is, among other things, to be excluded from the places where the earlier parts of the story took place. It is partly the context of other people. What I did was done with them or done in response to what they did or said. I still carry their hopes and expectations with me. The values that guided what I have done (and that color the tone of the narrative) inevitably were shaped partly by them.

Because both the people and the places we have known are intrinsic to the story, loss of either is a complex deprivation. We lose the pleasures of being with those people in those places. We also lose some of the grip we had on the reality of our earlier story, more of which now has to rely on fugitive memory images. And we lose people who were part of our story's perhaps unconsciously half-intended audience. After someone has died, we may later become aware of this role he or she had when we do something and notice that the deceased is not there to see or be told about it. Not only do particular people shape the content and narrative tone of the story, but also we may see them partly as libraries in which our lives' stories are safely kept. And as we tell the story or act it out, we need these people to listen, and we hope for their recognition of what we are like.

The role of places in our self-creative story makes the emotional pull of territory unsurprising. This makes it more natural to identify with the interests of a geographically based nation than, for instance, with the interests of farmers.

And the role of particular people in our self-creative story makes our identification with them natural, too. (This is of course just one reason why we identify with people we know. Other, less egocentric reasons are usually at least as strong.) But this account of the role of people close to us faces a problem parallel to that faced by the sociobiological account of tribalism. Just as the nations and other groups with which we identify are far larger than the group of those we are genetically related to, so they are far larger than the group of people who have a role to play in our personal story.

The relationships that are so important to us, both for our sense of identity and for other reasons, normally draw heavily on a shared cultural background. A shared frame of reference, a common history (passed on by a common education), and a shared sense of humor all create a context in which relationships and identity can flourish. And in turn this cultural context is tied up in obvious ways with a shared language. (Anyone who knows, as I do, what it is to speak another language badly will know how this coarsens the texture of relationships and forces you to present a drastically simple and crude version of what you want to say and hence of yourself.)

The ways in which we think of our identity and shape it are in these different ways bound up with a shared language and culture. Because of this, we care about the survival of our language and cultural traditions. We want what has mattered to us to survive. The nation is often seen as at least the best defense of these things and sometimes as their embodiment.

It is also within a particular culture and language that our created identity is validated by the recognition bestowed by others.[12] So any lack of respect for our culture and language in turn devalues our personal self-respect.

Nationalism and the Roots of Conflict

Tribes are marked off from one another by some combination of ethnicity, religion, shared territory, language, and shared culture. Needs linked to creating and maintaining personal identity are part of the explanation of why these particular differences between people are the basis of tribal identification. (Other needs and interests, for instance economic ones, may also play a part. The interaction between economic and deeper psychological needs can be very complex.)[13]

Mazzini's nationalist slogan could be rephrased as: "Every tribe a nation-state, only one nation-state for the entire tribe." Tribal loyalties both find expression in nationalism and are partly created by it. These loyalties and this way of expressing them bring both benefits and risks. The questions are whether the benefits are worth the risks and whether there are ways of reducing the risks.

Benevolent Nationalism: Self-Respect and Moral Identity

There is little doubt that people's sense of their own worth is enhanced by feeling that they run their own affairs. To live in a country ruled by a colonial power or in one leaned on heavily by a big neighbor (whether the neighbor is the United States or the former Soviet Union) may create the feeling of being deprived of what is rightfully yours, perhaps even of being treated like a child. Whether it comes as formal independence after colonial rule or as release from the domination of a large neighbor, national independence may bring a gain in self-respect. This can give support to people's sense of their own moral identity: the sense of being a person of a particular kind, who lives by some values rather than others.

Moral identity is sometimes bound up with national identity in impressive ways. During the Nazi occupation of most of Europe, many Jewish children were hidden in convents. One nun, asked afterward why she had risked hiding some children, replied, "Je suis française a la fin." Guelfo Zamboni, as the Italian consul general in Salonika in 1943, saved the lives of many Jews by issuing false Italian documents to them. When rebuked by the SS chief in Salonika for his defense of Jews, Zamboni replied, "As long as the Italian flag flies here, under this flag I am the only one who decides what to do or what not to do." When the Jews in Denmark were about to be rounded up by the Nazis, Danish non-Jews gave massive support to the Jews and saved over 90 percent of them. Jews were stopped on the streets and offered keys to people's flats and houses. Some Jews were hidden in hospitals by doctors and nurses who gave them false medical records. Taxis, ambulances, fire engines, and cars were used to take them to the coast for their escape to Sweden. In the public statement made by the Danish church, the roundup was described as being "in conflict with the sense of justice inherent in the Danish people and inseparable from our Danish Christian culture through centuries."

Some of the benefits of national consciousness are real. But there is also the conflict risked by the more competitive kinds of nationalism.

Some Causes of Nationalist Conflict

What turns benevolent nationalism into the more menacing version of nationalism? Blurred boundaries and disputed territories play an obvious role. But there are other causes. Sometimes politicians have their own motives for whipping up competitive nationalism. Sometimes it results from fear and entrapment. Sometimes views of a Social Darwinist kind make people think conflict between national groups is unavoidable. And closer to the heart of nationalism are some tendencies toward conflict in the very processes by which national identity is socially constructed.

Political Manipulation

Sometimes nationalist rivalries are whipped up by politicians for domestic political reasons. There was at least an element of this in the German naval expansion that made a contribution to the outbreak of World War I. The German government and its supporters were worried by the growing support for the radical policies of the Social Democrats. In the 1890s, Adm. Alfred von Tirpitz had advocated a bigger navy, giving as one reason that "the great patriotic task and the economic benefits to be derived from it will offer a strong palliative against educated and uneducated Social Democrats." Bernhard Bülow, the chancellor when the naval arms race began, took the same view. He urged "a policy which appeals to the highest national emotions," mentioning the need to "regain the sympathies of the Social Democrat workers for the state and the monarchy."[14]

The events of 1914 are of course a spectacular case of "the highest national emotions" contributing to catastrophe. But this pattern has been repeated many times. Most recently, Slobodan Milosevic chose to base his own power on the appeal of "Greater Serbia," while Franjo Tudjman manipulated Croatian national feeling in a parallel way.

Fear and Entrapment

In many countries, some politicians like to play the patiotic card for their own purposes. Something more needs to be said about when this finds a response. One explanation of the case of Yugoslavia appeals to fear. In the former Yugoslavia, most people cannot have wanted ethnic conflict. Close to half of all families were ethnically mixed. But the communist period had not allowed the development of a political culture in which people learned how to settle differences peacefully. And with the collapse of Tito's federation, ethnic national units seemed the only protection against threats from other groups.

The Hobbesian picture of people subordinating themselves to any government able to provide safety and security may apply here. And the manipulation of ethnic and religious tribalism by politicians only added to the fear in other groups and thus made escape from the trap of conflict harder. When the conflict starts, its psychology entraps almost everyone. The Croatian writer Slavenka Drakulic wrote of an airplane flight from London: "I hear a girl next to me, no older than twelve, say to her friend as the aeroplane flies over Croatia: 'If we were forced to land in Zagreb, I would have to lie about my Serbian nationality, or those Croats would kill me on the spot.' We are all trapped. The two girls are at war, too, and even if hostilities were to cease instantly, how long would it take for these girls not to be afraid of landing at Zagreb?"[15]

Hobbesian fear leads to the creation of a new state for protection. Different kinds of fear and entrapment play a part in conflicts between already-existing nations. Going back again to 1914, the mutual sense of entrapment clearly played a part in bringing about World War I. Russia, France, and Britain feared the growth of German power and formed an alliance to "contain" it, which was in turn seen in Germany as "encirclement." The newspaper *Der Tag* wrote of "enemies all around —permanent danger of war from all sides." The son of Bethmann Hollweg, the

German chancellor, reported that his father thought it pointless to plant new trees on his estate near Berlin because "in a few years the Russians would be here anyway."[16] Sir Edward Grey, the British foreign secretary, later wrote that "armaments were intended to produce a sense of security in each nation. . . . What they really did was to produce fear in everybody."[17]

A similar story is found still further back. Thucydides said of the Peloponnesian War: "What made war inevitable was the growth of Athenian power and the fear this caused in Sparta."[18]

Social Darwinism

Sometimes the sense of entrapment in unavoidable conflict is reinforced by an unarticulated Social Darwinism. Those who accept the sociobiological hypothesis that a disposition to group loyalty is genetically programmed as a result of its contribution to inclusive fitness may be tempted to go further. The Social Darwinist extrapolation sees nations as the units engaged in a Darwinian struggle for survival. Nations unwilling to fight will go under.

The heyday of explicit Social Darwinism was the period before World War I. In England this Social Darwinism was expressed by Karl Pearson, who said that the nation should be "kept up to a high pitch of external efficiency by contest, chiefly by way of war with inferior races, and with equal races by the struggle for trade routes and for the sources of raw materials and food supply."[19] Lord Salisbury said that "you may roughly divide the nations of all the world as the living and the dying. . . . The living nations will gradually encroach on the territory of the dying and the seeds and causes of conflict among civilised nations will speedily appear."[20]

In Germany at that time, Social Darwinism was even more influential. The Kaiser thought Germany had to face an "imminent struggle for existence." Admiral Tirpitz thought a bigger fleet "essential if Germany is not to go under swiftly." When Sir Edward Grey proposed an end to the naval arms race, Chancellor Hollweg saw this as a sign of weakness. He rejected the idea in these terms: "The old saying still holds good that the weak will be the prey of the strong. When a people will not or cannot continue to spend enough on its armaments to be able to make its way in the world, then it falls back into the second rank. . . . There will always be another and a stronger there who is ready to take the place in the world which it has vacated."[21]

The fact that the Social Darwinism of that period has fallen into disrepute is one of the few ways in which nationalism has grown less menacing. We must hope that the doctrine is not revived.

National Identity and Perceived Characteristics

Political manipulation, together with entrapment in mutual fear, contributes to national conflict. And a residual Social Darwinism may make it seem inevitable. But these explanations do not go deep enough. Other causes are found in the fact that national consciousness is itself a social construct. National consciousness draws on a narrative about national history. It also draws on people's perception of what they take to be their own nation's distinctive characteristics.

One can only respect and admire the Danes who stood up to the Nazis because they believed the sense of justice was inherent in the Danish people. But there is another side to the belief in the good qualities of one's own nation.

National self-images require the selection of some features rather than others. Unsurprisingly, the preferred traits are characteristically favorable. We are intelligent and witty, open-minded and brave. But these are comparative characteristics. It is a daunting conceptual feat to maintain the view that we score so well on them without thinking that by comparison our neighbors are stupid and humorless, bigoted and cowardly.

We are rightly uneasy about the idea of racial pride, seeing at best a murky boundary between that and objectionable racism. But the same considerations should make us ask questions about national pride. It is true, as Benedict Anderson has argued, that racial hostility is often dehumanizing in a way that national hostility is not. Racism tends to define people in terms of biological categories such as skin color, while national insults at least focus on human cultural creations.[22]

But the boundary between national or cultural stereotypes and racial ones is less well defined than this suggests. A student at a university in Northern Ireland told me that her fellow students knew each other by first names only. Surnames would give away which communities they came from, and they wanted their student life to escape the community divisions (though sometimes first names were a giveaway, too). But when friendships were secure, the community membership could be revealed, presenting a rare chance for stereotypes to be compared in an atmosphere of goodwill. The student mentioned one of the stereotypes she had been taught as a child, that the primitiveness of the members of the other community was shown by their having one long eyebrow rather than two brows with a gap between them. Her friends in the other community reported exactly the same stereotype in reverse. These mirror images were not racist; the two communities were not of different races. Yet the hostile physical stereotype is the stuff of which racism is made.

Because national self-image is often (even if misleadingly) cast in terms of the tribal nation, the favorable national characteristics are easily thought of as ethnic ones. And from thinking of one's own ethnic characteristics as particularly good, the slide to the evils of "ethnic cleansing" can too easily take place.

National Identity and Narrative

National identity, like personal identity, is constructed partly by means of a story about the past. The narrative used to shape national consciousness can contribute to conflict in a way not completely separate from the contribution of perceived characteristics.

Much of the story of a nation is made up of its relations with other nations, who often turn out to have behaved ingloriously. The narrative of the Croats emphasizes the stifling nature of communism, conceived as a system primarily imposed by Serbs. The narrative of the Serbs emphasizes the period of Croatian fascism, the evils of the Ustasi, and the Serbian part in defeating the Croats and their Nazi allies. (The Croatian government reinforced this narrative by renaming streets after fascist leaders.) These are only the more recent chapters of the two stories. And new chapters are now being written.

The effect of such narratives, this time in Ireland, is captured by William Butler Yeats in "The Stare's Nest by My Window":

We had fed the heart on fantasies,
The heart's grown brutal from the fare;
More substance in our enmities
Than in our love.

The narratives do not have to be entirely "fantasies." A selective reading of the past, a Serb one or a Croat one, can have the same effect on the heart.

There are narratives of victory and narratives of defeat. Narratives of victory can slide into a triumphalism that arouses resentment in those whose ancestors were on the other side. The Orange parades in Northern Ireland, which celebrate the defeat of the Catholics by William of Orange, are an extreme case of this.

Narratives of defeat, kindling a desire to redress a grievance, also play an obvious part in entrapping people in a spiral of hostility. Slavenka Drakulic says: "After the war the role will be reversed and the victims will judge not only the executioners, but their silent accomplices. I am afraid that, as we have been forced to take sides in this war, we—all of us, on both sides—will get caught in that cruel, self-perpetuating game for ever."[23]

Isaiah Berlin quotes Schiller's "bent twig" theory of nationalism as a reaction to oppression or humiliation and suggests that the nationalism of Israelis and Palestinians may be so intractably strong because both are reacting against having been victims.[24]

In South Africa, Afrikaner nationalism can also be seen as something springing back like a bent twig. The brother of John Vorster, the former prime minister, described being at school a decade and a half after the Boer defeat: "If you were caught speaking Afrikaans, you had to carry a placard round your neck bearing the words 'I must not speak Dutch.' When the bell went for school to start again the last man with what was called the Dutch mark had to write out one thousand times 'I must speak English at school.'"[25] It is not hard to see how this sort of thing contributed to the stubborn defensiveness whose effects black Africans later were to feel.

One of the strengths of nationalism is the contribution it can make to self-respect. But the strengths and the weaknesses are closely interwoven. Slights to self-respect are often the first step in the spiral of conflict.

Defusing Nationalism

If the account given here is for the most part correct, nationalism is partly the expression of a tribalism that goes very deep in our psychology. It is linked partly to a general disposition to group loyalty and partly to the way distinguishing tribal features play a role in our creation of identity. In principle, this could all be harmless. But, for reasons we have seen, this tribalism is dangerous. Yet because it goes so deep, it is very hard—perhaps impossible—to eliminate. This casts doubt on the expectation among thinkers of the Enlightenment that national loyalties would fade away.

The best strategy is to attempt to contain the tendencies toward hostility and conflict within nationalism. Because nationalist conflict has a variety of sources, there is no single "solution" to the problem. A variety of strategies can be adapted to fit different cases.

One central point, which may appear paradoxical, is that often the best way to contain tribalism is to grant the demands of nationalism. This applies particularly where there is the prospect of a tribal nation or of something close to it. The former Czechoslovakia provides a model. If the Slovaks want to separate from the Czechs, both groups will live more happily together without the tribal conflict generated by the refusal of a divorce. And this applies to many other possible cases. If the majority of Scots or Basques or Quebecois really want their own independent nation, "yes" is the answer that defuses tribal conflict, and "no" is the answer that starts the spiral of resentment.

The Soft-Edged Nation-State

In many cases, the tribal nation is not possible. Shared or disputed territory necessitates some sort of pluralism. We need to be more imaginative about the kinds of pluralism that are possible.

A worthwhile response to the problem of blurred or disputed geographical boundaries may be the blurring of the conceptual boundaries of the nation-state. Northern Ireland might benefit from thinking along these lines. Northern Ireland is nearly always seen either as a duck or as a rabbit. "The six counties belong in the Republic" versus "Ulster is part of the United Kingdom" is a classic duck-rabbit figure, and no solution is likely to work unless it takes account of both ways of viewing Northern Ireland. Ideally, a solution would encourage tolerance of ambiguity, a recognition that Northern Ireland is not quite a duck, nor quite a rabbit.

One approach would be to give up the assumption that nation-states must have hard borders, that any piece of territory is either part of one country or part of another. Avishai Margalit once proposed that Jerusalem should be the capital both of Israel and of a Palestinian state. If the possibility of soft-edged countries is introduced, the territory of Northern Ireland could be part of both the Republic and the United Kingdom. People already have the choice of citizenship of either country (or of dual nationality). There could be autonomous local administration, with internationally backed guarantees of respect for minority rights. Policing this could perhaps be done by the European Community. It should not be done by the British, who are one of the historically involved tribes.

Any approach of this kind is obviously going to raise many questions and problems: Can two independent countries harmonize sufficiently to share a province or a city? What happens when they disagree? What should be left to local administration, and what limits on majority decisions should be set in the interests of the minority? I am not putting forward a detailed policy but suggesting that some scheme of this sort is worth looking into. It will be messy. But duck-rabbit figures are messy. The policies tried so far have been of duck fanciers trying to twist the figure one way and rabbit fanciers trying to twist it the other way. These policies have not been such a success that messy alternatives should be excluded.

Northern Ireland is just an example. Around the world enough places are shared between tribes to make some experiments worth trying. In such places the hard-edged nation-state can be Procrustean. Adapting states to fit people rather than making people fit states is a policy that might make use of nation-states with soft edges.

Limits to National Autonomy

In other ways, too, the concept of the nation-state is sometimes too rigid. As Henry Shue suggests in chapter 20 of this volume, we need to think in terms of limited sovereignty. World government has been proposed as a solution to national conflicts, a suggestion often dismissed as either utopian or undesirable. But there are many gradations between world government and the unlimited sovereignty of autonomous nation-states. We are already growing accustomed to a degree of policing of conflicts between nations by the world community. And because of our common interest in the avoidance of nuclear war, many of us accept the idea of some international policing of nuclear proliferation.

After years of accepting that the United Nations cannot interfere in a country's "internal affairs," we are starting to think in terms of international intervention to prevent genocide, "ethnic cleansing," and other horrors. This is an important development of the principle of limited national sovereignty. A strong enough policy of this kind is the Hobbesian solution to the fear that generates nationalist conflict, for instance in Yugoslavia.

International intervention does not have to use military force. Different kinds of breach might call for different degrees of response. Linkage of respect for minority rights with loans from the World Bank or the International Monetary Fund is a weaker form of international pressure. Given the principle that national sovereignty is limited, we need a debate on what the limits are and on what forms of intervention are justified in different cases. Clear answers to these questions could help avoid some of the horrors we now see.

Limited sovereignty, like the soft-edged nation-state, blurs traditional conceptual boundaries. This is occurring through the development of groups such as the European Union. It could be taken further with the aim of reducing nationalist conflict. For instance, a constitution for the European Union might have provisions for minority rights within member nations.

This constitution might include the rights of "subnations" to vote to secede from their parent nations, provided that these subnations in turn respect the rights of minorities within their borders. (There are, as Allen Buchanan points out in chapter 18 of this volume, other problems about secession that would also need to be resolved.)

States in Eastern Europe wanting to join the Union would have to accept the constitution. In some cases this acceptance might substitute the Czechoslovak model for the Yugoslav one. Minorities in the countries of the existing Union might benefit, too.

Again, this is not intended as a blueprint for detailed policy. I am gesturing toward the kind of conceptual and political innovations that may be worth considering if we want to reduce nationalist conflict.

The Long, Slow Strategy

These possible strategies for containing the dangers of nationalism start by accepting our tribal psychology as a fact of life. At present, this is the only realistic option.

But I am reluctant to abandon the hope of the Enlightenment that in the long run these tribal loyalties may take second place to a more general humanism. Immediate strategies for containing conflict could be supplemented by greater self-consciousness about the tribal loyalties themselves. In the long run, this could lead these simpleminded commitments to evolve into something more complex.

Some of the changes of outlook I hope for may come through the growth of intellectual understanding. One instance is something already under way: the growing appreciation of the limitations of Social Darwinism.

Today considerably more people grasp the fact that we do not have to see nations as fighting each other to the death in a Darwinian struggle for survival than in 1914. Even if there is some truth in the sociobiological hypothesis of a genetic disposition to group loyalty, this by no means entails the Social Darwinist view. It entails nothing about nations being the units loyalty must attach to. And, in particular, it does not entail genetic determinism: the view that our genetic composition makes certain behavior, for instance group conflict, inevitable. Especially with modern weapons, cooperation may do more than conflict for inclusive fitness. And even where some menacing trait has biological origins, the best strategy of containment may be environmental, for instance by making sure that conflict does not pay.

Our understanding could usefully grow in other ways, too. The spread of a more sophisticated understanding of the way national self-images and narratives are constructed could slowly erode uncritical nationalism. And seeing the ways in which modern pluralist nations differ from tribal nations may have the same effect. Belief in "Greater Serbia," and so forth, depends on myths that are unlikely to survive the growth of a more critical outlook.

Greater awareness of the links between tribalism and identity might accompany an awareness of the variety of other resources we can draw on for self-creation. We have more than just our tribal membership. We are mothers and fathers, sons and daughters, brothers and sisters, friends, architects, scientists, fans of the Grateful Dead, supporters of the Liverpool Football Club, mountaineers, vegetarians, amateur photographers, lovers of Mozart, admirers of Tolstoy, and haters of Heidegger. To have a self-conception only in terms of being a Serb or a Croat would be a great impoverishment. Slavenka Drakulic has expressed this result of the Yugoslav conflict:

> I had fought against treating nationality as a main criterion by which to judge human beings; I tried to see the people behind the label; I kept open the possibility of dialogue with my friends and colleagues in Serbia even after all telephone lines and roads had been cut off and one third of Croatia had been occupied and bombed. . . . In the end none of that helped me. Along with millions of other Croats, I was pinned to the wall of nationhood—not only by outside pressure from Serbia and the Federal army but by national homogenization within Croatia itself. That is what the war is doing to us, reducing us to one dimension: the Nation. The trouble with this nationhood, however, is that whereas before, I was defined by my education, my job, my ideas, my character— and, yes, my nationality too—now I feel stripped of all that. I am nobody because I am not a person any more. I am one of 4.5 million Croats.[26]

As more people see this for the impoverishment that it is, we may hope that tribal psychology itself may be changed. Perhaps self-creation will become less centered on the narrow range of charged tribal characteristics. Because this hope of tribalism being weakened depends on long-term changes of consciousness, it may seem utopian. Year by year, changes of consciousness are imperceptible, just like the day-by-day growth of children. But children do grow up, and our consciousness really has changed from that of medieval people.

The thinkers of the Enlightenment did not see the importance of tribalism or the contribution national loyalties make to our psychology. Seeing what they missed makes us, in one way, more sympathetic to nationalism. The case for this greater sympathy is based on the contribution of national loyalties to people and their sense of identity. This makes nations only of instrumental value. They are to be judged by the good and bad contributions they make to the lives of people. In this way the Enlightenment thinkers who kicked nations off their pedestal got it right. A good Enlightenment principle might be: Always treat nations merely as means and never as ends in themselves.

For the present we have to accept the strong psychological pull of nationalism as a fact of life. But if we are lucky, we may move toward a rather different world. I hope for a world of many small countries, which are only relatively autonomous. I also hope that many of them may be like W. H. Auden's Arcadia, where the only statues allowed are of great dead chefs.

NOTES

In the final version of this essay, I have been helped a great deal by perceptive comments from David Little, Michael Hechter, Jeff McMahan, and Robert McKim.

1. Quoted in Eric Hobsbawm, *Nations and Nationalism since 1780: Programme, Myth, Reality* (Cambridge, 1990) p. 101.

2. Benedict Anderson, *Imagined Communities; Reflections on the Origin and Spread of Nationalism* (London, 1983); Ernest Gellner, *Nations and Nationalism* (Oxford, 1983); Hobsbawm, *Nations and Nationalism.*

3. Hobsbawm, *Nations and Nationalism*, p. 44.

4. Basil Davidson, *The Black Man's Burden: Africa and the Curse of the Nation-State* (New York, 1992).

5. Ibid., p. 206.

6. C. Haney, C. Banks, and P. Zimbardo, "Interpersonal Dynamics in a Simulated Prison," *International Journal of Criminology and Penology*, 1973.

7. Konrad Lorenz, *On Aggression* (New York, 1974), p. 20.

8. W. D. Hamilton, "The Evolution of Altruistic Behavior," *American Naturalist* 97 (1963): 354–56; W. D. Hamilton, "The Genetical Evolution of Social Behavior, I and II," *Journal of Theoretical Biology* 7 (1964): 1–52.

9. R. Paul Shaw and Yuwa Wong, *Genetic Seeds of Warfare: Evolution, Nationalism, and Patriotism* (Boston, 1989).

10. Derek Parfit, *Reasons and Persons* (Oxford, 1984), pp. 211–12, 339, 340.

11. Jeffrey Masson, *Against Therapy* (London, 1993), pp. 134–64.

12. Charles Taylor, *Multiculturalism and "The Politics of Recognition"* (Princeton, 1992).

13. Michael Hechter, "The Dynamics of Secession," *Acta Sociologica*, 1992.

14. V. R. Berghahn, *Germany and the Approach of War in 1914* (London, 1973), pp. 29–31.

15. Slavenka Drakulic, *Balkan Express: Fragments from the Other Side of War* (London, 1993), p. 20.

16. Berghahn, *Germany and the Approach of War*, pp. 172, 186.

17. Viscount Grey of Falloden, *Twenty-five Years, 1892–1916*, vol. 2 (London, 1925), p. 52.

18. Thucydides, *The Peloponnesian War*, trans. Rex Warner (Harmondsworth, 1986), pp. 35–49.

19. James Joll, *The Origins of the First World War*, 2d ed. (London, 1992), p. 179.

20. Zara Steiner, *Britain and the Origins of the First World War* (London, 1977), p. 16.

21. Michael Howard, "The Edwardian Arms Race," in *The Lessons of History* (Oxford, 1993), pp. 81–96.

22. Anderson, *Imagined Communities*, chap. 8.

23. Drakulic, *Balkan Express*, p. 55.

24. Isaiah Berlin, "The Bent Twig," in *The Crooked Timber of Humanity: Chapters in the History of Ideas* (New York, 1992), pp. 238–61.

25. David Harrison, *The White Tribe of Africa* (Johannesburg, 1981), p. 54.

26. Drakulic, *Balkan Express*, p. 51.

3

Nationalism and Modernity

CHARLES TAYLOR

Nationalism is much talked about these days. I suppose it's obvious why. The postcommunist massacres in the ex–Soviet Union and ex-Yugoslavia are reason enough. And suddenly this kind of frightening outburst seems in danger of becoming more the rule than the exception. For some people this is all the more shocking in that it seems like a throwback. The Bosnian savagery comes across to these people as an atavistic return, as though primeval identities and ageless mutual hatreds were being resurrected at the end of the twentieth century. But this can't be quite the right take on things, because so much in nationalism is quintessentially modern. The Serb-Croat wars disconcert us because they mix an unquestionably modern discourse—self-determination, rule by the people, et cetera—with other elements that seem to us alien to (what we understand as) modernity.

Can we hope to understand this? Is there even a "this" to understand here? Is there a single phenomenon? Maybe we're making things even harder for ourselves by assuming that there is something called "nationalism" that is the same wherever people make demands in the name of ethnic/cultural self-determination, so that Bosnian Serbs and Québécois are placed in the same category.[1] The differences are explained by the first being more "extreme" than the second, just as neat whiskey knocks you out, but diluted whiskey makes you mellow.

I want to argue that there are big differences here but also some links. Sorting this out will require thinking in more than one register. One-line theories of nationalism are as bad as such theories invariably are in social science. I am going to try to explore the ways in which various nationalisms are linked to modernity, both to central features of its political culture and to the stresses and malaise to which it gives rise.

Some explanations take up this topic from this latter perspective. Nationalism is an outbreak of emotion that is understandable when people are under strain because of, say, a disorienting social and economic transition, especially if this is accompanied by hard times. So we understand why lots of Russians voted for Zhirinovsky in the last election, even though we deplore it, just as we understand why Algerians voted for the Islamic Salvation Front in their last election. Now if things had been going better, if people had felt more secure, or if there hadn't been so much unemployment and hardship, these extreme and dangerous parties wouldn't have made the headway they did.

There is very often a lot of truth in this last counterfactual proposition. But it doesn't tell us what is really interesting to know: why nationalists or Islamic "fundamentalists" are the candidates waiting to take up the angry, disoriented protest vote. And this has a lot to do with the progress of what I am calling "modernity," even, perhaps especially, where it seems to take "antimodern" forms.

So I want first to trace the ways in which nationalism arises out of modern society and the modern state form. Ernest Gellner has an interesting theory of just this kind.[2] His is in a sense a functional account. It concentrates on modern societies as economies, which by their very nature need to be serviced and (to some degree) managed by the state.

A modern economy is by definition one undergoing growth and change. As such it requires a population that is mobile, both occupationally and geographically. People no longer will necessarily stay in the same métier throughout their whole careers, and certainly there cannot be the hereditary handing down of métier from parent to child that characterized many premodern societies. This flexibility can be attained only by a high level of general education, literacy, and numeracy, one unmatched by any previous society in history. The modern division of labor is multiform but shallow. That is, it is taken for granted that people can be retrained or at least that their children can. Vocations are no longer linked with the standing status divisions that marked many earlier societies, of which the extreme case is the traditional Indian caste system.

Moreover, this generalized and high level of culture has to be homogeneous. We need people who can communicate with each other and generally understand each other without having to rely heavily on familiarity with particular contexts of family, clan, locality, provenance, et cetera. To "do business" with each other, operate a system of courts, run a bureaucratic state apparatus, and the like, we need millions who can communicate without difficulty in a context-free fashion. A standard language must replace all the local and class dialects that abounded earlier.

Society needs in a sense a homogeneous culture, one into which people have to be inducted to be able to do business with each other across all the particularities of context and background. But how can they be inducted into this culture? Here is where the modern state takes on an especially important role.

In earlier "agro-literate" societies, the high culture was confined to a class, the literati and perhaps other top strata. The job of handing on this culture could be assumed by families in some cases or by special institutions that might be at some distance from the state (for example, the Church in premodern Europe). But in the modern context, the task of educating everybody up to scratch is too imposing and too vital to be left to the private sector. Both the scale of the educative enterprise and its essential uniformity dictate that it be assumed by the state. Modern societies/economies are all serviced, inescapably, by a state system of education.

A homogeneous language and culture is fostered and diffused and hence also to some degree defined by the state. Modern societies necessarily have official languages, almost official cultures. This is a functional imperative. Gellner takes issue with Elie Kedourie: it is not so much that nationalism as a sentiment, as a political aspiration, has imposed homogeneity. Rather, homogeneity is a requirement of the modern state, and it is this "inescapable imperative [that] eventually appears on the surface as nationalism."[3]

Now up to this last quote, I think Gellner is basically right. There can be differences in the detailed account, but it seems to me an undeniable feature of modern market, growth-oriented, industrial economies, embedded as they are in bureaucratic polities, that they force a kind of homogeneity of language and culture, both designedly, as through the education system, and by the very way they operate, as through their media. And it seems that this couldn't very well be otherwise. The demands of this kind of society in trained personnel—above all in *retrainable* personnel, capable of taking on ever-new technologies and operating by ever-new methods—and the need for intercommunication across vaster and vaster networks push inevitably to the diffusion of standardized, context-free languages, embedding within themselves a multiplicity of expert "language games." As a consequence of this, earlier "network" identities, linked to family, clan, locality, and provenance, tend to decline, and new "categorical" identities, which link us to a multitude of others nationally or even globally—on the basis of confession, profession, citizenship—take on more and more importance.[4]

Compared to earlier societies, which tended to be divided between a "high" culture, and appanage of a restricted class, and a set of partly overlapping "folk" cultures, this modern form tends to universalize a species of "high" (literate) culture, putting a larger and larger proportion of its population through tertiary education, inculcating into many of them a "canon," as "high" cultures have always tended to do to their initiates. As Gellner puts it, "a high culture pervades the whole of society, defines it, and needs to be sustained by that polity. *That* is the secret of nationalism."[5]

All this seems true, but how does it account for nationalism? This seems evident enough to Gellner. If a modern society has an "official" language, in the fullest sense of the term—that is, a state-sponsored, -inculcated, and -defined language and culture, in which both economy and state function—then it is obviously an immense advantage to people if this language and culture are theirs. Speakers of other languages are at a distinct disadvantage. They must either go on functioning in what to them is a second language or get on an equal footing with speakers of the official language by assimilating. Or else, faced with this second distasteful prospect, they demand to redraw the boundaries of the state and set up shop in a new polity/economy where their own language will become official. The nationalist imperative is born.

People have raised objectives to Gellner's theory on a number of grounds, most notably that it seems to have trouble explaining the rise of nationalism in preindustrial contexts, such as nineteenth-century Eastern Europe, and twentieth-century Africa. But I don't want to dwell on these difficulties, for which there are probably answers anyway. What concerns me is the incompleteness of the explanation.

Some people assimilate; they go without much protest into the mix-master of school and army and lose their regional dialects. They enter as peasants and emerge as Frenchmen.[6] Why do some put up a fight and create nationalist movements while others do not? Or again, if there are two languages widely spoken in a given state, why is it so difficult to come to some arrangement around a form of bilingualism? This does happen, of course, but alas, much more rarely than it should, and it is often fraught with strife and difficulty even where it has been adopted. Why should this be so?

Some people might think that the problematicity of bilingualism needs no explanation. It's so much easier to operate in a single language. The answer is: easier than what? If everyone were willing to agree happily to operate in a single language, we'd be crazy to insist on two. But if the alternative is strife, resentment, separatist movements, perhaps even the dissolution of the state, well, bilingualism isn't really that complicated. In my (admittedly jaundiced) experience of living in a bilingual state, pleas about the trouble and expense of bilingualism are generally technological pretexts for a chauvinism that dares not declare itself openly.

But if that is so, then the crucial explanatory bit is missing from Gellner's account. The reason why some minorities assimilate and others fight back has to be referred to the nationalism of the latter. The reason bilingual solutions are hard isn't because they're so complicated and expensive but because they're resisted (for example, under the bad faith pretext that they're complicated and expensive) on fundamentally nationalist grounds. That is, nationalism is still figuring in the account as an explanans, not as a successfully accounted for explanandum.

What Gellner has done, which is very valuable, is define some of the very important stakes of nationalist struggle. Just because the modern state does sustain an official language/culture, it becomes of ultimate significance to those with a strong national identity to get some kind of control of a state. The state focus of so much modern national sentiment and national identity, which Gellner makes a matter of definition, is thereby partly explained, and this is no small matter. But the original energy fueling these struggles remains to be understood. Unless one takes the cynical view (espoused, for instance, by Pierre Trudeau in relation to Quebec independentism) that the whole thing is powered by the ambition of so- cial elites to establish a monopoly of prestigious and remunerative jobs. The re- fusal of bilingualism is then easily explained: Under this regime, members of our gang get 50 percent of the jobs; under unilingualism, we get 100 percent.

Once again, this certainly explains something but far from everything. It can't explain, for instance, why nonelites are so easily recruited into the nationalist en- terprise. Nor does it explain the solidarity of the elites themselves. If you are one of those holding down a top job within the 50 percent allocated to your language group, why should you upset everything so that some as-yet-unfavored compatri- ots can take over the other 50 percent? Why side with compatriots against fellow top jobholders? Of course, not everybody does, but one of the remarkable things about the moral pressures of nationalism is that many feel they should and lots do. Where does nationalism get its moral thrust? Totally cynical explanations are pow- erless to illuminate this.

Last, I wonder if we should make the state focus definitional for modern na- tionalism as Gellner does. Granted, nationalism overwhelmingly takes this form, but not invariably. Thus French-Canadian nationalism, from the nineteenth into the twentieth century, had two forms, of which the dominant one was turned away from the state and promoted nonstate institutions, especially the Church. The more familiar state-centered mode was also there, at least since the rebellion of 1837, but it remained the less powerful strand—that is, until the turnover of 1960, after which it has taken over the whole field, with the resultant rise of in- dependentism and the identity switch from "Canadien-français" to "Québécois." Nevertheless, during those many decades before 1960, there were people whom everybody, including themselves, referred to as "nationalistes" who lacked the state focus. The emotional and moral sources on which they drew were different but not totally distinct from those drawn on by Quebec nationalists today. We gain nothing by excluding this phenomenon from our purview by definitional fiat.

So the ultimate sources of modern nationalism still escape us. (Perhaps they al- ways will.) But at least we understand better some of the things at stake in modern nationalist struggles, and hence their focus, thanks to Gellner's account. Before I try my hand at defining the sources, I would like to supplement Gellner's picture of what is at stake by bringing to the fore other functional requirements of the modern state.

Modern nation-states are "imagined communities," in Benedict Anderson's celebrated phrase.[7] We might say that they have a particular kind of social imaginary—that is, socially shared ways in which social spaces are imagined. There are two important features of the modern imaginary, which I can best bring out by contrasting them in each case with what went before in European history.

First, there is the shift from hierarchical, mediated-access societies to horizontal, direct-access societies. In the earlier form, hierarchy and what I am calling mediacy of access went together. A society of ranks—"society of orders," to use Alexis de Tocqueville's phrase—like seventeenth-century France, for instance, was hierarchical in an obvious sense. But this also meant that one belonged to this society via belonging to some component of it. As a peasant, one was linked to a lord who in turn held power from the king. One was a member of a municipal corporation that had a standing in the kingdom or exercised some function in a parliament with its recognized status, and so on. By contrast, the modern notion of citizenship is direct. In however many ways I am related to the rest of society through intermediary organizations, I think of my citizenship as separate from all these. My fundamental way of belonging to the state is not dependent on or mediated by any of these other belongings. I stand, alongside all my fellow citizens, in direct relationship to the state that is the object of our common allegiance.

Of course, this doesn't necessarily change the way things get done. I know someone whose brother-in-law is a judge or an MP, and so I phone her up when I'm in a jam. We might say that what has changed is the normative picture. But underlying this, without which the new form couldn't exist for us, is a change in the way people imagine belonging. There were certainly people in seventeenth-century France and before for whom the very idea of direct access would have been foreign, impossible to clearly grasp. The educated had the model of the ancient republic. But for many others, the only way they could understand belonging to a larger whole, like a kingdom or a universal church, was through the imbrication of more immediate, understandable units of belonging (parish, lord) into the greater entity. Modernity has involved, among other things, a revolution in our social imaginary, the relegation of these forms of mediacy to the margins, and the diffusions of images of direct access.

This has come about in a number of forms: the rise of a public sphere, in which people conceive of themselves as participating directly in a nationwide (sometimes even international) discussion; the development of market economies, in which all economic agents are seen as entering into contractual relations with others on an equal footing; and, of course, the rise of the modern citizenship state. But we can think of other ways as well in which immediacy of access takes hold of our imaginations. We see ourselves as in spaces of fashion, for instance, taking up and handing on styles. We see ourselves as part of the worldwide audience of media stars. And while these spaces are in their own sense hierarchical—they center on quasi-legendary figures—they offer all participants an access unmediated by any of their other allegiances or belongings. Something of the same kind, along with a more substantial mode of participation, is available in the various movements (social, political, religious) that are a crucial feature of modern life and link people trans-locally and internationally into a single collective agency.

These modes of imagined direct access are linked to—indeed, are just different facets of—modern equality and individualism. Directness of access abolishes the heterogeneity of hierarchical belonging. It makes us uniform, and that is one way of becoming equal. (Whether it is the only way is the fateful issue at stake in much of today's struggles over multiculturalism.) At the same time, the relegation of various mediations reduces their importance in our lives; the individual stands more and more free of them and hence has a growing self-consciousness as an individual. Modern individualism, as a moral idea, doesn't mean ceasing to belong at all—that's the individualism of anomie and breakdown—but imagining oneself as belonging to ever wider and more impersonal entities: the state, the movement, the community of humankind. This is the same change—seen from another angle—that I described above in terms borrowed from Craig Calhoun: The shift from "network" or "relational" identities to "categorical" ones.

The second important feature of the modern social imaginary is that it no longer sees the greater translocal entities as grounded in something other, something higher, than common action in secular time. This was not true of the premodern state. The hierarchical order of the kingdom was seen as based in the Great Chain of Being. The tribal unit was seen as constituted as such by its law, which went back "since time out of mind" or perhaps to some founding moment that had the status of a "time of origins" in Mircea Eliade's sense. The importance in premodern revolutions, up to and including the English civil war, of the backward look, of establishing an original law, comes from this sense that the political entity is in this sense action-transcendent. It cannot simply create itself by its own action. On the contrary, it can act as an entity because it is already constituted as such, and that is why such legitimacy attaches to returning to the original constitution.

Seventeenth-century social contact theory, which sees a people as coming together out of a state of nature, obviously belongs to another order of thought. But it wasn't until the late eighteenth century that this new way of conceiving things entered the social imaginary. The American Revolution is in a sense the watershed. It was undertaken in a backward-looking spirit, in the sense that the colonists were fighting for their established rights as Englishmen. Moreover, they were fighting under their established colonial legislatures, associated in a Congress. But out of the whole process emerged the crucial fiction of "we, the people," into whose mouth the declaration of the new Constitution was placed.

Here the idea is invoked that a people or, as it was also called at the time, a "nation" can exist prior to and independently of its political constitution so that this people can give itself its own constitution by its own free action in secular time. Of course, the epoch-making action rapidly comes to be invested with images drawn from older notions of higher time. The "Nova Ordo seclorum," just like the new French revolutionary calendar, draws heavily on Judeo-Christian apocalyptic beliefs. The Constitution founding comes to be invested with something of the force of a "time of origins," a higher time, filled with agents of a superior kind, which we should ceaselessly try to reapproach. But nevertheless, a new way of conceiving things is abroad. Nations, people, can have a personality, can act together outside of any prior political ordering. One of the key premises of modern nationalism is in place, because without this the demand for self-determination of nations would make no sense. This just is the right for peoples to make their own constitution, unfettered by their historical political organization.

What is immensely suggestive about Anderson's account is that it links these two features. It shows how the rise of direct-access societies was linked to changing understandings of time and, consequently, of the possible ways of imaging social wholes. Anderson stresses how the new sense of belonging to a nation was prepared by a new way of grasping society under the category of simultaneity:[8] society as the whole consisting of the simultaneous happening of the myriad events that mark the lives of its members at that moment. These events are the fillers of this segment of a kind of homogeneous time. This very clear, unambiguous concept of simultaneity belongs to an understanding of time as exclusively secular. As long as secular time is interwoven with various kinds of higher time, there is no guarantee that all events can be placed in unambiguous relations of simultaneity and succession. The high feast is in one way contemporaneous with my life and that of my fellow pilgrims, but in another way it is close to eternity, the time of origins, or the events it prefigures.

A purely secular time understanding allows us to imagine society "horizontally," unrelated to any "high points," in which the ordinary sequence of events touches higher time, and therefore it does not recognize any privileged persons or agencies—such as kings or priests—who stand and mediate at such alleged points. This radical horizontality is precisely what is implied in the direct-access society, where each member is "immediate to the whole." Anderson is undoubtedly right to argue that this new understanding couldn't have arisen without social developments like that of print capitalism, but he doesn't want to imply by this that the transformations of the social imaginary are sufficiently explained by these developments. Modern society also required transformations in the way we figure ourselves as societies. Crucial among these has been this ability to grasp society from a decentered view that is no one's. That is, the search for a truer and more authoritative perspective than my own doesn't lead me to center society on a king or sacred assembly, or whatever, but allows for this lateral, horizontal view, which an unsituated observer might have—society as it might be laid out in a tableau without privileged nodal points. There is a close inner link between modern direct-access societies, their self-understandings, their refraction in categorical identities, and modern synoptic modes of representation in "the Age of the World Picture": society as simultaneous happenings, social interchange as an impersonal "system," the social terrain as what is mapped, historical culture as what shows up in museums, et cetera.[9]

What light can these considerations about the social imaginary throw on modern nationalism? They can help illuminate what is at stake in nationalist struggles, just as Gellner's account did, an account that these considerations in a sense complement. Gellner showed the phenomenon of a state-fostered official language as a functional requirement of a modern state and economy. And in an analogous way there are functional requirements that attend the modern social imaginary.

The horizontal, direct-access society, given political form by an act of the people, forms the background to the contemporary source of legitimate government in the will of the people. This principle is getting harder and harder to gainsay in the modern world. It comes close to being the only acceptable basis for any regime that doesn't declare itself as merely temporary or transitional, with the partial exception of so-called Islamic regimes—although this doesn't prevent it from being used to justify the most terrible tyrannies. Communist regimes were also supposedly based on popular sovereignty, and fascism was supposed to emanate from the united will of a conquering people.

Now this has certain functional requirements. Let's first of all take the case where the attempt is made to live out the principle of popular sovereignty through a representative democracy. The nature of this kind of society, as in any other free society, is that it requires a certain degree of commitment on the part of its citizens. Traditional despotisms could ask of people only that they remain passive and obey the laws. A democracy, ancient or modern, has to ask more. It requires that its members be motivated to make the necessary contributions: of treasure (in taxes), sometimes blood (in war); and it expects always some degree of participation in the process of governance. A free society has to substitute for despotic enforcement with a certain degree of self-enforcement. Where this fails, the system is in danger. For instance, democratic societies where the level of participation falls below a certain threshold cease to be legitimate in the eyes of their members. A government elected in an election with a turnout of 20 percent can't claim to have the mandate of the people. In can only claim to have gotten there by the rules, which is a much weaker defense if ever it faces a crisis.

So democracies require a relatively strong commitment on the part of their citizens. In terms of identity, citizenship has to rate as an important component of who they are. I am speaking in general, of course; in any society, there will be a wide gamut of cases, stretching from the most gung-ho and motivated to the most turned-off internal exiles. But the median point of this gamut has to fall closer to the upper than the lower limit. This membership has to be one that matters. In particular, it has to matter more than the things that can divide the citizens.

In other words, the modern democratic state needs a healthy degree of what used to be called "patriotism," a strong sense of identification with the polity, and a willingness to give of oneself for its sake. That is why these states try to inculcate patriotism and to create a strong sense of common identity even where it did not previously exist. And that is why one thrust of modern democracy has been to try to shift the balance within the identity of the modern citizen, so that being a citizen will take precedence over a host of other poles of identity, such as family, class, gender, even (perhaps especially) religion. This may be promoted in a deliberate way, on the basis of an express ideology, as in the case of French Republicanism. Or it may be fostered in more indirect ways, as a consequence of the injunction to render other modes of description—gender, race, religion, et cetera—irrelevant in the operation of public life.[10]

But the effect is the same, and we can see that it complements the factors Gellner highlights. Parallel to the homogeneity of language and culture that the modern state economy can't help fostering is this homogenization of identity and allegiance that it must nourish for its survival. In both cases, the features that divide us, that distinguish us into subgroups and partial publics, fade, either altogether or at least in their importance and relevance.

How does this connect with nationalism? One obvious link is that nationalism can provide the fuel for patriotism. So much so that we can have trouble distinguishing them. But it is important to keep them distinct if we want to understand our history. If we think of patriotism as a strong citizen identification, then nationalism is one basis for patriotism but not the only one. We can speak of nationalism when the ground of the common political allegiance is some ethnic, linguistic, cultural, or religious identity that exists independently of the polity. If I am a nationalist, I owe allegiance to this state because it is the state of the X's, where X is my national identity, one I would bear whether or not we were lucky enough or strong enough or virtuous enough to have a state. The whole nationalist idea supposes this prepolitical identity, as I said above.

But patriotism can also have the meaning it had for the ancients. I love my fatherland, and what makes it essentially mine is its laws. Outside of these, it is denatured and no longer really mine. There is no reference to a prepolitical identity here; on the contrary, the patria is politically defined. Now this is important, because this was the form that patriotism took initially in the two great inaugural revolutions of the liberal age, the American and the French. Neither was initially nationalist. The nation was taken as given out of previous history or constructed, in the American case, out of an alliance based on an obvious commonality of historical predicament, and in both cases the patriot was one who sought the nation's freedom. It was later, when (the elites of) other peoples began to feel that they couldn't attain real freedom by simply revolutionizing the existing (often imperial) political structures or finding their place within a liberal empire (of Napoléon), that nationalism raised its head.

But subsequently, so much did nationalism become the rule, as a basis for patriotism, that the original prenationalist societies themselves began to understand their own patriotism in something like nationalist terms. Instead of seeing liberal institutions as uncomplicatedly universal, nationalism accredited the idea that in each society they must be tailored to the particular genius of the people. But then even in their original countries of origin where they were at first understood universalistically, they now come to be seen as colored by particular circumstances and history.

Be that as it may, nationalism has become the most readily available motor of patriotism, so that when leaders want to unite a country and lift people out of their warring partial allegiances they appeal to a broader national identity, telling a story that makes this central to the history of their society rather than the partial identities they are trying to supersede. Thus Nehru, in his *Discovery of India*, tells a narrative of Indian identity, the basis of a pan-Indian secular nationalism that would take precedence over the potentially warring communal allegiances, Hindu and Muslim.

There is thus a sort of dialectic of state and nation. It is not just that nations strive to become states; it is also that modern states, in order to survive, strive to create national allegiances to their own measure. This is a point parallel to Gellner's correction of Kedourie above. Nationalism is not only the motor behind the homogenization of modern societies; it can also sometimes be the upshot. In order to see this, we have to keep in mind the functional requirement of patriotism.

But this still doesn't "explain" modern nationalism because lots of nationalisms arise outside of this state-building process,[11] and we still have to explain why some state-sponsored enterprises of patriotism succeed and other founder on unconquerable existent identities. (Is the Nehruvian secular Indian nationalism among the casualties?) The ultimate insight still eludes us.

It does, however, further define the form of the struggles to which nationalism gives rise and clarifies what is at stake in them in a way parallel and complementary to Gellner's account. This showed how the modern economy and bureaucratic state pushed toward a state-fostered common language and culture and thus showed that if a given minority group didn't want to assimilate and the majority was unwilling to give them a place through some regime of bilingualism, then the minority faced the unenviable position of being forever disadvantaged. Feeling the assimilative pressure on their members inseparable from this position, they ultimately risked the feared outcome of assimilation. Trouble and strife are built into such a situation.

Analogously here, we see that the modern state must push for a strong common identity. And thus if a group feels that this identity doesn't reflect it and the majority will not accommodate it by modifying the definition of common identity to include this group, then its members feel like second-class citizens and consequently experience an assimilative pressure. Trouble of some sort must follow.

What this doesn't tell us is what makes these if clauses true when they are. What it does help us to see is that once they are true, the distressing scenarios of nationalist struggles—separatist movements, assimilation policies, tense compromises, and the like—are not just the result of gratuitous bloody-mindedness, even less the result of some regression to premodern tribal identities, but are very much the product of a situation of rivalry that is quintessentially modern in its structure and stakes.

A further word here might be helpful about how this latter kind of struggle plays itself out, based on further reflections on the functional requirements of democratic rule. The model of democratic legitimacy requires that the laws we live under in some sense result from our collective decisions. "The people" for these purposes is thought to form a collective unit of decision. But we do more than decide on issues that are already clear-cut. If that were the case, the best way to do things would be to put everything to a referendum. We also have to deliberate, clarify things, make up our minds. So "the people" also has to be conceived as a collective unit of deliberation.

Now in the meaning of the act "the people" is also seen as made up of equal and autonomous members, because to the extent that this is not the case and some are dependent on others the decision would be held to emanate from the influential part and not from the whole people.

If we put these two together, we have the idea of a process of deliberation and decision in which everybody can be heard. Of course, if we were very exigent, this would always turn out to be utopian. In fact, democratic societies are usually satisfied with some approximation of principle to this norm. But if it appears that, in some systematic way, there are obstacles to certain sections of the population being heard, then the legitimacy of democratic rule in that society is under challenge.

Now there are a number of ways a case can be made that a certain segment of the population is being systematically unheard. A case of this kind was made on behalf of the working class in earlier times, could be made today with great plausibility on behalf of the nonworking marginalized poor, and is often vigorously made on behalf of women. What concerns me here is the way that a case of this kind can be made in relation to an ethnic or linguistic group.

A minority group can come to feel that their way of seeing things is different from the majority, this is generally not understood or recognized by the majority, and, consequently, the majority is not willing to alter the terms of the debate to accommodate this difference, and therefore the minority is being systematically unheard. Their voice cannot really penetrate the public debate. They are not really part of the deliberative unit.

Understanding of how this feeling could arise must emerge from our ever-deferred search for the sources of nationalism. But we can see from here how destabilizing this type of challenge is in a modern democratic society, because it strikes at the very basis of legitimacy in this kind of society. Part of understanding modern nationalism is seeing how vulnerable our societies are to it.

That being said, can we now come to the sources of nationalism? If I could listen to the voice of prudence, I would now plead lack of space and leave this to some other occasion. But I'm going to ignore the trembling of angels and rush in anyway. Nationalism, I have wanted to say, can't be understood as an atavistic reaction. It is a quintessentially modern phenomenon. One might think that the above discussion clears the way for a picture of it as both. What is modern would be the context of nationalistic struggles, the stakes and predispositions to struggle, given national sentiment, as these have been outlined by Gellner, supplemented by my remarks (in turn inspired by Anderson). What is primeval would be the sentiment itself, and so the two can be neatly combined.

But I think that even the sentiment is one that could only arise in modernity, and that is what I now want to explain. Why does nationalism arise? Why couldn't the Germans just be happy to be part of Napoléon's liberalizing empire, as Hegel would have liked? Why didn't the Algerians demand the full French citizenship to which they would have been entitled according to the logic of "l'Algérie, c'est la France" instead of going for independence? And so on, through an immense range of similar questions.

First, it's important to see that in a great many situations the initial refusal is that of certain elites, generally the ones who are most acquainted with the culture of the metropolis they are refusing. Later, in a successful nationalist movement, the mass of the people is somehow induced to come on board. This indicates that an account of the sources of such a movement ought to distinguish two stages.

So let me try to tackle the first phase. Why do the elites refuse metropolitan incorporation, even, perhaps especially, when they have accepted many of the values of the metropolis? Here we have to look at another facet of the unfolding process of modernity.

From one point of view, modernity is like a wave, flowing over and engulfing one traditional culture after another. If we understand by modernity, inter alia, the developments discussed above—the emergence of a market-industrial economy, of a bureaucratically organized state, of modes of popular rule—then its progress is, indeed, wavelike. The first two changes, if not the third, are in a sense irresistible. Whoever fails to take them or some good functional equivalent on will fall so far behind in the power stakes as to be taken over and forced to undergo these changes anyway. There are good reasons in the relations of force for the onward march of modernity so defined.

But modernity as lived from the inside, as it were, is something different. The institutional changes just described always shake up and alter traditional culture. They did this in the original development in the West, and they have done this elsewhere. But outside of those cases where the original culture is quite destroyed and the people either die or are forcibly assimilated—and European colonialism has a number of such cases to its discredit—a successful transition involves a people finding resources in their traditional culture to take on the new practices. In this sense, modernity is not a single wave. It would be better to speak of alternative modernities, as the cultures that emerge in the world to carry the institutional changes turn out to differ in important ways from each other. Thus a Japanese modernity, an Indian modernity, and various modulations of Islamic modernity will probably enter alongside the gamut of Western societies, which are also far from being totally uniform.

Looking at modernity from this perspective, we can see that it—the wave of modernity—can be felt as a threat to a traditional culture. It will remain an external threat to those deeply committed against change. But there is another reaction among those who want to take on some version of the institutional changes. Unlike the conservatives, they don't want to refuse the changes. They of course want to avoid the fate of those aboriginal people who have just been engulfed and made over by the changes. What they are looking for is a creative adaptation, drawing on the cultural resources of their tradition that would enable them to take on the new practices successfully. In short, they want to do what has already been done in the West. But they see, or sense, that that cannot consist in just copying the West's adaptations. The creative adaptation using traditional resources by definition has to be different from culture to culture. Just taking over Western modernity couldn't be the answer. Or otherwise put, this answer comes too close to engulfment. They have to invent their own.

There is thus a "call to difference" felt by "modernizing" elites that corresponds to something objective in their situation. This is part of the background to nationalism. But there is more. The call to difference could be felt by anyone concerned for the well-being of the people involved. But the challenge is lived by the elites concerned overwhelmingly in a certain register, that of dignity.

Western modernity has been a conquering culture because the changes described above confer tremendous power on the societies adopting them. In the relation of conquest, there grow presumptions of superiority and inferiority that the conqueror blithely accepts and the conquered resist. This is the challenge to dignity. To the extent that traditional elites can remain insulated from the relationship, they feel the challenge less. But those involved in modernization, whether it be in a colony or a country overshadowed and threatened, have before them constantly what they also see as a state of backwardness that they are concerned to make up for. The issue is whether they can.

Thus the urge on the part of elites to find their own path is more than a matter of concern for their compatriots. It is also a matter of their own dignity. Until they can find their own creative adaptation and take on the institutional changes while remaining themselves, the imputation of inferiority against the culture they identify with remains unrefuted. And, of course, the imputation is liberally made by members of the dominant societies. Their word tends (irrationally but understandably) to have weight just because of their success and power. They become, in a sense, important interlocutors whose recognition would count for a lot if they gave it. In the face of nonrecognition, this importance will frequently be denied, but sometimes with a vehemence that makes the denial suspect.

I am trying to identify the source of the modern nationalist turn, the refusal—at first among elites—of incorporation by the metropolitan culture, as a recognition of the need for difference but felt existentially as a challenge, not just as a matter of valuable common good to be created but also viscerally as a matter of dignity, in which one's self-worth is engaged. This is what gives nationalism its emotive power. This is what places it so frequently in the register of pride and humiliation.

So nationalism can be said to be modern because it's a response to a modern predicament. But the link is also more intimate. I said above that nationalism usually arises among "modernizing" elites. The link can be understood as more than accidental. One facet of nationalism, I have been arguing, is a response to a threat to dignity. But modernity has also transformed the conditions of dignity.

These in effect could not but change in the move from hierarchical, "mediated" societies to "horizontal," direct-access ones. The concept of honor, which was in place in the earlier forms, was intrinsically hierarchical. It supposed "preferences," in Montesquieu's terms. For me to have honor, I had to have a status that not everyone shares, as is still the case with an "honors list" of awards today. Equal direct-access societies have developed the modern notion of "dignity." This is based on the opposite supposition that all humans enjoy this equally. For instance, the term as used by Kant designates what is supposed to be the appanage of all rational agents. Philosophically, we may want to attribute this status to all, but politically, the sense of equal dignity is really shared by people who belong to a functioning direct-access society together.[12] In this typically modern predicament, their dignity passes through their common categorical identity. My sense of my own worth can no longer be based mainly on my lineage, my clan. A goodly part of it will usually be invested in some other categorical identity.

But categorical identities can also be threatened, even humiliated. The more we are inducted into modern society, the more this is the form in which the question of dignity will pose itself for us. Nationalism is modern because it is a typically modern way of responding to the threat represented by the advancing wave of modernization. Elites have always been able to experience a dramatic loss of dignity in the face of conquering power. One way of responding is to fight back or come to terms with the conquerors out of the same traditional identity and sense of honor. Another is to force a new categorical identity to be the bearer of the sought-for dignity. It is (a subspecies of) this second reaction that we call nationalist. But it is essentially modern. The 1857 rebellion in India was in part an attempt to expunge this perennially available loss of dignity in a premodern context. In this sense, it was not a nationalist movement, as the later Congress was.

The modern context of nationalism is also what turns its search for dignity outward. No human identity is purely inwardly formed. The other always plays some role. But it can be just as a foil, a contrast, a way of defining what we're not, for better or for worse. So the aboriginals of the newly "discovered" world figured for post-Columbian Europeans. The "savage," the other of civilization, provided a way for Europeans to define themselves, both favorably (applying "civilized" to themselves in self-congratulation) and sometimes unfavorably (Europeans as corrupted in contrast to the "noble savage"). This kind of other reference requires no interaction. Indeed, the less interaction the better, or else the stereotype may be resisted.

But the other can also play a role directly, where I need his or her recognition to be confident of my identity. This has been standard for our relation to our intimates, but it wasn't that important in relation to outsiders in the premodern period. Identities were defined by reference to the other but not out of the other's reactions. Where this latter becomes so, of course, the way we interact is crucial. Perhaps we should correct this statement: because of the big part played by illusion, the way the interaction is seen by the parties is crucial. But the key point is that the interaction is understood to be crucial by the identity bearers themselves.

I would like to argue that identities in the modern world are more and more formed in this direct relation to others, in a space of recognition. I can't argue the general case here,[13] but I hope that this is evident for modern nationalism. Modern nationalist politics is a species of identity politics. Indeed, the original species: national struggles are the site from which the model comes to be applied to feminism, to the struggles of cultural minorities, to the gay movement, et cetera. The work of someone like Frantz Fanon,[14] written in the context of the anticolonial struggle but whose themes have been revived in the other contexts, illustrates the connections. Strong national sentiment among elites usually arises in the first phase because an identity is threatened in its worth.

This identity is vulnerable to nonrecognition, at first on the part of the members of the dominant societies, but later there has developed a world public scene, on which peoples see themselves as standing, on which they see themselves as rated, and which rating matters to them. This world scene is dominated by a vocabulary of relative advance, even to the point of having to discover periodic neologisms in order to euphemize the distinctions. Hence what used to be called the "backward" societies began to be called "underdeveloped" after the war, and then even this came to be seen as indelicate, and so we have the present partition: developed/developing. The backdrop of modern nationalism, that there is something to be caught up with, each society in its own way, is inscribed in this common language, which in turn animates the world public sphere.

Modern nationalism thus taps into something perennial. Conquest or the threat of conquest has never been good for one's sense of worth. But the whole context in which this nationalism arises—that of successive waves of (institutional) modernization—and the resultant challenge to difference—that of the growth of categorical identities—as well as the creation of the world public sphere as a space of recognition—are quintessentially modern. We are very far from atavistic reactions and primal identities.

Hence the first phase of modern nationalism, the refusal of incorporation, arises from the felt need for difference in the context of modernization, but lived in the register of dignity, of an identity potentially threatened in its worth, and in a growing space of recognition.

Let's suppose this is all true (a proposition with a very low antecedent probability); it still only accounts for the first phase. How does nationalism become generalized and galvanize whole populations? How does it spread beyond the elites?

The answer to this question will be even more unsatisfactory than the answer to the previous question. There doesn't seem to be a single mechanism. Sometimes a charismatic leadership with great imaginative power can make nationalism a mass movement by linking the national aspiration to a host of existing complaints. This was true in the case of Gandhi during the Salt March, for instance. Often the movement spreads slowly down from the original elites to those who strive to emulate them, accede to them, and take them as their model. And when we take account of the fact that modernity itself, as we saw above, tends to generalize a transformation of the original high culture, we can understand how more and more strata of the population may come to experience their situation in the terms originally espoused by elites.

These are ways in which the mass of the people can come to share in the original nationalist aspiration and sense of vulnerable identity. But there are other ways in which nationalism can become a mass movement, in which ordinary people are recruited into it without necessarily sharing the original outlook. Sometimes active minorities, themselves actuated by nationalist fears and aspirations, can contrive to sow discord, distrust, and hatred between populations that hitherto had lived in some amity side by side. Terrorist killings can accomplish this, or atrocities committed by armed gangs, identified as from one group, against the members of the other community. Then uninvolved people can begin to mistrust their neighbors, even though these may be uninvolved as well. Each community draws together among its own members, in fear and for protection. But the result is that they begin to condone or at least not protest the action of their self-appointed "self-defense" squads, as these perhaps begin to clear out the now-untrustworthy neighbors. The scenario is all too depressingly familiar from recent developments in Croatia and Bosnia.

At the end of the day, each community is ranged against the other, perhaps even geographically separated into "ethnically cleansed" pockets, full of a hatred and fear fed on atrocity stories and often feeling betrayed and bewildered. Each community is now in the grip of a powerful nationalism, hell-bent on its own form of ethnically pure "self-determination," but for the masses the motivation may have little to do with a call to difference and a sense of threatened identity. This is a nationalism born of a sense of physical threat, of the fear of displacement, even extermination, by a hostile other. Each community has the sense that the other united first against its unsuspecting members and that its own mobilization is secondary and defensive in nature. The tragedy is that often neither is right; the split was in a sense engineered by determined and violent minorities, playing a game of provocation and counterprovocation, objectively allied in gradually unraveling ties of conviviality, even intermarriage, which may be of centuries' standing.[15]

Many of today's mass nationalisms are of this secondary and defensive variety, a response to the perceived threat of expulsion or genocide. The infernal circles of killings between Armenians and Azeris, Georgians and Abkhazi, and so on, are of this kind. But this is not to say that such nationalisms are of an entirely different kind. Because somewhere in the causal story is usually the action of minority elites, who were actuated by the classic motivation to difference I described above. What does distinguish them, however, is that the diffusion of the nationalist movement doesn't come through more and more strata coming to share the original aspiration, through a conversion to the nationalist vision, as with Gandhi and the Salt March, but rather through the (often-manipulated) politics of division and mutual threat—not an identity threat in this case but a physical threat of exile or annihilation. I want to call this kind of mass nationalism defensive, but we have to remember that usually at its origin lies a minority nationalism of aspiration. And of course it may also happen that over time, in a third phase, a mass nationalism of defense can be gradually won over to some version of the original aspiration.

The rise of communal "nationalisms" in India illustrates these mechanisms. Before the mass agitations of the twentieth century, Hindus and Muslims often enjoyed a degree of conviviality difficult to imagine today. Both communities participated in a form of syncretism. In certain parts of the subcontinent, Hindus would attend the celebration of Moharram and Muslims would attend Dussehra feasts. Protests around the turn of the century began to come from elites in both communities, who wanted to create and propagate a purer, more consistent version of their respective religious identities.

The motivations for religious reform and purification are, of course, always plural and complex. But I would maintain that part of the motivation is the one I described above. Hindu reform, for instance, from Rammohan Roy on, was partly stimulated by the fact of domination, by admiration for the powers of discipline and organization of the dominators, and by the desire to find Hindu sources for an identity that could sustain the same reformed practices. It was an unavoidable by-product of this that popular syncretism, along with many other practices of popular Hinduism, was judged unacceptable. In Arya Samaj terms, it was "idolatry."

A similar approach, couched in the same terms, comes from the side of Muslim reform. These reform movements, which turned to a purer, often more Sharia-oriented Islam and condemned various popular practices, sometimes including various aspects of Sufism, have been a feature of the last century or so. Indeed, they began somewhat earlier if we include the Wahhabi. Again, it would be a wild oversimplification to explain them entirely as the response to a "call to difference." But the need to respond to a conquering West and the wounds to Islam's self-esteem as itself an erstwhile conquering civilization have almost certainly given a stimulus to these movements.

The move to sever syncretic conviviality, then, comes from elites concerned, at least in some important part, with the call to difference and the threat to identity. And indeed, the Arya Samaj did call for Hindus to cease participating in Moharram, and to complete the connection, members of the Arya Samaj formed part of the nucleus out of which emerged the Rashtriya Swayamsevak Sangh and later the Bharatiya Janata Party, standard-bearers of contemporary Hindu communalism.

But between pure-minded calls to renounce syncretism and the present communal violence and mistrust lies the second phase. My argument is that, unlike the pan-Indian nationalism of Gandhi, followed by Nehru, which was popularized by diffusion of the aspiration concerned, communalism made inroads into syncretic conviviality mainly through clashes and conflicts that raised ever-stronger reactions of defense. For Jinnah and those around him, the impulse to form Pakistan had a lot to do with the preservation of a modernized (and, in Jinnah's case, rather secularized) Muslim identity against the danger of being overwhelmed in a Hindu state. Their own "call to difference" risked being drowned out, they feared, by India's answer to its own call. But when the Muslim League swept the Muslim areas of India in the elections of 1941, the popular slogan was "Islam in danger!" What was being conjured up here was a threat of a more direct and aggressive kind. The ideology of Pakistan propagated itself as a defensive nationalism.

Of course, since then, in a third phase, the original positive aspiration may have propagated itself downward in Pakistani society. It is not easy to judge the extent to which this is so because defensiveness and threat still seem important mainstays of Pakistani unity.

I have been trying to plug the explanatory hole that I saw in Gellner's account and my Anderson-inspired complement to it. These told us something about the context of modern nationalist struggles, even about what can make them virtually inevitable. But the sources of nationalist aspirations escaped us. They offered us Hamlet without the prince. I have tried to explain the missing bit by invoking the context of expanding modernity and the call to difference it raises among peoples in the path of that expansion. This call, lived by elites in the register of dignity, can become the basis of a mass movement in a number of ways, including some rather sinister and destructive ones that have little to do with the call itself.

What does this tell us about the kinds of nationalism? Can we think of it as something homogeneous? Here there are lots of difficulties, and I can see my theory already in danger of unraveling because it places phenomena like the various modes of Islamic "fundamentalism" in the Third World (Iran, Algeria) in the same category as nationalism. Indeed, insofar as I am trying to account for nationalism as a call to difference in face of the wave of "modernization," lived in the register of threatened dignity, and constructing a new, categorical identity as the bearer of that dignity, I could also be talking of the rise of Marxist parties in certain Third World contexts.

This doesn't by itself worry me. As Liah Greenfeld argues (and I feel my account has a lot in common with hers),[16] this may even be a plus for the account. We shouldn't make a fetish of our preliminary vocabulary of distinctions. So what if the categories that emerge from the explanation include more than what we antecedently called "nationalism"? If some common element is really illuminated, then we have gained.

Now with the very important reservation that I don't want to reduce Islamic integrism to a single mode of explanation, as we are dealing with a complex, many-sided, overdetermined, reality, I nevertheless would like to argue that its various manifestations have some features of the profile I have just outlined. The sense of operating on a world scene in the register of threatened dignity is very much present, as are the overvehement rejection of the West (or its quintessence, America, the "great Satan") and the tremendous sensitivity to criticism from this quarter, for all the protestations of hostility and indifference. Islamic societies are perhaps, if anything, more vulnerable to a threat to their self-esteem from the impact of superior power in that Islam's self-image, as indicated above, was of the definitive revelation, destined to spread outward without check. The Islamic sense of Providence, if I may use this Christian expression, can cope with the status of conquerors but tends to be bewildered by the experience of powerlessness and conquest.

Again, for all the protestations of faithfulness to the origins, this integrism is in some respects very modern. It mobilizes people in a modern fashion in horizontal, direct-access movements; it thus has no problem using the "modern" institutional apparatuses of elected legislatures, bureaucratic states, and armies. While it would reject the doctrine of popular sovereignty in favor of a species of theocracy, it has also delegitimated all the traditional ruling strata. The Iranian revolution was carried out against the Shah. Those enjoying special authority are exclusively those who "rationally" merit this, granted the nature and goals of the state—namely, the experts in God's law (not to speak of Ayatollah Khomeini's media-oriented abuse of the Islamic judicial forms in issuing his *fatwa* against Salman Rushdie).

Indeed, it seems true of all fundamentalisms that they paradoxically are most modern when they think they are most faithful to tradition, starting with the original home of the term, in the Protestant sectarian doctrines of biblical inerrancy. This is, in fact, a doctrine only defended in recent centuries. But more important, one can doubt that the issue would even have been clearly understood by Christians in earlier centuries. It supposes a modern conception of the literal truth in secular time that owes something to our social imaginary and our science. Christians of earlier centuries lived in a world in which secular time was interwoven with various orders of higher time, various dimensions of eternity. From within this time sense, it may be hard to explain just what is at stake in the question whether "day" in Genesis means "literally" the twenty-four hours between sunset and sunset, let alone convince someone that he or she should be concerned about it.

Moreover, seeing nationalism, proletarian internationalism, and religious fundamentalisms in the same register may help us to understand their interaction, that they are so often, in fact, fighting for the same space. Arab nationalism gives way to Islamic integrism,[17] just as the demise of Soviet Marxism opens the way for virulent nationalisms. The search for a categorical identity, to answer the call to difference and be the bearer of the sought-for dignity, can take many forms. It is understandable that the discrediting of some strengthens the appeal of others.

Moreover, this kind of diversity and rivalry shades into that between different definitions of nationalism. In many countries, fewer and more inclusive national identities have vied for people's allegiance: Quebecois and Canadian, Slovak and Czecho-Slovak, Scots and British. Indeed, one could class the struggle between Nehruvian and "Hindutva" nationalism in India as another such rivalry rather than as a struggle between a national and a religious identity. In all the struggles invoked in this and the preceding paragraph, it is as though there were a space waiting to be filled. It is this that I am trying to cast light on.

So I'm not unduly worried that my account may lead us to bring together things that we now class under different headings. Understanding nationalism in terms of a "call to difference" allows for a great variety of different responses. The aspiration to take on certain forms of modernity on the basis of one's own cultural resources can obviously be played out in many different ways, depending on what you want to take over and what cultural resources you hope to sustain it with. The considerations Gellner adduces, as well as others, certainly explain why one thing people generally want to take over is state power; hence the near-universal validity of his definition of nationalism. But we can also see why in special circumstances a phenomenon like pre-1960 Quebec "nationalism" can arise.

But one difference is worth noting here—that between liberal nationalism like, for example, contemporary Quebec independentism on the one hand and what we now see raging in Bosnia on the other. There are some common roots, as captured in my scheme, but there are also clear qualitative differences. The idea that these are both manifestations of the same force but differing in virulence is a serious mistake. It is not just that the second phase in Bosnia was a purely "defensive" one, in my sense. More fundamentally, nationalisms differ, as I have just said, in regard to what they want to take over.

Now in some nationalisms part of what is defined as the desirable modernity is the liberal regime of rights and equal citizenship, attributed to all members of the political unit, regardless of differences, even of ethnicity. These nationalisms have taken over—one might better say, have never lost—the aspirations to patriotism of the founding revolutions anterior to nationalism. The original "nations" these revolutions sought to liberate were held to consist of all free men living in the historically defined societies. The fact that "free men" excluded women in one way and Afro-American slaves in another, more grievous way didn't totally blunt the force of this principle. On the contrary, this force was part of the complex of factors that eventually led to the lifting of these exclusions.

The first wave of nationalisms in Europe that grew up in opposition to the Holy Alliance were of this liberal sort. They retained the original *Verfassungspatriotismus* of the revolutions; their sense of nation incorporated the constitutional principles of liberalism. Contemporary Quebec nationalism is of this kind.

Of course, liberal nationalism suffers strains. All are citizens without distinction, and yet the state has its raison d'être in a cultural nation to which not all citizens belong. There are tensions here to be managed. But there is no question of sacrificing universality on the altar of the nation, for this would be a betrayal of identity.

Quite different are the modes of nationalism where what is to be taken over does not include this liberal patriotism, even in some cases, as in proto-Nazi German movements, where this patriotism is rejected as an alien element, a bit of "Zivilisation" that is contrary to the "Kultur" of the nation, or where liberal politics has never had a toehold, as in the Balkans. There one can have forms where the aspiration includes state power, economic development, even something like an abolition of traditional hierarchies in the name of popular sovereignty. But nothing stands in the way of defining the nation purely ethnically, even racially. Where this is so, the elements of modern politics taken up are no help. Rather, they aggravate things. At least traditional societies recognized some moral limits, however frequently transgressed, in the treatment of outsiders. But in the face of the sovereign national will, source of all right, nothing else can stand.

Premodern societies often incorporated different groups in a sort of hierarchy of complementarity, where each one had its niche—as Greeks, for instance, were frequently merchants in the Ottoman Empire. This was a far cry from equal rights, but it did confer a semisecure status. But the outsider has no place in a regime of popular sovereignty, where the people are ethnically defined. Moreover, under the rules of self-determination, outsiders in sufficiently large numbers can contest one's right to the territory. Add to this the sense of threat in defensive nationalism and the scene is set for ethnic cleansing.

It is clear that this type of nationalism, while having partly similar roots to the liberal one and growing and operating within the context of modernity, is nevertheless a wholly different animal, obeying a different dynamic. The account I'm offering should not only lead us to see other phenomena (for example, some "fundamentalisms") as very similar to nationalism but also help us to distinguish rather different modes within the category.

I have not addressed all sorts of other objections. But enough is enough. I have tried to present an account of nationalism on two levels, as it were: on one level, I have attempted to describe the social and state context in which national struggles are played out and by which the stakes of these struggles are defined; and on a second level, which it was more foolhardy to venture onto, I have tried to say what gives rise to nationalist aspirations and national movements. Whatever the inaccuracy of my remarks on this second level (or indeed, on the first), I am convinced that nationalism needs to be tackled in this two-pronged way, and I hope to have helped clarify some of the thorny issues that impede our vision of this absorbing, disturbing, but seemingly inescapable feature of our modern world.

NOTES

1. We might follow Ernest Gellner in defining nationalism as the "political principle, which holds that the political and the national unit should be congruent" (*Nations and Nationalism* [Ithaca: Cornell University Press, 1983], p. 1). The basic idea is that a people, defined antecedently by unity of culture, language, or religion, should be allowed to give themselves their own political forms. This certainly picks out a class of movements, sentiments, political *idées-forces* in the contemporary world, namely, those related to that principle. The question I'm raising is whether they all have the same causes and are moved by the same dynamic.

2. I am drawing here on ibid.

3. Ibid., p. 39.

4. I have borrowed this terminology from Craig Calhoun. See, for instance, his "Nationalism and Ethnicity," *American Review of Sociology*, no. 19 (1993): 230. I have drawn heavily on Calhoun's work in my characterization of "direct-access" societies below.

5. Gellner, *Nations and Nationalism*, p. 18. I have dwelt at length here on only one facet of Gellner's theory, the emphasis on the homogenization functionally essential to a modern economy. But the move to modern, homogenized society was driven by other things as well. The modern European bureaucratic state has been growing for a number of centuries, increasing its outreach, invading the lives of its citizens, administering its territories, far and near, by uniform principles. Not all of this was powered by economic motives (though much undoubtedly was). But the upshot essentially provides the basis from which Gellner's account takes off: this historical development has given us the homogeneous state with its

uniform official language and culture, indispensable to our kind of economy as well as to our type of polity and our administrative procedures. And it is this that accounts for nationalism.

6. Eugen Weber, *Peasants into Frenchmen* (Stanford: Stanford University Press, 1976).

7. Benedict Anderson, *Imagined Communities: Reflections on the Origin and Spread of Nationalism*, rev. ed. (London: Verso, 1991).

8. Ibid., p. 37.

9. Calhoun, "Nationalism and Ethnicity," pp. 234–35. I want to reiterate how much the discussion in this section owes to Calhoun's recent work.

10. I haven't discussed the case of nondemocratic regimes based on popular will, but these plainly push in the same direction, indeed, even further and faster. Because their emanation from the common will is essential to their legitimacy, they cannot leave their citizens alone in a condition of obedient passivity, as earlier despotic regimes were content to do. They must always mobilize the citizens into repeated expressions of unshakable, unanimous will: phony elections, demonstrations, May Day parades, and the like. This is the essence of modern "totalitarianism" in its distinction from earlier despotism.

Calhoun in "Nationalism and Ethnicity" stresses, however, how easily the search for national identity, even in democratic contexts, leads to an attempt to induce people to suppress their other (gender, religious, minority-cultural) identities in favor of a "national" one. The modern quest for patriotism is full of dangers.

11. Many are "produced," however, at an earlier phase in which a movement begins to unite disparate populations under the same banner in the name of a supposed common history. Thus many official languages today have resulted from the imposition of one dialect as the "true" language on whole peoples who earlier spoke a scattering of similar dialects. National vernaculars have almost always had to be "invented" in this sense.

Too much has perhaps been made of this point in a spirit of debunking nationalist claims. A lot of nationalist history hovers between myth and lies. But as Calhoun cogently argues, this doesn't by itself invalidate the claims that contemporaries may make in terms of their shared sense of national identity: "Ethnicity or cultural traditions are bases for nationalism when they effectively constitute historical memory, when they inculcate it as habitus, . . . not when (or because) the historical origins they claim are accurate" ("Nationalism and Ethnicity," p. 222).

12. This doesn't have to be a political society. It can be a dispersed common agency, like a religious or ethnic group.

13. See Charles Taylor, "The Politics of Recognition," in *Multiculturalism and "The Politics of Recognition,"* ed. Amy Gutmann (Princeton: Princeton University Press, 1992), pp. 25–73.

14. Especially Frantz Fanon, *Les Damnés de la Terre* (Paris: Maspéro, 1975).

15. Fortunately, this tactic doesn't always succeed. There are signs that ties between Hindus and Sikhs in the Punjab were in many cases strong enough to withstand the atrocities perpetrated by murderous bands of Khalistan supporters, though a self-feeding process of distrust and division was clearly the aim of these terrible acts. Again, after the massacres of partition in 1947, the communities in India seemed to draw back from the brink. Secularism was strengthened for a while. It took some time for the forces of Hindu chauvinism to make the progress they have registered recently.

16. See Liah Greenfeld, "Transcending the Nation's Worth," *Daedalus* 122, no. 3 (Summer 1993): 47–62. A fuller account of her view is given in *Nationalism: Five Roads to Modernity* (Cambridge, Mass.: Harvard University Press, 1992).

17. See Martin Kramer, "Arab Nationalism: Mistaken Identity," *Daedalus* 122, no. 3 (Summer 1993): 171–206.

4

The Sources of Nationalism
Commentary on Taylor

WILL KYMLICKA

Charles Taylor's chapter has two main sections: an account of the modern "context" of nationalist movements, drawing on the work of Gellner and Anderson, and then an account of the "sources" of nationalism, applying Taylor's own earlier work on the idea of "a politics of recognition." I found the first section to be insightful and helpful, but I'm puzzled about the second section and, indeed, about the distinction between the "context" and "sources" of nationalism.

I will start by identifying and elaborating some of the most important points in the first half of the chapter. I hope to show that if we have a fuller view of (what Taylor calls) the "context" of modern nationalism, then the sorts of questions we face regarding the "sources" of nationalism are different from the ones Taylor identifies and require different sorts of answers.

Taylor rightly argues that an essential component of modernization is the diffusion throughout a society of a common culture, including a standardized language. This occurs for a variety of reasons, of which Taylor emphasizes two. First, it is a functional requirement of a modern economy, with its need for a mobile and educated workforce. Second, it reflects the need for a high level of solidarity within democratic states. The sort of solidarity needed by a welfare state requires that citizens have a strong sense of common identity and common membership so that they will make sacrifices for each other, and this common identity is assumed to require (or at least be facilitated by) a common language and history. A third reason, which Taylor does not emphasize but which may be equally important, is that the diffusion of a common culture seems essential to the modern commitment to equality of opportunity. The provision of standardized public education through-out a society, for example, has been seen as necessary to ensure equality of oppor-tunity for people from different classes and regions of the society.

So the process of modernization involves, inter alia, a process of "nation build-ing"—that is, a process of promoting a common language and a sense of com-mon membership in and equal access to the social institutions based on that language.

What this clearly shows, I think, is that modern political life has an inescapably national dimension to it. This is reflected in decisions regarding official languages, core curricula in education, and the requirements for acquiring citizenship, all of which involve diffusing a particular national culture throughout society and all of which seek to promote a particular national identity based on participation in that national culture.

Some people think that the United States provides an exception to this rule, since it has no constitutionally recognized official language. But this is misleading. The fact is that the U.S. government promotes a common language and culture as much as any other state does. Thus it is a legal requirement for children to learn the English language and American history in schools; it is a legal requirement that immigrants (over the age of fifty) learn the English language and American history in order to acquire American citizenship; it is a de facto requirement for employ-ment in government that the applicant speak English; court proceedings and other government activities are typically conducted only in English; and the resulting legislation and bureaucratic forms are typically only provided in English. All lev-els of American government—federal, state, and municipal—have insisted that there is a legitimate governmental interest in promoting a common language, and the Supreme Court has repeatedly affirmed that claim in upholding laws that mandate the teaching and use of English in schools and government functions. In-deed, as Gerald Johnson put it, "It is one of history's little ironies that no polyglot empire of the old world has dared to be so ruthless in imposing a single language upon its whole population as was the liberal republic 'dedicated to the proposition that all men are created equal.'"[1]

Some theorists seem to think that modern governments can and should avoid supporting any particular national culture or national identity. Hence some theo-rists talk about a state that is "neutral" with respect to national identity. They sug-gest that governments should treat culture the same way they treat religion—that is, as something people should be free to pursue in their private lives but that is not the concern of the state. Just as liberalism precludes the establishment of an official religion, so, too, there cannot be official cultures that have preferred status over other possible cultural allegiances.

For example, Michael Walzer argues that liberalism involves "a sharp divorce of state and ethnicity." The liberal state stands above all the various ethnic and na-tional groups in the country, "refusing to endorse or support their ways of life or to take an active interest in their social reproduction." Instead, the state is "neutral with reference to language, history, literature, calendar" of these groups.[2]

But this is incoherent. The idea that the government could be neutral with respect to cultural groups is patently false. One of the most important determinants of whether a culture survives is whether its language is a language of government—that is, whether its language is used in public schooling, courts, legislatures, welfare agencies, health services, et cetera. When the government decides the language of public schooling, it provides what is probably the most important form of support needed by cultural structures, since it guarantees the passing on of the language and its associated traditions and conventions to the next generation.

Conversely, it is very difficult for languages to survive in modern industrialized societies unless they are used in public life. Given the spread of standardized education, the high demands for literacy in work, and widespread interaction with government agencies, any language that is not a public language becomes so marginalized that it is likely to survive only among a small elite, in isolated rural areas, or in a ritualized form, not as a living and developing language underlying a flourishing culture.

This shows that the analogy between religion and culture is mistaken. It is quite possible for a state not to have an established church. But the state cannot help but give at least partial establishment to a culture when it decides which language is to be used in public schooling or in the provision of state services. And there are many other ways in which governmental decisions and institutions help to sustain particular cultures—for example, decisions about immigration, public holidays, school curricula, the drawing of political boundaries, or the division of powers between different levels of government.[3]

Once we recognize this inescapably national dimension to political life, we have taken the first steps toward an explanation of the rise of nationalist movements. As Taylor rightly notes, the process of nation building inescapably privileges members of the majority culture: "If a modern society has an 'official' language, in the fullest sense of the term—that is, a state-sponsored, -inculcated, and -defined language and culture, in which both economy and state function—then it is obviously an immense advantage to people if this language and culture are theirs. Speakers of other languages are at a distinct disadvantage." This means that minority cultures face a difficult choice. To avoid perpetual marginalization, minorities must either integrate into the majority culture or start a movement to gain official status for their language and culture.[4]

Faced with this choice, most immigrants will choose to integrate. After all, they have already voluntarily left their own culture with the expectation of integrating into another national society. That's what it means to become an immigrant. If they found the idea of integrating into another culture repugnant, they would not have chosen to become immigrants. Moreover, since they typically emigrated as individuals or families, rather than as entire communities, immigrants lack the territorial concentration or corporate institutions needed to form a linguistically distinct economy and society alongside the mainstream economy and society. Any attempt to re-create such a distinct parallel society would require tremendous support from the host society—not only in terms of language rights but also in terms of settlement policy and even the redrawing of boundaries so as to enable some form of self-government—support that no host government would be inclined to offer. So the nationalist option is neither desirable nor feasible for immigrants. And indeed there are very few (if any) examples in the modern world of immigrant groups forming nationalist movements for self-government or secession.[5]

The case of nonimmigrant minorities, however, is very different. By nonimmigrant minorities I mean historically settled, territorially concentrated, and previously self-governing cultures whose territory has somehow become incorporated into a larger state. In the North American context, this would include the indigenous Indians and Inuit, Québécois, Puerto Ricans, native Hawaiians, and other groups whose territory has been conquered or colonized. These groups at the time of their incorporation into the larger state had already formed culturally and linguistically distinct societies, and unlike immigrants, they had not chosen to leave their culture and homeland.

The project of nation building has very different implications for immigrants and settled minorities, both factually and normatively. Immigrants rarely object to the imposition of a common language, since they have already chosen to leave their old culture behind and since the option of re-creating a culturally distinct society alongside the existing national culture is not feasible. For incorporated minorities, however, the imposition of the majority language threatens their existing culturally distinct society. Such groups almost inevitably resist integration and seek official recognition of their language and culture.

As Taylor notes, this demand for official recognition needn't take the form of a secessionist movement for a separate state. It could instead take the form of demanding some form of local autonomy, perhaps through a system of federalism and/or a system of official bilingualism. But whatever the exact form, it typically involves the demand for the sorts of legal rights and legislative powers necessary to ensure the survival of a culturally distinct society alongside the majority society.

As Taylor rightly notes, such nationalist movements are a distinctly modern phenomenon, not only in the sense that they are a natural concomitant to the modernizing project of nation building, but also in the sense that they are themselves a form of nation building. Nationalists in Quebec or Catalonia also believe in the importance of diffusing a common culture and language throughout their society so as to diminish class and regional differences. And they use the same tools that the majority nation uses in its program of nation building—that is, standardized public education, official languages, including language requirements for citizenship and government employment, et cetera.

So nationalist movements by national minorities are not rejecting the dynamic of modernization and nation building. They accept the idea that a modern economy and democratic community require a diffused common culture. They are simply arguing that they form their own distinct economy and society within the boundaries of the larger state. They are arguing that some countries are not nation-states but multination-states, containing two or more national societies.

To my mind, this claim is perfectly understandable and, indeed, eminently fair. The fact that a previously self-governing society has been incorporated (often involuntarily) into a larger state does not mean that it ceases to form its own distinct national society.

In the case of immigrants, I think it is fair for governments to say that individuals who voluntarily choose to come to a new country are expected to integrate into the existing national society. But to forcibly incorporate a national minority into a larger state and then deny that group language and self-government rights because they are now a minority is to compound one injustice with another.

So far, I have simply been restating and amplifying Taylor's comments, in the first part of the essay, that help explain the context for the emergence of nationalist movements. However, Taylor insists that these considerations are not yet sufficient to explain nationalism because we still need to know why "some put up a fight and create nationalist movements while others do not." To answer this question, he argues, we need a deeper theory of the "sources" of nationalism.

At this point, I begin to lose the thread of Taylor's essay. To begin with, I'm not sure I understand his question. If Taylor is asking why immigrants integrate while national minorities do not, then that seems to be fairly obvious—part and parcel of the process of uprooting oneself from one's culture and immigrating to another society is leaving behind the potential (and motivation) for national claims. If instead Taylor is asking why some national minorities resist while others do not, then I think the question is misleading. The fact is that virtually every national group in this century has put up a fight. Indeed, Walker Connor goes so far as to suggest that there are no examples of recognized national groups in this century having voluntarily assimilated to another culture.[6] (There are many examples from earlier centuries of national groups disappearing without a fight, but both the means of nation building and the scope for organized resistance were very different then. For example, the issue of the language of public schooling obviously could not arise before there was public schooling.)

So the question is not why some national minorities resist and others do not but rather why virtually all such minorities put up a fight. The answer again seems quite obvious—the desire to live and work in one's own language is, I think, very natural and understandable. Why *wouldn't* national minorities wish to maintain their culture?[7]

Indeed, the idea that people have a deep attachment to their own language and culture has been widely accepted by theorists from all points of the political spectrum. This idea is sometimes said to reflect a communitarian or conservative view of self-identity. But in fact it is widely accepted, implicitly or explicitly, by liberals as well. Consider John Rawls's argument about why the right to emigrate does not make political authority voluntary:

> Normally leaving one's country is a grave step: it involves leaving the society and culture in which we have been raised, the society and culture whose language we use in speech and thought to express and understand ourselves, our aims, goals, and values; the society and culture whose history, customs, and conventions we depend on to find our place in the social world. In large part, we affirm our society and culture, and have an intimate and inexpressible knowledge of it, even though much of it we may question, if not reject. The government's authority cannot, then, be freely accepted in the sense that the bonds of society and culture, of history and social place of origin, begin so early to shape our life and are normally so strong that the right of emigration (suitably qualified) does not suffice to make accepting its authority free, politically speaking, in the way that liberty of conscience suffices to make accepting ecclesiastical authority free, politically speaking.[8]

Because of these bonds to the "language we use in speech and thought to express and understand ourselves," cultural ties "are normally too strong to be given up, and this fact is not to be deplored." Hence for the purposes of developing a theory of justice, we should assume that "people are born and are expected to lead a complete life" within the same "society and culture."[9] According to Rawls, then, the ties to one's language are normally too strong to give up, and this is not to be regretted. We can't be expected or required to make such a sacrifice, even if some people voluntarily do so.

Of course, Rawls is not talking in this passage about a national minority but rather about the members of the majority nation. Or, more accurately, he is actually assuming that the boundaries of the country coincide with the boundaries of a single national society and that people who share the same citizenship share the same language and culture. Throughout his work he equates a "country" with a "society" with a "people" with a "culture" with a "language." Thus he presents the passage above as an argument about the difficulty of leaving one's political community. But this is misleading since his argument does not rest on the value of specifically political ties (for example, the bonds to one's government and fellow citizens). Rather it rests on the value of cultural ties (such as bonds to one's language and culture). And in countries with national minorities, cultural boundaries do not coincide with political boundaries. While Rawls himself never addresses the case of multination countries, his argument above explains and supports the desire of national minorities to live and work in their own culture. One could find virtually identical arguments and assumptions about the value of national identity in many other liberal theorists, from Humboldt and Mill to Berlin and Dworkin and Raz.[10]

Taylor seems to think that this sort of explanation of nationalist movements is insufficient, and so he seeks to provide a deeper explanation of the "sources" of nationalism, in terms of the need for "dignity" and "recognition." To my mind, Taylor's argument here takes a fairly clear and commonsense phenomenon and obscures it in unnecessary complications. Of course it is true that nationalist movements involve a demand for recognition and employ the rhetoric of dignity. But the rhetoric of dignity is used to express a prior attachment to their language and culture; it is not an explanation of that attachment. To suggest, as Taylor seems to do, that people generate an attachment to their language and culture as a way of protecting their dignity seems deeply implausible to me.

Moreover, Taylor's account is misleading in focusing so exclusively on the nationalism of minorities (or other disadvantaged national groups in the Third World), as if the puzzle is to explain why minorities have this strange and unusual attachment to their own language and culture. The fact is that national minorities are no different from the members of majority nations in this regard. Anglophones in Ontario (or Illinois) are as deeply attached to their language and culture as Francophones in Quebec or the Flemish in Belgium. If the demographics were reversed, and Anglophones in the United States were outnumbered by Francophones or Hispanics, then they, too, would mobilize to gain official recognition and support for their language and culture. The only difference is that Anglophones in North America can take their national identity for granted. As Hugh Seton-Watson put it, national identity is "passively treasured by nearly all citizens of modern societies, even if they do not know it," since they take it for granted. But were their identity to be threatened, national majorities would mobilize in just the same way as minorities.[11]

By focusing on the dignity of disadvantaged national groups, Taylor implies that there is a qualitative difference in the sources or motivations of minority and majority nationalisms. But I see no evidence that there is such a qualitative difference.

Put another way, the fact that national minorities wish to retain their culture is no more puzzling than the fact that national majorities wish to retain theirs. In each case, there may be significant economic or other advantages to integrating into another culture. For example, Czechs might gain economically from replacing Czech with German as their official language. Yet no one thinks it puzzling that Czechs maintain Czech as their official language. On the contrary, we would probably be shocked if they voluntarily relinquished their language and adopted the language of a neighboring country, even if that neighbor was larger and wealthier. And indeed, to my knowledge, no examples of that have occurred in this century. Why then should we find it puzzling that the Québécois or Flemish wish to maintain their language and culture? Taking it for granted that majority nations will maintain their language and culture while expressing puzzlement at the desire of national minorities to do the same applies a double standard.

So it seems to me that Taylor's account of the "sources" of nationalism is otiose. The explanation for nationalist movements is both simpler and deeper than Taylor suggests. The desire to live and work in one's culture is simpler than the complicated psychodynamics of maintaining one's "dignity" in the face of external forces, and it is deeper and wider, since it is found equally in the members of larger and powerful national groups.

Of course, this not yet a full explanation of nationalism, because, as Taylor emphasizes, nationalist movements come in various shapes and sizes. In particular, they can be either liberal or illiberal. An illiberal nationalist movement will aim not only to maintain the ability to live in one's own culture but also to oppress dissidents or racial minorities inside the culture and/or dominate nonmembers outside the group.

For example, some nationalist movements say that membership in the national group depends on not only knowing the language and history but also having a particular skin color or sharing a particular religion Thus the "coloreds" in South Africa are excluded from membership in the Afrikaner "nation," even though they speak the same language and learn the same history and conventions as white Afrikaners in school. Similarly, the children of Turkish guest workers are denied membership in the German nation because of their ethnicity. In Yugoslavia and Iran, national membership includes religious belief, so that non-Christians and non-Muslims, respectively, are excluded from possible membership in the nation. In contrast, being accepted as a member of the American nation requires only a knowledge of the English language and American history and is otherwise open to people of all religions and races. The same is true of Quebec, where the government actively recruits black emigrants from Haiti or French West Africa and requires only that they know French and something about Quebec history to become accepted as Québécois.

Some nationalist movements not only wish to ensure that they can maintain themselves as a distinct society but also seek to dominate others and deny their rights as national minorities. This leads to campaigns of ethnic cleansing or prohibitions on the use of minority languages.

These are all illiberal forms of nationalism, and they are clearly unjust because these internal restrictions or external oppressions are not required to fulfill people's legitimate interest in maintaining their own cultural membership. It is reasonable and fair for national groups to seek some sort of official status. Given the centrality of the state in modern life, this status is needed to sustain one's language and culture. But once one has that official standing, then any racialist, oppressive, or self-aggrandizing measures are unnecessary and unjust.

It is essential to figure out why some nationalist movements take a liberal form and others do not. And this is what Gellner's and Anderson's accounts leave unexplained. Their explanations of the emergence of nationalism are clear enough, I think, but we still need to identify the "sources" of this difference between liberal and illiberal forms of nationalism.

But I don't think that Taylor's references to dignity and recognition are much help here. For one thing, Taylor's focus on minority or disadvantaged groups is too narrow. The fact is that majority and powerful national groups are just as likely to adopt illiberal forms of nationalism as minority and disadvantaged national groups. (The Germans have a more racialist conception of national membership than the Québécois.) Any account that focuses exclusively on the dynamic of minority nations cannot explain a phenomenon that is found as much among national majorities.

Moreover, as Taylor admits, his account applies to illiberal fundamentalist movements as much as to liberal nationalist movements. Taylor concedes that the rhetoric of dignity and recognition is as much at play in illiberal Iranian nationalism as it is in liberal Flemish nationalism. So obviously we need some other explanation of why some nationalist movements develop in a liberal way and others do not.

I do not have any well-worked-out answer to this question. But let me conclude by throwing out one tentative suggestion. I suspect that the extent to which a nationalist movement is liberal will largely depend on whether or not it arises within a country with long-established liberal institutions. Flemish, Scottish, and Quebec nationalisms are liberal because Belgium, Britain, and Canada are long-standing liberal democracies. Any nationalist movement that seeks to impose illiberal practices on a population accustomed to the benefits of liberal governance will not acquire any popular support. In contrast, Serb, Ukrainian, and Slovak nationalisms are illiberal because they emerged in illiberal states. Nationalist movements, then, tend to take their cue from the political culture around them.

In short, the fact that national minorities seek state recognition and use of their language and culture doesn't really need much explaining—it reflects a pervasive and commonsensical attachment to one's language and culture that is also found among national majorities. What does need explaining is why nationalism often takes an illiberal form, with membership defined along racial or religious lines or with a desire to dominate others inside or outside the group. Taylor's theory of dignity and recognition is unnecessary to explain the former and inadequate to explain the latter.

NOTES

1. Gerald Johnson, *Our English Heritage* (Westport: Greenwood, 1973), p. 119.

2. Michael Walzer, "Comment," in Charles Taylor, *Multiculturalism and The Politics of Recognition*, ed. Amy Gutmann (Princeton: Princeton University Press, 1992), pp. 100–101.

3. I discuss these examples in depth in *Multicultural Citizenship: A Liberal Theory of Minority Rights* (Oxford: Oxford University Press, 1995), chap. 6. Parenthetically, this also shows that familiar accounts of the distinction between "ethnic" and "civic" nationalism—according to which the former is concerned with the protection and promotion of a language and culture, whereas the latter is concerned solely with upholding certain principles

of liberal democracy—are misconceived. Civic nationalisms, as much as ethnic nationalisms, have involved the protection and dissemination of a common language and societal culture. For further discussion of this point, see my "Misunderstanding Nationalism," *Dissent* (Spring 1995): 130–37.

4. I don't mean to imply that these two options are logically exhaustive. One could imagine a political system that distinguished several types of power—economic, political, military, et cetera—and allocated each to a separate ethnocultural group. This was indeed how some premodern political systems worked. But that is not the way modern liberal democracies have operated.

5. My focus here is on immigrant groups, but much the same applies to refugees within Western democracies. While their decision to leave their homeland was not voluntary, they, too, typically lack the territorial concentration and institutional structures needed to form viable societal cultures in their new country.

6. Walker Connor, "Nation-Building or Nation-Destroying," *World Politics* 24 (1972): 350–51, and "The Politics of Ethnonationalism," *Journal of International Affairs* 27, no. 1 (1973): 20. For a more recent survey of ethnocultural conflicts around the world, which shows clearly the profound differences between immigrant groups and national minorities, see Ted Gurr, *Minorities at Risk: A Global View of Ethnopolitical Conflict* (Washington, D.C.: Institute of Peace, 1993).

7. It is also natural and understandable that people want to learn from other societies and to adapt and integrate some of these societies' accomplishments into their own culture. But it is important to distinguish the willingness to adapt and integrate foreign influences so as to enrich one's own society from the willingness to leave one's culture and integrate into another society. For further discussion, see my *Multicultural Citizenship*, pp. 101–5.

8. John Rawls, *Political Liberalism* (New York: Columbia University Press, 1993), p. 222.

9. Ibid., p. 277.

10. I collect some representative examples in *Multicultural Citizenship*, chaps. 4, 5. See also Yael Tamir, *Liberal Nationalism* (Princeton: Princeton University Press, 1993).

11. Or as George Bernard Shaw put it, "A healthy nation is as unconscious of its nationality as a healthy man of his bones. But if you break a nation's nationality, it will think of nothing else but getting it set again" (*John Bull's Other Island* [London: Constable, 1907], pp. xxxiv–xxxv).

5

Nationalism in a
Comparative Mode
A Response to Charles Taylor

WALTER FEINBERG

I will make three points in this chapter. The first is that Charles Taylor is right in viewing dignity as an essential feature of nationalism, but he is wrong in thinking that it can help us very much in understanding contemporary nationalist movements. Dignity functions at a very deep level within the nationalism issue and not at the level of explanation that Taylor addresses. The kind of social imagination that Taylor attaches to dignity involves the constitutive conceptual features of nationalism, but it will not get us very far when we seek to understand particular nationalisms. In other words, the idea that dignity is tied to national identity tells us about the meaning of nationalism. It does not tell us a great deal about the cause of this or that nationalist movement.

Second, the concept of dignity as Taylor develops it provides a psychological spin on the explanation of nationalism, but this spin is incomplete. It places too much emphasis on the individual psychology of elites, and it neglects other equally important considerations. Moreover, neglecting these other considerations may well add to the misunderstandings and conflicts that often accompany nationalist movements.

Third, different forms of nationalism require different explanations. Here I show how the idea of dignity relates to these different forms in different ways.

Modernity and Nationalism

The rise of nationalism involves the development of a specific form of collective identity, one that is seen to originate in a shared language, culture, and historical experience. People who express particular nationalist sentiments usually hold that they are obliged to favor conationals[1] and that their nation has a right to recognition by others. This recognition entails, among other things, acceptance by outsiders of the special moral obligation that people within the nation have to one another.

Although recent events in the former Soviet Union and especially in Bosnia and other parts of the former Yugoslavia have displayed many of the negative aspects of nationalism, they do not serve to define it. Nationalism, as Taylor indicates, can be liberal as well as conservative and democratic as well as authoritarian. While there are differences about whether nationalism is a relatively new phenomenon, as Anderson suggests,[2] or a more ancient one, as Roger Scruton proposes,[3] it is not simply to be understood and dismissed as an anachronistic remnant of a tribal morality superimposed on modern needs, practices, and institutions.

The conditions that give rise to nationalism today are essentially modern and include the pressure toward economic and political homogeneity and a felt need for differentiation and recognition. Thus, as Taylor correctly notes, whatever its origins, nationalism today arises from the demands that the modern state makes on its population and develops in response to economic, cultural, and social conditions that are unique to modern life.

The most important of these conditions include the rapidly expanding global economy that places a strain on local labor and leads some to seek state protection from global economic forces on the grounds that co nationals have a special responsibility to one another; the spread of popular global culture, a spread that threatens to marginalize local forms of cultural expression and leads to demands to set up special cultural boundaries, such as official languages and restricted immigration based on national preferences or nationalistic educational programs; and a unique combination of cultural and racial integration at the higher ends and class stratification and immobility at the lower end. This means that for a large number of people the modern multinational, cosmopolitan state is unable to deliver on promises of upward mobility and a better life—promises that have served as legitimizing principles for more universalistic, cosmopolitan societies and have served to justify compulsory schooling and the development of a cosmopolitan identity. The effect is a challenge to the legitimacy of schooling as an instrument of fairness and mobility and a reassertion of more culturally specific, nationalistic educational goals.

These conditions are acknowledged by Taylor in a general way when he sees nationalism as "a call to difference in face of the wave of 'modernization,' lived in the register of threatened dignity, and constructing a new, categorical identity as the bearer of that dignity." However, in Taylor's explanation of nationalism, he puts these conditions to the side in order to highlight the conceptual framework and imaginative innovations to which he sees them giving rise.

The Difference between an Explanation of Nationalism and an Explanation of Nationalisms

Taylor explains modern nationalism as a reformulation of collective imagination that enables people to conceive of themselves as equal members of one and the same national unit, as opposed, say, to unequal participants in a cosmic plan interpreted by church authority and enacted by princely powers. Given this long-range perspective, the reformulation of collective imagination is certainly an important consideration in explaining nationalism as such. However, an explanation of the rise of contemporary nationalism in, say, Bosnia, the former Soviet Union, or Quebec must also provide an account of why this way of imagining collective identity has, in these instances, come to take priority over other imaginative possibilities. After all, it would be quite conceivable to have all of the imaginative apparatus of nationalism in place but still see one's primary affiliation connected to race, religion, gender, humankind, or any other possible forms of organization. Imagination sets a range of possibilities for us; it does not determine which of the possibilities we will choose to act on or organize our lives and commitments around. Certainly nationhood requires the kind of imaginative frames described by Taylor, but nationalism requires more. It requires a commitment to bring this imagined world into being for oneself and for others "like oneself." Hence an explanation of nationalism in the modern age requires a comparative framework. The question is not simply, "Why nationalism?" It is why nationalism rather than something else such as, say, transnational racism or classism or religious fundamentalism.

The Problem with Dignity as an Explanatory Concept

The need for the comparative perspective also suggests one of the reasons why Taylor's concern for dignity is not sufficient to provide an account of nationalism. Dignity may be slighted for many different reasons—because one is a woman, a Jew, a working person, or an older citizen. Seeing a slight to dignity as the fuel for nationalism does not tell us how it is that the appeal to nationhood comes to have priority over other appeals when dignity is at stake.

It is true, as Taylor's criticism of Gellner emphasizes, that the homogenizing effect of modern state bureaucracies and educational systems is not a sufficient explanation for the rise of modern nationalist movements. Even if the push toward homogenization is as strong as Gellner suggests, this does not tell us why some people and groups work hard to accommodate themselves to the standard model while others strive to resist it. An account of nationalism requires that we understand why some groups resist official definitions and reconceptualize the boundaries of the state in ways that are consistent with modern nationalism while others are more content to accept official standards and definitions and to strive to over-come their own "deficits" in an attempt to assimilate into the larger multiethnic, cosmopolitan state. Yet if Gellner fails to answer this issue, so, too, does Taylor. Why, we may ask, in the tone of the bewildered white, Anglo-Christian male, are some groups so willing to accept our standards while others feel they are an impo-sition and a slight to their dignity?

The explanatory shortcomings of the concept of dignity should lead to some concern regarding Taylor's view that elites form the spark for nationalist move-ments. In the first place, if the concept of dignity is not fine enough to distinguish between national resistance and, say, gender or class resistance, it does not help to say that it is the slighting of the elite that starts the process. The question we want answered is which process does it start. Is it the affirmation of gender, class, race, or nation? However, there are other, more fundamental problems that the focus on elites raises.

Taylor's account serves to highlight conceptual and psychological questions while neglecting economic ones. In raising this criticism I am not suggesting that economic causes are real and psychological ones artificial. Nor am I arguing that elites are always a secondary element in nationalistic movements. I am saying that sometimes economic causes are significant and that when they are we need explanatory schemes that can capture this. I am also saying that sometimes elites are responding not to slights to themselves but to the deteriorating conditions, under modernization, of the masses and that when this happens we also need ex-planatory schemes that can capture this dynamic. In order to address this issue, I return to the question of the character of nationalism and the forms that it takes in the modern world.

Two Forms of Nationalism

Nationalism takes at least two different forms, which it is helpful to dis-tinguish. There is the nationalism of exclusion, in which a dominant group within an established state seeks to maintain its own identity. It may do this either by en-forcing uniformity on different groups within its boundaries or by preventing those outside its boundaries from entering and becoming fully participating citi-zens. The attempts by the right wing to establish an official national language and provide a common and dominantly coded curriculum in the schools is an expres-sion of the former. The exclusionary policies of the Japanese toward their long-standing Korean residents is an example of the latter.

There is also a nationalism of resistance. Here a dominated group within a local area may seek to forge an identity that separates it from a more cosmopolitan unit, as in Quebec. Or a nationalism of resistance may take the form of the opposition of one subordinated group against other, equally subordinated groups in a struggle for dominance and power, as in Bosnia. Dignity is not unimportant as an element in the explanatory process, but it needs to be examined in detail in each instance in order to understand the factors involved in its loss.

Each form of nationalism has its own explanations, but suggesting that they all pivot in the same way on a deprivation of dignity on the part of elites overstates the importance of elites and short-circuits other important explanatory elements. Dignity works differently in the nationalism of resistance than it does in the nationalism of exclusion. In the nationalism of resistance, some elites are educated to identify with norms of modernization. They are schooled in the curriculum or even on the soil of the cosmopolitan sector. A rebellion against these norms emerges, according to Taylor, when the dominant forms threaten to overwhelm local culture and hence to defile that which is different.

Yet even when restricted to resistance movements, Taylor's focus on elites only takes us part of the way toward an explanation of any particular expression of nationalism. What Taylor does not tell us is why elites should experience a loss of dignity, especially when they have been singled out as special and often treated to the best education that the cosmopolitan sector can provide. Why should they not be satisfied to model or enforce the standards of the dominant culture on their "own" people?

A considerable body of literature suggests that when elites begin to resist they do so not merely in terms of their own individual dignity—although this is a factor—but to give voice to the situation of "their" people where political influence or economic well-being or both are eroding. Consider the case of Fanon, educated and trained as a psychiatrist in France. When he was appointed to minister to government officials in Algeria, where he was born, he questioned whether he should be using his skills to comfort his people's torturers, who were suffering from bad dreams and lack of sleep. If these nationalistic sentiments were accompanied by a felt loss of dignity, it was not because of any assault on his status as a professional. It resulted from the fact that he was placed in a position where his professional know-how was used to mend the pain of colonialists who were harming the Algerian people.

To fail to see this connection between the elite and the people is to provide an explanation that focuses too heavily on individuals and could wrongly imply that national movements of resistance could be stemmed by simply providing elites with a bit more dignity—perhaps a clinical promotion for Fanon or a college professorship for Castro.[4]

This way of looking at national movements of resistance is likely to intensify the misunderstandings. Whereas one group seeks recognition as a collective unit, the other seeks to explain the movement as a problem with individual leaders. The critical question, then, is how this identification with "their" people develops, given that so much educational energy has been spent creating an elite that is intended to be loyal to the principles and institutions of the modern, cosmopolitan sector.

There are a number of different answers to this question. One approach involves distinguishing between different kinds of elites and how they have obtained their legitimacy. For example, given my earlier remarks regarding integration and mobility at the upper end of national life and stagnation and immobility at the lower end, then elites themselves will have different sources of legitimation, and those who are accepted by the cosmopolitan culture may be different from those accepted by indigenous groups.

In addition to the possibility of a dual elite, there is the likelihood that local elites, even those educated and legitimized through the educational avenues of the cosmopolitan center, have a dual perspective. On the one hand, their education informs them of the refined explanations and justifications for the existing distribution of power, wealth, and status, and on the other hand, they have access to the "folk" explanations that are transmitted through informal local educators such as grandmothers, priests, and barroom gossipers. In both of these cases, the assault is experienced not just to one's self or one's private position but to the self as a member of a national group whose lower standing and limited opportunities have become the focus of a collective grievance. Through both personal history and day-to-day contact, the chosen, locally originated elite comes to reidentify with this national grouping and takes its identity on again. The process is often intensified by markers such as skin color, accent, "body language," or taken-for-granted elements of day-to-day conversation that serve to distinguish locally grown elites from cosmopolitan ones, thus limiting the extent to which identity can be shaped by professional or cultural status.

Similarly, the nationalism of exclusion may also be understood by exploring conditions that connect dignity to the lives of people as they are lived in our rapidly changing world. Consider the vast change that has occurred in the last decade and a half in the relations of power between capital and labor due in large part to the globalization and mobility of capital and the national boundaries of organized labor. Organized labor is still nationally based while capital can be moved with great swiftness to different parts of the globe, enabling it to rent a labor force first in this country and then in that one, as the need and the climate for capital accumulation allow. This imbalance has placed nationally based labor unions in a very vulnerable position, as industry after industry can make good on promises to move operations abroad should labor become too aggressive. One response to this vulnerability is to seek to protect the economic situation by emphasizing membership in the "national family" and by insinuating that such membership entails certain economic rights that those outside the family should not be entitled to. True, dignity, as Taylor conceives it, is involved in these developments, but it is situated in some very important structural changes taking place worldwide. To view the nationalism of exclusion in terms of a response to global forces and to the immobility of organized labor is to begin to approach a comparative explanation by which we can see some of the factors that are lending themselves to the nation rather than, say, the class as the organizing principle in this instance.

It may also be useful to recall that different modes of organization—class, religion, nation, gender—are not necessarily exclusive of one another and that different combinations are possible. It is important to build an explanatory scheme that can capture some of these combinations. For example, many patriots see their nation's mission as wider than just establishing an organization that gives voice to a unique people. The national voice is important not just because it expresses the desires of a people but also because the message itself is believed by them to have global implications. Israel stands to exemplify the laws of Moses; the former Soviet Union to advance the cause of the working class worldwide; Iran to fulfill the prophecies of Muhammad. We can best understand these possibilities by developing fluid explanatory schemes that capture both the horizontal and the hierarchical, the deontological and the teleological aspects of the modern drive for nationalism.

Conclusion

What Taylor's account tells us is that nationalism is not always traced back to simple economic causes and is not reducible to tribal impulses that will be overcome by more modernization. He is quite right in seeking to understand expressions of nationalism in the first instance in what nationalists tell us about themselves—that they seek a voice for their collective uniqueness. However, if our understanding of nationalism is to be as comprehensive as Taylor wishes, it will be important to allow that sometimes larger forces spark the spirit of nationalism and that these forces will be different in different cases. Dignity can serve as a reminder that nationalism is about identity and recognition as long as it does not mask cases in which nationalism is also about a reduction in economic well-being and political or cultural influence. In other words, explanations of nationalism must be explanations of nationalisms, and these will take different forms in different situations.

NOTES

1. See chapter 8.

2. Benedict Anderson, *Imagined Communities: Reflections on the Origin and Spread of Nationalism* (London: Verso, 1991), pp. 9–46.

3. Roger Scruton, *The Philosopher on Dover Beach* (New York: St. Martin's, 1990), p. 304.

4. Although this reading is possible given Taylor's present essay, it is not consistent with the body of his work. See Charles Taylor, *Philosophy and the Human Sciences: Philosophical Papers 2* (Cambridge: Cambridge University Press, 1995), pp. 15–58.

6

The Moral Psychology
of Nationalism

AVISHAI MARGALIT

Nationalism Was Not Foreseen

The "prophets" of the nineteenth century, claims Isaiah Berlin, foresaw many of the central trends of the twentieth century: Burckhardt foresaw the importance of the military-industrial complex, Weber the growth of bureaucracy, Bakunin the revolutions in Third World countries, Durkheim the anomie of industrialized society, Tocqueville the conformism of egalitarian societies, and Marx the accelerated rate of technological change and the concentration of the means of production in the hands of the few. Yet no one foresaw the centrality of nationalism in twentieth-century life.

Nineteenth-century thinkers—especially those who lived through the 1848 revolutions—were obviously aware of the force of nationalism in Europe, but toward the end of the century it was generally believed that nationalism was on the decline and would soon disappear. And there was solid justification for this belief— namely, the cosmopolitan character of the market economy. Neither production nor the financial system could be confined by the straitjacket of national borders. The expansion of the market economy in its capitalist form was expected to diminish the grip of nationalism. The market systems would be larger than the national units in production and especially in finance. Nationalism would evaporate in competition with the market. *The Communist Manifesto* expresses these views clearly: "National differences and antagonisms between people are daily more and more vanishing . . . owing to freedom of commerce, to the world market, to uniformity in the mode of production and in the conditions of life corresponding thereto."

Early in the nineteenth century the economist Georg Friedrich List already understood the antinationalist potential of the free market economy.[1] List's criticisms of Adam Smith and David Ricardo focused on the fact that they ignored nationalism as an independent economic factor—that is, they disregarded the nation as an organic economic unit. As List saw it, for market economists microeconomics deals with the individual and macroeconomics with the world as a whole while the most important intermediate unit—the nation—vanishes. But List, like the Romantic "economist" Adam Müller, believed that in the absence of the nation the individual consumer's life has no meaning. The consumer's choices within the market are generally determined by parameters of the national culture. Only such a culture can give meaning to the individual's choices. Moreover, the nation itself has its own goals and is not merely a means for improving the lot of individuals or of humanity as a whole. Although List believed that the economists of his day tended to ignore the nationalist aspect of the decisions made by producers and even more so by consumers, he also believed that an international market free of borders and constraints would hurt national interests. There are mutual constraints between the nation and the market.

List's own career provides ambiguous evidence for his claims. He was one of the most consistent and efficient advocates of the German Zollverein, a customs union that forged the German economy into a single unit (excluding Austria). Since the Zollverein is rightly considered to have been the crucial step in the unification of Germany, this would seem to confirm List's theory that economics serves the nation. On the other hand, one might say that the abolition of customs duties within the market and the imposition of customs on goods from the outside actually show that it is economics that determines the nature of the political unit rather than the other way around. According to this last claim, the existence of the German Zollverein should support the belief that the European Common Market, for example, will dissolve nationalism in Western Europe.

The greatest threat to nationalism, however, is not international trade, which involves the transfer of goods and money, but the international economy, which involves the unlimited transfer of workers. A migration of workers from one state to another that is determined only by the needs of the market is liable to change the national character of nation-states and turn them into immigrant societies in which the makeup of the population changes constantly according to these needs.

In general, the fear that a competitive international market may be a threat to nationalism is based on the awareness that competitive markets are founded on achievement relations that do not take people's belonging relations into account. The basis of the nationalist orientation, in contrast, is the belonging relationship between members of the same nation. The more sophisticated the international market becomes, leading to increased transfer of workers and managers, the more the achievement relations of the market take their toll on the belonging relations of the nations involved.

I maintain that those thinkers who considered the nature of the market and production at the end of the nineteenth century a reason for believing that nationalism would be weakened and possibly even disappear had a weighty reason for their belief. Even at present it seems to me that the direction of influence between the market and nationalism remains an open question.

Friedrich List does not belong to the variegated arsenal of figures discussed by Isaiah Berlin, but it is not a coincidence that I have been using List as a critic of the cosmopolitan economy in the name of the nationalist idea. He was greatly influenced by Romantic thought, and Romanticism forms the basis of Berlin's thinking about nationalism.

Romanticism and Nationalism

To understand Berlin's thought, it is important to distinguish between the value system of a worldview and its psychological underpinnings. Berlin believes that in political philosophy the right value system does not necessarily go together with the right psychology. Indeed, one almost gets the impression that he believes there is an inverse relationship between them: the better the value system, the shallower the psychology, and vice versa. At any rate, in Berlin's view the counter-Enlightenment, with Romanticism at its center, had a deeper insight into human psychology than the Enlightenment itself. It thus follows that the ideologies that issued from the Enlightenment, such as liberalism and socialism, were based on a shallow psychology. In contrast, Romantic nationalism, even in its most dangerous manifestations, had deep insight into the makeup of the human psyche, if not into the human soul. Any social theory that aspires to relevance—Berlin himself is interested mainly in liberalism—must therefore take into account the psychological needs that were uncovered by the Romantics and are assumed to be fulfilled by nationalism.

The influence of Romanticism on European nationalism has been discussed by many thinkers, but Berlin inverts the causal order, seeing German Romanticism itself as a response to national humiliation. It was Hegel who claimed that Solger, Novalis, and Kleist provided the Romantic response to the French Revolution. But Berlin dates the events even earlier than that, seeing Germany's humiliating situation as a result of the fact that the armies of Richelieu and Louis XIV had crushed a large part of the German populace, thus stifling the development of the Protestant Renaissance, leaving Germany a backward land with feelings of inferiority in the face of French culture. In Berlin's view, the French Revolution was only an additional event that emphasized Germany's backwardness in contrast with the French Enlightenment that rode the waves of the revolution.

The effects of national humiliation include both compensatory illusions and sensitive insights. People who have been humiliated see themselves as representing some sort of "great spirituality" in contrast to the materialistic humiliators whom they see as the embodiment of efficiency, coldness, intellectualism, and human estrangement. As they see it, they themselves embody human sensitivity, warmth, a poetic soul, and spiritual closeness to "what is really important in life," and so their inferiority is artificial and transient. Humiliated people see themselves as spontaneous, generous, and capable of intense emotions and bold gestures, as opposed to the calculating, intellectualizing character of the oppressors. In short, they are like the bent twig in Schiller's poem that will soon spring erect and whip its torturer.[2] There is much that is illusory in this familiar self-image of people in humiliated nations and classes. On the other hand, such people may well have some insights as a result of being humiliated or, more precisely, because their subordination requires of them a human sensitivity that is generally lacking in the oppressors. The latter, due to their position of superiority, are liable to be haughty and arrogant, making them humanly insensitive.

Very few trends of thought had such a deep influence on the culture of feeling as Romanticism. Its influence on the culture of nationalist feeling was particularly great. Understanding Romanticism means knowing something important about European nationalism. Of course, Romanticism should not be identified only with the German variety, just as the Enlightenment should not be identified only with the French variety, although Germany and France remain the outstanding representatives of these two trends of thought. Still, it should be remembered that Rousseau's influence on Romanticism was perhaps greater than that of anyone else. Rousseau also had a great influence on Romantic nationalism. It was not the political nationalism of Rousseau, however, that influenced Berlin's thought but rather the cultural nationalism of Herder, who was born in the same city as Berlin—Riga, the capital of Latvia.

Political nationalism is centered on the idea that a nation's supreme expression is its sovereign political will as embodied in the nation-state. Individuals participate in the nation by being citizens of the nation-state. According to this conception, obeying the commands of the state and being loyal to it are considered the outstanding expressions of belonging to the nation. Only a member of the nation can be a "true" citizen of a nation-state, while minority members are at best nominal citizens.

Cultural nationalism, in contrast, considers the nation an organic entity whose supreme expression is the national culture—particularly the national language. For this sort of nationalism, politics is not an essential expression of the nation but only a means for ensuring independent and creative cultural expression in cases where the culture and the language are threatened. According to this conception, politics is a means rather than an end. The culture, rather than the manifestations of political will, is the focus of national identity.

Berlin was aware of cultural nationalism not only in its Herderian version but also in its Zionist version, as expressed by Ahad Haam. Berlin's mentor in the Zionist movement was its longtime leader Chaim Weizmann. Weizmann himself spent most of his life in Zionist diplomacy and political activity, but he was greatly influenced by Ahad Haam's cultural Zionism.

Berlin supported the political Zionism that aimed at establishing a state for the Jews, but he considered the state only a means for securing the national existence of the Jewish people. Under the historical circumstances in which the Jews were living at the time, the state was perhaps the only means for achieving this goal, but it was still a means and not an end. Berlin considered the state only one possible framework for national existence and by no means its goal. He was certainly very distant from the nationalism of blood and soil—like Karl Kraus, Berlin believed that this lethal combination only causes tetanus.

Herder's cultural nationalism is in an important sense the topic that appears today under the label of "multiculturalism" rather than that of "nationalism." When anti-Enlightenment thinking emphasizes political nationalism, it involves a different sort of psychology than when the emphasis is placed on cultural nationalism. The anti-Enlightenment that focuses on political nationalism criticizes the Enlightenment's covert assumption that future societies will be able to abandon politics. In "laissez-faire" liberalism, the market is supposed to replace politics. The only legitimate sort of struggle in laissez-faire thinking is economic bargaining. According to this view, contractual agreements between individuals and firms are supposed to settle all conflicts. The assumption is that all conflicts between rational people can be settled if and when they are allowed to communicate freely with one another.

Socialists, too, recognized the principled possibility that politics could disappear. This was supposed to occur in socialist societies, in which class conflicts would be eliminated. Carl Schmitt is the outstanding contemporary exponent of the counter-Enlightenment critique of this assumption.[3] Schmitt defines areas of human activity according to their fundamental dichotomies. Logic is organized around the contrast between truth and falsity, aesthetics around the contrast between beauty and ugliness, ethics around the contrast between good and evil, and religion around the contrast between holy and profane, while politics is organized around the basic contrast between friend and foe. The claim that politics could disappear implies that the polarity between friend and foe could be dissolved in the realm of social organization. In Schmitt's opinion, however, this is a utopian, illusory assumption. There is nothing like nationalism to sharpen the basic political dichotomy between friend and foe.

Let me present a parable. Human beings are like creatures navigating across an unknown land, not knowing where they are on the map. They are trying to find out where they are by triangulation. What they must do is locate two salient points on the map that they can see in their actual surroundings. They first draw imaginary lines from these two points that intersect at the point where they are in reality, then draw lines from the two points on the map that are angled in the same direction as the imaginary lines in their real surroundings. The point of intersection of the two lines on the map then tells them where they are. Thus in Schmitt's view we need enemies for the "triangulation" that tells us what we are. Having an enemy is our principal means of acquiring an identity.

Only political nationalism, in Schmitt's opinion, does justice to the basic human need to stick together with friends and fight enemies. The contrast between friend and foe cannot be reduced to any other. The political realm is not only an autonomous one but also the most basic of all the areas of human activity. In other words, it is easier to reduce truth and falsity, beauty and ugliness, good and evil, holiness and profanity to the basic political contrast between friend and foe than the other way around. This pessimistic idea that there is no possibility of eliminating the division of humanity into friend and foe means that there is in principle no chance of achieving harmonic relations among all human beings. One can change sides so that yesterday's enemy becomes today's friend, and vice versa, but people cannot exist without "we" and "they."

Berlin may be skeptical about the possibility of creating harmony among people, but he certainly does not believe that humans have an ontological need for enemies. On the other hand, Berlin believes that it is impossible even in principle for there to be harmony between all human values. In Berlin's view, nationalism is based not on human hostility toward the other but on the incommensurability of values.

Not All Good Things Go Together

Henri Bergson claimed that all philosophical systems are based on one fundamental intuition. Each philosopher sees "one point" in a way that no one else has seen it. Berlin's fundamental intuition—the "one point" that he saw differently from everyone else—was the realization that not all of the values that are important to us are reconcilable, and therefore not all of these values can be actualized in one form of life. This realization is Berlin's most important justification for cultural and social pluralism, which sees other forms of life as possessing internal value. This is because each of us ought to be aware that other forms of life embody values that are important to us but cannot be realized at all in our own form of life, or at least not to the same degree. The sort of nationalism that is based on pluralism is a special case of this awareness and perhaps the best expression of it. Liberalism, as the form of government most likely to ensure a pluralism of values and forms of life, is thus also justified by the claim that a plurality of mutual irreconcilable values is important to us.

The irreconcilability of values is both a psychological and a conceptual claim in Berlin's view. It is psychologically difficult to reconcile a contemplative life and an active life in the same form of life. It is both conceptually and psychologically difficult to reconcile a monastic life with a family life.

Berlin's claim is not that values are relative—that other people value different things than we do. The relativity of values is at best a justification for tolerance, not pluralism. Berlin's idea is that the values that are actualizable by other forms of life are very important to us and not only to the people who belong to that form of life.

Leibniz's God was supposed to have chosen "the best of all possible worlds," where each possible world is the totality of all compossible things—all the things that can exist together. For Leibniz's God the best of all possible worlds is the world that optimally embodies two values that are in tension: order and variety.[4]

Berlin's basic intuition is that even God cannot choose the best form of life because there are no supervalues, such as variety and order, that can be used to measure the totality of values that a society actualizes. The values embodied in each society exhaust all of the justifications we have for a form of life. There are no supervalues of a higher order that provide us with a way of comparing the collections of values that are embodied in each society. We cannot choose between different ways of life that we consider valuable on the basis of rational considerations or justifications—we can only perform an existential act of choice that expresses our freedom to live this way rather than some other way, where both this way and the other way are valuable to us. But more often than we choose a way of life, we are born into one. National belonging is the outstanding example of this truth.

The idea that there are no dimensions for comparing national forms of life that embody desirable values is also a reason to avoid seeking national supremacy. There is no point in such an effort, just as there would be no point in the winner of a dog beauty contest entering a beauty contest for cats. The criteria are noncomparable.

Berlin often uses the term "incommensurability" to express the idea of the irreconcilability of some desirable values. "Incommensurability" literally means the lack of a common measure, but I'm not sure whether Berlin uses the term literally or metaphorically. I do believe that there is a need to distinguish between Berlin's idea that desirable values are often irreconcilable and the claim that there is no common basis for measuring them.

When we are faced with a decision—even a fairly trivial one, such as whether to go abroad for our vacation or buy a new dining-room table—we try to compare two options that seem very different and have very little in common, except perhaps for being in the same price range. We do indeed have reasons for choosing each of the options, but we don't know how to compare the reasons either.

The modern theory of utility begins with the fact that people's behavior and choices reveal preference relations between options even if they are very different from one another. If these preference relations obey certain formal constraints, such as transitivity, then there is a function that expresses them numerically. The question is how to interpret this function. One interpretation is that it is a utility function—that is, a function measuring the utility to the chooser of each of the various options, utilities that enable him or her to choose among very different alternatives. A consumer chooses the vacation abroad rather than the dining-room table because the vacation seems to provide more expected utility than the table. Berlin gives enough indications to show that he is skeptical about utilitarianism—that is, about the power of the concept of utility to explain the nature of our choices among alternatives. Another interpretation is that the numerical function describes the fact of preference relations without explaining the reasons for the preferences. They are simply brute facts.

Commensurability is the mathematical result that is obtained when preference relations satisfy certain principles. I don't think Berlin wants to quarrel with mathematics. I therefore believe that it is necessary to distinguish between the metaphorical sense of incommensurability, or the lack of reasons for preferring one thing to another, and the literal sense of the term, or the impossibility of finding a common measure for the two things.[5]

Unity and Multiplicity

Berlin notes that some of our most familiar values nowadays, such as sincerity and integrity, are actually quite new. This is also true of the value of variety: "The view that variety is desirable, whereas uniformity is monotonous, dreary, dull, a fetter on the freely-ranging human spirit . . . stands in sharp contrast with the traditional view that truth is one, error many, a view scarcely challenged before—at the earliest—the end of the seventeenth century."[6] Is this true? One of the well-known fathers of linguistic structuralism, who was also an important although less well known philosopher of twentieth-century nationalism, was N. S. Trubetzkoy. He expressed the view that in the story of the Tower of Babel the Bible demonstrated a clear preference for the variety of languages and cultures over one language and culture. The fact that they had only one language and culture brought the tower builders to the boring emptiness that ended in the arrogant project of building the tower. In Trubetzkoy's opinion, the "confounding of the languages"—that is, the imposition of cultural variety—is not a curse or a punishment but a solution to the problem of the sin that results from cultural homogeneity:

> The Holy Writ depicts mankind speaking one language, that is, a linguistically and culturally homogeneous mankind, and it turns out that this single, universal culture, devoid of national characteristics, is extremely one-sided: an enormous development of science and technology (which is indicated by the project of the tower) is coupled with spiritual emptiness and moral decay. The result is excessive arrogance and pride, whose embodiment is the godless and senseless project.[7]

This can serve as a nice rabbinic-style homily, but it cannot undermine Berlin's claim. The simple, literal meaning of the biblical story is that the "confounding of the languages" is a punishment. The prophet Zephania hints at the story of the tower in his consolation prophecy (3:9): "For then will I turn to the people a pure language, that they may all call upon the name of the Lord, to serve him with one consent" (King James Version). The biblical ideal is clearly one language and one culture. I believe Berlin is right in his historical observation that multiplicity and variety were not considered valuable in Western culture before the start of the modern age. One sometimes gets the impression that Berlin is a sort of enthusiastic ecologist who sees value in the very existence of human variety, independent of its content: a variety of human forms of life, like a variety of species of plants and animals, is a good thing in and of itself. But this Whitmanesque sense is not the main trend of Berlin's thought. The main trend involves the notion that more than one form of life must exist in order for values we consider worthwhile to be fulfilled.

National Forms of Life

Brother can you spare a paradigm?
—Sidney Morgenbesser

Forms of life in general, and nationalist ones in particular, are frames that present the individual with a range of choices among options, giving meaning to the person's choice and thus forming his or her identity. A convenient context for explicating this notion is one that Trubetzkoy helped found—namely, structuralism. Structuralism is based on two organizing principles: equivalence groups and chaining. For example, a restaurant menu is organized into a group of similar or equivalent items constituting the appetizer, another group of items constituting the main course, and so on. We choose one item from the group of equivalent items (paradigmatic class) called appetizers, say the soup, and we concatenate it with an item from the equivalence class of main courses, which is then concatenated with an item from the class of desserts, so that our order to the waiter constitutes a sort of sentence.

There are limitations on possible concatenations. It would be very unusual to concatenate a restaurant-order sentence composed solely of desserts or to change the order of the items so as to begin with coffee and end with soup. Every form of life has its own constraints. But what is a form of life? I shall try to explicate it in structuralist terms. A form of life is determined by the collection of equivalence classes available for choice within a society, as well as the constraints on the concatenations acceptable in that society. The personal style of individuals in that form of life is expressed in their choice of items from the equivalence classes. According to this view, even people with exceptionally individual styles are dependent on the particular equivalence classes their society provides for them to choose from.

Forms of life differ from one another not only in their equivalence classes and acceptable concatenations but also in the degree of freedom they grant to the individual. Items of clothing, for example, can be divided into the equivalence classes of head coverings, upper-body coverings, lower-body coverings, and foot coverings. Some societies obligate their members to choose a head covering, while others make this choice optional. There are significant differences in the degree of openness of the classes. A closed society defines its choice classes rigidly and applies rigid constraints to the acceptable concatenations. For example, it does not permit any optional choices (it requires a head covering, say); moreover, it imposes heavy sanctions on deviant concatenations. A national form of life is determined by the equivalence classes (paradigms) and concatenations the nationalist society offers its members in every area of life. In some societies there can be applicable overlap among different forms of life—for example, the Catholic, Irish, and proletarian forms.

It might seem that the "structuralist" account used here for explicating the idea of forms of life is appropriate at best for explaining differences in cuisine and dress. But what does it have to do with the tension between values?

Values enter the picture in two ways: as side-constraints and as metaphorical features of the alternative items for choice. Values as side-constraints determine, for instance, which items are not permitted in the equivalence classes. Mustafa Kemal forbade Turkish men to wear the fez and introduced European headdress into the equivalence class of head coverings instead. His reason was that the fez symbolizes servitude, traditionalism, and lack of modernity. In contrast, the act of changing the veil from an optional to an obligatory item of dress for women in Iran was an expression of a value change. In other words, prescribing what is available for choosing and prescribing what must be chosen are examples of side-constraints.

Another way to look at the issue is to say that the veil exemplifies modesty. That is, the veil has the property of modesty—not literally, since a piece of cloth cannot be modest or immodest, but metaphorically.[8] Thus values are metaphorically exemplified by the items available for choice. A clash between values such as modernity and traditionalism may thus be manifested in the items exemplifying these features—the European hat versus the fez.

Belonging to a national form of life means being within a frame that offers meaning to people's choice between alternatives, thus enabling them to acquire an identity.

The Needs Fulfilled by Nationalism

Nationalism, in Herder's view, fulfills a deep need in human beings—the need to belong to a society that provides them with a complete form of life. A distinction can be made between three different but related senses of the notion of belonging.

The first, Herderian, sense is the sort of belonging that makes expression possible. Every person, in Herder's opinion, has the need to express his or her selfhood. A person's selfhood is also the clearest expression of his or her humanity. In the context of nationalism, this means supporting what I have called elsewhere "an adverbial approach" to nationalism.[9] The idea is that people make use of different styles to express their humanity. The styles are generally determined by the form of life to which they belong. There are people who express themselves "Frenchly," while others have forms of life that are expressed "Koreanly" or "Syrianly" or "Icelandicly."

An analogy may make this clearer. Painters generally express themselves in a variety of painting styles, and many even belong to various schools. There are schools of figurative painting and abstract painting, realistic and surrealistic painting, impressionistic and expressionistic painting, yet the members of all of these schools share the effort to express themselves in painting despite the differences among their ways of doing so. There are also eclectic painters who do not belong to any school. They simply paint. Analogous to the eclectic painters are "cosmopolitan" people who do not belong to any group. But most people express themselves by belonging to a trend that determines the contours of their expression. The need for belonging in the first sense is the need for the provision of means of expression. This need is therefore parasitic upon human beings' basic need to express themselves. A nation is a sort of school of human expression. There are also other sorts of schools—tribal, class, religious, and the like.

The second sense of the term (in the nontechnical sense of "sense") is related not to the expression but rather to the feeling of belonging as contrasted with achievement. To belong in this sense means to be accepted by others as you are, not as the result of some deed or misdeed of yours. The family is the paradigm example of a unit based on belonging in this sense, while a professional football team is an example of belonging based on achievement (as opposed to merely being a fan on the team, which is a matter of belonging in the family sense). National belonging, like family belonging, is not based on achievement. It seems to me that Berlin's concept of belonging is close to the sense in which it is opposed to achievement. Belonging to a nation, in Berlin's view, needs to be manifested in a feeling of being at home, where this means being able to act freely and naturally. Berlin assigns great importance to acting naturally and spontaneously rather than artificially. In this sense he resembles Tolstoy of *War and Peace*, who considers the natural/artificial contrast a very basic one.

The third sense of national belonging bridges the gap between belonging and achievement. This sort of national belonging provides you with reflected glory based on the achievements of gifted members of your nation. Mickiewicz bestows glory on those who belong to the Polish nation, while Yeats bestows glory on the

Irish—each nation has its own stars; each person chooses the achievements in whose glow he or she wishes to bask.

Berlin greatly values people's need to feel at home precisely because this is a feeling that Jews have lacked in the Diaspora. There is a strong association between the feeling of being at home and the feeling of belonging. Robert Frost's poem "The Death of the Hired Man" presents all of the motifs of this association (they have to accept you irrespective of your achievements):

> Home is the place where when you have to go there they have to take you in.
> I have called it something you somehow haven't to deserve.

The reason Berlin considered Zionism justified as a national movement of the Jewish people was because it would provide a home for a nation that had lost the feeling of being at home. Many Zionist thinkers described the Jews as a people who were ill, while Berlin considered them "ill at ease"—that is, lacking the feeling of being at home, which is built on unconditional acceptance and the lack of any need to constantly prove oneself through achievement. I believe that Berlin's idea of the human need for belonging in all three senses is derived from his idea of the need for feeling at home, which he projected from the Jewish experience onto humanity in general. The rootless Jew has become a metaphor for modern human existence in Western society as a whole.

What May We Hope For?

Berlin is well aware that nationalism is an active force in our world. He is well acquainted with its dangerous manifestations. He believes that one of the psychological forces that shape nationalism, especially the political sort, is the sense that the other is "naturally" inferior—in other words, that those who do not belong to one's own nation (generally one's neighbors) are inferior. This psychological sense of one's own nation's superiority versus the inferiority of the other places nationalism on a continuum whose extreme is fascism: "If Fascism is the extreme expression of this attitude, all nationalism is infected by it to some degree."[10]

The inferiority of the other (whether someone who does not belong to one's nation, as in fascism, or to one's race, as in Nazism) is an essential trait in the sense that there are "natural" slaves in Aristotle's view. This is the sense in which in Shakespeare's *Tempest* Caliban, the deformed slave on the enchanted island, is a natural slave while Prospero, the deposed prince of Milan, is a natural master, even as a shipwreck survivor on the same island. Since one's nation is considered superior to others, this means that there is no need to justify its national purposes to such inferior people, since they are not open to noble aims in any case. Caliban is incapable of understanding Prospero.

Berlin is clearly aware of the feelings of superiority and patronizing attitude that accompany nationalist thought and emotions, but he does not believe, as Schmitt does, that such feelings are inevitable. These feelings are a historical given. They are liable to deteriorate into fascism, but this does not have to happen.

The sense of essential superiority, in Berlin's view, is not only a product of particularist outlooks: fascism, Nazism, or nationalism. Even movements with universalist pretensions, such as Marxism, have developed a dangerous version of superiority. It is not, to be sure, a "natural" superiority but rather one based on class origins. According to this view, anyone who does not come from the working class is presumed to belong to the forces of "yesterday," or, as in the case of the intelligentsia, a suspect until proven innocent, while anyone who does come from that class is presumed to belong to the forces of "tomorrow." The aristocracy of history can be a dangerous source of superiority and inferiority, as the Stalinist purges demonstrated—even when it speaks in the name of human universality.

The connection between fascism and particularism is also very complex. Berlin discusses Joseph de Maistre's contribution to the sources of fascism. But de Maistre's brand of "radical conservatism" testifies to the possibility of nonparticularist fascism, since it is of the "catholic," universalist sort.

A distinction is lacking in Berlin's thought, the distinction between ecclesiastical and political fascism—that is, between fascism that has as its end service to the Church (for example, the regimes of Salazar in Portugal and Franco in Spain and some of the fascist regimes in South America) and fascism of the Mussolini sort, which, although it does have an agreement ("Concordat") with the Church, considers the state rather than the Church the embodiment and ultimate end of fascist values. From a practical standpoint, the difference between the two sorts of regime is often marginal. Ecclesiastical fascism in its concrete manifestations has generally used the Church as a tool for the advancement of the regime rather than the other way around. Perhaps this is why Berlin does not ascribe any importance to the distinction between the two sorts of regime. Yet from the conceptual standpoint this is a distinction that makes a difference. It is also important for the issue at hand, since ecclesiastical fascism is not particularist but aims to defend a universalist Church—the Catholic Church—which it places at the center of its concerns. In other words, even though there is justifiable basis for opposing the idea of nationalism because its particularism—which includes the notion of essential superiority—is liable to have destructive political consequences, the basis for the opposition is not so much the particularism as the sense of superiority itself. This sense may just as easily be nourished by universalist considerations, whether religious or secular.

In his *Logic*, Kant lists the four great "cosmopolitan" philosophical questions. The crucial question in his view ("What is man?") can be asked only after the other questions ("What can I know?"; What may I hope for?"; and "What ought I to do?") have been answered appropriately. For Berlin the order is different. The prerequisite for answering the question "What is man?" is a sense of empathy, a feeling of identification with Kant's assertion (which Berlin quotes as the source of the title for his book *The Crooked Timber of Humanity*): "Out of timber so crooked as that from which man is made nothing entirely straight can be carved."

This sense about what man is should, in Berlin's view, provide constraints on the answers to the two questions "What may we hope for [from human society]?" and "What ought we to do [for its welfare]?" For Berlin, psychology precedes ideology. This is not psychology as a strict science. Berlin does not believe that psychological laws exist that make psychology such a science. What he means is ordinary, everyday psychology as the empathic understanding of the other's point of view. Berlin sees this sort of empathic understanding in the area of nationalist feeling as centered on the need for being at home and the need for belonging but also the dangerous need to feel essential superiority.

What may we hope for? We may hope for a world in which cultural nationalism will flourish without being fed by a sense of essential superiority. This is not the reality today, but there isn't anything essential in human beings that makes Herderian nationalism impossible.

NOTES

1. Georg Friedrich List, *Das nationale System der politischen Oekonomie* (Stuttgart, 1840), trans. S. S. Lloyd, *The National System of Political Economy* (London, 1885).

2. Isaiah Berlin, "The Bent Twig," in *The Crooked Timber of Humanity: Chapters in the History of Ideas* (New York, 1991), p. 246.

3. Carl Schmitt, *Der Begriff des Politischen* (Munich, 1932).

4. In the social realm, the best social order, in Leibniz's view, is the one that leads to the greatest amount of freedom, which ensures variety, that can be reconciled with the greatest degree of order, which is embodied in the rule of law.

5. There is an interesting interpretation of Berlin's concept of commensurability in John Gray's excellent book, *Isaiah Berlin* (Princeton, [1996]).

6. Isaiah Berlin, *Against the Current: Essays in the History of Ideas* (New York, 1980), p. 333.

7. N. S. Trubetzkoy, "The Tower of Babel and the Confusion of Tongues," trans. K. Brostrom, in *The Legend of Genghis Khan*, pp. 148–49.

8. Nelson Goodman, *The Languages of Art* (London, 1969).

9. I discuss this idea at length in *The Decent Society* (Cambridge, Mass., 1996)

10. Berlin, *Crooked Timber*, p. 176.

7

Conventions and Conversions, or, Why Is Nationalism Sometimes So Nasty?

ROBERT E. GOODIN

In the terms dominating contemporary social and political philosophy, nationalists are paradigmatic communitarians and liberals paradigmatic cosmopolitans.[1] Nationalists, like communitarians more generally, emphasize the various and nefarious ways in which individuals are embedded within particular communities—communities constituted in turn by self-consciously shared identities, defined in terms of race or place or history or religion or whatever. Liberals, like cosmopolitans more generally, emphasize what is common across all those communities—universal standards and a shared humanity.

Liberals are perfectly capable of explaining, in perfectly liberal terms, why their aspirations might sometimes be frustrated. Defined in terms of their normative values rather than their empirical analytics, though, liberals are insistently universalist; and universal ideals of a liberal sort, applicable to all and shared by all, are at root incapable of providing any good grounds for going to war with one another. Even in terms of its empirical analytics, liberalism's paradigmatic "war of all against all" is properly classed as a "cooperative game," one admitting of mutually profitable compromise.

Nationalism, construed in communitarian terms, constitutes a contrasting case. Nothing says that national communities necessarily *must* be locked in constant and mortal combat with one another. Nothing, however, in communitarian doctrine says that they must not be. It is all a matter of national taste, and national communities' tastes sometimes run very bloodthirsty indeed. Nor is there anything within the nationalist communitarian doctrine to restrain such communities from acting with utmost brutality on that blood lust.

Saying that something is "just a matter of taste," however, puts the phenomenon beyond rational analysis and explanation. There is, as the saying goes, "no accounting for taste": *de gustibis non est explanandum*. Talk of "tastes" thus relegates the phenomenon to the realm of the irrational and arational, the world of collective identities and historical grievances (often more imagined than real), of collective neuroses and psychoses.[2]

In the end, Gellner may well be right that the conflict between liberalism and nationalism really is nothing more than just such "a tug of war between reason and passion."[3] But that would be a pessimistic conclusion. It would imply that we cannot appeal to either to restrain itself in the name of the other precisely because (in some deep sense) neither can understand or make sense of the claims of the other at all. That analytic disjuncture prevents either from getting any normative leverage on the other, and Gellner's "tug of war" would then be all that is left. Before we proceed to such a pessimistic conclusion, it is well worth seeing what might be done to close that analytic gap.

This chapter is devoted to trying to understand the phenomenon of nationalist comunitarianism, including its sometimes-bloody excesses, within a rationalistic framework more commonly associated with the liberal side of the debate. Obviously, that is not the only place to start. Clearly, it is not where commited communitarians would themselves start; equally clearly, there is more to the phenomena than my model will be able to capture.[4] Still, it is analytically well worth our while to see just how much of rogue phenomena such as the bloodier forms of nationalist communitarianism can be incorporated within a unified model grounded in rationalist analytics alone.

Toward a Credibly Modest Communitarianism

In its more extravagant forms, recent communitarianism makes some plainly crazy claims. It asserts that we are all so embedded in our own particular communities, their values and viewpoints, that we can never transcend them. Were that true, however, national communities would never experience schisms, much less revolutions—even outside agitators would be unable to find anything within us to grip onto and agitate. Were those wilder communitarian claims true, we could never even carry on meaningful conversations across national or any other communal boundaries. Polish-Americans would have nothing to say to Italian-Americans, much less Poles to Italians in the UN cafeteria. Not only would each have nothing of interest to say to the other, but each would not even be able to say anything *sensible* to the other, anything that the other would (in some deep sense) understand at all. That claim seems to be patent nonsense.

While rejecting offhand those wilder claims of communal embeddedness, we nonetheless ought to explore various weaker senses in which the claims of communitarianism may (yea, must) be true. Everyone has to start somewhere, and where you end up or, anyway, how easily you get there clearly depends upon where you start. There are traces of the past in the present. We have memories, and recollections of past experiences significantly shape future reactions.

All that is undeniably true. But that is a much more modest claim that yields none of communitarianism's more radical conclusions. It provides no grounds for thinking that national or communal cultures are inscrutable, one by the other; it provides no grounds for regarding every community's values as incommensurable with every other's, in consequence. All it says is that conversations across some national, communal, and cultural divides will require a little more work, that disputes across some of those divides will take a little longer to resolve, than others.

Precisely because it poses so modest a challenge to transcendent liberal universalism, this more modest form of the communitarian claim is one that communitarians themselves are relatively uninterested in developing. That task necessarily falls to their opponents—who, understandably exasperated with the absurdities of nationalists' and communitarians' bolder claims, are typically disinclined to pick up their pieces, either.[5] That, I think, is a mistake. There is considerable value in exploring the grounds and implications of this more modest form of the nationalist-cum-communitarian claim.

Toward a Rational Reconstruction: The Bayesian Story

In providing a rational (which is to say, liberal) reconstruction of these more modest communitarian foundations of nationalism and cognate phenomena, I see two tasks before me. First, I must provide an account of "differentiation" of communities, nations, and such groups from one another. Second, I must provide an account of the "blood and guts" hostility that all too often characterizes relations between different communities, especially national ones.

Accounting for the sheer fact of differentiation proves to be the easier task. The central tenet of the more modest communitarian claim, as I have characterized it, is simply that everyone has to start somewhere, and depending on where you start, it proves easier to go in some directions than others. Differentiation of that sort among separate groups of people admits of a perfectly straightforward explanation along broadly Bayesian lines.[6] In those terms, different groups of people would come to have different beliefs (about what is "true," what is the "best way of doing things," and so on) based purely upon the logic of information processing.

A stylized model along those lines would go roughly as follows: (1) Everyone starts with free access to certain limited "information" (facts about what is true, the best way of doing things, or whatever). (2) Acquiring more information is costly. (3) People rationally decide whether to seek more information or stop seeking more information on the basis of their best guess as to whether the additional information will be such as to change their minds about the question at issue.[7] (4) People discount information (and by extension sources of that information) according to how well that information accords with their preexisting information.[8]

Communities and indeed nations (especially insofar as they are culturally closed and distinct national communities) fit well into this model of self-contained and mutually reinforcing information networks. On that account, what is going on within national communities is just this: people within the same community enjoy free access to the same information; those within different communities have access to correspondingly different bits of information. Given the costs of acquiring further information, most people would rationally stop well short of a thoroughgoing questioning of all preconceptions that form the natural inferences from such free information as is common within their own communities. Discounting information that does not fit with preexisting information, in itself a perfectly rational practice, increases both insularity within communities and differences between them; new information that is seen as crucially confirmatory in one community, organized around one body of preexisting information, would equally rationally be regarded as an "outlier" by another community, organized as it is around a different body of preexisting information.[9]

In short, it is perfectly rational for different self-contained communities, starting with different information (colloquially, "taking different things as given" or "starting from different premises"), to become increasingly differentiated from one another as more and more information comes in.[10] That is how my broadly Bayesian analysis accounts for *differentiation* across different national and culturally distinct communities, not so much as misunderstandings as mere differences in understandings.

The great accomplishment of my broadly Bayesian model, as developed so far, lies in rationalizing those differential understandings. My model shows why such differences should exist—and why, even with the best will in the world, they might sometimes persist. And it does so (pleasingly enough for anyone who harbors liberal-Enlightenment values of theoretical parsimony) by assimilating the genesis of distinct "communities" to the genesis of all sorts of other institutions and organizations within society. All of those, on this model, are likewise seen as products of asymmetrical information and transaction costs of one sort or another.[11]

That strength is also a weakness, though. There is something suspicious about any model that attempts to assimilate the warring communities of Ulster and Lebanon to anything so tame as competing work teams or Lions Clubs. Furthermore, upon reflection it seems we have good grounds for being suspicious. It seems crazy to suggest that the differences between those warring factions derive, purely and simply, from informational asymmetries that transaction costs prevent them from ironing out. No one could seriously suppose that those conflicts would be at an end if the United Nations could just organize an airdrop of enough encyclopedias or even of enough fantastically lucid informational broadsheets. Clearly, something more remains to be said on the subject.

Toward Social Significance: Conventions as Shared Understandings

On my broadly Bayesian information-processing model of communal attachments, groups like nations have different understandings born of different information. Within a group there is a "shared understanding," in the sense that everyone has a broadly similar stock of information that they interpret in broadly the same way. When communitarians—especially nationalist communitarians—talk of "shared understandings," however, they seem to have in mind something richer, fuller, larger. They seem to be thinking more of something like a whole "way of life" that is being shared: language and literature, morals and religion, history and humor.

Of course, "information" is itself a rich and elastic concept. Nowise exhausted by mundane things like tide tables or train times, it can (at least in principle) be expanded to incorporate most, if not quite all, of what communitarians want. It makes perfectly good sense to talk in terms of our having "information about" language and literature, morals and religion, history and humor. Recasting the point in that way seems somehow to trivialize the point communitarians were trying to make, however. Someone who merely "knows" jokes may be able to recall and retell them without sharing any sense of what makes them funny. Thus this model conflates "knowing how" with merely "knowing that."[12] Communities, especially national communities, share "understandings" not just in the trivial sense of sharing certain "bodies of information" but also, more important, in the sense of sharing some idea of the *significance* to be attached to those things.[13]

Conventions

National communities share something else that I think comes closer to the communitarian point, in this respect. That is *conventions*. Different groups have different "ways of doing things," different ways of construing and confronting shared problems. The grandest example of such conventionally shared understandings is language systems themselves—and of course language conflicts lie at the heart of many national and subnational ethnic divisions. But all sorts of other shared codes of conduct, ranging from etiquette to ethics, can arguably be construed on much the same model.

Many of the things that differentiate national communities, in particular, seem to be little more than conventions of just this sort. Consider those things constituting the "British cultural identity"—things "such . . . as drinking tea and patronising fish and chip shops, an enthusiasm for gardening, a love of the countryside, and so on."[14] Those, clearly, are all purely conventional. But equally conventional are key components of what David Miller goes on to distinguish as constituting the "British national identity"—things like shared political institutions and various constitutional settlements, old and new.[15] The "conventions of the constitution," clearly, are as conventional as anything else.[16]

Conventions such as these are perfectly amenable to ordinary rationalistic analysis. It is analytically inherent in the notion of a convention that everyone must converge on much the same convention for anyone to benefit. There may or may not be good external reasons for adopting one convention rather than another. Be that as it may, there are internally compelling reasons for everyone to abide by the same convention as everyone else around them. And, even externally, there is an overwhelming reason for everyone within an interacting group to converge on some convention or another—even if it is not necessarily the best one that might be logically possible.[17]

Conventions such as these characterize a community's shared understandings in roughly the sense communitarians want. Within any given community (defined as a group of individuals frequently interacting with one another), there is a good, rational reason for the conventions to be broadly similar. Across different communities (defined as groups of individuals who do not interact with one another very frequently), there is no particular reason for sharing the same conventions. Once conventions are in place within any given community, there is good reason for people to persist in following them and to resist even moderately good reasons for changing them. And so on.

Furthermore, this analysis of what unites communities also provides a tolerably good account of what divides them. Where conventions happen to be shared across different communities, such occasional interactions as do occur across communal boundaries will be made easier. Being easier, they will become more frequent; and communities sharing broadly similar conventions will grow closer together.[18] Conversely, interactions will be harder and hence less frequent among communities with dissimilar conventions, which will grow further apart in consequence. In these ways the simple dynamics of conventions might go far—as far, perhaps, as the earlier "asymmetrical information" story—toward explaining communal polarization.

Arbitrariness

An analysis couched purely in terms of "differing conventions," however, goes only part of the way toward accounting for the significance that communitarians in general, and nationalists in particular, attach to the differences between themselves and others in the "understandings" communities share. The story about "conventions" explains well enough why people within a community are supposed to be operating from *within* its shared understandings—why they are supposed to partake of them rather than simply having information about them, why they are supposed to "know how" rather than merely "know that." But nothing that has been said so far explains why anyone should be particularly *hostile* toward other people's conventions (so long, at least, as there is no risk of these conventions disrupting their own). The "conventions" story, as elaborated so far, leaves out the "blood and guts" viciousness that characterizes the most troublesome forms of nationalism.

That is inevitably so, or so it might seem. After all, conventions—by their very nature—are essentially arbitrary. Broadly speaking, it does not matter which convention we settle upon. Or even if it matters, even if some convention would be better (even much better) than others, what matters ever so much more is that we settle on one and that it is the same one followed by everyone else with whom we are interacting.

Of course, this at-root arbitrariness of our conventions is rarely acknowledged in public discourse. That is hardly surprising, given the importance of whipping everyone into line behind the same convention. It is more compelling to say not just that French is *our* language but also that it is a uniquely beautiful tongue, not just that pounds/shillings/pence is *our* currency but also that its clumsy practice of counting in twelves has certain unique commercial advantages.[19] Thus it is common to say of most sorts of conventions that while they are just conventions, some conventions are better than others—and, not incidentally, ours are better than most.

Even national cultural chauvinists, however, are often prepared to concede that much that is distinctive about their own national and cultural community is at root the product of their unique traditions and conventions. And the recognition of conventions as conventions necessarily carries with it acknowledgment of their artificiality and hence of their arbitrariness in that minimal sense. Conventions are human constructions. Some might serve us better, some worse; there might be good reasons for us collectively to adopt certain conventions in preference to others. But even if those advantages of alternative conventions are given externally, their status as conventions can only be given internally by and within our community.

Conventions to "Treat as True"

This is *not* true, however, of those conventions whose artificiality cannot be openly acknowledged without undermining their capacity to perform their function. My aim here is to draw attention to that class of conventions and to discuss their role in defining and dividing nations and communities.

Conventions ordinarily do not themselves aspire to any objective truth status. Of course, some conventions might be better or worse, more or less useful, than others. Be that as it may, however, conventions are inherently arbitrary human artifices. As such, they cannot literally be (or pretend or claim or aspire to be) true.

Sometimes, however, we adopt conventions about what to *treat as true* for purposes of our collective interactions. We thereby politicize our epistemology in at least two senses. First, the theory of knowledge here in view is one that is itself essentially political in character: how we come to "know" the "truth" about these things (the scare quotes in both cases being genuinely scary) is essentially a political process. Second, and following from that, there is a distinctive theory of knowledge—a distinctive epistemological style—associated with the distinctively political realm.

In developing these thoughts, I shall be developing a thesis parallel to what has elsewhere been dubbed the "consensus theory of truth." The standard way of describing that story is to say that "consensus betokens truth." Supposing everyone is observing the same external reality, if everyone's subjective report of it is broadly the same, then what all those subjective reports converge upon is probably a broadly true account of the objective properties of that external world.[20] In the cases here in view, the story runs in the opposite direction. In the standard case, truth is the end and consensus the means to it. In the more politicized cases here in view, consensus is the end and "truth" (so to speak) is the means.[21]

Toward Blood and Guts: Our Truths and Theirs

If the broadly Bayesian account I previously developed provides a rational reconstruction of the differentiation of national and ethnic communities, implacable hostilities between certain national and ethnic communities might be broadly explained precisely in terms of that notion of conventions we collectively decide to "treat as true."

The underlying idea is simple enough. Suppose there are certain things upon which we need broad agreement across the whole community in order to get on with the rest of our lives. Suppose, furthermore, that those things aspire (perhaps necessarily so) to truth status. Then those two suppositions, joined together, would necessarily entail that there are some things that we must all be prepared to "treat as true" (whether or not objectively they are or can be shown to be true) if we are to be able to get on with the ordinary business of life together.

Ex hypothesi, however, that choice of what to treat as true in these domains is purely conventional. As such, it is inherently arbitrary, and that being so, different communities will inevitably choose differently. Yet by the nature of this particular sort of convention, it cannot acknowledge its own essential arbitrariness. Each community is thus led to *claim* itself to be in possession of the one uniquely true account, the one uniquely right way of doing things, in this respect.

"True for you" is necessarily a slur or a taunt. Truth is true universally. It is not indexed to particular individuals or particular nations or particular communities. To say something is "true for you" is to accuse you of having made a category mistake, ascribing truth to something that cannot actually possess it. By the same token, to admit something is merely a convention is to say that it is "true for us"—which is to confess to our having made a similar category mistake ourselves. Whatever is true, really and truly true, must necessarily be true for everyone else as well as for us.

A Manichaean struggle thus necessarily emerges between "our truths" and "theirs." By the very nature of the claims, both truth claims cannot be right. And if being right in these respects matters—if the "truths" in view are invested with social significance on all sides—the groundwork is laid for genuinely implacable hostilities between nations (and races and ethnic groups more generally) organized around and through these conventions.

Here I shall play out these themes through a pair of sustained examples, religion and history. Both figure centrally in nationalist self-identity. Both figure even more centrally in chauvinistic struggles of various national communities against one another.

Religion

The paradigm of a convention that needs to be "taken as true" in the way I have been discussing would be religion, according to a neo-Hobbesian account of the role of religion in political life.[22] In that neo-Hobbesian account, we all agree to be Roman Catholics (or whatever) in this country not because we all necessarily think that that faith is uniquely correct—much less that it can be shown to be so—but merely because we cannot afford to embroil ourselves in inherently undecidable and endlessly absorbing theological disputes.

Neo-Hobbesian arguments for a state religion thus invite us to pluck arbitrarily some religion or another and establish it as authoritative within our community.[23] Within the terms of that model, that choice is recognizable as inherently arbitrary. The lived reality is, and must necessarily be, very much otherwise. From within, the claims of religion must by their nature be treated as true. The necessity of doing so derives not just from the exigencies of selling salvation (how best to propagate and instill the faith and so on). It derives, more fundamentally, from the nature of religious claims themselves.

Religious claims purport to represent objective truths about the nature of the world—that there *is* a God (or gods), with just these properties, who has issued precisely these commandments. The community may have decided upon a convention to proceed "as if" Catholicism were true. But the claims that convention treats "as if" true are claims that themselves purport to *be* true. Given the nature of religious claims, taking any particular faith "as given" is necessarily tantamount to taking the faith "as *true*."

Those imbued with traditions of religious tolerance—from the earliest Dutch burghers through American heirs of the First Amendment—are used to fudging these differences. But everyone who takes their faith seriously must necessarily be offended at, for example, the way in which the 1707 Act of Union that linked the two British crowns made the selfsame sovereign an Anglican when in England and a Presbyterian upon crossing into Scotland. Such a mystical transformation makes a mockery of any absolute truth claims on behalf of either denomination.

Religious controversies may be virtually unique in these crucial respects. There may not be all that many propositions upon which we need broad agreement across a whole community (ones that, absent such agreement, would lead to disputations that are both undecidable and unignorable, all-consuming) and upon which we need agreement of a sort that necessarily purports to assert truth claims.

Still, it is only right that religious conflicts should occupy a privileged place in the study of nationalist, ethnic, and communal conflicts. Historically, wars of religion were the dominant mode at least for long stretches of human history. In today's world, religious difference still underlies (or overlays) the vast majority of communal conflicts that threaten human life on a grand scale. Certainly they seem at the very heart of all the nastiest of the nationalist struggles that have broken out with the waning of the Cold War. Thus it seems right that we should take them as a paradigm of the sorts of claims that undergird the nastiest face of nationalism and the most serious sort of intercommunal conflict.

History

Other nonreligious aspects of intercommunal (national, racial, or ethnic) strife sometimes take on something of the same cast, however. "Origin" claims, both individual and collective, often lie at the core of national and other communal identities. National and other communities are, quite literally, constituted by the conjunction of a certain story about where we as a People came from and a story about where each of us individually sprang from that makes us part of that People. But histories are complex and multifaceted and can be read in many different ways. So, too, can anyone's lineage, depending on which line you follow and how far back. Picking out one telling of either of these tales as the definitive account amounts to privileging, more or less arbitrarily, one version over all others.

If the choice of histories is largely arbitrary, it is nonetheless crucial that everyone claiming to be one People by virtue of a shared history and lineage settle on the *same* story. A single person cannot have two quite different histories. Spatiotemporal location is a unique identifier; no given person could have been in two different places doing two different things at the same time. The same is true for those national and other communities defining themselves in terms of shared experiences. We cannot, in those terms, be one People if we have had divergent experiences. So, too, for those communities defining themselves in terms of a shared ancestry. We cannot, in those terms, be one People if we have sprung from different roots.[24]

Conventions are the obvious solution in such situations. They enable us all to converge on the same story, among the many possible stories we might tell about our individual and collective backgrounds.[25] These conventions, like all conventions, are certainly human artifices—and largely arbitrary ones at that. Undeniably, history is a purely human artifact, a story we tell ourselves. Undoubtedly there are some constraints on what stories we tell ourselves. Bloodlines and battlegrounds constitute hard facts about the world, whatever social construction we might put on them. Some stories may fit those hard facts better than others; some may form more pleasingly coherent narratives than others. Still, which story we settle upon among the many eligible ones is indeed largely an arbitrary choice from among that admittedly circumscribed set of almost equally viable options.[26]

Those national and other communities that constitute themselves essentially by reference to their histories have trouble admitting that fact, however. It is in the very nature of the thing that *history happened*, just as it is in the nature of the thing that truth is true. Imagined histories are not history at all, any more than imagined communities are communities—except in the sociological sense that that imagining makes them real in their consequences. The point, however, is that they will be deprived of that power once they are seen as mere figments of the collective imagination.

Of course, not all national or other communities attach all that much importance to shared histories and lineages. But for those that do try to constitute themselves out of such notions, the open acknowledgment of many equally valid ways of reading the past—open acknowledgment of the fact that it is essentially arbitrary which events or which branches of the family tree we pick out as especially salient—is powerfully subversive of the shared identity. Thus, in these communities, conventionalized histories and lineages represent another instance of the special sorts of conventions here in view. Just as with conventionalized religion, the convention is not just to settle upon something to which we can all agree but, moreover, to treat those conventionalized claims as possessing a truth status that, as mere conventions, they necessarily lack.

Rationalizing the Unreasoning

The aim of this chapter has been to "rationalize" nationalist communitarian sentiments, to try to assimilate them to ordinary liberal-Enlightenment accounts of social life. These sentiments were always destined to be a special case of that more general sort of account. They have turned out, in the latter respect in particular, to be a very special case indeed.

The question that inevitably emerges is what, if anything, has been gained by this exercise in shameless reductionism. "Understanding," of course, is the principal response. And that may in itself contribute toward the damping down of at least certain forms of communal conflicts and nationalist fracases.

The first step in my analysis—seeing national and other communal differentiation in terms of sheer information dynamics—might have some clear practical payoffs of just that sort. Others are not wrong, just different, and different in ways that are themselves eminently reasonable, even in terms of our own canons of rationality. We might hope that message will be a powerful palliative to nationalist and other forms of intercommunal strife.

Equally hopeful is the second step in my analysis—seeing essentially arbitrary conventions at the core of the social life of nations and other communities. Differing conventions, openly acknowledged as such, need not themselves be particularly divisive. Our conventions *matter* to us in ways that the gaps and biases in our information base do not. But these conventions just represent *our* way of doing things, which no one else should be expected necessarily to share. That acknowledgment, too, might help nations and other communities see how they can have a strong sense of their own distinctive identities and at the same time legitimately adopt a "live and let live" attitude toward other communities very different from themselves.

Less hopeful is the message of the final step in my analysis—seeing implacable hostilities between national and other communities in terms of conventions unable to admit their own conventionality. Objectively, they are arbitrary and hence differ across the various national and other communities. Subjectively, though, those communities cannot admit the arbitrariness of their conventions and hence that others might reasonably differ. Those conventions purport to represent universal truths, which others who differ can only be seen as positively denying. There is no scope for reasoning across differences such as these. It is a case for conversion, not reason—with potentially all the bloody connotations of wars against infidels that that term conjures up.

Of course, it does not always come to that, precisely because not all communities care that deeply about issues (of the "one true faith" or "one true history") that can be resolved only by conventions that cannot admit their own conventionality. The upshot of my analysis is that the less nasty forms of nationalism occur where issues such as that are off the national agenda. But my analysis offers little insight into questions of how to get or keep them off the agenda. Specifically, simply pointing out in a publicly compelling way the arbitrariness of the conventions involved will not work to damp communal conflict.

Conventions are needed to resolve questions of religious difference only among peoples who take their religion seriously. Only there, absent some conventional resolution, would the religious question threaten to prove so utterly fixating as to stymie all other forms of social intercourse; only there do we really need to settle upon a common religion, any religion, in order to get on with the rest of life. Likewise, conventionalized common histories and lineages are only needed among people keen to constitute themselves as one in terms of mythically shared histories. Clearly, the logic at work in such cases is the logic of convention, pure and simple, but the language cannot be. Given such a population and given the truth status to which the central propositions of religion or history aspire, what is chosen as a convenience must necessarily be presented as The Truth.

In such circumstances, pointing out that the religious settlement or whatever within any given national community is, after all, merely an arbitrary convention would be decidedly ill advised. It might end wars of religion with other national communities but on the pain of reopening wars of religion within the national community.

In the end, then, mine is a story about the inherent hazards of politicizing epistemology and epistemologizing politics. Much in nationalist politics is perfectly amenable to rationalist analysis; and in many respects those rationalist analyses tend both to predict and to contribute toward "live and let live" approaches to national differences. The real problem, according to my analysis, lies with conventions to "treat as true" the claims (like those of religion and history) that, by their nature, insistently assert truth status. Where truths such as these are disputed and where such disputes are invested with social significance and hence cannot simply be ignored, conventions to finesse those quarrels may sometimes be useful. In such cases, however, the inevitable price paid for internal peace is apparently a serious risk of external strife.

Overrationalizing: An Epilogue

Here ends my rationalistic account of differences across nations and the ways in which those differences sometimes cause us to come to grief. Many differences can be analyzed in those terms, and at least some of the grief might be avoided if people can be brought to see things that way. Having said that, however, I must also frankly acknowledge that there is more to nationalism than admits of rational analysis or reform.

Attachments to one's own nation, culture, and community—and hatred of those constructed as "the other," opposing nations, cultures, and communities— can and sometimes clearly do serve deeper and more disreputable psychological functions than any essentially Enlightenment model of humanity cares or dares to consider. The rationalistic model sketched above also omits any mention of the essentially strategic functions that national/ethnic/communal attachments and oppositions might serve. The former proposition suggests that communal attachments are less rational than I am here supposing; the latter suggests that they are rational in some different way.[27]

In short, national, ethnic, and other civil strife really is sometimes just the product of madness or badness, compulsion or cunning, on the part of some or all parties to it. The model that I have been developing analyzes nationalist and cognate intercommunal strife, more charitably, in terms of understandable (albeit perhaps irreconcilable) differences among reasonable, nondevious peoples. Clearly, we cannot stop there. But it seems, quite simply, irresponsible not at least to start there.

By the same token, it must also be admitted that sometimes there really are wicked people who must be stopped. Some truths of international law and morality are not at all conventional—or if conventional are such important conventions to uphold, for all concerned, that it is well worth going to war over them.[28] Some struggles of nationalists, just like some struggles against nationalists, are conducted in the name of much larger truths nowise peculiar to the conventions of any particular tribe alone.

At that point, however, we have begun adjudicating national claims rather than merely analyzing their formal structures. That, too, is an important task—and one for which liberalism is far better equipped than certain excessively relativistic, nonjudgmental forms of communitarianism cast in a postmodernist mode. While we certainly ought not to shrink from that task, it is, quite simply, a separate story from the more formalistic one that this chapter has been devoted to telling.

NOTES

An earlier version of this chapter benefited from comments at the Conference on the Ethics of Nationalism, University of Illinois at Urbana-Champaign, April 1994. I am particularly grateful for comments, then and later, from Brian Barry, Russell Hardin, Tom Hurka, Judy Lichtenberg, Robert McKim, Jeff McMahan, Philip Pettit, and Yael Tamir.

1. Will Kymlicka, *Contempory Political Philosophy* (Oxford: Clarendon, 1990); Chris Brown, *International Relations Theory: New Normative Approaches* (Hemel Hempstead: Harvester-Wheatsheaf, 1992), pp. 21–106. The nonparallelism in this formulation is deliberate. "Communitarian" is a broader class than just "nationalist," though nationalists are a paradigmatic instance of that broader class; "cosmopolitan" is a broader class than just "liberal," though liberals are a paradigmatic instance of cosmopolitans.

2. For an excellent survey of work in this tradition, see Shmuel Noah Eisenstadt and Bernhard Giesen, "The Construction of Collective Identity," *Archives Europeénnes de Sociologie* 36 (1995): 72–102.

3. Ernest Gellner, *Thought and Change* (London: Weidenfeld and Nicholson, 1971), p. 149, quoted in Yael Tamir, *Liberal Nationalism* (Princeton: Princeton University Press, 1993), p. 5.

4. In *Liberal Nationalism*, Tamir pursues a similar goal to mine working from the oppo-

site direction, trying to assimilate liberal values to nationalist ones, whereas I assimilate nationalist sentiments to liberal logic.

5. A notable exception, upon which I build here, is the discussion in Russell Hardin, *One for All: The Logic of Group Conflict* (Princeton: Princeton University Press, 1995), chap. 7, to which this chapter was originally cast as a reply.

6. These connections are elaborated by Russell Hardin in *One for All* and "The Street-level Epistemology of Trust," *Politics and Society* 21 (1993): 505–29. It is only "broadly" Bayesian for reasons discussed in note 10 below.

7. These components of the model are familiar from discussions of "rational ignorance" in Anthony Downs, *An Economic Theory of Democracy* (New York: Harper, 1957), and of "satisficing" in Herbert Simon, "A Behavioral Theory of Rational Choice," *Quarterly Journal of Economics* 69 (1954): 99–118.

8. David Hume charmingly anticipates this aspect of the model in his essay "Of Miracles," *Enquiry concerning Human Understanding*, sec. 10.

9. I offer a parallel analysis in *Manipulatory Politics* (New Haven, Conn.: Yale University Press, 1980), chap. 2. For a striking contemporary example, consider the differential response of the black and white communities to the O. J. Simpson trial. Blacks, who were more likely to have had experience with police malpractice, were thus more inclined to discount police testimony than whites.

10. Ordinary Bayesian models, of course, tend toward convergence as more information comes in. (In ordinary Bayesian terms, how you set the "a priori probabilities" does not matter, in consequence.) My model differs from ordinary Bayesianism insofar as it allows people to weight evidence according to how much credibility they attach to it and for that in turn to be a function of how well it fits their a prioris—that is, ordinary Bayesian models do not contain clause 4 above. That departure from ordinary Bayesian logic seems eminently justifiable for purposes of analyzing social phenomena: the socially more typical case seems to be more one of someone claiming to have just seen someone walking on water (a report that might well make us want to query the credibility of the reporter) than that of someone reporting the color of a ball drawn from an urn (which typically arouses few such worries).

11. Within this essentially economic way of thinking, the most notable example is the firm. Perfectly informed actors in a perfect market would have no reason to internalize the production process within a firm rather than buying those products in the market. Firms make sense, on this account, only because of informational imperfections—specifically, our being less able to monitor the quality of outputs bought in the market than inputs to the production process within the firm. See R. H. Coase, "The Nature of the Firm," *Economica* 4 (1937): 386–405, and Oliver E. Williamson, *The Economic Institutions of Capitalism* (New York: Free Press, 1985).

12. Gilbert Ryle, *The Concept of Mind* (London: Hutchinson, 1949), chap. 2.

13. This "significance," furthermore, is not well captured in my quasi-Bayesian terms of "differential weighting for information-processing purposes."

14. David Miller, "Reflections on British National Identity," *New Community* 21 (1995): 161.

15. He itemizes these as traditionally embracing, principally, values of "Protestantism, limited government and free commerce overseas" (ibid., p. 158).

16. A. V. Dicey, *The Law of the Constitution*, 7th ed. (London: Macmillan, 1908); Geoffrey Marshall and Graeme C. Moodie, *Some Problems of the Constitution*, 5th ed. (London: Hutchinson, 1971), chap. 2.

17. David K. Lewis, *Convention* (Oxford: Blackwell, 1969).

18. The paradigm here is a shared language—the old jibe about America and Britain being "two cultures divided by a common language" notwithstanding. See more generally James S. Coleman, *Foundations of Social Theory* (Cambridge, Mass.: Harvard University Press, 1990), pt. 2.

19. One A. C. Aitken, professor of mathematics at the University of Edinburgh, cast his *Case against Decimalisation* (Edinburgh: Oliver and Boyd, 1962) in terms of the fact that "twelve [is] a number divisible by 2, 3 4 and 6," which makes it more suitable for "use in parcelling, packaging, geometrical and physical construction" (pp. 6–7).

20. This line is particularly associated with Jürgen Habermas. See especially Philip Pettit, "Habermas on Truth and Justice," in *Marx and Marxisms*, ed. G. H. R. Parkinson (Cambridge: Cambridge University Press, 1982), pp. 207–28.

21. For a very different account of the instrumental, functional value of treating certain propositions as if they could have objective truth value—according to his analysis, in order to encourage argumentation and debate—see Huw Price, *Facts and the Function of Truth* (Oxford: Blackwell, 1988).

22. Thomas Hobbes, *Leviathan* (London: J. Cooke, 1651), chap. 31. Hobbes himself attempts to conjure up the necessity for a single state religion from certain necessary features of language and community. Signs of respect, in religion as elsewhere, are necessarily conventional; the conventions of language are necessarily public; the public, in any given community, is necessarily singular. For a more straightforward case for a state religion, frankly Hobbesian in spirit, see Jean-Jacques Rousseau, *Social Contract*, bk. 4, chap. 8.

23. Picking rather than choosing, in the terms of Edna Ullmann-Margalit and Sidney Morgenbesser, "Picking and Choosing," *Social Research* 44 (1977): 757–85.

24. The impossibilities in view here are more psychological and sociological than purely logical. Logically, Peoples could be constructed in more realistic terms of partly overlapping group experiences and kinship systems, but groups constructed out of people who share "any of many" membership criteria are unlikely to meet the sociological and psychological needs of people who need to construct themselves as part of a historically given People. Much the same is also true, mutatis mutandis, about individuals' own personal histories; anyone attaching great importance to what he or she has *done* is unlikely to have much time for reflecting upon mixed motives and the multiple descriptions under which each of those various acts might have been chosen.

25. Or broadly the same story. There can be disagreements over many of the core tenets of Judaism without undermining its central role as the defining feature of the state of Israel. So, too, can there be differences in the interpretation of our shared past, as long as we agree that a shared past of some sort or another (and, furthermore, broadly the same sort) is what defines us as a People.

26. On the ways in which nationalist myths constitute "partial" truths, historically, see particularly David Archard, "Myths, Lies and Historical Truth: A Defence of Nationalism," *Political Studies* 43 (1995): 472–81.

27. What drives that latter model is not the rationality of information processing and

decision making but rather the rationality of strategic game playing and coalition politics and sharing spoils. In that latter model, people emphasize certain similarities (certain "primordial ties") not because they are psychologically compelling but only because they are strategically useful. They emphasize these communal ties when, but only when, it is in their interest to do so. Consider the compelling case of the way Chinese communities emphasized their ethnicity on one island in the West Indies where it would promote their trading opportunities but not on another where it would not. See Orlando Patterson, "Context and Choice in Ethnic Allegiance: A Theoretical Framework and Carribbean Case Study," in *Ethnicity*, ed. Nathan Glazer and Daniel P. Moynihan (Cambridge, Mass.: Harvard University Press, 1975), pp. 305–49. Claus Offe, in "Ethnic Politics in East European Transitions" (Australian National University, March 1994, mimeograph), analyzes East European ethnic revivals in similar fashion.

28. Michael Walzer, "World War II: Was That War Different?," *Philosophy and Public Affairs* 1 (1971): 3–21.

II

NATIONALISM AND
THE DEMANDS OF
IMPARTIALITY

The Limits of National Partiality

JEFF McMAHAN

One million Arabs are not worth a Jewish fingernail.
— Rabbi Yaacov Perin, quoted in the *New York Times*, February 28, 1994

Partiality and Impartiality

Nations and Nationalism

Nations are human groups distinguished by both objective and subjective criteria. The objective relations that may bind the members of a nation together include a history of mutual association and common occupancy of the same territory, common ethnic origins, use of the same language, shared religious beliefs, a common commitment to certain political institutions, a common culture involving shared values and customs, and so on. Although most nations are united in several of these ways, no single objective commonality or any particular combination of these commonalities is necessary for the existence of a nation.[1] At the subjective level, most adult members of a nation must share a sense that together they constitute a distinct group and that belonging to this group is a constitutive element of each member's individual identity. They must, in other words, recognize one another as sharing a collective identity.[2]

Because some of these criteria admit of degrees or invoke concepts that are vague (for example, culture) and because many of the criteria are also characteristic of other collective entities (such as clans, tribes, ethnic groups, and certain political associations), it is not surprising that there are frequent disputes about whether certain groups are actually nations. Some observers, for example, hold that the population of the United States has all the hallmarks of nationality, including a distinctive historical culture; others accept that it is a nation but one that embraces many cultures; while still others hold that the United States is a multinational state.[3]

"Nationalism" refers to a cluster of beliefs about the normative significance of nations and nationality. Those who are called nationalists typically hold, inter alia, that the continued existence and flourishing of their own nation is a fundamental good, that the members of the nation ought to control their own collective affairs, and that membership in the nation makes it not only permissible but in many instances morally required to manifest loyalty and partiality to fellow members. Some nationalists are "radically particularist"; they restrict the scope of these beliefs to their own nation, which they may regard as uniquely worthy of partisan sentiment and devotion. Other nations, they may believe, suffer from a variety of defects, among which is a tendency to entertain delusions as to their own merits. But not all particularist nationalists disparage the nationalism of other nations. There are some whose particularism is theoretically motivated. A morality, according to their view, is a communal product whose range of application is properly restricted to the community in which it evolved. One's own morality, therefore, should neither condemn nor endorse the nationalism of others. Whether others ought to be nationalists depends on the deliverances of their particular morality.[4]

Other nationalists hold that, with perhaps a few exceptions, all people are morally entitled to value their own nation, to seek to ensure its self-determining character, and to show partiality to its members. These "universalist nationalists" are typically, as individuals, highly partial to their own nation. They are, one might say, "partisan universalists." There are, however, universalist nationalists who lack strong national attachments themselves yet endorse the nationalism of those they regard as fortunate enough to have them. My concern in this essay is primarily with universalist nationalism in general, whether partisan or detached.

Some theorists have claimed that nationalism insists that "the political and the national unit should be congruent."[5] But there are two ways to make national and political units coincide. One is to redraw the boundaries of existing political units so that they conform as closely as possible to the geographical contours of nations. The other is to preserve existing political configurations while seeking to forge the populations of states into nations—what is sometimes referred to as "nation building." Since the latter may require breaking down national identities whenever two or more nations are encompassed within a single state, it is anathema to nationalists. Thus insofar as nationalists believe that nations and states should coincide, their view must be that states should be molded to fit nations rather than nations to fit states. Even this, however, is not a defining feature of nationalism. While it does seem that nationalists necessarily favor some form of political self-determination for their own nation (and, if they are universalists, for other nations as well), they do not have to believe that self-determination requires sovereign statehood. Thus many nationalists in Quebec, Scotland, and elsewhere repudiate secessionist aspirations; some, indeed, embrace the anarchist doctrine that no state can be legitimate and thus none should exist.

The defining characteristic of nationalism that will be the focus of this inquiry is its insistence that members of the same nation—*conationals*—are in many contexts permitted or even required to be partial to one another—that is, that they generally may and often must give some degree of priority to one another's interests over those of foreigners or nonmembers. This commitment to partiality within the nation appears to render nationalism incompatible with the guiding principle of liberalism that all persons are of equal worth and as such are entitled to equal concern and respect.[6] It is, indeed, an axiom of modern moral thought that "no one is more important than anyone else. . . . [E]veryone counts the same. For a given quantity of whatever it is that's good or bad—suffering or happiness or fulfillment or frustration—its intrinsic impersonal value doesn't depend on whose it is."[7] But to give priority to conationals is to show greater concern and respect for them than for others; it is to count one's conationals more than others.

The conflict here is not quite as stark as it may initially seem. The claim that partiality may be permitted or required among conationals does not necessarily deny that people have equal worth; it may instead deny that an individual's worth is the sole determinant of how he or she ought to be treated. It is possible to acknowledge that all persons have equal worth, and thus matter equally sub specie aeternitatis, while also holding that a person's moral status vis-à-vis a particular moral agent may depend not just on the intrinsic properties that determine this person's objective moral worth but also on the ways in which he or she is related to the agent. What the nationalist claims is that we are not all morally equidistant from one another—that a special relation between two people may give each a special moral reason to favor the other that neither has with respect to others outside the relation. These reasons are "agent-relative," specific to those who share a certain relation rather than universal. They do not imply that anyone is owed partiality by virtue of an objectively superior moral worth.

Still, nationalism does insist that conationals should have greater concern for one another than for others and should, other things being equal, give priority to one another's interests over the interests of others. And this is at least prima facie incompatible with the idea that all persons are entitled to equal concern and respect or that no one's interests count more than the equivalent interests of another.

Various responses to this conflict compete for our allegiance. Two are radically particularist. One holds that national partiality is justified, though only in *our* case. Although we may give priority—perhaps even absolute priority—to our own conationals, others lack a similar justification. Their duty is to submit to us. This view is not worth discussing. Nor will I discuss the somewhat more tenable view that there is no general answer to the question whether (or how much) national partiality is justified since different answers are given by different and equally valid local moralities. According to this view, whatever the local morality determines to be the appropriate degree of partiality within the community is authoritative for the members of the community. There is no neutral, external standpoint from which the local morality's determinations can be challenged or overruled.

I am interested in what can be said about the legitimacy of partiality at the universal level. I will simply assume that if any form of nationalism is defensible, it will be of the universalist variety. There are, of course, universalist responses to the conflict between equality and partiality that are also implausibly extreme. It might be held, for example, that all people should give absolute priority to their own conationals, that there are no constraints on what may be done to others in advancing the interests of one's own nation. Or, at the other extreme, it might be held that no degree of partiality can ever be directly justified, that no departure from equal concern and respect can be justified by appeal to the intrinsic significance of special relations. This latter view is, indeed, fairly widely held among philosophers, if not among people generally; I will return to it presently.

Here, as elsewhere, however, I believe that common sense should not be lightly dismissed. What most of us in fact believe is that there are at least two distinct sources of moral reasons, neither reducible to the other. First, an impartial core to morality imposes duties on all of us to respect the worth of others irrespective of whether or how we are related to them. But, second, the basic duties that we owe to one another may be supplemented by special moral reasons that arise from our relations with one another. The reasons deriving from these different sources compete for our attention, time, and resources.[8] It is therefore one of the central tasks of moral and political philosophy to seek a coherent, determinate, and stable reconciliation of the competing demands that issue from these divergent sources.[9] It is important to determine, in particular, what sorts of relation are capable of legitimizing partiality as well as how extensive the justified departures from strict impartiality are.

The Spectrum of Special Relations

The sentiment of partiality toward particular individuals is elicited by a variety of relations that one may bear to those individuals. One may be partial to members of one's family, friends, acquaintances, coworkers, coreligionists, members of one's local community, citizens of one's state, members of one's race, or even the members of one's species. In some instances—for example, friendship—the sentiment of partiality is partly constitutive of the nature of the relation. But manifestations of these various forms of partiality are not all equally defensible. Partiality within the family is almost universally recognized as paradigmatically legitimate. Parents are not only permitted to give a certain priority to the interests of their own children but also morally required to do so in a wide variety of circumstances. At the other end of the spectrum, partiality toward members of one's own race is widely condemned as a paradigmatically arbitrary, illegitimate, and pernicious form of discrimination. (Solidarity among the members of races that are the victims of discrimination or oppression is an exception. I will later suggest that there is a special reason why partiality seems legitimate in these cases.)

Where does partiality within the nation lie along the spectrum from familial to racial partiality? Is conationality a legitimate or illegitimate basis for partiality? Intuitively, nationalism is an intermediate case. It is a phenomenon about which many are profoundly ambivalent. We tend to judge it by its effects, which are mixed. On the positive side, nationalism summons forth many virtues: loyalty, commitment, and self-sacrifice. Those who share the bonds of nationality enjoy the security of belonging as well as the self-esteem that is the paradoxical concomitant of self-transcendence; and when the nationalist ideal of self-determination is achieved, members of the nation typically find a measure of dignity and autonomy that they are denied by even the most benign paternalism that fails fully to share and therefore to understand or respect their culture. But to understand the moral ambiguity of nationalism one must also note its darker side, and each positive feature casts a deep shadow. The nationalist virtues are inherently truncated: it is betrayal to exercise them equally on behalf of outsiders. The comfortable sense of identity and belonging is obtained at the expense of those who are necessarily excluded. And even national pride and self-esteem may depend on a judgment, implicit or explicit, of the lesser worth of outsiders. Viewed thus, the pursuit of national self-determination may seem less an assertion of human dignity than a meretricious expression of atavistic tribal impulses that threaten endless political fragmentation and conflict. We therefore find it heartening when barriers between nations give way to recognition, cooperation, and integration—as seemed, until recently, to be happening in much of Europe. For, in general, it is better that people concentrate their attention on what they have in common than on what divides them. (The exception is when another group is united around an identity or project that is evil; then a public assertion of difference may be necessary.) While it is true, of course, that nationalism, also, encourages the members of a nation to focus on their commonalities rather than their differences, nationalism seeks a heightened unity within the nation by stressing the otherness of those without. It unites some by dividing them from others.

A common defense of nationalism consists in comparing nations to families, thereby assimilating national partiality to the paradigm of partiality within the family. Opponents of nationalism have followed a parallel strategy by highlighting the similarity between nationalism and racism. But nationalism is not closely analogous to either. Indeed, all the various special relations that have been thought to justify departures from impartiality—love, friendship, parenthood, conationality, citizenship, and so on—seem sui generis; none is relevantly quite like any other. Each has to be understood on its own terms, though our understanding of one may be enhanced by comparing or contrasting it with another whose moral nature is intuitively clearer.

The Justification of Partiality

Before we can assess any relation as a foundation for partiality, we must understand the different forms that the justification for partiality may take. Different relations may justify partiality for different reasons. In some cases, several distinct justifications may coalesce around a single relation.

The Personal Point of View

One defense of partiality appeals to our nature as persons. We are not disinterested and impartial spectators; each of us has a distinct identity, is variously related to some individuals and not to others, and views the world from a unique perspective that naturally generates a pattern of concern and valuation that is inherently partial. Since morality must respect and reflect our nature as persons, it must acknowledge that each person has reasons for action that are generated by or within his or her own personal point of view. The personal point of view is thus an autonomous and authoritative source of moral reasons, though most theorists concede that it is not the only such source. According to one prominent theory, while our fundamental moral reasons are independent of the personal point of view, morality nevertheless accommodates the personal point of view by permitting each person to give somewhat greater weight to those things that specially matter from his or her own point of view than they would be assigned from the impartial point of view.[10]

This is an important view, about which it is impossible to say anything decisive in the short space of an essay. But there are reasons for skepticism about its ability to justify national partiality. It seems, for example, to make the permissibility of partiality toward a person depend upon subjective factors, such as whether one specially cares or is concerned about that person. But while this may be the principal basis for partiality in the case of certain comparatively rare personal relations, it is at most an ancillary factor in the case of most special relations. It is, for example, not because a mother specially cares about her son that she is justified in giving him priority over others; rather, it is the objective nature of the relation she bears to him that both warrants her special concern and grounds the special reasons she has to favor him. If merely caring more about some person were a sufficient reason for giving that person priority, then racist and other pernicious forms of partiality could be readily defended.

It is possible, of course, that reasons deriving from the personal point of view do not always have their origin in purely subjective considerations. The personal point of view might, for example, encompass a person's objective interests, so that one would have reasons stemming from one's personal point of view to pursue these interests irrespective of whether one cares about them.[11] But even if this is right, it does not offer the right sort of defense for many forms of partiality. While it is true that being engaged in certain special relations may contribute to one's objective good, one's reasons for being partial to those to whom one is so related are not typically reducible to reasons of self-interest. Parents, for example, normally benefit from the relation they bear to their children, but their interest in preserving the relation is at most a marginal element in the justification of parental partiality. A parent's reasons to devote special care to his or her child have a different source from that parent's reasons to protect or promote his or her own interests.

The idea that one's reasons for partiality toward those to whom one is specially related derive from the personal point of view is difficult to reconcile with the idea that there are special *duties* regarding those to whom one is specially related. That there are duties of this sort is an axiom of common sense as well as an integral component of nationalism, which insists that there are duties of loyalty and partiality to one's nation and conationals. But it is difficult to see how these duties could have their source in the personal point of view, irrespective of whether the latter is explicated in wholly subjective terms or whether it also incorporates objective interests. Duty is not contingent on inclination or subjective concern. The presence or absence of parental concern has no bearing on whether a parent has special duties to his or her child. Nor is self-interest commonly supposed to generate duties to oneself, though even if it did, those duties would be a poor counterfeit for genuine associative duties. The duties that arise from special relations are owed to those to whom one is specially related. These people are more than merely the incidental beneficiaries of duties owed to oneself.

The general problem with the appeal to the personal point of view is that one's moral reasons for showing partiality to those to whom one is specially related do not, in fact, emanate from oneself or one's own personal point of view. How things appear to one is largely irrelevant to whether one may or must show partiality to certain people. One's reasons derive instead from one's relations with these people—relations that are objective features of the world and in principle recognizable from any point of view. This does, of course, mean that the source of these special moral reasons is personal to the individual: the relation is something that ought to matter, and typically does matter, to that person but matters less, if at all, to others. But that is not to say that these reasons are the *products* of the individual's personal point of view. To say that is to confuse the fact that the *content* of the reasons is specific to the person with the idea that the person is the *fons et origo* of these reasons or that the reasons derive their normative authority from the prominence they assume when viewed from that person's point of view. To assess whether it is legitimate for one person to show partiality to another, it is more important to understand the objective moral significance of the relations that obtain between them than to know what the one person's perceptions, sentiments, or interests are.

Instrumental Considerations

Special relations may be morally significant in various ways. Many special relations are, for example, instrumental to or even partially constitutive of human well-being. This is most obvious in the case of relations involving love. A life devoid of either the bestowal or the receipt of love would be incalculably impoverished. But love is discriminating or selective and involves a powerful disposition to favor those who are its objects; it is therefore necessarily partial. This form of partiality must be permitted, since it is an ineliminable concomitant of a relation that is necessary for human flourishing.

Against this, some have claimed that one should love impartially by loving everyone equally. But this is a psychological and perhaps conceptual impossibility. The empathetic bond established by love imposes a limit to one's capacity to endure the emotional strains of loving. No one could bear for long the death of a loved one each day. More important, a set of dispositions that could be evoked by anyone, whatever his or her personal characteristics, would have to be wholly undiscriminating and largely uncharged by emotion. Perhaps agape could be like this, or *caritas*, compassion, or even respect. But nothing that anemic could be so critical to individual well-being. We need not only to love selectively but also to be loved with a degree of exclusivity, in a way that distinguishes us as special. We need more than to be faintly illuminated by the diffuse light of a universal affection or to be ministered to by the cold hand of impartial benevolence. Thus even those who now suffer most from lack of love would surely prefer a world in which each person is specially loved by a few to a world in which each is cared about equally and impartially by everyone else. George Orwell was right when he observed that "love means nothing if it does not mean loving some people more than others"— and, one might add, loving some not at all.[12]

This defense of the partiality attendant upon love assumes that the moral significance of love is instrumental. This is not to say that love is merely a *means*, since it is as much an ingredient as a causal condition of well-being. But the significance of love, according to this view, lies in the contribution that it makes to something else—namely, individual well-being.

Moral theories that insist on impartiality must take into account that many relations, like those based on love, have instrumental significance. Unless these theories treat impartiality as an end in itself, they must accept that it is often best, from the impartial point of view, to encourage participation in special relations that require partiality. Rule Consequentialism, for example, may approve rules that enjoin the formation of friendships and require loyalty and fidelity to one's friends. Similarly, other theories require that we cultivate certain dispositions and traits of character that will cause us to favor some people over others if our having those characteristics will, over time, have consequences that are best from the impartial point of view.[13]

Dispositions that it is overall and impartially best for one to have will sometimes cause one to do what, in the circumstances, is worse from an impartial point of view—for example, succoring one's ailing spouse rather than working overtime in order to make a larger contribution to Oxfam. Some impartial theories imply that being guided by one's disposition in these circumstances is wrong, though this is an acceptable price to pay for having the disposition.[14] In this respect, these theories clearly diverge from commonsense morality. But this is also true, though to a lesser degree, of those impartial theories that accept that it cannot be wrong to be compelled to act by dispositions that it is overall and impartially best for one to have. For given the vast inequalities between rich and poor in the contemporary world, the dispositions that it would be best in impartial terms for those in affluent countries to have are not those that are presently approved by commonsense morality. It would clearly be better, from the impartial point of view, for those in affluent societies to be less strongly disposed to care for family and friends and correspondingly more strongly disposed to make sacrifices to benefit the poor in other countries. Doubtless this would significantly impoverish our lives, but our losses would be amply counterbalanced by the gains to the poor.

Even if the rules or dispositions enjoined by the variants of Indirect Consequentialism were to coincide with those approved by commonsense morality, the convergence would be contingent and the theories would require the right acts for the wrong reasons. The suggestion that parents ought to cultivate strong dispositions to favor their own children because this arrangement is more conducive to the general happiness than the alternatives is a grotesque caricature of the sources of parental obligation.

The same objections apply to another common argument for the view that it is best in impartial terms for people to form strong personal attachments and to devote special care and concern to those to whom they are closely related. According to this argument, the most efficient way to ensure that people receive the care they need is to assign each person special responsibility for those to whom he or she is specially related. Although it has been repeatedly echoed in the recent literature, the classic statement of this argument appears in William Paley's *Principles of Moral and Political Philosophy*, which contends that "the good order and happiness of the world are better upholden whilst each man applies himself to his own concerns and the care of his own family . . . than if every man, from an excess of mistaken generosity, should leave his own business, to undertake his neighbour's, which he must always manage with less knowledge, conveniency, and success."[15]

It is of course true that, in general, one is better situated than most others to promote the well-being of those to whom one is specially related, for typically one has a superior understanding of the nature of their interests, one is naturally motivated by ties of affection to enhance their well-being, and one's physical proximity gives one the capacity to assist in ways that those who live elsewhere cannot. But the affluent in the contemporary world are again an exception. The affluent are in a better position to care for the needs of millions of impoverished people in other countries than are those people's families, friends, or conationals. They know that what the impoverished most need is food and medicine, and they have the ability to fulfill these needs via such organizations as Oxfam. At least in the case of the affluent, therefore, the impartial perspective requires a distribution of responsibility that is radically different from that demanded by commonsense morality; they must divide their care and concern, and more particularly their resources, more evenly between those to whom they are specially related and those who are utter strangers.

One could dispute the details. But again the more important point is that this account fails altogether to capture our understanding of the moral significance of special relations. Could any parents really suppose that it is simply a matter of administrative efficiency that they have special responsibilities to their own children and that they would be relieved of those responsibilities were there an alternative distribution of duties that would be better for children generally, even if it would be worse for their own?

To deny that instrumental considerations are the essence of the morality of special relations is not to say that they have no moral significance. In many instances it may be part of the moral case for permitting partiality within special relations that these relations are important in various ways to human flourishing. In some instances this may indeed be the sole reason. But in general instrumental considerations are only a small, though conspicuous, part of the story.

Formal and Substantive Impartiality

Many writers have thought it possible to reconcile the demands of impartiality with the permissibility of partiality by distinguishing two levels at which partiality and impartiality may operate. Impartiality, they say, is required by respect for the moral equality of persons. But equality is sufficiently recognized if impartiality functions at the *formal* level by governing the evaluation, formulation, selection, or defense of moral principles. This means, as Thomas E. Hill, Jr., puts it, that moral principles must be assessed "from a point of view that requires temporary detachment from the particular desires and aversions, loves and hates, that one happens to have; . . . principles must be defensible to anyone looking at the matter apart from his or her special attachments."[16] But this formal impartiality, as Hill stresses, does not entail a requirement of impartiality at the *substantive* level—that is, the level at which principles are implemented in action.[17] In other words, the principles arrived at within the constraints of formal impartiality do not necessarily rule out substantive partiality—that is, giving priority to some people over others, for example, because of the relation they bear to oneself.

While this seems true, it is not helpful in assessing the challenge to nationalism, which comes not from the requirement of formal impartiality but from the demand for substantive impartiality. Universalist nationalism seems compatible with the requirement of formal impartiality. The principle that each person should be loyal and partial to his or her own nation does not appear to be biased in favor of any individual or group. But no form of nationalism seems compatible with substantive impartiality, which forbids giving preference or priority to one person over another for reasons that are private or peculiar to oneself or one's group. And substantive impartiality, it may be argued, is required by the principle of equal concern and respect. For if all people have a right to equal respect, then even from the standpoint of the individual agent, no one must count more than another.

The important question, then, is whether strict impartiality is required at the substantive level. If so, can some attenuated form of nationalism be defended on purely instrumental grounds? If strict impartiality is not required, what forms and degrees of partiality are permitted or required? In particular, is conationality a legitimate basis for partiality, and if so, what degree of priority is it acceptable to give to conationals over others? It does not help, in answering these questions, to insist on formal impartiality. A great many methods of generating or defending moral principles, including numerous varieties of contractarianism, are compatible with formal impartiality. Some of these may yield principles requiring substantive impartiality, while others will surely grant that varying forms and degrees of partiality are defensible.

Yet none of these methods, I believe, can generate a detailed account of the conditions in which substantive impartiality is required, or of the forms and degrees of partiality that are either permitted or required, without considerable substantive moral argumentation. Thus, for example, Brian Barry's favored form of contractarian methodology bids us ask: "What would rules and principles capable of attracting general agreement require in the way of impartial behaviour"—or permit or require in the way of partial behavior?[18] But the agreement sought is *reasonable* agreement—that is, agreement whose terms no one could reasonably reject. And I see no way of determining what people could reasonably agree to on these matters that would not require an independent and probing exploration of the morality of special relations. This essay is intended as a modest contribution to that necessary inquiry.

The Intrinsic Significance of Special Relations

I have acknowledged that many special relations have a profound instrumental significance. Nothing could be more obvious than that our relations with one another, and particularly our close personal relations, are vital and indispensable elements of our happiness and well-being. In many cases, however, the moral significance of special relations is not exhausted by the valuable contributions they make to our lives. It seems, rather, that the territory marked out by certain relations between people constitutes an autonomous area within the domain of morality, so that the existence of these relations and the forms of behavior that are appropriate within them do not require justification in terms of anything else. It is part of the meaning or significance of these relations that they legitimize certain forms of partiality. The relations themselves are fundamental or foundational sources of moral reasons, including permissions and requirements. These reasons coexist and in some instances compete with reasons that arise in response to people's intrinsic or nonrelational properties.

The radical particularist gives one account of the reasons stemming from special relations: a morality just *is* a set of norms that evolve within and govern the various fundamental human relations. But many relations, I believe, have a universal moral significance, though of course they may take somewhat different forms in different settings, with each variant absorbing some of its moral flavor from the surrounding culture. Mutual love, for example, demands partiality wherever it occurs—which is to say, virtually everywhere. A relation that did not, given opportunities, both call forth and require partial behavior on at least some occasions would not be love at all. And while loving relations are among the essential ingredients of a good human life, the primary justification for love and its associated partiality is not instrumental. Morality urges us to foster loving relations and to care specially for those we love not just because this is good for both us and them, making all our lives richer and deeper, but because this is the *right* way to live. Loving relations are not just essential to the good life but are also partly constitutive of the *moral* life. Within certain constraints that morality also imposes, expressions of love and special caring represent fundamental virtues whose justifiability does not depend on the contribution they make to any other good.

The relation that a parent bears to his or her child is similarly of intrinsic moral significance. This is not to say, however, that parental duties are morally primitive or unanalyzable. There seem, rather, to be multiple sources of parental duties: for example, the genetic or biological connection between parent and child, the voluntary assumption of responsibility (as in the case of adoption), responsibility for the child's need for aid arising from the act of having caused the child to exist, and so on. The list is undoubtedly incomplete (though what else it might contain is surprisingly obscure, for the foundations of parental obligation have not been carefully investigated and are not well understood). The important point for our purposes is that none of these possible bases for parental duties is instrumental in character. Purely instrumental considerations—for example, that the natural affection of parents for their children tends to make parents more competent caregivers for their own children than others—cannot, as we have noted, provide an adequate account of the grounds of parental duties.

We should recall, however, the multiplicity of human relations, some of which appear to legitimize partiality while others do not. Can we identify the features that tend to give certain relations their intrinsic significance? Are there any features that the various significant relations have in common? I will begin to explore these questions below, focusing particularly on the question whether conationality is a relation that has intrinsic moral significance. Before that, however, I will consider some arguments for nationalism that appeal to the instrumental significance of conationality. Even if there is much more to certain relations than their positive instrumental significance, the contribution they may make to certain goods, such as individual well-being, may alone be sufficient to justify our engaging in them and practicing the forms of partiality they require. This might be true of nationalism, independently of whether conationality itself has intrinsic moral significance.

The Instrumental Case for Nationalism

The literature is replete with claims about the importance that membership in a national community and participation in its culture have in the lives of individuals. It is argued, for example, that particular cultures provide "horizons of significance," background standards of value by reference to which individuals are able to assess their options and choices.[19] National identification and solidarity are also held to be necessary in large and otherwise impersonal modern societies in order to motivate the forms of cooperation and self-sacrifice that are needed to ensure a decent material standard of living.[20] Finally, and most important, various claims have been made about the psychological significance of national affiliation.[21] We all seek some measure of self-transcendence, an enlargement of the self beyond its narrow boundaries, an escape from the isolation and insignificance of singularity. Group membership offers an accessible mode of self-transcendence, and the nation, for reasons that remain somewhat obscure, offers a particularly compelling focus for collective identification. In the modern world, the nation has superseded the family and the religious community as the primary locus of collective self-identification and has become a fecund source of self-esteem. By investing our egos in it, we ensure that its triumphs become our own; by making its goals our own, we partake in its greater permanence; it becomes a continuer of the self, bestowing vicarious survival. It provides a sense of belonging, security, strength, and stability. (In the case of many people, nationalist sentiments may indeed be sublimated religious impulses. For these people, the nation—being transcendent, superpersonal, permanent, protective, authoritative, and so on—functions as an effective substitute for a deity.)

These and other claims about the value that national affiliation has within the lives of individuals form the basis of an argument that parallels that given above for the partiality that goes with love. The second step in this argument is to note that, like love, participation in national life necessarily involves partiality. Social psychologists have long known that people naturally tend to favor fellow members of any groups to which they belong, however arbitrarily those groups may be distinguished from others.[22] And the impulse to partiality is that much stronger in national communities, whose members tend to share certain values and to be engaged in the pursuit of common goals. Therefore, we may conclude that national partiality must be accepted as an unavoidable aspect of arrangements that are necessary for the good human life.

Matters are, however, more complicated than this. We may grant that national affiliation and partiality contribute much of value to the lives of individuals. But their darker side—the exclusivity, chauvinism, and hostility to outsiders—must also be taken into account. And even if the good features do outweigh the bad, that alone is insufficient to establish an instrumental justification for nationalism if there are alternative forms of collective identification that would fulfill the same needs that national membership does but without some of nationalism's more disturbing features. (If, moreover, it is assumed that conationality has no intrinsic moral significance, so that the instrumental argument must stand on its own, then the net benefit that people derive from national attachments must be sufficiently great to override the objection that it is unjust to discriminate among people on the basis of relations that lack intrinsic significance.)

Some, of course, have argued that the cosmopolitan ideal of identification with humanity as a whole—of being, as Diogenes put it, "a citizen of the world"—can offer much the same range of benefits that identification with one's nation provides. But this is improbable. Given that people have always tended to bond together in bounded communities, there are doubtless evolutionary mechanisms that make an eradication of particularist identities unfeasible. Moreover, the sense of identity and belonging that accompanies membership in a nation may crucially depend on the contrast between one's own nation and others. Without others to serve as foils, there would be nothing distinctive about one's own nation and thus no basis for identification. Similarly, the enhanced self-esteem that accompanies the enlargement of one's ego through identification with the nation may require an implied comparison with other nations, a sense that one's own nation is superior, at least in certain respects, to others.

But nationalism and cosmopolitanism are not exhaustive of the possibilities. There is no necessity to choose between, for example, being simply a Serb and being a citizen of the world. While it is impossible to avoid being to some extent a child of one's culture, it is also the mark of a drone to accept with docility or without reflection a ready-made, mass-manufactured, one-dimensional conception of oneself as a Serb, Hutu, Chechen, or whatever. This is the stuff of which impoverished lives are made. Thus Schopenhauer noted that "the cheapest form of pride is national pride; for the man affected therewith betrays a want of *individual* qualities of which he might be proud, since he would not otherwise resort to that which he shares with so many millions."[23] To acquiesce in a vision of oneself in which nationality overshadows the other variegated dimensions of one's life, character, and relations with others is to suffer a miserable reduction of the richness of one's identity. Other elements of one's actual identity, as well as further possibilities for self-creation, get crowded out of one's self-conception and may, from inattention and neglect, eventually fade from one's identity altogether.

It is not only the distinctive individual qualities of which Schopenhauer wrote that may be displaced from one's conception of oneself by a hypertrophied, metastasizing national identity; other forms of group identification may be withered as well. In most cases, there are numerous social and political dimensions to a person's identity; we are all mongrel to a greater or lesser degree.[24] One may be, for example, a pacifist, a philosopher, a socialist, a southerner, a vegetarian, a ruralist, a belletrist, a squash player, or all of these at once. Membership in and identification with a range of groups may enrich one's life, extend one's sympathies and bonds with others, and thereby lessen the potential for incomprehension of and conflict with others. Both prudence and an impartial concern with consequences therefore suggest that it is desirable for people to cultivate complex, multilayered individual identities, built around distinctive individual qualities *and* multifarious group identifications.

Let us call this model of self-identification "complex identification" and contrast it with "national identification," in which nationality has a commanding role in shaping a person's identity. Complex identification does not, of course, exclude nationality as an element of individual identity; it merely denies nationality the preeminent importance assigned to it by the nationalist. (As Walzer has observed, one may naturally shift back and forth between national identification and a more complex identification, depending upon, inter alia, whether one feels threatened or secure.)[25] The possibility of complex identification suggests that national identification is not necessary for the goods that it often provides: a cultural context, the security of belonging, self-esteem, social solidarity, and so on. These goods seem compatible with complex identification. Culture, for example, need not be monolithic. One may participate in and draw sustenance from a variety of overlapping cultures. And nations are only one source of culture. Many subnational cultures can exist within a single nation, whose unity may be more political or religious than cultural, and there can also be a union of nations whose historical cultures coexist within and contribute to a larger, encompassing culture based in part on respect for diversity. Who can say, in advance of experience, where the limits to what is possible lie? Collectivities other than the nation can, moreover, provide a sense of belonging, security, self-esteem, and so on. A robust sense of connectedness with others can be achieved though identifying oneself with a variety of collectivities.

In addition to offering richer, more distinctive individual identities, complex identification has the advantage of recognizing and fostering diverse attachments that cross national boundaries, thereby broadening people's understanding of and sympathy with others and reducing the propensity for conflict characteristic of more exclusive national identities. While complex identification preserves the disposition to loyalty and partiality, it generates a more complex pattern of differentiation and commonality in one's relations with others and thus gives partiality a more diffuse focus than national identification allows.

Complex identification also calls for different political and institutional structures from those that are appropriate to national identification. Complex identification is naturally expressed not by molding political life to fit the national unit but by separating the two. Political units should be built around explicitly political rather than national or cultural identities. Thus solidarity in political life should to the maximum extent be based on shared political ideals and commitments, not on inherited national or ethnic ties. Correlatively, national life should be relegated, insofar as possible, to the private sphere, with national self-determination expressed more in cultural than in political terms.[26]

Because nations and states do roughly coincide in many areas of the world, it is necessary, if political life is to be wrested from the grip of nationality, to create political institutions both above and below the level of the state. This could involve both a devolution of political power within the state and the transfer of various forms of political authority (for example, over certain matters of economic, environmental, or military policy) to bodies representing states seeking greater integration (such as the European Union).[27] Each level of political organization could become a focus of collective identification, thereby enhancing the multidimensional nature of people's individual identities and further reducing the barriers between people of different nationalities.

We must acknowledge, however, that a shift from national identification to complex identification would not be without costs. As events in recent years amply attest, national identification can be quite intense, and this magnifies both its virtues and its vices. At its greatest intensity, it generates a solid and stable sense of self, an unshakable sense of belonging, and preternaturally strong bonds of solidarity. But the fierce loyalty and partiality that are corollaries of this solidarity involve an extreme sensitivity to threats to the nation, a tendency to dehumanize outsiders, and a willingness to commit atrocities in what one believes to be the defense of the nation. While a shift away from national identification toward complex identification would diminish both overt and latent hostility to members of other nations, it would also involve a corresponding diminution of the solidarity within social groups. Still, although it is difficult to substantiate a generalization of this sort, it seems likely that the trade-offs would be on balance beneficial. With complex identification, people would be less willing to die for the groups to which they would belong, but they would also be less willing to kill, and there would be less reason for them to do either.

If it is true that the effects of complex identification would be better, impartially considered, than those of national identification, then the instrumental case for nationalism that appeals to the good effects of national identification fails. It remains to be determined, however, whether complex identification is psychologically possible for most people and also whether its associated political program is feasible. This requires further inquiry that is beyond the scope of this essay.

Another instrumental argument for nationalism deserves mention. This argument claims, roughly, that cultural pluralism is good, that respect for cultural pluralism requires the preservation of existing nations since each embodies a unique culture, and that each nation must therefore be politically self-determining in a way sufficient to enable it to survive and flourish. There are at least four distinct reasons for thinking that cultural pluralism is important. One appeals to the familiar liberal claim that there is no single best way of living. If that is right, then it is important that a variety of cultures exist so that people may have alternatives to the cultures in which they find themselves and dissidents may have sanctuaries or places of refuge. Second, the existence of diverse cultures facilitates imaginative reflection about different modes of life, thereby aiding individuals in the revision or expansion of their own conceptions of the good. This enables cultures to avoid stagnation and instead evolve and mature through creative assimilation from other cultures. Third, individual cultures may have impersonal value, value that is independent of the contributions that they make to the lives of individuals. Thus, as Charles Taylor has pointed out, people normally desire for their culture to continue to exist and flourish long after they themselves have ceased to exist, and this desire may be independent of their natural tendency to see in the continuation of the culture the survival of some element of their own identities. There is, moreover, no reason to suppose that only those within the culture are capable of appreciating its intrinsic value. Most of us are capable of perceiving in a particular alien culture a variety of merits that may not be replicated in any other culture. Fourth, and finally, cultural diversity is itself an impersonal value. Just as there are two distinct impersonal reasons for preserving a biological species, one deriving from the intrinsic value of the species itself and the other deriving from the contribution that the species makes to the value of biodiversity, so individual cultures are worth preserving both because of their own intrinsic value and because of the contribution they make to the independent value of cultural diversity.

The appeal to the value of cultural pluralism does support the preservation of existing nations but not in a way that would satisfy the nationalist. The protection of national cultures seems compatible with the rejection of the nationalist view

that political life must be organized around the national unit. It is possible for diverse cultures to thrive within liberal political structures that remain, so far as possible, neutral among them and committed to the protection and (in limited ways)
promotion of each.[28] Indeed, in one respect liberal politics seems more hospitable
to cultural pluralism than universalist nationalism is. The unity and solidarity that
nationalists seek within the nation are threatened by the presence of non-national
subcultures within the nation; hence nationalists typically seek the absorption of
subcultures into the larger national culture. Liberal politics, by contrast, is tolerant
of cultural diversity at the subnational level.

The Intrinsic Significance of Conationality

In the preceding section we concluded that the instrumental moral significance of conationality may be less than the nationalist supposes since it seems
that it would be better for people generally if they were to treat conationality as
only one of many relations that may serve as sources of collective identification
and focuses of loyalty and solidarity. But the idea that we should seek to diminish
the role national identification plays in our lives loses force if conationality is a relation that has deep intrinsic moral significance. In this section, we will consider
whether conationality is indeed a source of moral reasons that are underived from
anything other than the nature of the relation itself.

Commonalities

Conationality is not a simple relation but is compounded out of the various relations mentioned earlier that unite people into nations—relations involving commonalities of language, ethnicity, religion, culture, custom, and so on.
Conationality consists in these *relations of commonality* and typically does not involve *personal* relations at all, for most of a person's conationals are strangers to
him or her. It is the various ways in which one's conationals are *like oneself* that
primarily distinguish them from others. Are these various commonalities of intrinsic or foundational moral significance and thus capable of generating special
moral reasons for those who share them to favor one another in certain contexts?

Clearly many forms of commonality are utterly without moral significance.
Suppose, for example, that a person believes him- or herself to be one of a number of people who consistently overestimate the number of dots flashed on a
screen. The relation that such people believe to obtain between themselves and
these others is clearly of no moral significance. Yet, interestingly, it has been shown
in controlled experiments that simply telling people that they belong to such a
group (even if, in fact, they do not) is sufficient to elicit partiality from them toward other members of their group and make them less kindly disposed toward

those who they think underestimate the number of dots flashed on a screen.[29] So the fact that one feels warmly toward the members of some group to which one belongs need not even be evidence that comembership in the group is a morally significant relation.

Which commonalities, if any, do have intrinsic moral significance? *Commonalities of value*—that is, shared values, ideals, commitments, or even interests (in the sense of *being* interested in the same thing rather than *having* an interest in the same thing)—seem more likely to be morally significant than commonalities that do not involve any congruence of values. Of course, obvious restrictions apply. Shared values that are perverse or evil do not legitimize partiality.[30] Nor, it seems, do shared values that are utterly trivial. Assuming that commonalities of value can be intrinsically significant, the degree to which they are significant depends on the worthiness or importance of the relevant values. It also depends on how large a role the values have in people's lives. Consider two relatively insignificant commonalities of value: the bond shared by fans of *Star Trek* and that shared by fans of the Chicago Bulls. The relation that unites *Star Trek* fans seems the more significant of the two, since it involves deeper affinities of character, taste, and value than a shared enthusiasm for the Bulls. A taste for *Star Trek* is indicative of a range of interests and concerns that may be integral to a person's identity, whereas enthusiasm for the Bulls is often determined not by a sense that the team instantiates or embodies some ideal with which one identifies oneself but by the contingency of residence. A Bulls fan who moves to Houston may soon transfer his or her loyalties to the Rockets.

Another relation binding the members of a nation that may have moral significance is mutual esteem. Because conationals are typically molded by the same culture, they will tend both to share and to instantiate its values. They therefore tend to find more to admire in one another than they find in others. Of course, admiration is wholly subjective and I have suggested previously that subjective factors are in general a weak foundation for partiality. What matters primarily is the objective character of the relations that obtain between people. It is, however, characteristic of conationals that among their commonalities of value—that is, things they value in common—are traits that they themselves tend to instantiate. They tend, in other words, to share certain traits that they also tend to admire. These *valued commonalities* are objective commonalities that ground mutual esteem among conationals.[31]

Is it a reason for being partial to conationals that they share one's values or share with oneself certain features or characteristics that one values or admires? Certainly commonalities of value and valued commonalities constitute a basis for harmony, compatibility of character, and mutual understanding, sympathy, and esteem—things that draw people together and make them comfortable with one another. These commonalities are therefore elements in the psychological basis for partiality within nations. But as we have seen, the fact that a relation elicits partiality is no guarantee that it is a legitimate basis for partiality.

Racial partiality, or racism, often appeals for justification to the claim that members of the same race—*coracials*—are united by commonalities of value and in particular by valued commonalities. Racists value certain attributes they take to be characteristic or definitive of their race, certain valued commonalities. These are not the biological determinants of race, such as the color of the skin, texture of the hair, or gross morphology generally. The latter are, to borrow (and distort) the Lockean category, only the nominal essence of the race. The surface features are what guide us in practice in distinguishing between members of different races, but these features are not the object of racists' valuations. For racists, the nominal essence is only the visible marker of a deeper real essence that is primarily psychological. Other races are inferior not because their members are different morphologically but because they share various deficiencies of character or intellect. Racists are bound to the members of their race by commonalities that they believe set them above the members of other races.

The problem for racists, of course, is that there is an inevitable failure of correlation between the nominal essence and the supposed real essence, a misalignment between the criterion for discrimination and the object of evaluation. There is no race whose members all share the same psychological or moral profile. For any set of intellectual or moral virtues, there will be some members of a given race who fail to possess them and a vast number of members of other races who do possess them. Racists thus face a dilemma. Either they must treat the nominal essence (certain biological markers) as the ground for partiality, in which case their partiality will be grounded on a genuine objective commonality, but one that is obviously insignificant, or they must persist in the claim that the nominal essence, which provides the basis for discrimination, is an infallible indicator of the presence of the real essence, in which case the commonality to which racists appeal is illusory.

The error that racists make is moral, not intellectual. If they were simply mistaken about the facts, racism would not be as odious as it is. But the falsehood is too obviously false. Racism involves self-deception motivated by, among other things, a desire to see oneself as superior to others. Racists' contempt for those who are unlike themselves and admiration for the qualities supposedly characteristic of their race are transparent, though unmerited, compliments to themselves. Racists embrace and act upon what, at some level, they know to be fantasies—fantasies that degrade others as a spurious means of exalting themselves.

This objection to racial partiality does not discredit the idea that commonalities of value or valued commonalities are legitimate bases for partiality, but it does suggest that commonalities of these sorts cannot provide a foundation for national partiality. Typically, nationalists also believe in a real essence that underlies the superficial markers of nationality. This is the "national character," conceived as a superior set of moral, spiritual, and intellectual virtues. Nationalists often believe that the possession of this character by the members of their nation constitutes an agent-neutral ground for partiality toward them. But this is supplemented, within the nation, by an agent-relative ground, which is that each member of the nation is related to his or her conationals by virtue of their common possession of the national character. The national character is, in short, a valued commonality, which consists in part of commonalities of value. But the national character, like the essence of a race, is at best a statistical generalization. The correlation between membership in the nation and possession of the national character is inevitably imperfect when membership is normally a matter of birth, with no screening or selection. There may, of course, be a rather higher correlation between the nominal and the putative real essence in the case of nationality than in the case of race since those who belong by birth to a particular nation will be socialized and acculturated within the national culture, which imprints its own features on its members. Certain similarities and affinities of character are thus statistically likely.

This fact, however, has its negative aspect as well, for if valued commonalities are to provide a foundation for partiality, the commonalities must, at a minimum, be genuinely worthy. But to the extent that there is a national character that is the result of cultural conditioning, it will also tend to be the case that the nationalist's admiration for that character is a product of the same process. The national character will *of course* be superior *relative to the values of the national culture*. But if the members of the nation value the national character because they have been indoctrinated by the culture to do so (and of course because it flatters them to believe in their own excellence), this casts doubt on the objective defensibility of their evaluation.

(It is worth noting that there are cases in which what appears to be racial or national partiality may be based only superficially or obliquely on commonalities that are constitutive of coraciality or conationality. If a racial or national group is subjected to discrimination or persecution, its members will often become more cohesive and mutually supportive as a result, and most of us believe that this is a morally acceptable response. But the defense of their mutual partiality need not appeal to the commonalities that make them members of the same race or nation. It may instead appeal to their common fate as victims of prejudice or injustice. Consider, for the sake of comparison, the fact that many members of the deaf community in the United States share a sense of identity and solidarity akin to and perhaps stronger than that typically found among conationals. Many do not regard their deafness as in any way a disability, have no desire to be able to hear, are pleased rather than distressed if their own children are born deaf, and are strongly disposed to favor other deaf people and to distrust those who hear.[32] It seems obvious, however, that deafness is a morally insignificant commonality, comparable to left-handedness. But what unites the deaf is not deafness per se but the fact that they share a common exclusion from full participation in American society as a result of their deafness. It is their common fate as victims of social neglect that justifies their banding together. And if this is true, it offers a way of reconciling our condemnation of racial and other forms of discrimination with our sense that it is appropriate for certain minority groups to take pride in their distinctness and to maintain certain discriminatory practices that preserve their distinctness and benefit their members to the exclusion of others. For *their* discriminatory partiality need not be based on an insignificant commonality such as race but may instead appeal to their shared status as victims. Whether this commonality has intrinsic significance is uncertain and perhaps doubtful, but it has genuine instrumental significance.)

The general point is that even if we can detect certain broad and general commonalities of value or valued commonalities among the members of a nation, a significant number of members will not share the relevant values or manifest the national character and many nonmembers will. Suppose, however, that certain commonalities of value or valued commonalities are intrinsically significant, and suppose that some of these were to bind all and only the members of a particular nation together. How much would this pair of assumptions yield? It seems that commonalities of these sorts could at most make it *permissible* for those who share them to show a limited degree of partiality to one another. These commonalities could not support special *obligations*. Suppose that two philosophers both value rational argument and that both excel at it. Between them there is both a commonality of value and a valued commonality. While this might make it permissible for them to be partial to one another in certain contexts, it clearly does not *require* them to, even if the value they share is a worthy one. Special obligations cannot, it seems, be contingent on something as changeable as an individual's personal values. If there really were special obligations between the two philosophers, neither could be released simply by converting to mysticism.

In sum, what seem to be the most intrinsically significant commonalities within nations cannot provide the justification for the forms of partiality essential to nationalism. For the relevant commonalities are not universal within the nation and are, in fact, shared by many outside the nation. And even if they were possessed by all and only the members of the nation, they would be incapable of grounding special obligations rather than mere permissions. And nationalism certainly holds that loyalty to and partiality within the nation are duties rather than mere options.

Does the admiration that one typically has for the qualities characteristic of one's conationals add anything at all to the case for national partiality? There is rather a dilemma here. If the positive evaluation of one's conationals is based on values that are not recognized by others but are instead highly specific to the national culture, then this casts doubt on the validity of the evaluation, and so tenuously supported an evaluation seems a flimsy basis for partiality. If, however, one's admiration is for genuinely objective and worthy qualities that are widely shared by one's conationals and if possession of these qualities constitutes an intrinsic justification for partiality toward those who possess them, then it seems that one's reason for partiality must be agent-neutral in character. But then members of other nations would have the same reason for partiality toward one's conationals that one's conationals have for partiality among themselves, and this takes us away from universalist nationalism, which asserts a universal justification for *agent-relative* partiality.

It seems reasonable to conclude, therefore, that any conspicuous virtues characteristic of the members of one's nation do not contribute to the case for partiality within the nation. (Thus a nation whose members were, in general, more admirable than those of some other nation would not have stronger reasons for mutual partiality, other things being equal, than the members of the other nation.) Yet it also seems that a group that is conspicuously unworthy of allegiance forfeits any claim to legitimize partiality among its members. Hence it may be that the general possession of some minimum set of admirable traits by the members of a nation, while not a positive reason for mutual partiality among them, is nevertheless a necessary condition of justified partiality within the nation.

Reciprocity, Gratitude, and Devotion

The relations of commonality that obtain between conationals, as individuals, do not seem intrinsically sufficiently significant to ground duties of mutual partiality. However, other aspects of their relations do seem capable of generating special duties among them that are not merely instrumentally justified. I will suggest that there are two distinct sources of special duties among conationals, one found in their relations with one another, the other in each individual's relation to the nation as a whole.

One source of special duties among conationals is familiar from the theory of political obligation. One who engages in voluntary cooperative endeavors with others normally benefits from the contributions that others make to these endeavors and thereby acquires duties of fair play to reciprocate. Conationals are typically engaged with one another in multifarious, continuing cooperative activities. Salient among these are the normal political, economic, and social forms of cooperation necessary among citizens of the same state, for conationals are usually, though obviously not invariably, citizens of the same state. To this extent, the account of permitted and required partiality among conationals overlaps with the theory of political obligation. (I am assuming that the duty of fair play is one element, though not the only one, in a complete account of political obligation.) But conationals also engage in various common projects and activities that are nonpolitical or unconnected with citizenship. For insofar as they together constitute a nation, which is an active association spanning many generations, they are necessarily involved in sustaining and continuously re-creating their culture and way of life as well as transmitting the cultural heritage to their descendants. These various activities that make up the life of a nation are a further source of duties of reciprocity.

The second source of special duties among conationals is related to the first. As we just noted, a nation is, among other things, a grand collective project spanning many generations that furnishes countless profound and indispensable benefits to its members. However much one may repudiate certain elements of it, one is nevertheless deeply indebted to one's nation and its culture. They have provided the language in which one thinks and speaks, the intellectual and artistic heritage that informs one's sensibility and one's understanding of both oneself and the world, many of the values that give purpose to one's life and structure one's relations with others, numerous elements of the material and social infrastructures that make a decent life possible, and so on, almost indefinitely. In short, the nation itself, as a transhistorical entity, is one's benefactor, and there are duties that one owes to it in consequence. One has duties of gratitude to the nation—moral reasons, in acknowledgment of the benefits one has received through the nation, to cherish, sustain, and strengthen the nation and its culture; to preserve its physical treasures and its institutions as well as the heritage of its values, traditions, and customs; and to pass these on to subsequent generations that they may benefit in the same manner in which one has oneself benefited. This is true even if one's national culture is in no way superior to neighboring cultures. Just as one may have duties of gratitude to one's own parents even if they have been unremarkable in their role as parents, so one may have debts to one's nation even if one regards it as deficient in many respects or inferior to others. In that case, one's duty might be to seek its improvement through the creative assimilation from other cultures of the virtues that it lacks. (There may, of course, also be duties to support the national values, to the extent that they are objectively defensible, and this, too, may involve directly or indirectly benefiting one's conationals.)

Duties involving partiality among conationals that derive from this source are not ones that people owe directly to one another. The duties are, in the first instance, owed to the nation itself. It is only derivatively that duties owed to the nation as a whole take the form of duties to benefit individual members of the nation. There are some contexts, in other words, in which one has special reasons to benefit one's conationals not because of one's individual relations with them but because benefiting them contributes to the flourishing of the nation. One benefits them not qua individuals but in their capacities as members, creatures, cocreators, or fragmentary instantiations of the nation. These duties are therefore quite unlike duties of partiality within the family, which are owed to specific individuals by virtue of their individual relations with oneself.

This is a highly abbreviated sketch of what seems to me the most plausible account of the noninstrumental foundations of partiality within the nation. If I am right, duties of loyalty and partiality within the nation are not really *associative* obligations at all—that is, obligations that arise simply from "identity and relatedness."[33] It is not a shared sense of collective identity or a set of commonalities from which the sense of identity flows that grounds these duties. The duties are instead more closely analogous to political obligations as the latter are understood in traditional accounts that appeal to considerations of reciprocity and gratitude for benefits received. The moral significance of "identity and relatedness" is instrumental rather than intrinsic.

Domesticating Nationalism

In the previous two sections, I have advanced two claims. First, I suggested that it would be better, where considerations of consequences are concerned, if we were to foster more complex individual identities, with the present intensive focus on national identification yielding to a richer, more varied pattern of collective identifications. This would result in people's having more diversified group affinities and loyalties and thus a diminished inclination to national partiality. Second, I claimed that people are bound by duties of gratitude to endeavor to preserve and to promote the flourishing of their nations and that the fulfillment of these duties often requires people to favor their conationals over others. It may be doubted, however, whether these claims are compatible. For it may seem that to fulfill one's duties of gratitude to one's nation one must manifest a degree of loyalty and partiality to its members that would exceed what the proposal for complex identification regards as desirable.

These are not matters that can be readily quantified. But it is reasonable to suppose that the diminution of national identification and partiality required by complex identification is compatible with the fulfillment of one's duties of gratitude to one's nation. The central goals of complex identification are to diminish national chauvinism and exclusivity and to facilitate and encourage mutual understanding and recognition, cooperation, and mutual aid among nations. And what these goals require is mainly that people's individual identities should accord appropriate recognition to the numerous profound commonalities that span divisions between nations and that national life and culture should be confined to a greater degree to the private rather than the political sphere. To see that this is compatible with extensive loyalty to the nation and partiality to its members, consider the case of the family.

There have been times when families were more like nations are now. Clans, family dynasties, and landed aristocratic families have at times had many of the characteristic features of modern nations: they have been important sources of individual identity, boasted of mythical bloodlines traceable back to ancient heroes, endowed their members with an invincible conviction their of superiority to others, and even been territorially based and often expansionist. But the family as a social unit and locus of partiality has now, with some exceptions in certain countries, been tamed. In contemporary Western societies, families are neither competitive nor antagonistic, are not a basis for political organization, do not compete with one another for power, and are considerably less important as sources of individual identity than they once were (for example, it is now rare for one to identify oneself as "one of the Shropshire Smiths" or "the Virginia Joneses"). Yet the family retains a vital role in people's lives, and family members remain intensely loyal and partial to one another. This shows, I think, that people may care intensely about one another, share a way of life together, and recognize an array of special duties to one another without regarding other groupings of the same sort as "outgroups" that are appropriately despised as alien and inferior.

What we should seek through complex identification is a transformation of the nation that parallels, in relevant respects, that which the family has gradually undergone. The nation must be tamed and domesticated. This requires action at the individual and institutional levels. Individuals must be encouraged to see themselves as more than drones in the national hive, and institutions must be arranged, both within and between states, to enable nations to coexist harmoniously while at the same time retaining their autonomy and cultural integrity. Provisions for self-determination, for example, would correspond to the assignment to families of a sphere of privacy that may be invaded only for the gravest reasons.

The proposal to reshape the nation so that it more closely resembles the family reminds us of one vitally important point: even paradigmatically justified partiality is not unlimited. For there are obviously limits to the degree of priority that one is permitted to give even to one's closest family members. The degree of permissible partiality, even within the family, is determined in part by considerations of agency. The kind of case in which there is greatest scope for partiality is that involving the distribution of benefits. In many cases, the bestowal of benefits is supererogatory. In these cases, the scope for partiality is literally unlimited. It may be permissible, for example, to give one's own child an expensive gift even if the money one spends could do more good if it were used to buy toys for children whose parents are less well off. (Even if one accepts a conception of morality as highly demanding, there may still be limited room for supererogation.) In some cases, of course, the distribution of benefits is not supererogatory. The proper distribution of a benefit may, for example, be determined by desert or need. Or it may be governed by norms designed to serve social purposes. Partiality in cases of the first sort is unjust, while in cases of the second sort it may defeat the governing purposes and therefore constitute pernicious favoritism or nepotism.

Special relations may also justify some degree of partiality in choices involving the prevention of harms. Most of us believe, for example, that a parent may save his or her own child rather than two children who are strangers if the parent cannot save them all. The moral significance of special relations begins to diminish, however, when we come to cases involving the causation of harm and, in particular, cases in which an act causes harm as a means of preventing a different harm or providing a benefit. A parent may not, for example, intentionally kill an innocent child, even if this is the only way the parent can save his or her own two children (for example, because they both require organ transplants). Analogous restrictions apply in the case of partiality among conationals, except that in this case the restrictions are likely to be stronger since relations among conationals are a weaker basis for partiality than relations among family members.

Although in general it is desirable to seek to refashion relations within and among nations so that relations among nations come to resemble more closely those among families, there is one respect in which the nation ideally ought to be less like the family and more like an association of friends. While membership in the family is typically nonvoluntary, so that the boundaries between families may be crossed only through special events such as marriage and adoption, the aim of domesticating nationalism will be better achieved if the boundaries between nations become more permeable. At present, of course, membership in a nation is largely nonvoluntary and nationalists tend to regard the nonvoluntary relations that are constitutive of membership as having a deeper significance and authenticity than most voluntary relations. Those who belong to a nation by birth generally have a more secure status within the nation than those who have, for example, married into it or sought membership after renouncing or leaving the nation of their birth. Other members of the nation tend to feel a stronger affinity with the former than with the latter; they will feel the pull of loyalty and partiality more strongly toward those who belong by birth, even those who have publicly rejected the national values or the national culture, and less strongly toward those who, coming originally from another culture, have voluntarily, autonomously, and even passionately embraced the national values and culture.

Those who belong by birth are also regarded as being under a stronger obligation of loyalty to the nation. This may be so even when a person has emigrated and sought assimilation into another nation. In a piece of spy fiction by Agatha Christie, a naturalized German is caught spying in England for the Nazis. One of the protagonists observes that the captured spy is, "I'm sorry to say, English by birth," to which the heroine replies, "Then I've no pity or admiration for her—it wasn't her country she was working for."[34] According to this view, merely by being born a member of a country or nation one acquires obligations of loyalty and partiality from which one cannot be released even by emigration. This, admittedly, is a rather extreme conception of the nonvoluntary character of national membership and consequently of national duties. No one thinks that Einstein was a traitor for helping the United States defeat the Nazis. But the extreme view does help us to understand the more moderate and extremely common view that birth alone is a powerful source of duties and that a great deal is required in order for one to be freed from their demands.

This view draws support from the fact that there are other special relations, nonvoluntary in character, that are widely regarded as legitimate bases for partiality. The relation of a parent to a child, for example, is nonvoluntary. While two people may choose to have a child, they cannot, in most cases, choose a particular person to be their child.[35] And the relation of the child to the parent is even more obviously nonvoluntary. Yet these relations are paradigmatically legitimate bases for partiality. There are, moreover, reasons why nationalists feel that the nonvoluntary character of full membership is important. Benedict Anderson suggests, for example, that "because [national] ties are not chosen, they have about them a halo of disinterestedness."[36] Avishai Margalit and Joseph Raz note that the sense of identity and belonging that one derives from national membership will be "more secure, less liable to be threatened" if membership is "determined by nonvoluntary criteria" than if it depends in some way on one's accomplishments.[37] If membership is guaranteed by birth, then nationality offers a source of acceptance and approval that is automatic and unconditional. Finally, nonvoluntary relations may also have a greater claim to be constitutive of an individual's identity. If one cannot help but be x, then x seems to be more securely a part of what one really is than y, where y is an attribute that one can choose either to have or not to have.

Yet, despite all this, one recoils from the view that, among our various nonpersonal relations, our deepest allegiances are determined by inescapable ties of blood and birth. The liberal impulse is to insist that, beyond the intimate sphere of the family, special relations provide a more legitimate foundation for partiality to the extent that they are chosen autonomously or entered into freely. The voluntariness of a special relation is no obstacle to its being integral to one's individual identity, provided (as complex identification presupposes) that some degree of self-creation is both possible and desirable.

The argument for greater permeability of national boundaries, or greater interpenetration among nations, appeals to considerations of consequences. The aim is enhanced mutual understanding, appreciation, and respect, which will be facilitated by the recognition that some members of another nation were originally members of our own, while still other members of that nation have joined us and are not really such bad people after all. Against this, the nationalist might argue that communities bound together by nonvoluntary relations will be less inclined to believe themselves superior and more disposed to be tolerant of others. For when membership is a matter of birth, there can be no screening of members and therefore no guarantee that members generally will meet any criterion of excellence. And it might also seem that tolerance would be the appropriate stance toward outsiders who could not help being members of their group rather than one's own. This a priori reasoning is, however, at variance with the facts, as the case of racial prejudice shows. Indeed, when membership is largely nonvoluntary, a group's claim to superiority may become a dogma that it clings to all the more desperately for its evident indefensibility and that it can assert only through the exercise of power. What is necessary is a diminution of both people's need to find self-esteem through identification with the nation and their sense of the utter alienness of nations other than their own. And the achievement of the latter aim may be facilitated by seeking to make national communities less exclusive, allowing other paths to membership than birth and blood.

Summary

In this essay I have explored the question whether conationality is a legitimate basis for partiality. I argued that while relations among conationals certainly have instrumental significance, there are alternative patterns of individual identification and social organization in which nationality would have a less prominent role than nationalists would find acceptable but that would better serve people's needs overall. I argued further that while the various commonalities that are constitutive of conationality seem unable to provide an intrinsic justification for partiality within the nation, conationals do have special duties to one another that are based on considerations of fair play and gratitude to the nation. And I sought to reconcile these claims about the instrumental and intrinsic bases for partiality by appealing to the example of the family, a social unit within which there are strong special duties as well as intense mutual partiality but which is not a basis for political organization and no longer serves as an important source of collective identification and self-esteem. I am aware that my proposals are vulnerable to powerful objections. I have endorsed the view that we should seek, as far as possible, to confine national life to the private rather than the political sphere but am aware both that national unity is a potent source of political unity and that in many cases beliefs about political organization are integral to people's conception of the nature of their nation. And I have advocated increased permeability of national boundaries but am aware that wholly unregulated entry may be incompatible with the preservation of a nation's distinct identity and culture. I wish that I had compelling answers to these objections, but I do not. My one certainty is that the philosophical exploration of nationalism is still in its early phase, and others more competent than I will address the many issues and problems that I have ignored.

NOTES

Versions of this essay were presented at the University of Colorado at Boulder, the United States Military Academy at West Point, and Tel Aviv University in Israel. I am grateful to the audiences on those occasions for suggestions and to Hugh LaFollette, Robert McKim, Arthur Ripstein, Samuel Scheffler, and Noam Zohar for comments on an earlier draft. I have also learned much from my commentator at the conference in Urbana, Thomas Hurka.

1. See Henry Sidgwick, *The Elements of Politics* (London: Macmillan, 1891), pp. 213–15.
2. Compare David Miller, "The Ethical Significance of Nationality," *Ethics* 98 (1988):

647–62, esp. p. 648; David Miller, "In Defence of Nationality," *Journal of Applied Philosophy* 10 (1993): 3–16, esp. pp. 5–8; and Avishai Margalit and Joseph Raz, "National Self-Determination," *Journal of Philosophy* 87 (1990): 439–61, esp. pp. 443–47. Miller's illuminating study *On Nationality* (Oxford: Clarendon, 1995) appeared too late to be taken into account here.

3. For the view that the United States constitutes a nation with a single culture, see Roger Scruton, "In Defence of the Nation," in *The Philosopher on Dover Beach* (New York: St. Martin's, 1990), p. 323. The view that the United States is a nation with a multiplicity of distinct cultures is defended in Kwame Anthony Appiah's Tanner Lecture, "Race, Culture, and Identity: Misunderstood Connections," a version of which appears in *Color Conscious*, ed. Anthony Appiah and Amy Gutmann (Princeton: Princeton University Press, 1996).

4. Walzer has advanced a qualified particularism according to which there is a minimal universal core to morality, which effectively takes the form of a requirement to respect the autonomous development of other cultures, with their own distinctive moralities. See Michael Walzer, "Nation and Universe," in *The Tanner Lectures on Human Values*, vol. 11, ed. G. B. Peterson (Salt Lake City: University of Utah Press, 1990), esp. pp. 533, 551–52; and Michael Walzer, *Thick and Thin* (Notre Dame, Ind.: University of Notre Dame Press, 1994), chaps. 1, 4.

5. Ernest Gellner, *Nations and Nationalism* (Ithaca: Cornell University Press, 1983), p. 1.

6. See, for example, Ronald Dworkin, *Taking Rights Seriously* (London: Duckworth, 1977), pp. 180–83.

7. Thomas Nagel, *Equality and Partiality* (New York: Oxford University Press, 1991), p. 14.

8. For a fuller discussion, see chapter 12.

9. Compare Thomas Nagel, *The View from Nowhere* (New York: Oxford University Press, 1986), chaps. 1, 8, 9, and *Equality and Partiality*, esp. chaps. 1, 2, 15.

10. See Samuel Scheffler, *The Rejection of Consequentialism* (Oxford: Oxford University Press, 1982).

11. This possibility was suggested to me by Samuel Scheffler.

12. George Orwell, "Reflections on Gandhi," in *The Collected Essays, Journalism, and Letters of George Orwell*, vol. 4, *1945–1950*, ed. Sonya Orwell and Ian Angus (Harmondsworth: Penguin, 1970), p. 527.

13. See Peter Railton, "Alienation, Consequentialism, and the Demands of Morality," *Philosophy and Public Affairs* 13 (1984): 134–71.

14. Ibid.

15. William Paley, *The Principles of Moral and Political Philosophy*, vol. I (London: Longman, 1814), pp. 339–40. The more rigorously developed echoes are in Robert Goodin, *Protecting the Vulnerable* (Chicago: University of Chicago Press, 1985), chaps. 3–5, and "What Is So Special about Our Fellow Countrymen?," *Ethics* 98 (1988): 678–86; Frank Jackson, "Decision-Theoretic Consequentialism and the Nearest and Dearest Objection," *Ethics* 101 (1991): 472–75; and Martha Nussbaum, "Patriotism and Cosmopolitanism," *Boston Review* 19 (1994): 6.

16. Thomas E. Hill, Jr., "The Importance of Autonomy," in his *Autonomy and Self-Respect* (Cambridge: Cambridge University Press, 1991), pp. 45, 46.

17. Ibid., p. 45. Also see Brian Barry, *Justice as Impartiality* (Oxford: Clarendon, 1995),

pp. 7–12; and Alan Gewirth, "Ethical Universalism and Particularism," *Journal of Philosophy* 85 (1988): 283–302.

18. Barry, *Justice as Impartiality*, p. 11. Similarly, Gewirth ("Ethical Universalism and Particularism") claims that among the principles that are approved at the formal level there must be some that grant all people the right to form particular associations within which a certain degree of mutual partiality is essential. But he does not say how one discriminates, at the formal level, between acceptable and unacceptable associations or how one determines the limits to partiality within those associations that are acceptable.

19. See, for example, Charles Taylor, *The Ethics of Authenticity* (Cambridge, Mass.: Harvard University Press, 1992), chap. 4; Will Kymlicka, *Liberalism, Community, and Culture* (Oxford: Clarendon, 1991), chap. 8; and Allen Buchanan, *Secession: The Morality of Political Divorce from Fort Sumter to Lithuania and Quebec* (Boulder, Colo.: Westview, 1991), pp. 53–54.

20. See, for example, Miller, "In Defence of Nationality," p. 9; and, for a contrary view, see chapter 13 of this volume.

21. Some of these claims are developed in more detail in chapters 2, 10, and 13.

22. See, for example, Henri Tajfel, "Experiments in Intergroup Discrimination," *Scientific American* 223 (1970): 96–102; and Jacob M. Rabbi and Murray Horwitz, "Arousal of Ingroup-Outgroup Bias by a Chance Win or Loss," *Journal of Personality and Social Psychology* 13 (1969): 269–77.

23. Arthur Schopenhauer, "Aphorisms on the Wisdom of Life," in *Parerga and Paralipomena*, vol. I, trans. E. F. J. Payne (Oxford: Oxford University Press, 1974), p. 360.

24. For an independent articulation of this idea, see Appiah, "Race, Culture, and Identity."

25. Walzer, *Thick and Thin*, p. 82.

26. The idea that political unity should be divorced from bonds of nationality is defended in Yael Tamir, *Liberal Nationalism* (Princeton: Princeton University Press, 1993), and in chapter 13 of this volume. It is subject to pungent criticism in Scruton, "In Defence of the Nation."

27. Compare chapter 20.

28. This claim is defended by Walzer in chapter 15 and challenged by Kymlicka in chapter 8.

29. Tajfel, "Experiments in Intergroup Discrimination."

30. A similar claim is defended in chapter 9.

31. There is a curious paradox in the efforts of the "nation builders" to forge a population into a national unit. They recognize that people will converge on a common identity only to the extent that the nation builders can get them to believe that they are bound by various commonalities and can rouse in them a robust mutual admiration. Hence the tendency of nationalist leaders to embellish freely what little there may be in the way of a national history or national character. While they recognize that people generally require commonalities, including valued commonalities, in order to be strongly cohesive, their own activities, such as fabricating mythical histories, presuppose the desirability of cohesion even in the absence of significant objective commonalities. The key to the paradox is probably quite simple—that their interest is in personal power rather than the reality of the nation.

32. See Edward Dolnick, "Deafness as Culture," *Atlantic Monthly*, September 1993, pp. 37–53.

33. Tamir, *Liberal Nationalism*, p. 99.

34. Agatha Christie, *N or M?* (New York: Dodd, Mead, 1941), p. 217.

35. The limited exception is adoption, where there may be an element of choice. And, of course, there may be more scope for choice in biological reproduction as advances in genetic engineering progress. Even here, however, there is a deeper philosophical question: whether greater control over the genetic character of one's child will ever enable one to choose a particular child or just an increasingly specific *type* of child.

36. Benedict Anderson, *Imagined Communities: Reflections on the Origin and Spread of Nationalism*, rev. ed. (London: Verso, 1991), p. 143.

37. Margalit and Raz, "National Self-Determination," p. 447.

9

The Justification of
National Partiality

THOMAS HURKA

The moral issues about nationalism arise from the character of nationalism as a form of partiality. Nationalists care more about their own nation and its
members than about other nations and their members; in that way nationalists are
partial to their own national group. The question, then, is whether this national
partiality is morally justified or, on the contrary, whether everyone ought to care
impartially about all members of all nations. As Jeff McMahan emphasizes in
chapter 8, a philosophical examination of this question must consider the specific
features of nationalism as one form of partiality among others. Some partiality—
for example, toward one's spouse and children—seems morally acceptable and
even a duty. According to commonsense moral thinking, one not only may but
also should care more about one's family members than about strangers. But other
instances of partiality, most notably racial partiality, are in most circumstances
widely condemned. Is national partiality more like familial partiality or more like
racial partiality? To answer this question, we must know what in general justifies
attitudes of partiality. Caring more about certain people is appropriate when one
stands in certain special relations to those people. But what are these relations, and
to what degree do they hold among members of the same nation? Assuming they
are present within families and not within races, to what degree are they present
within nations?

In addressing these questions, I will consider only "universalist" nationalism,
the view that *all* people ought to be partial to their own nation and conationals.
This is a more interesting and plausible position than the "particularist"—one

could equally well say "chauvinist"—view that only one's own nation, say, only Canada, deserves special loyalty. And I will consider only intrinsic justifications of nationalism. There are various instrumental arguments for national partiality, ones claiming that, starting from impartial moral principles, we can show how people's being partial to their conationals will have good effects impartially considered. I do not find these instrumental arguments very persuasive. In any case, the more interesting philosophical question is whether national partiality can be justified noninstrumentally, or at the foundational level of morality. Many people believe that familial partiality is justified not just as a means to benefits for all but intrinsically or in itself. My question will be whether national partiality can be justified in the same foundational way.

My discussion will cover three separate topics. First, I will challenge one widely accepted view about the moral foundations of nationalism. Second, I will suggest that a full discussion of nationalism must recognize that it has two components, which raise distinct moral issues. Finally, I will sketch a moral defense of one of these aspects of nationalism. This defense will concede that along one important dimension the relations among conationals have less of the character that justifies partiality than do the relations among family members, but it will argue that along another dimension they have roughly as much. The result is not that we should be as partial to our conationals as we are to our children—that would be absurd— but that we may properly be partial to some degree.

Nationalism and "Embedded Selves"

I have said that the moral issues about nationalism turn on whether certain relations hold within national groups. But many writers connect these issues to more abstract debates about the nature of morality and of moral agents. They say the impartialist view that we ought to care equally about all humans goes with the "Enlightenment" conception of morality as universal and impartial, whereas the defense of nationalism goes with a different "particularist" or "communitarian" conception of morality. According to this latter conception, moralities necessarily arise within the life of particular communities and therefore inevitably distinguish centrally between members and outsiders, requiring a certain priority to the interests of the former. David Miller expresses this kind of view. He says that moral impartialism sees the subject "as an abstract individual, possessed of the general powers and capacities of human beings—especially the power of reason," whereas a nationalist ethic sees the subject as "partly defined by its relationships, and the various rights, obligations, and so forth that go along with these, so these commitments themselves form a basic element of personality."[1] But although nationalism is often said to rest on these communitarian ideas about morality—let me summarize them in the slogan that "moral selves are embedded"—I do not see any connection between the two. Despite their prominence in the recent literature on nationalism, claims about the "embedded self" are not relevant to the intrinsic justification of national partiality. I can detect two arguments in defense of nationalism that may be suggested by the talk of embedded selves, which I will call the *cultural perfectionist* argument and the *metaethical particularist* argument. The cultural perfectionist argument does not go far enough to justify a universalist ethic of nationalism; the metaethical particularist argument goes too far. Let me start with the cultural perfectionist argument.

Perfectionism as a general normative view holds that the good for human beings consists in developing their "nature" or "identity."[2] More specifically, it holds that certain properties make an individual what he or she is and thereby constitute that person's nature or identity, and that his or her good consists in developing these properties to a high degree. In many classical versions of perfectionism—for example, those of Aristotle, Marx, and Nietzsche—the relevant nature is generic human nature, one shared by all human beings. But those who talk of "embedded selves" sometimes suggest a different perfectionist view. According to this view, human beings have natures or identities based on their membership in particular cultures, and their good consists at least partly in developing these narrower cultural identities. According to this "cultural" perfectionism, I as a Canadian have a specifically Canadian identity, a German has a German identity, and in each case our good consists at least partly in developing this cultural identity. One argument suggested by the talk of "embedded selves" is that this cultural perfectionism provides the justification for national partiality. If human beings had just an abstract or common human nature, this argument runs, a purely impartialist or cosmopolitan morality would be reasonable. But if, instead, their identities depend on their belonging to particular cultures, morality demands that they be specially loyal to those cultures.[3]

Though this is a less central point, I do not believe that cultural perfectionism is a very plausible version of perfectionism. In the most attractive versions of this general normative view, the properties that it is good for a human to develop constitute his or her identity in a strict or metaphysical sense. They are essential to the person in the strong sense that he or she could not exist as numerically the same individual without having these properties. This condition is satisfied by the classical perfectionisms of Aristotle, Marx, and Nietzsche; since I am essentially a human, no being that did not have the properties that make humans human could be identical to me. But the condition is not satisfied by cultural perfectionism. I was born in Canada and raised in Canadian culture. But we can easily imagine a different course of events, one in which, a few months after my birth, my parents return to their native Czechoslovakia and raise me there. And what we imagine in this course of events is that *I*, the very same individual, am raised in Czech culture. My being a Canadian, therefore, is not metaphysically essential to me and constitutes my identity in only a weaker, nonmetaphysical sense. And nonmetaphysical identities, it seems to me, cannot generate a plausible version of perfectionism.

As I said, however, this is a less central point. What is more important is that even if we accept cultural perfectionism, it does nothing to justify national partiality. Let us grant that humans have different goods based on their membership in different cultures. How does it follow that I should care more about the achievement by my conationals of their specific cultural good than about the achievement by people in other cultures of their specific good? What rules out the view that I should care impartially about all people's realizing their different cultural identities—that is, what rules out an impartialist cultural perfectionism? Such a perfectionism would recognize that the good of Canadians is different from the good of Germans but direct both Canadians and Germans to care equally about both. How does accepting cultural perfectionism as a general position rule this specific view out?[4] I am not suggesting that the writers who embrace cultural perfectionism do so in an impartialist way. Most, it seems to me, endorse national partiality. But the partiality they affirm does not follow from their cultural perfectionism, which is equally consistent with an impartialist approach. Their position therefore combines cultural perfectionism with claims about partiality that are independent of any ideas about cultural identities and cannot be justified by them.

Cultural perfectionists may object that I have ignored a crucial feature of their argument. This argument does not claim only that people in different cultures have different identities; it claims, beyond that, that those identities involve, as one component, a demand for partiality toward the culture's members. Thus my identity as a Canadian demands partiality toward Canadians, a German's identity demands partiality toward Germans, and neither of us can fully achieve his or her good by following an impartial morality.

If it takes this form, the cultural perfectionist argument requires a strong additional assumption. To show that national partiality is justified in *every* culture, it must assume that *every* culture involves as one component a demand for partiality, so there could never be a culture of pure impartialists. I find this assumption dubious, but let us grant it and ask what follows. If my identity involves as one component a demand for national partiality, I cannot fully achieve my good if I do what is right by impartialist standards. But this is no embarrassment or difficulty for an impartialist cultural perfectionism. It is merely one instance of the familiar fact that to do what is right, or has the best consequences impartially considered, agents must sometimes sacrifice some of their own good. Doing what is right often involves omitting what is best for oneself; here it involves omitting that part of one's good that consists in being partial. This familiar fact does not tell against impartial cultural perfectionism, and there is still no justification for national partiality.[5]

The difficulty with the cultural perfectionist argument is that it operates at the wrong level to justify national partiality. The affirmation of partiality concerns the *form* of an ethically appropriate concern. It says that whatever people's good consists in, we should care more about our conationals' good than about other people's. But cultural perfectionism makes claims about the *content* of our ethical concern, or about what people's good consists in. And no claims about what people's good consists in can justify the idea that we ought to care more about some people's good than about others'.

The second argument suggested by the talk of "embedded selves," which I called the metaethical particularist argument, does address issues about form. It claims that an impartialist morality, one requiring all humans to care equally about all others, is inconsistent with the true nature of moral codes and principles. These codes and principles, the argument says, always arise within particular cultures; they are addressed to the members of a culture as having the particular cultural identities they have and as occupying particular roles within that culture. Morality is always *our* morality, in these circumstances here. This means that the standpoint presupposed by impartial morality—outside all cultures and making judgments about them all—is not available. Morality must be partial because the impartialist alternative is conceptually incoherent.

The problem here is that the particularist argument excludes not only impartialist morality but also a universalist ethic of nationalism. For universalists, too, make claims about what is right in all cultures, namely, partiality toward them; their judgments, too, do not arise from their particular culture but apply equally to all cultures. Consider Alasdair MacIntyre's lecture, "Is Patriotism a Virtue?" As its title indicates, this lecture asks a question about the value of patriotism in all cultures everywhere. And MacIntyre ties an affirmative answer to this question to what looks like a particularist metaethical view. On the view that underwrites patriotism, he writes, we never learn "morality as such, but always the highly specific morality of some highly specific social order." Later he claims that impartialist morality requires something that cannot be justified, namely, that we "assume an abstract and artificial—perhaps even an impossible—stance, that of a rational being as such, responding to the requirements of morality not *qua* peasant or farmer or quarterback, but *qua* rational agent who has abstracted him or herself from all social particularity."[6] But someone who really accepted this metaethical particularism could not ask the universalized question of MacIntyre's title. Such a person could only write a lecture titled "Is Canadian Patriotism a Virtue in Canada?" (if he or she was Canadian) or "Is German Patriotism a Virtue in Germany?" (if he or she was German). This person would not make any claims but would deny the intelligibility of claims about the value of patriotism in cultures other than his or her own. Any such universalist claims, no less than those of impartialist morality, issue from a standpoint that the particularist says is not available—namely, one abstracted from any particular social identity and addressed to all humans or all members of cultures as such. As I have said, the interesting affirmation of national partiality is the universalist one; it is also the one that all writers on this subject discuss. But this universalist affirmation cannot be supported by metaethical particularism; on the contrary, it is excluded by it.

Let me summarize my discussion of the "embedded self" by introducing some technical terminology. The interesting nationalist doctrine is both universalist and agent-relative. It is universalist because it claims that partiality toward one's nation and conationals is appropriate for all humans in all cultures. It is agent-relative because it says that what different humans should be partial to is different—namely, their *own* conationals. The cultural perfectionist argument does not go far enough to justify this doctrine, because it does not rule out an impartialist view according to which we ought to care equally about the realization of their different cultural identities by people in all the cultures in the world. The metaethical particularist argument goes too far to justify the doctrine, because it rules out not only impartialist but also all universal moral claims. Neither of the two arguments that I can see suggested by the talk of "embedded selves" does anything to justify national partiality. The real issues about the ethics of nationalism do not concern the nature of morality or of the self but are those I introduced at the start of this chapter. Assuming that special relations sometimes justify partiality, are the relations among conationals of the kind that do justify partiality, like those among family members, or of the kind that do not, like those among members of a race?

Nationalism and Impersonal Goods

My second topic is the content of national partiality, or exactly what nationalists are partial to. Many writers speak simply of being partial to one's nation without explaining further what that means. Some speak, more specifically, of being partial toward one's conationals—that is, of giving more weight to the interests of individuals in one's nation than to those of other individuals. This is certainly one aspect of nationalism, but I believe there is often another aspect.

In a number of writings Charles Taylor has emphasized the importance of cultural survival as a good and value for minority groups. In *Multiculturalism and "The Politics of Recognition,"* for example, he writes: "It is axiomatic for Quebec governments that the survival and flourishing of French culture in Quebec is a good."[7] Noting the importance of this insight, McMahan says it shows how for participants in a culture its survival has "impersonal value."[8] I agree that in one important sense the survival of a culture is an "impersonal" value or good, but in another sense, which seems to be the one McMahan has in mind, it is not, or is not most importantly, impersonal.

The survival of a culture is an impersonal good in the sense that is not reducible to the goods of individual persons, or to goods located in individual persons' lives. Consider francophone Quebeckers who care deeply that there be a French culture in Quebec three generations from now. Do they believe that the survival of French culture is a good because better human lives will be lived if French culture survives than if it does not? Do they believe, more specifically, that their great-grandchildren will lead better lives if they are born and raised in a French culture than if, that culture having disappeared, those great-grandchildren are born and raised as full members of an English culture? I do not believe these Quebeckers need or even should, if they wish to avoid chauvinism, believe this. They should grant that after enough time the disappearance of French culture would not be worse for persons in the sense of making the lives lived by persons worse. If, despite this, they continue to view the survival of their culture as a good, they must view it as an impersonal good in the following sense: it would be better if French culture survived even if this would not make the lives persons live more valuable.[9]

Valuing cultural survival in this way does not require the metaphysical view that cultures or nations exist separately from, or over and above, their individual members. It is fully compatible with the reductionist view that facts about nations consist entirely in facts about individuals and the relations between them. According to this reductionist view, for French culture to survive in Quebec is only and entirely for individuals in Quebec to live and interact in certain ways. But while holding that the *existence* of a culture is reducible to facts about individuals, a nationalist can deny that the *good* of the culture's existing is reducible to the *goods* of individuals. The fact that people interact in certain ways can have a value that is separate from the values present in their individual lives.[10]

Cultural survival, then, is an impersonal good in the sense that it does not consist in the goods of individual persons. But the word "impersonal" is often used in another sense, one equivalent to "impartial." In this sense, an impersonal good is one it is appropriate for all agents to desire and pursue and to weigh impartially against other similar goods. This seems to be the sense McMahan has in mind when he calls cultural survival an "impersonal value." He introduces the topic of survival while discussing the instrumental arguments that can be given, from an impartialist standpoint, for endorsing some degree of national partiality, and he considers it alongside a value that cannot but be impersonal in this second sense—namely, that of the overall cultural diversity of the world. But it seems to me that cultural survival is valued by nationalists, and is thought by them appropriately valued, in a highly partial way. Who is it who cares about the survival of French culture in Quebec? It is surely, above all, francophone Quebeckers. And they do not care about their culture's survival only in an impartial way, or merely as contributing to a universal good such as overall cultural diversity. If they did, they would gladly accept the disappearance of French culture in Quebec if that somehow allowed the survival of two other cultures elsewhere in the world. This is not their attitude; they care specially about the survival of *their own* culture. In the same way, it seems to me, people outside a culture do not have nearly as much reason to care about its survival as a good. McMahan writes that people outside a culture "are capable of appreciating its intrinsic value" and of "perceiving in a particular alien culture a variety of merits that may not be replicated in any other culture." But these remarks, though true, do not suffice to establish the appropriateness of impartial concern for another culture. I can appreciate that the well-being of someone else's children is a good while believing that I ought to care much more about my own children's wellbeing. And in my view commonsense nationalism does not give people outside a culture much moral duty to care directly about the culture's survival. This is obscured in many actual situations by the fact that the members of the culture do desire its survival. Thus if francophone Quebeckers care deeply about their culture's survival, this gives other people, and especially anglophone Canadians, a reason of a more familiar kind to support measures that will ensure the culture's survival—namely, that Quebeckers desire it. But what if a majority of Quebeckers ceased to care about their culture's survival and instead preferred assimilating into English culture? In this situation I believe Quebeckers in the minority would still feel a strong duty to fight for their culture and to try to persuade the majority to change their minds. But non-Quebeckers would surely not feel any such strong duty, nor would they be failing in not feeling it. They might appropriately feel some mild regret about the loss of a distinctive culture and the loss of some overall diversity in the world, but they would not feel strongly bound to prevent the assimilation, for example, by offering subsidies to Quebeckers who retain their French culture. When it is considered in itself and apart from the desires it gives rise to in members, the survival of a culture does not seem to be something that, according to commonsense nationalism, nonmembers have a strong reason to care about or pursue.

I have suggested that cultural survival, though an impersonal good in the sense that it is not reducible to the goods of individuals, is the object of highly partial attitudes. The same can be true of other impersonal goals associated with a culture. For example, nationalists can care that their cultures not only survive but also achieve the full flowering or self-expression that comes through sovereignty and independent statehood. In this case the importance of the impersonal good may be harder to see because there can also be personal goods at stake in sovereignty. Thus nationalists may believe that the individuals in their culture will engage in more valuable political activity or live under more culturally sensitive institutions if their government is entirely their own. But if it is possible to value the survival of one's culture apart from any benefits to individuals, it is surely possible to value sovereignty and statehood in the same way, and I think those active in independence movements do commonly have this impersonal desire. They value their nation's sovereignty, as they value their culture's survival, as something good partly in itself. Thus a central force in the Quebec sovereignty movement has been the desire that francophone Quebeckers affirm their status as *un peuple* by establishing their own nation-state. In fact, nationalists can have many impersonal goals that they value in a partial way: that their culture flourish in the arts and sciences, that it be economically vigorous, that it produce athletes who win medals at the

Olympics. Beyond this, nationalists can have impersonal political goals that they value partially: that their nation occupy a large territory, that it be militarily powerful, that it dominate its neighbors and even dictate to the world.

In this list of impersonal goals, there is a large moral difference between the innocuous first goal, cultural survival, and the politically threatening ones that come later, such as military power and world domination. But this is nothing new in the study of nationalism, which is often described as Janus-faced, attractive in some forms and terrifying in others. And our responses to the list may be guided by the view, which many writers on this subject endorse, that any acceptable form of national partiality must be constrained by respect for the basic rights of all individuals, no less in other countries than in one's own. One may pursue one's own nation's good and do so in preference to other nations' good but only in ways that respect fundamental rights.[11] As it happens, the more acceptable impersonal goals, such as cultural survival, can usually be pursued successfully without violating anyone's rights, whereas it is hard to see territorial expansion or world domination achieved without violating rights. The different impersonal goals may differ morally not so much in themselves, therefore, as in the means likely to be necessary for their achievement.

I do not claim that every form of nationalism involves concern for impersonal goods; some nationalists may favor only the interests of their individual conationals. But it seems to me that the two forms of partiality often go together, and I will therefore define *full-blooded nationalism* as combining a greater concern for the impersonal goods of one's own culture, such as its survival and flourishing, with a greater concern for the interests of one's conationals. In a phrase I have used above, full-blooded nationalism involves partiality both toward one's nation, seen as having certain impersonal goods, and toward one's conationals. If this characterization is correct, it has an important implication for the morality of nationalism.

If full-blooded nationalism involves two components, a successful moral justification of it must address both. It must show the appropriateness of partiality toward one's conationals and also toward one's nation's impersonal good. Here the difficulties facing the two justifications seem interestingly different.

Consider, first, partiality toward one's conationals. There is no doubt that one ought morally to care about one's conationals; they are people, and one ought in general to care about people. The difficulty is to show why one should care more about these people than about others who are not members of one's nation, or why partiality toward this particular group is appropriate. In the situation where partiality seems most clearly justified, that of the family, it rests on a special relationship between people that is both rich and intense. The members of a family care deeply about each other, have lived together for many years, and have to a significant degree shaped each other's characters. Their interactions have been as close as people's typically ever are. But the relations among conationals are nothing like this. I have never met the vast majority of my fellow Canadians and do not know who they are; the causal links between our lives are tenuous at best. Especially worrisome is the fact that these links do not seem closer than my links with many non-Canadians—for example, with Americans living just across the Alberta-Montana border. In fact, with respect to closeness, the relations among conationals seem comparable to those among members of a race, who likewise mostly have not met. If the relations between conationals hold only to a limited degree, and not much more than between non-nationals, how can they justify any substantial degree of partiality?

The justification of the second form of partiality, toward one's nation's impersonal good, faces the opposite difficulty. Here there does not seem to be a large problem about justifying the attitude's partiality. Only one culture or nation in the world is mine; all the others are not mine. This is not just a small difference in degree but a large difference, perhaps a difference in kind. So if the justification of strong partiality requires a large difference in linkage or connectedness, we have that here. The problem, rather, is to show that impersonal goods are morally appropriate objects of any concern in the first place. What can be called "individualist" theories of the good deny this. Individualist theories hold that the only goods there are, and thus the only objects of rational concern, are personal goods, or the goods of individuals.[12] According to individualism, nationalists who value the survival or flourishing of their culture apart from any effects on individuals are being irrational and fetishistic. Their attitude is objectionable not because of its partiality but because of its object, which is not a genuine good because it is not a feature of individuals' lives. Nor is it only individualism in the strict sense that counts against the second form of partiality. A more moderate view allows that there can be impersonal goods and rational concern for them but insists that these goods are always relatively minor and the concern they call for always of less weight than the concern required for individuals. According to this moderate view, a partial attitude toward one's nation's impersonal good is allowed but not in a strength that often allows promoting that good at the expense of benefits to individuals.

To summarize: If there are two forms of national partiality, they need two justifications, and the difficulties facing these justifications are different. That one should care somehow about one's conationals is not in doubt; the question is whether it is right to care more about them than about non-nationals. As for a nation's impersonal good, if some concern for it is appropriate, it seems plausible that this is a highly partial concern. The difficult question here is whether that initial concern is appropriate: whether impersonal goods are worth caring about or whether the only, or only important, goods are those of individuals.

Partiality and History

Having suggested the importance to nationalism of impersonal goods, I will now set them aside and consider the more commonly recognized aspect of nationalism: partiality toward one's conationals. This partiality has many more specific manifestations. Nationalists typically care much more about relieving economic hardship within the nation than outside it; compare what nations spend on domestic welfare programs with what they spend on foreign aid. Nationalists also want immigration policy decided primarily by considering the effects on people already within the nation rather than on those who want to join. These various positions may receive some support from concern for impersonal goals like the nation's flourishing as a collective, but they are primarily directed at individuals. Setting aside the impersonal component of nationalism, therefore, I will consider the moral justification of partiality toward one's individual conationals. When partiality toward certain individuals is justified, it is because certain special relations hold between oneself and them. To what degree do these relations hold between members of a nation?

Because the arena in which partiality seems most clearly justified is the family, defenders of nationalism often try to assimilate the relations among conationals to those among family members. As we have seen, however, this assimilation is problematic; especially in the degree of interaction they involve, nations are not like large families. To many writers, therefore, it has seemed that the degree of national partiality that is justified is even in the most favorable circumstances much less than most nationalists desire.

In this section I will sketch a reply to this widespread skepticism about national partiality. This reply concedes that along one important dimension the relations between conationals have much less of the character that justifies partiality than do familial relations, but it claims that along another dimension, which most writers ignore, they have roughly as much.

First, however, I must state a presupposition of my argument: that the basis of partiality among conationals must be an objective rather than a subjective relation and, in particular, cannot be just the fact that conationals care more about each other than about non-nationals. It may be, as is sometimes argued, that certain subjective facts—that is, certain attitudes on the part of individuals—are necessary for a nation to exist. For example, it may be that individuals must view membership in a group as an important part of their identity before the group constitutes a nation. But questions about when a nation exists are different from questions about when its members should be partial toward each other, and the latter questions cannot turn on mere facts about caring. There are two decisive arguments for this conclusion.[13] One is that a purely subjective basis could not rule out the racial partiality that most of us find morally offensive. The fact that racists care more about people with their own skin color would by itself make it right for them to do so. The second argument is that a subjective basis cannot justify what nationalists typically affirm—namely, a duty to favor one's conationals that is binding even on those who do not now care about their conationals. I will assume, then, that the basis of national partiality must be some objective relation—that is, some relation that holds independently of people's attitudes. To determine which relation this is, we must look more closely at the objective side of personal or familial relations.

Consider my relation to my wife. If I love her specially, it is partly for certain qualities that she has. Some of these qualities I am attracted to without judging them to be intrinsically good, such as her appearance and the sound of her voice. Others I do judge to be good, such as her trustworthiness, her intelligence, and her concern for other people. Especially with these latter qualities it is important that my beliefs about them be true, that she, in fact, have the qualities, and that they truly be good. But even if all my relevant beliefs are true, my wife's having these qualities does not explain all my emotional attachment to her. If it did, I would abandon my wife the moment someone else came along with the same properties to a higher degree. Or if, just before dying, my wife had a clone of herself made to stay with me, I would think myself no worse off for the exchange. But of course I would not trade in my wife in this way. Though I love her partly for her qualities, I do not do so in a way that would accept substitution. I also love her, in the common phrase, "as an individual," or for herself.

What does it mean to love a person "as an individual"? In my view, it does not mean loving a person apart from any qualities at all but rather loving the person for qualities that no one else can share. More specifically, it involves loving the person for certain historical qualities, ones deriving from his or her participation with one in a shared history. Thus I love my wife not only as trustworthy, intelligent, and so on but also as the person who nursed me through that illness, with whom I spent that wonderful first summer, and with whom I discovered that hotel on Kootenay Lake. These historical qualities focus my love on my wife as an individual, since no substitute, not even a clone, can be the very person who did those things with me.

A highly romantic view of love and friendship holds that once these historical qualities are established they entirely determine the relationship, which should therefore never end and always imposes duties of partiality. This is the view expressed in Shakespeare's line: "Love is not love / Which alters when it alteration finds." But I think most of us believe that historical qualities, though part of the basis for love and friendship, are, again, not the entire basis. If my wife changes radically, losing the general or shareable qualities I admire and taking on ones I find despicable, I will no longer feel attached to her or bound by duties of partial concern. My love, in other words, has a dual basis. My wife's role in a shared history with me explains why I love her more than other people with similar general qualities, but her general qualities matter, too. If those qualities changed enough, our history would not be a sufficient basis to maintain my love or to continue to demand partiality toward her.

We can see the same dual basis in nationalists' attachment to their nation and conationals. Nationalists are, first, attracted to their culture and the activities that define it, thinking them to a considerable degree good. They need not believe that their culture is superior in the sense of being the single best in the world. That chauvinist belief would not be credible and, in any case, would justify not universalist nationalism but the belief that everyone in the world should promote the one best culture. Instead, nationalists need only believe that their culture is one of perhaps many in the world that are good. What attaches them specially to this culture and its members are historical facts: that this is the culture *they* grew up in, that their conationals share *with them* a history of being shaped by, participating in, and sustaining this culture. The favorable evaluation of their conationals' cultural activities is a necessary basis for this nationalist attachment, but it is not sufficient. There is also, and distinguishing their conationals from other people whose culture is equally good, the crucial fact of a shared cultural history.

This dual basis can lead to conflicts about national attachment. As Yael Tamir writes, "Citizens of a state involved in an unjust war may be torn between the feeling that they have an associative obligation to serve in the army together with their enlisted fellows, and their commitment to a moral code dictating they should refuse."[14] In the situation Tamir describes, the citizens' state is not now good; it has at least some general qualities that are evil. But the citizens are still historically connected to this state as the one they grew up under. How they resolve this conflict depends on which of the two bases of national attachment they find more important, which in many particular cases will depend on how evil their state currently is. If it is not irredeemably evil, the citizens may continue to feel special duties toward it and work harder to reform it than to reform other equally evil states elsewhere. But if their state degenerates too far, their historical connection to it may be outweighed and their feelings of national attachment, like love for an individual whose character has changed utterly, may end.

If national attachment rests partly on the belief that one's culture is good, it is important that that belief be true, which requires the culture to be, in fact, good. This is one point where evaluative considerations bear on the justification of national partiality, but there is another point as well. Considerations about good and evil also help determine when a shared history is of the right kind to justify partial concern and, when it is, what degree of partiality is justified.

Consider again a personal relationship like that between spouses. Here the shared history is predominantly one of mutual benefit or beneficence; two people have helped each other through difficult times and also shared good times, giving and taking pleasure in each other's company. And I think a history of reciprocal benefit or, alternatively, one where people have jointly benefited others, such as the students in a school where these people taught, can be a legitimate basis of partiality. The same is true of a history of shared suffering; people who lived in the same barracks in a Nazi labor camp and suffered the same evils there can appropriately feel on the basis of their shared history some greater concern for each other's well-being. But I do not think a shared history justifies partiality when it is a history of doing evil, as for former members of an SS unit that ran and terrorized a labor camp. Many of us find something obscene in the idea of nostalgic re-unions, even at this late date, of former SS colleagues, and there is a similar ob-scenity in the idea of partiality toward former SS colleagues. If an SS veteran re-ceives a letter from one of his former colleagues claiming financial hardship and requesting a loan of $1,000, should he feel a special duty to honor the request or to help his former colleague before helping others who are equally in need? It seems to me that he should not, even if his former colleague is now morally re-formed. If anything, given the evil of the history they share, he should feel a duty not to associate with his former colleague and should contribute first to others who did not participate in that aspect of his past. Whereas a shared history of doing good or suffering evil can justify duties of partiality, a shared history of doing evil cannot.

These points suggest a general account of the basis of duties of partiality. Some activities and states of people, most notably their doing good or suffering evil, call for a positive, caring, or associative response. Others, such as their doing evil, call for a negative or dissociative response. Partiality between people is appropriate when they have shared in the past in the first kind of activity or state. For example, if two people have a shared history of doing good, either reciprocally or to others, partiality between them in the present is a way of honoring that good fact about their past. (This is why partiality among former SS colleagues is troubling; it seems to honor a past that properly calls for dishonor.) One should, in general, care more about people who have shared with one in activities and states that call for a caring response. This account does not claim to justify partiality of concern as a general moral phenomenon; on the contrary, it assumes it. It assumes that one has a spe-cial duty to honor past doings of good or sufferings of evil *that involved oneself.* But it does give particular duties of partiality a more abstract basis. In the many realms where partiality is appropriate—the family, private clubs, perhaps the na-tion—it is an appropriate response to a history that joins oneself and other people in activities or states that are good or that call for association.

This general account can explain our attitudes to racial partiality. As McMahan notes,[15] while we condemn racial discrimination by members of a dominant racial group, we often think it appropriate for minority races to celebrate their distinct-ness and even to implement discriminatory policies that benefit their members at the expense of others. In current conditions, black and aboriginal solidarity move-ments have a different moral status than white supremacy movements. The expla-nation, I would argue, is that minority racial groups have a shared history of the kind that makes partiality morally appropriate—namely, a shared history of suf-fering evil because of one's racial membership. But the history of dominant racial groups, which is largely one of oppressing the minority, is not of the kind that jus-tifies partiality. Among members of the minority, there is a shared history that morally warrants partiality toward other members; among members of the ma-jority, there is one that positively precludes it.

More important, the account suggests a defense of national partiality against the skeptical argument mentioned above. If certain people have a shared history of doing good, what determines the degree of partiality that is justified between them? Two factors suggest themselves: the degree to which the people's history is shared or involves interaction between them, and the amount of good their interaction produced. Other things being equal, people whose history involves closer relations or more intimate contact have stronger duties of partiality. Also, other things being equal, people whose interactions produced more good, for themselves or for others, have stronger duties of partiality.

The history of family members scores extremely high on the first of these dimensions—namely, closeness of contact. Family members interact intimately on a daily basis, with large effects on each other's lives. Family history also scores high on the dimension of good done, given the large benefits given by parents to their children, spouses to each other, and even children to their parents. Surely family members benefit each other as much as they do any individuals.

A nation's history, by contrast, scores very low on the first dimension. As I have said, I have not met the majority of my fellow Canadians and do not know who they are. But a nation's history does much better on the second dimension. Consider another example from my history. In the 1960s Canadians created a national health care system that continues to provide high-quality medical care to all citizens regardless of their ability to pay. The benefit this medicare system provides any one citizen is probably less than that provided by his or her family, but it is still substantial, and it is one Canadians have provided together. Canadians derive equally substantial benefits from many other aspects of their political activity. When these benefits are added together, they constitute a significant counterweight to the weakness of national relations on the first dimension, that of closeness of contact. The critique of national partiality considers only this first dimension, of closeness. But if we believe that a necessary basis for justified partiality is a shared history, that this history must be good rather than evil, and that the degree of partiality a history justifies depends partly on the quantity of goodness it produces or embodies, we have some response to the critique. On the one dimension, a national history does indeed have much less of the character that justifies partiality than a family history. But on another dimension, the national history has roughly as much.

This account of the basis of national partiality fits most obviously those many nationalisms that point to glorious deeds in the nation's past, such as saving Europe for Christendom or inventing representative democracy. But the account should not be too closely tied to these nationalisms, for two reasons. First, if the basis of national partiality is objective rather than subjective, it must depend on the nation's actual history rather than on beliefs about that history that are all too often false. A national mythology with no basis in fact cannot justify nationalist policies today.[16] Second, the benefits produced in a nation's history need not be specially grand; on the contrary, they can be perfectly ordinary. Consider again familial partiality. The benefits my wife and I have given each other, such as companionship and love, are also given to each other by countless other couples. What ties my wife and me specially together is not that we have produced unique goods but that we have produced familiar goods jointly, in interactions with each other. The goods in a nation's history can likewise be familiar. Before enacting medicare, Canadians together maintained political institutions and through them the rule of law in Canada, which ensured liberty and security for all Canadian citizens. The same liberty and security were produced in other nations, but only my fellow Canadians produced them with me, and it is that historical fact that is decisive. According to the account I am proposing, it is important that a nation's history have produced significant benefits, but these benefits need not be the grand ones of national mythologies or even at all different from those produced in other nations' histories.

Nations as defined by political institutions[17] are not the only large groups that can have this kind of history. Consider a linguistic and cultural group. Its members have together sustained a language and through it the possibility of beneficial communication for all its speakers. Other groups have also sustained languages, but this group has done it here. They have also, as writers and readers, sustained a literature and an artistic tradition that provide further benefits. When political and cultural groups coincide, these two grounds of partiality reinforce each other. The nation's members have two separate reasons for being partial to the same individuals. But when political and cultural boundaries do not coincide, there can be conflicts about partiality. Consider francophone Quebeckers. They share a political history with all Canadians and a cultural history with a smaller number of francophone Canadians. Which group they feel more partial to will depend on how good they think the groups' present qualities are and how beneficial they think the groups' histories have been. Those who think of Canada as a successful country with an admirable political history will be strongly attached to the larger group; those who see present failure and a past of suppressing minorities will not.

Whether a nation is defined politically or culturally, its history differs from a family's in involving many more people, both as recipients of its benefits and as participants in producing them. If only the first of these differences, in the number of beneficiaries, mattered morally, the nation's history would score much higher on the dimension of good done than the family's, since its benefits are much more widely dispersed. The total good resulting from Canadian medicare, for example, is vastly greater than any produced in a family. But it is more plausible to count both differences about numbers, so that what matters for this dimension is not the total benefit produced in a history but something closer to the average benefit per participant, which in the national case roughly equals the average benefit per recipient.[18] Even when we take this view, however, the good produced in a national history is comparable to that in a family history. If we consider the benefits each

Canadian receives from living under the rule of law and with social programs such as medicare, they are surely of similar size to those that person receives from his or her family. If this is so, a national history scores roughly as well on the dimension of good done as a family history. Since the national history scores less well on the dimension of interaction, the result on balance is that less partiality is justified toward one's conationals than toward one's family members. This is an intuitively plausible result. Not even the most ardent nationalist claims that one should care as much about one's conationals, as conationals, as about one's spouse or child. And the degree of concern that is justified toward conationals is considerably greater than toward non-nationals, since one's history with the latter scores very poorly on both dimensions. One not only has had no close interactions with non-nationals but also has produced no significant goods with them. The political and cultural institutions of a nation enable its members to cooperate, however indirectly, in producing significant benefits. But there are no comparable institutions joining non-nationals, even ones living just across a national border, and therefore no comparable goods they can be said jointly to have produced.

I wish I could say more precisely what degree of national partiality this historical account justifies. Unfortunately, that would require weighing against each other more precisely the two dimensions of closeness of contact and good done in a history, which I cannot now do. Nor do I see that more precise weightings of these dimensions follow from the general ideas I have advanced. So I will content myself with two more modest conclusions. The first is that, whatever degree of national partiality is intrinsically justified, it is more than the limited degree that the comparison with families initially suggested. Though a national history scores less well on one dimension than a family history, it scores comparably well on another and therefore justifies at least a moderate degree of partiality. It may be that any morally acceptable national partiality must be constrained by respect for the basic rights of all persons, both within one's nation and outside it. But familial partiality is likewise constrained by respect for rights, and it still has considerable room to express itself. The second conclusion is that it is no surprise that nations and cultures are prime objects of partial attitudes. According to the historical account, partiality is justified when the members of a group have worked together in the past to produce significant benefits. But nations and cultures embody just the institutions that make such beneficial interactions possible. My nation is an appropriate object of partial attitudes because it more than other similarly sized groups has allowed me to act with others to produce significant human goods.

NOTES

An earlier version of this essay was presented as a commentary on Jeff McMahan's "The Limits of National Partiality" at the Conference on the Ethics of Nationalism, University of

Illinois at Urbana-Champaign, April 1994. Many of its ideas were stimulated by McMahan's fine essay; I am also grateful to him and to Robert McKim for helpful comments.

1. David Miller, "The Ethical Significance of Nationality," *Ethics* 98 (1988): 649–50. The same view is defended in his *On Nationality* (Oxford: Clarendon Press, 1995).

2. See my *Perfectionism* (New York: Oxford University Press, 1993).

3. This argument is suggested in Michael Sandel, "The Procedural Republic and the Unencumbered Self," *Political Theory* 12 (1984): 81–96; and Yael Tamir, *Liberal Nationalism* (Princeton: Princeton University Press, 1993), chap. 1.

4. As an analogy, consider a different version of perfectionism defended by Rousseau, Humboldt, and Mill. They hold that the nature whose realization constitutes a person's good is not one shared with all other humans or even one shared with all members of one's culture but rather a nature distinctive of that person as an individual. Each person has a unique individual identity, by realizing which the person achieves "individuality." But do these writers say that each person ought to care only or even more about his or her own achievement of individuality than about other people's? They do not. They say that each person ought to care impartially about the achievement of individuality by all and to support those institutions, especially liberal institutions, that will permit individuality for all. But if this individualist perfectionism is compatible with full impartiality, surely cultural perfectionism is as well.

5. Could the cultural perfectionist claim that the demand for partiality is not just one component of every cultural identity but an essential component, so that if I do not care more about my conationals I do not realize my cultural identity to any degree at all? This claim surely is, as a claim about identities, utterly implausible. And even if it is accepted, it still does not show why, at a foundational level, I should care more about the realization to some rather than no degree of my nation's identity than of others'.

6. Alasdair MacIntyre, *Is Patriotism a Virtue?*," Lindley Lecture (Lawrence: University of Kansas, 1984), pp. 9, 12. A weaker version of metaethical particularism is defended by Michael Walzer in *Spheres of Justice* (New York: Basic Books, 1983), chaps. 1–2, and *Interpretation and Social Criticism* (Cambridge, Mass.: Harvard University Press, 1987).

7. Charles Taylor, *Multiculturalism and "The Politics of Recognition,"* ed. Amy Gutmann (Princeton: Princeton University Press, 1992), p. 58.

8. See chapter 8.

9. The importance of goods that are impersonal in this sense for the morality of war is brought out in Jeff McMahan and Robert McKim, "The Just War and the Gulf War," *Canadian Journal of Philosophy* 23 (1993): 522. Note that what Derek Parfit calls an "impersonal," as against a "person-affecting," principle of beneficence does not involve reference to impersonal goods in my sense (see his *Reasons and Persons* [Oxford: Clarendon, 1984], pp. 386–87). Parfit's "impersonal" view holds that the best outcome is the one in which the best lives are lived, even though the people living those lives may be numerically different from the people in alternative outcomes. (Numerical nonidentity is especially likely when the outcomes involve large-scale and long-lasting changes, as the survival and disappearance of a culture do.) But Parfit's "impersonal" view still holds, with other versions of beneficence, that the relevant goods in the different outcomes are all states of individual persons. It is this latter claim that the affirmation of what I call impersonal goods denies. This affirma-

tion rejects not only person-affecting beneficence but also the individualism about value still present in Parfit's "impersonal" view.

10. If the impersonal view accepts metaphysical reductionism, it embodies G. E. Moore's principle of "organic unities," according to which the value of a whole need not equal the sum of the values its parts would have if they existed alone. See Moore, *Principia Ethica* (Cambridge: Cambridge University Press, 1903), chap. 6.

11. See, for example, chapter 8.

12. Individualism is affirmed in Avishai Margalit and Joseph Raz, "National Self-Determination," *Journal of Philosophy* 87 (1990): 439–61; and Tamir, *Liberal Nationalism*, pp. 83–84. Interestingly, Margalit and Raz allow that the interest of a group is not reducible to the interests of its members (p. 450) but insist that only individual interests are relevant to the justification of national rights.

13. See chapter 8.

14. Tamir, *Liberal Nationalism*, p. 102.

15. See chapter 8.

16. It is also relevant that these beliefs usually concern the distant past, which in my view counts less in justifying partiality than does the recent past. Immediately after World War II, national partiality on the part of Germans would have been morally unthinkable because of the evil their nation had just done. It is much less so today, after fifty years of the Federal Republic.

17. Those of us who live in multicultural states, especially ones like Canada where two cultures are geographically separated, are much more likely than others to define "nation" in political rather than in ethnic or cultural terms. If we did not, we would be barred by language from any pan-Canadian "nationalism." The Canadian understanding of "nation" is nicely illustrated by an incident from the 1968 federal election campaign. The Progressive Conservatives, seeking to reverse decades of electoral failure in Quebec, announced a *deux nations* policy, according to which Canada was composed of French-speaking and English-speaking *nations*. Pierre Trudeau, recently elected leader of the Liberal party, said he rejected this "two nations" policy. He did not favor the separation of Quebec but wanted Canada to remain one nation. Though Trudeau's reply benefited him electorally in English Canada, it was widely regarded as linguistically mischievous. The English word "nation," it was said, is not equivalent to the French *nation*. While the French word has a primarily cultural significance, the English word is political. The correct translation of *deux nations* is therefore "two [founding] peoples," which does not carry, as "two nations" does, any implication of separate political institutions.

18. I owe this point to Jeff McMahan. Note that treating both differences as significant plausibly implies that members of small nations have just as strong duties of partiality as members of large nations. If only the number of recipients were significant, citizens of the United States would have a duty of partiality ten times as strong as that of Canadians because their history has benefited ten times as many people.

10

Nationalism, For and (Mainly) Against

JUDITH LICHTENBERG

To many people, the very idea of nationalism smacks of ethnocentrism or even racism. They suspect that violence, hatred, and distrust of the Other, embodied in a sharply divided world of "us" and "them," always lurk within the nationalist's heart. Recent world events have done nothing to allay these suspicions. Nationalism, according to this view, is an evil to be overcome by a cosmopolitan stance that denies the significance of national boundaries.

Yet positive values have also been associated with the nationalist idea, as some recent accounts remind us.[1] Democracy, autonomy, community, pluralism—these goods have been connected with the development of nationalism over the past several centuries. Some of the values underlying nationalism also manifest themselves today in its dilute and more respectable cousin, multiculturalism. And it goes without saying that whatever its merits, nationalism exerts enormous power on the aspirations of many people around the world.

My aim here is to make explicit both the genuine attractions of nationalism and its disturbing features. I begin with some preliminary observations concerning the confusing and contested terms "nationalism" and "nation." I then explore what I believe are the five main arguments in support of nationalism. These I call the Flourishing Argument, the Self-Determination Argument, the Reparations Argument, the Pluralism Argument, and the Intrinsic Value Argument.

The serious controversies surrounding nationalism can be understood, I believe, in terms of two main problems. One is the Territory Question. It asks whether or under what circumstances the commitment to nationalism entails the commitment to a state—and thus a territory—as the nation's embodiment. The answer bears significantly on the meaning, viability, and acceptability of nationalism as a practical phenomenon. The second problem I call the Partiality Question. Everyone acknowledges that nationalism permits—some would say it requires—members of a nation to favor compatriots over outsiders in certain respects and that certain traits and practices characteristic of the nation be given priority. The question is how these forms of partiality are to be understood and whether they can be defended morally.

Does the term "nationalism" capture a single phenomenon? Despite the antiessentialist turn now fashionable, it is hard to avoid the urge to look for something common. In so doing, we should not preclude the possibility of several fundamentally different kinds of nationalism, some more acceptable than others.

So, for example, Ernest Gellner and, following him, E. J. Hobsbawm define nationalism as the view that "the political and the national unit should be congruent."[2] Yet, on the other hand, Yael Tamir has recently advocated a "liberal nationalism" that severs the connection between the national and the political. (By contrast, we cannot imagine a liberal racism.) The question dividing these approaches should not be decided by definitional fiat. Below we shall examine the reasons for and against conjoining nationalism with the political—that is, territorial—aim.

To know what nationalism is, we must first know what a nation is. The word is often used interchangeably with "state" or "country"; if you ask ordinary people what a nation is, they will point to states—those entities possessing political sovereignty, having control over their borders, eligible to join the United Nations, and the like. But this view is unsatisfactory for at least two reasons. First, groups that lack states sometimes harbor nationalistic aims; indeed, the argument for statehood often rests on the premise of nationhood. Second, many states today are multinational. A multinational state does not consist of a single group of the sort implied by the idea of a nation.

Nations are groups of a certain kind. But what kind? Much has been written about what makes for nationhood: whether it is common territory, bloodlines, ethnicity, language, religion, common belief. Hobsbawm, among others, has shown the inadequacy of any of the objective criteria if seen as definitive. Taking a plausible candidate such as language, for example, he points out that in 1789 only 50 percent of French people spoke French and that at the moment of Italian unification in 1860 only 2.5 percent of Italians spoke Italian! National languages are more often the consequence of nationalistic efforts than their foundation.[3] Some deny that any such objective criteria are sufficient, or even necessary, to define nationhood and instead emphasize mutual recognition and the belief that one belongs to the group.

Yet despite the importance of subjective elements, defining "nationalism" solely in terms of them seems incomplete, perhaps because the subjective connection is usually rooted in objective ones. For practical purposes, however, we can adopt Hobsbawm's "initial working assumption" that "any sufficiently large body of people whose members regard themselves as members of a 'nation'" are a nation.[4] But several further observations are important.

Our most common experience of nationalism today is of groups whose identity is connected to their ethnicity. And it is at least in part because it is not obvious how to avoid the slippery slope from ethnic identification to racism that many find nationalism troubling. It seems odd, furthermore, that ethnic identification can flourish where the distinction between "us" and "them" is hard for the outsider to observe.[5] Perhaps the explanation is that, like adolescents rebelling against their parents, people must struggle hardest to establish their identity when it is prone to confusion with that of others.

At the same time, nationalism need not take this ethnic/quasi-racial form.[6] The United States provides a clear example. It has no distinctive ethnic identity; indeed, its identity consists partly in its pluralistic mix. And despite its white Northern European roots, a legacy of racism, and an overwhelmingly Christian population, a certain kind of pluralism is important to its identity, and increasingly so. The United States as a nation is defined by a conjunction of its political culture and its larger culture, which possesses a distinctive character assimilable by people from a wide variety of ethnic backgrounds.

The example of the United States supports the view that a nation is best understood as a culture. This is not terribly illuminating, perhaps, because it isn't transparently clear what a culture is. (I shall not try to define it here.) Still, we have a good intuitive grasp of the concept—better than we do of "nation," which, as I have argued, is easily confused with "state." Cultures are often rooted in ethnic ties, but they need not be. Nationalists, we may then say, are those who aim for expression of their culture—although just what form this expression must take we shall leave open for now. When nationalists succeed in getting secure states, we tend to call the phenomenon "patriotism" rather than "nationalism."

The defense of nationalism can be understood in terms of five central arguments, distinct although not always distinguished or easily disentangled. They are:

1. The Flourishing Argument: the belief that human beings need to belong to or identify with some group beyond their immediate family or, in any case, that they flourish when they do.
2. The Self-Determination Argument: the claim that individuals possess a moral right, or that morally it is desirable for them to be able, to form self-governing associations with others of their choosing.

3. The Reparations Argument: the idea that nationhood is a means of rectifying historical grievances, of righting old wrongs.

4. The Pluralism Argument: the view that the world is a better or more interesting place if it contains diverse cultures. Even if some cultures are correctly judged superior to others, a diverse world is better than a homogeneous world.

5. The Intrinsic Value Argument: the view that the existence of a given culture is a good that ought to be promoted. In contrast with the Pluralism Argument, here a culture ought to exist and flourish because of its *particular* value.

These five grounds constitute an attempt both to justify nationalism rationally and, in some cases at least, to explain its actual appeal to people. I shall examine them in turn.

Let us concentrate on a common understanding of the Flourishing Argument: the psychological claim, often taken as self-evident, that people need to identify with or belong to some group beyond their immediate family.[7] Obviously, a judgment of this sort does not lend itself to straightforward empirical verification; more often than not, the judgment is rendered with nothing but anecdotes by way of support. Yet it seems to many to capture something undeniable.

Much depends on how we understand identification or belonging. I am (among other things) a woman, a mother, a wife, a Jew, a New Yorker, an American, a philosopher, a baby boomer, a teacher, a music lover, and a jogger. Only some of these groups satisfy the criteria relevant to national belonging. It isn't helpful to say the relevant categories are *social* groups; that only begs the question. We tend to think of the relevant kind of belonging as unchosen—as gender, ethnicity, and sexual orientation are conventionally thought to be—but this is more complicated than it appears.[8] Must I take pride in such connections? Does identification mean identity—that I would not be me were I not American, Jewish, or whatever?[9] Does it mean that I would act (even die) for my group as I would for myself? Or may it be something less than this? To what extent does the need to belong involve hostility to outsiders? Those who appeal to the centrality of belonging owe us answers to these questions.

Defenders of the Flourishing Argument must confront the question: Why not the human race as the object of identification? Humankind is too large, it seems, and presumably too indistinct to lend itself to the appropriate feelings. But are nations small and differentiated enough to serve the purpose? The idea that one can identify with 260 million Americans but not with 5 billion human beings may seem implausible. We can appreciate the significance of the line between those with whom one has face-to-face relations and those with whom one does not. Even if we expand the circle to a larger community, it is hard to see how it can be extended to many millions of people and still serve the functions the Flourishing Argument emphasizes.

One response to this skeptical line is to distinguish two features of groups conflated in the argument. One is the absolute size of the group, the second its differences from other groups. So, for example, it has been said that the invasion of Earth by alien creatures might produce that human-to-human bond that has so far been wanting. We do not identify with the human race now because it's the only race there is.[10]

How far does this response go in allaying doubts about the explanatory power of identification with very large groups? It is difficult to answer this question without a fuller appreciation of the ways belonging to groups is supposed to contribute to human well-being. To the extent that mere differentiation is key, identification with hundreds of millions of people could serve the purpose. But presumably belonging serves goals besides allowing people to distinguish themselves from *some* others. To that extent, the foregoing criticism stands.

So far our discussion has centered on the *object* of identification. But there are also questions about the *subject*—about the universality of the need to identify with or belong to a nationlike entity or about the extent to which such identification contributes to a person's flourishing. Surely some people feel such a need; the persistence of ethnic, religious, racial, and national loyalties perhaps serves as proof. But it is probably safe to say that others do not. Is it simply that the former so outnumber the latter? Or are they merely that much more zealous? To what extent is the need to belong alterable—subject to social influence?

Clearly, the Flourishing Argument is central and requires a deeper analysis than is possible here. We will return to some of the questions raised in this section in the discussion of Partiality toward Members. But here two points are important. First, much of the force of the argument depends on psychological claims that are difficult to make precise and to which no one has hard answers. It is easy to be dismissive, raising eyebrows at the vagueness and lack of hard evidence or arguing (as philosophers are wont to do) that these are empirical questions that normative treatments have to ignore. They *are* empirical questions, of course, but ones that no one interested in nationalism can reasonably neglect. And although the issues are not sharp, we cannot hope to resolve the political and philosophical questions without a better understanding of them.

Second, although it is hard to doubt that there is some truth in the Flourishing Argument—that most people need to belong to or identify with certain kinds of social groups—the crucial question is what follows with respect to forms of political organization. In part, this is a matter of fleshing out answers to the questions: "Belong in what sense?" and "Identify how?" However we answer these questions, there is a very large leap between the claim that people need to belong to groups and the conclusion that nationalism is either inevitable or desirable.

According to the Self-Determination Argument, individuals have the moral right, or morally ought to be able, to form self-governing associations with others of their choosing. National self-determination can be understood both by analogy with and as deriving from individual self-determination. In the latter sense, nations are collections of individuals who are entitled to determine their individual lives; when such individuals form groups their entitlements transfer to the group. If we understand individual rights in this way, we can see the connection between national self-determination and prized liberal values such as autonomy, liberty, and democracy. On the other hand, insofar as we acknowledge the existence of groups not wholly reducible to individuals and group rights and goods not wholly reducible to individual rights and goods, then groups may be thought to possess the right of self-determination "in their own right," so to speak. The power and plausibility of this latter view derive, I believe, from the Pluralism Argument or from the Intrinsic Value Argument. To say that the group ought to be able to determine its own course, if this is not a statement about the joint entitlements of the member individuals, is to make a judgment either about the culture's intrinsic appeal or else about the value of pluralism and diversity. I shall say more about these below.

Let us focus here, then, on the argument from self-determination rooted in the individualistic values of autonomy, liberty, and democracy. The appeal of this view can be reconstructed as follows. Individuals should be free to choose those with whom they will share their lives. If I don't want to live in a household or even in a society with certain others, I am free to leave, barring my having undertaken obligations that I may not simply renounce. If I can get others to agree to live with me—in a household or in some other voluntary association—I may do so. In the ideal case we can imagine multiple self-contained voluntary societies of self-governing individuals. This libertarian picture of human assocation has its attractions.[11] And it is, I think, part of the appeal of nationalism, despite its remoteness from many of the concrete nationalisms familiar to us.

One problem with this view is that we do not ordinarily choose our nationality in the way we choose our political affiliation or our profession. So the implication of voluntariness in self-determination does not seem to fit with the nature of national belonging. Still, one may choose to affirm one's nationality. That is precisely what the nationalist does, and this choosing may be thought to confer the appropriately voluntary character on nationalistic belonging.

Another apparent anomaly in the Self-Determination Argument is that the values it celebrates are often not upheld by nationalistic movements, which can be autocratic and oppressive. The contradiction is not as blatant as it appears, however, for insofar as people identify with their nation's leaders, they see these leaders as part of themselves, or vice versa. To that extent, this rule *is* self-rule. It is in virtue of this fact that we can explain why "men prefer to be ordered about, even if this entails ill-treatment, by members of their own faith or nation or class, to tutelage, however benevolent, on the part of ultimately patronising superiors from a foreign land or alien class or milieu."[12]

The deeper problem with the Self-Determination Argument emerges when we press for details. You may leave your country—but where will you go? You may form your own society—but where will you put it? Emigration is (for liberals) uncontroversial; but immigration is not. Similarly, secession may in principle seem unproblematic—"If a group decides it wants to secede, it should be able to; after all, people should be able to determine their own destiny"—until we realize that the group plans to take some land with them. The Self-Determination Argument is only as convincing, then, as the case for linking nationalism with the "territorial imperative."

The Reparations Argument is tied to self-determination but goes a step further. When a culture has been conquered or colonized by outsiders, when it has lost land or its members have been displaced, it may assert its right to be free of the yoke of oppression. As part of determining its own destiny, it may insist on the return of "the land of our forefathers," harking back to a time before the group was dispossessed of its rightful territory. For nationalists in quest of a state, this sense of historical grievance and the urgent need to right old wrongs is never far from the surface.

So, according to this view, at some past time the nation had land and a state and was wrongfully deprived of them. Often we can question whether such a golden age ever existed. As Ernest Renan remarked, "Getting its history wrong is part of being a nation."[13] But even when we agree that the nation got its history right, we might dispute the claim to reparations on the ground that too many events had intervened that extinguished or counteracted the claim. How are we to adjudicate the conflicting claims of groups to have been wronged years ago? The answer depends on whether the supposed injustice was real and significant, as well as on how much time has elapsed. Speaking generally, we can only say that sometimes reparations are appropriate and practical, sometimes not.[14]

In one sense, the appeal to reparations is not an argument for nationalism; it already presupposes the existence of a nation to which something is owed. Only when a group of the requisite sort exists or is believed to exist does the claim of reparations to it makes sense. At the same time, insofar as we identify nationalism with the territorial aim, we might view the appeal to reparations as an argument for nationalism. We find ourselves again confronting the Territory Question.

The Pluralism Argument and the Intrinsic Value Argument lead to the same door. The virtues of these arguments can perhaps be taken as obvious. Diversity and variety are good, other things being equal; a world of diverse cultures and styles is better and more interesting than a less diverse world. Given that a culture meets certain minimum moral standards, it is better for that culture to exist than not to. Over and above the value of diversity, some cultures possess qualities that are intrinsically valuable, morally or aesthetically. Their existence enhances the world. Of course, most cultures possess negative as well as positive qualities.

When the overall worth of the culture is positive, we have reason beyond the value of pluralism to promote that culture's existence and flourishing; the greater the overall intrinsic value of the culture, the more reason we have.[15]

The question, however, is what sort of entity we ought to promote if our goal is to foster the existence and flourishing of cultures. More specifically, should we promote the existence of nation-*states* as the embodiment of cultures that are valuable in their own right or that enhance diversity?

We saw earlier that Gellner, Hobsbawm, and others *define* nationalism as the view that "the political and the national unit should be congruent." And others, like Tamir, arguing that "it is the cultural rather than the political version of nationalism that best accords with a liberal viewpoint," sever the connection between nation and territory.[16] Tamir explicitly rejects the suggestion that instead of nationalism she choose a "less emotionally loaded term, such as 'people' or the much discussed 'community.'" She does not want to cede the concept of nationalism to conservative, reactionary, or racist political forces, she says, and she believes that rejecting the term "nationalism" means alienating oneself "from a whole set of values that are of immense importance to a great many people, including liberals."[17]

What matters, finally, are not the labels we use, although battles over terminology are not insignificant, especially where explosive terms like "nationalism" are concerned. But the important question is a substantive one. Can a culture secure those values it deserves to secure in the absence of a territorial state? The answer seems to be that some cultures can and some cannot.

Michael Ignatieff, criticizing Tamir's severing of the link between nation and territory, argues: "People seek nation-states of their own because they believe that these entities alone will protect them from the violence and the intimidation of their neighbors." Perhaps this is a generous view of the nationalistic impulse; some nationalists probably have more ambitious, and less defensible, aims. And some who fit Ignatieff's description may be mistaken or self-deceived in believing that a territorial state is the only way to protect their rights. Still, we can agree that a people may reasonably demand a state when they "have good reason to believe that statehood is their only security for the future."[18]

Taken as necessary and sufficient for justifying statehood, Ignatieff's criterion is at the same time demanding and modest: demanding insofar as a people must show that their very security depends on having a state; modest as it acknowledges no value more robust than security to justify statehood. But an important assumption is left only implicit in this view. For if a *people* has reason to believe that its only security lies in statehood, then it must be *as* a people that its security is threatened. It is not simply that individuals are endangered but that they are endangered *because* of their "peoplehood"—because they are Bosnian Muslims or Armenians or Kurds. At the same time, Ignatieff's view suggests that it is the basic physical security of individuals that serves as warrant for statehood.

Avishai Margalit and Joseph Raz defend a more robust view. They make a case for statehood (or what they call self-determination) when necessary to "protect the culture and self-respect" of the group.[19] Here it is not just that individuals are endangered because they belong to a certain group but that the existence of the group qua group is endangered. It follows that the culture itself is valuable and deserves protection and respect. And because its members' identity is tied up with the culture, their self-respect rises and falls accordingly.

Just what is required to protect the culture and self-respect of the group? There is no single or straightforward answer to this question. Still, we might assent provisionally to the following view: cultures have a strong claim to their own states when that is the only way they can protect their members' basic rights and interests and valuable characteristics of the culture itself.

Claims to statehood encounter two major problems. Both are in some sense practical, as opposed to philosophical or moral, problems, but they are deep practical problems. One is that all territory on the earth is already taken. (Were this not so, claims to statehood might almost be simple—except for the second problem below.) Thus claims to territory never go uncontested. Secession and the creation of new states can never be simple matters, for the property and other claims of the existing state and its members will have their merits, even when the culture demanding statehood has right and justice on its side. Complex negotiations, compromises, and agreements will always be necessary.[20]

The other difficulty is what Tamir aptly calls the "Russian doll phenomenon": "Every 'national territory,' however small, includes among its inhabitants members of other nations."[21] If every culture had, by the very fact of its being a culture (however this were determined), a right to statehood, we could face a practically infinite regress of states of diminishing size. This is not merely a serious obstacle to statehood. It seems a sufficient reason to deny that cultures per se have a right to statehood. To make the case for statehood, a culture must provide very good reasons why it *needs* a state. And to persuade us, an aspiring nation-state must also give assurances that it will not do to little nations within it what was done to *it* when it was a little nation within some other large state. Without such assurances it should not become a state.

But what may a nation-state not do to little nations within it (and to others outside)? And what must it allow *them* to do by way of affirming *their* culture? This brings us to some of the hardest questions, morally and philosophically, about nationalism.

What I am calling the Partiality Question encompasses two related but distinct issues. One, which we can call Partiality toward Members, is expressed in the questions: In what way and to what extent does nationalism warrant a person or group's favoring compatriots over nonmembers? Are there different conceptions of nationalism with different understandings of the meaning of partiality, some more palatable than others? These questions were left unresolved in the discussion of the Flourishing Argument.

The other issue emerged most clearly in the last section and is prominent in contemporary discussions of multiculturalism—the form nationalism takes when stripped of the territorial component. How and to what extent may a nation— that is, a culture—privilege its own traits and practices over those of other cultures within its borders? We can call this issue Partiality toward Practices. In this and the next section, I consider Partiality toward Members; in the last section, Partiality toward Practices.

How and to what extent may one favor members of one's nation over others? In trying to tame this question, we immediately fall back on the analogy with family. In myriad ways people favor members of their own family over nonmembers, and we cannot imagine things being different. The nationalist claims that partiality toward compatriots can be similarly grounded.

What is the grounding? In the case of the family, we might say two things. First, the emotional and psychological needs met by intimate familial relationships are among the most important we can imagine, and a form of social organization that did not allow for the flourishing of such relationships would be impoverished. Second, at least partly for this reason, a world organized into family units, in which people are committed to a small number of others with whom they have deep emotional and even biological connections, works better than other forms of organization to ensure people's basic well-being.

Can similar things be said about the relationships among members of a culture or nation? Let us take the second point first. Does a world of nations better secure people's well-being, on the whole, than some alternative arrangement? The blood that has been shed for the cause of nationalism is a central reason for doubting that it does. But it does not follow that all distinctions between people beyond the level of family should be abolished—that it would make sense, even in theory, to work toward a world of families, with no intermediate forms of association. For many reasons, the world demands a complex and multilevel structure of organization.

In some way, shape, or form, then, intermediate forms of association—states, cultures, tribes—must exist. They are practically necessary; they make the world a more diverse and interesting place; and—assuming some truth in the Flourishing Argument—they satisfy some important human needs. The question is what form the kind of loyalty and partiality bred by group belonging takes or must take. How great are the risks that it will degenerate into violence, xenophobia, and hatred? Obviously, this is a complex empirical question; I doubt that good answers are available. Is there anything constructive we can say about it? What weaker forms of loyalty and partiality can still be appropriately described in terms of nationalism?

Here are two different ways members of a culture might view themselves in relation to outsiders: (1) "We're superior. The world would be a better place if we dominated over others. We count more than they do." (2) "We're partial to our own. But we do not claim that we're better than anybody else; we expect members of other cultures to be partial to their own, too." Now it is clear how the first of these stances—a kind of egoistic partiality—can lead to hatred and violence and to the kind of fascism and racism with which nationalism is sometimes associated. But the second, universalized partiality could also lead to hatred and violence. People might have sufficient perspective to recognize that their commitment to their culture stems from its being *theirs* rather than from its inherent superiority, but this perspective might not moderate their zealousness. Such a stance might amount to abdicating judgment and the need for justification—to admitting that one has no justification for preferring one's own people, that one *just does*. But it need not be simply a denial of the need for justification. A person might defend this view by appeal to the Flourishing Argument: Everyone needs to identify with or belong to a group, and this justifies partiality, even though it justifies partiality equally among all groups.

One manifestation of this universalized partiality is expressed in "my country right or wrong." This slogan is often taken to assert the value of loyalty, which is inherent in the commitment to nationalism. But despite its familiarity, the slogan's meaning is not clear. The usual interpretation is that one should *defend* one's country no matter what it does. And that may seem persuasive because we imagine abandonment as the alternative. That this is a false dilemma becomes clear if we consider again the analogy of the family.

Suppose that my brother is accused of a serious crime, which he has in fact committed. Loyalty to my brother, in any sense worth valuing, does not require that I defend him—that is, insist on his innocence—no matter what the evidence or the truth of the matter. It may require that I stand by him; that I give him what resources I possess, consistent with the moral situation; that I help him to work through his guilt and suffering, help him to change himself. These demands on me may flow from my sense of identification with and connection to my brother. Similarly, loyalty to one's country might require that one stand by it, in much the same way; that one own up to one's connection and do what one can to set one's country straight. But this in no way implies that one must defend one's country no matter what it does.[22] And in the rare case where one's country, or one's brother, shows itself to be irredeemable, then abandonment may be the only acceptable course.[23]

Morally speaking, then, loyalty cannot be altogether content-neutral, blind to the nature of its object. But the hard case arises when one's own group is (for the most part) morally good enough, but so are outsiders. What form and degree of partiality toward members over nonmembers can be justified in this case?

We can simplify by stating the case in terms of negative and positive duties. Negative duties are duties of noninterference and nonaggression; positive duties are duties to aid and provide the means of well-being. One common approach is to argue that although people have negative duties to human beings in general, positive duties are incurred in virtue of particular acts, general agreements, or special relationships (of the kind one has to family members or fellow nationals).[24] Even many who would not defend this distinction in its pure form accept it as a rough practical guide.

Although I do not accept this view—because I believe one can have unincurred positive duties[25]—I believe it is important to see its implications for nationalism. On the one hand, it clearly prohibits aggression—and therefore, it seems, the kind of hatred and violence often associated with nationalism. Looked at in this way, this view might seem adequate to a moderate nationalism. Yet the laissez-faire attitude to strangers it endorses can turn to hostility at the slightest provocation. (And we know that often the provocations are not slight.) In part, this is because the duty of nonaggression is compatible with the right of self-defense; when strangers threaten one's security, or seem to, and when no positive ties bind the feuding parties, benign neglect easily turns to malign aggression. I believe that the framework of positive duties to members and only negative duties to strangers captures the psychology of a common variety of nationalism that stops short of fanaticism but nevertheless encourages a hostile and stereotyped view of outsiders.

Let me end this section with several points about the question of partiality toward members, construed in terms of negative and positive duties. The first is simply that the question whether we have unincurred positive duties is a deep and controversial one. Second, even if positive duties are always incurred by acts, agreements, or relationships, it doesn't follow that we have none to other nations or cultures. We do, and more every day.[26] This is even more true when members of different cultures reside within the same state. Thus we probably have duties to nonmembers within our state that are different from, and more extensive than, those to strangers outside.

Third, even assuming the foregoing framework, there is no consensus about how much we owe to members of our *own* culture. Two people who adhere to a nationalism that distinguishes positive duties to members and nonmembers could still disagree sharply about how much is owed to each.

A final point about the relevance of Partiality toward Members to nationalism returns us to some basic questions raised earlier. Nationalism is one form of groupism involving loyalty and partiality. But many other kinds of groups produce the same result. Evidence both anecdotal and experimental strongly suggests that people will form loyalties to artificially created groups, even those without characteristics significantly different from out-groups.[27] To the extent that loyalty and partiality occur wherever we find groups, any system of global political organization that subdivides people into smaller units than "human being"—that is, any viable system—will produce loyalties with their attendant problems.

This need not be as depressing as it sounds. Whether it is or not depends on whether Partiality toward Members must mean genuine hostility toward nonmembers or simply a differential of concern. We can assume, I think, that it does not *have* to mean hostility, even if all too often that is what we find. My special commitment to my family does not mean I dislike other families, nor even that I am unwilling to share resources with them. So even if national or other similar loyalties were inevitable, there is on the face of it no reason to think they must produce hostility or lack of concern for the welfare of other groups. The implication of the Robbers Cave experiment could be key: hostility declines where groups stand to gain by cooperation.

As we have seen, in our world not every nation—not every culture—can or ought to have its own state. But cultures that lack their own states or coexist with other cultures within a state also seek public self-expression. Questions about the legitimate constraints and powers of such cultures are therefore central.

"Culturalism," as we might infelicitously call this view, avoids the Territory Question, but it is saddled with the Partiality Question just as traditional nationalism is. Even more so, because in the multicultural state different cultures live in closer proximity (politically if not geographically) than in the pure, if idealized, homogeneous nation-state. In multicultural societies, the need for policies concerning the practices, within the public space, of both the dominant culture and minority cultures is the norm.

This brings us to the array of questions about multiculturalism that have recently become familiar. I cannot discuss them in detail here and shall try only to tie together some of the threads left unraveled in the foregoing discussion. The problem is to find our way from claims that seem uncontroversial: that generally it is good for individuals to be able to express their cultural commitments publicly and for cultures to survive and flourish. To what extent do these apparently innocuous assumptions explode in practice? The problem expresses itself in two ways, which are two sides of the same coin. There is the nationalism of those who have succeeded in securing a state, or at least dominance within one, and the nationalism of those—within this state but having a different culture—who have not. The questions are what legitimate claims each of these groups has and what to do when they clash.

One difficult issue concerns language.[28] Language is central to culture and to individual identity. Does the public life of a society require *a* language—or can it manage with two? More than two? May the dominant culture insist that everyone learn its language, whatever other language they learn? Suppose we ask whether members of a minority culture have a right to keep their culture alive by having its language taught. The answer depends partly on how such a right is understood. Would it be satisfied if members of the culture sent their children to private schools that teach the language? Few would dispute the right so conceived. But perhaps the question is whether the public schools ought to teach the language, perhaps even as the primary language. Surely not every (minority) culture has such a right as a matter of course.

Is the reason just that the acknowledgment of such a right is too impractical? At this point, the distinction between practicality and principle is hard to draw. But perhaps we can find a line. The dominant culture could have two different sorts of reasons for insisting that those within its borders who go to its schools learn, say, English. It could say: "This is an English-speaking culture, and we want to keep it that way. If you come here, you implicitly agree to participate in our culture." In that case the reasons for insisting all learn English are in some sense culturally biased—rooted in the particular traits or virtues of that culture. But the culture could instead argue: "As a matter of fact, you can't get along in this society without speaking English, just as you can't get along with knowing arithmetic. Therefore, it is our responsibility to make sure that you learn English." The latter is a neutral reason, it might be argued, that does not involve the domineering suppression of one culture at the hands of another. There's nothing special about English; it just happens to be the language spoken here.

We may suspect that, even when only the second kind of reason is expressed and even if it is sufficient to justify the imposition of language, the first lurks in the background. U.S. school districts with large Spanish-speaking constituencies might validly argue that a person needs English to get along in this society, but the less neutral reason would probably emerge if push came to shove: "This is our society, an English-speaking society, and we want to keep it that way."

Is this argument sound? If we admit that the minority culture has a legitimate claim to keep itself alive—if it may say, "We are valuable and want to maintain ourselves," and if this is precisely one of the legitimate appeals of nationalism—so, too, does the dominant culture. In principle, then, it is legitimate for the dominant culture to argue that things be done its way. A central question, however, is whether public support for the minority culture's language or other practices actually poses a threat to the dominant culture. When it does, the argument is legitimate. When it doesn't, the issue is more complex.[29]

Examples such as Quebec suggest that talk of the dominant culture and minority cultures needs further refining. What makes the argument for French-speaking education in Quebec plausible is that while countrywide the dominant culture is English-speaking, in a significant, well-defined region the majority culture is French-speaking.[30] So a great deal depends on how large a slice of the territory we look at.

How large a slice of the territory *should* we look at? And what other criteria should be required for a culture to make a successful claim? For a culture within a larger culture to make the case for the privileging of such crucial traits as language, it should satisfy several conditions: it should have majority status (and perhaps more) within its territory, some measure of self-sufficiency, and historical rootedness in the territory. But generalizations are risky; every case brings its own peculiar circumstances.

If the privileging of some cultural traits is an inescapable fact of public life, what are the consequences for the view that members of cultures or even cultures as a whole ought to be able to express themselves publicly? The latter view cannot mean, I have been arguing, that every (minority) culture in a society can claim equal footing with the dominant culture in matters such as language. What, then, does it mean?

First, we should note that the example of language is atypical both because it is absolutely central to cultural identification and because no society can be neutral with respect to it. Other cultural traits and practices—even central ones like religion—are less domineering, allowing for greater equality and diversity among cultures coexisting in a society. I would argue that insofar as the dominant culture can reasonably avoid privileging its peculiar traits and practices, it ought to do so. Now clearly this raises questions, currently much debated, about the extent to which a society (or a liberal society) can, or ought, to be neutral toward conceptions of the good. I do not mean to presuppose an answer to these questions here. But many of the issues confronting us about the survival and flourishing of cultures do not go so deep as to reach conceptions of the good in any interesting sense, even if some of them do. (There are enough mountains without making molehills into them.)

Let me make two further suggestions about how the claims of cultures to survive and flourish can be met, short of secession and statehood, in the face of a dominant culture. One is that in many cases negative duties—here in the form of nonpersecution—go a long way. To be allowed to practice one's culture, in the small and quasi-public ways most people typically do, and not be mistreated for belonging to a certain group is more than many peoples have enjoyed and as much as they would ask for. There are places where these seemingly modest goals cannot be met without statehood. But in many multicultural societies, nonpersecution is a possibility, even a fact.

Still, even in those societies, something more than the absence of persecution may be wanted. People, and peoples, want not simply to be allowed to practice their culture; they want its virtues to be recognized as valuable and its contributions represented in the public life of the society. How these desires can and should be met is a source of much discussion and disagreement. It is worth pointing out, however, that insofar as we incorporate the contributions of minority cultures into our public life (for example, in public education), we erode the boundaries between cultures—often artificial to begin with—that ground discussions of nationalism. We are then in the process of creating new cultures out of old ones. This should not be surprising; despite the grooves that the idea of nationalism has etched in our thinking, cultures are not static entities impervious to change.

Seen in this way, multiculturalism might be said to take from nationalism what is good, and turn it to cosmopolitan purposes.

NOTES

I have benefited from the comments and criticisms of many people on earlier drafts of this essay, among them participants in the University of Illinois at Urbana-Champaign Conference on the Ethics of Nationalism, the Yale Political Theory Workshop, and the New York University School of Law International Jurisprudence Colloquium, and colleagues at the Institute for Philosophy and Public Policy. In particular I would like to thank Lea Brilmayer, Robert Lane, David Luban, Stephen Nathanson, my commentator at the Illinois conference, and Jeff McMahan and Robert McKim, the organizers of the conference.

1. See, for example, Liah Greenfeld, *Nationalism: Five Roads to Modernity* (Cambridge, Mass.: Harvard University Press, 1992); Yael Tamir, *Liberal Nationalism* (Princeton: Princeton University Press, 1993); Avishai Margalit and Joseph Raz, "National Self-Determination," *Journal of Philosophy* 87 (1990); and Stephen Nathanson, *Patriotism, Morality, and Peace* (Lanham, Md.: Rowman and Littlefield, 1993).

2. Ernest Gellner, *Nations and Nationalism* (Ithaca: Cornell University Press, 1983), p. 1; E. J. Hobsbawm, *Nations and Nationalism since 1780: Programme, Myth, Reality*, 2d ed. (Cambridge: Cambridge University Press, 1992), p. 9.

3. Hobsbawm, *Nations and Nationalism*, pp. 51–63.

4. Ibid., p. 8.

5. Among those who have made this point are Michael Ignatieff, *Blood and Belonging: Journeys into the New Nationalism* (New York: Farrar, Straus, and Giroux, 1994).

6. Some, like Walker Connor, define nationalism as ethnonationalism. His reasons are interesting and illuminating but not, I think, decisive. See *Ethnonationalism* (Princeton: Princeton University Press, 1994). For the distinction between ethnic and civic nationalism, see Greenfeld, *Nationalism*, pp. 9–12, and Rogers Brubaker, *Citizenship and Nationhood in France and Germany* (Cambridge, Mass.: Harvard University Press, 1992), a study of two exemplars: French civic nationalism and German ethnic nationalism.

7. For a discussion of this view and its roots in the thought of Johann Gottfried Herder, see Isaiah Berlin, "The Bent Twig: On the Rise of Nationalism," in *The Crooked Timber of Humanity: Chapters in the History of Ideas* (New York: Knopf, 1991), esp. pp. 243–47. This sort of "groupism" or "tribalism" is of course much broader than nationalism, encompassing other phenomena as well. See further discussion of this issue later in this chapter. I suspect that moral philosophers are primarily interested in this larger question of group identity, while more historically minded thinkers are concerned with those features of nationalism peculiar to the modern period when nationalist movements developed. This may sometimes lead to misunderstandings and talking at cross-purposes, as became clear at the conference out of which this collection of essays grew.

For a discussion of the "modernist" and "perennialist" understandings of nationhood—and the defense of a middle ground—see Anthony D. Smith, *The Ethnic Origins of Nations* (Oxford: Blackwell, 1986), chap. 1.

8. For an interesting discussion, see Mary C. Waters, *Ethnic Options: Choosing Identities in America* (Berkeley: University of California Press, 1990). The dilemmas faced by blacks and members of other minorities for whom "passing" is an option illustrate the complexities of this issue.

9. For a defense of this view, see Michael Sandel, *Liberalism and the Limits of Justice*

(Cambridge: Cambridge University Press, 1982). Against it, see David Luban, "The Self: Metaphysical Not Political," *Legal Theory* 4 (1995): 401–37.

10. Jeff McMahan helped me to clarify some of the ideas in these paragraphs.

11. See Robert Nozick, *Anarchy, State, and Utopia* (New York: Basic Books, 1974), the last section especially, for a utopia of this kind.

12. Berlin, "The Bent Twig," p. 251.

13. "Qu'est ce que c'est une nation?," Conference at the Sorbonne, March 11, Paris, 1882, pp. 7–8, quoted in Hobsbawm, *Nations and Nationalism*, p. 12.

14. For an argument attempting to show that plausible nationalist claims are commonly claims of reparations for past injustice—colonialism and other illegitimate appropriation of territory—see Lea A. Brilmayer, "Is Nationalism Irrelevant?," paper presented at the American Philosophical Association, Pacific Division Meetings, March 1995, and "Secession and Self-Determination: A Territorial Interpretation," *Yale Journal of International Law* 16, no. 1 (January 1991).

15. Obviously, this is a vast oversimplification. I have not said how we decide which qualities are good and which are bad or how we weigh the good against the bad. In addition, there are questions about whether or when you must take the good with the bad or whether you can purge the bad and keep the good without destroying the culture. I shall not elaborate on these questions here. These are enormous issues in their own right, but I do not think that different answers affect the course of my argument.

16. Tamir, *Liberal Nationalism*, p. 58.

17. Ibid., p. 5.

18. Michael Ignatieff, "Boundaries of Pain," *New Republic*, November 1, 1993, p. 38. Statehood, he continues, must be justified prospectively, not as reparations for past suffering.

19. Margalit and Raz, "National Self-Determination," p. 457. Their criterion applies to what they call "encompassing groups," which correspond closely to what I have called "cultures" and what can also be called "peoples." See pp. 442–47 for a discussion of the characteristics of encompassing groups that illuminates the concepts of culture and people. Margalit and Raz qualify the case for statehood in two ways. The new state must be "likely to respect the fundamental interests of its inhabitants" (presumably minorities as well as its own people), and measures must be taken to "prevent its creation from gravely damaging the just interests of other countries" (p. 457).

20. For a discussion of these problems, see Allen Buchanan, *Secession: The Morality of Political Divorce from Fort Sumter to Lithuania and Quebec* (Boulder, Colo.: Westview, 1991), esp. chap. 3.

21. Tamir, *Liberal Nationalism*, p. 158.

22. It has been observed that a near-universal response among Jews to the Hebron massacre was shame, which implies this kind of identification: it is impossible to feel shame without feeling that you are connected to the person or group committing the act, so that in some sense when the person or group acts, you act. The same can be said of pride. But suppose I am an American who opposed the Vietnam War. Ought I to have felt shame at my country's actions? Embarrassment would be understandable, but shame seems to suggest some element of responsibility. This much, at least, seems plausible: to feel shame is to feel partly responsible; whether that feeling is well founded is another question.

For a persuasive defense of "moderate patriotism," which rejects "my country right or wrong" and justifies the sort of criticism described here, see Nathanson, *Patriotism, Morality, and Peace*, chaps. 3 and 4.

23. One might ask whether abandonment is even a possibility. Is it possible to disown the connection between oneself and one's family or one's nation? We might say that there is a sense in which one cannot, that these identities are not chosen and cannot be unchosen. But of course in another sense one can; one can renounce one's citizenship, for example.

24. Of course, we can imagine an even stronger view: that one owes nothing at all to people in general; that to strangers one does not even bear the negative duty of nonaggression. There are, no doubt, nationalists who hold this view. With them, discussion is pointless.

25. See my "The Moral Equivalence of Action and Omission," *Canadian Journal of Philosophy*, supplementary volume 8 (1982), reprinted in *Killing and Letting Die*, ed. Bonnie Steinbock and Alastair Norcross, 2d ed. (New York: Fordham University Press, 1994).

26. I have made this argument in more detail in "National Boundaries and Moral Boundaries: A Cosmopolitan View," in *Boundaries: National Autonomy and Its Limits*, ed. Peter G. Brown and Henry Shue (Totowa, N.J.: Rowman and Littlefield, 1981).

27. The anecdotal evidence includes loyalty to sports teams, residential colleges within a university, and fraternities and sororities. For interesting experimental evidence, see, for example, Muzafer Sherif et al., *The Robbers Cave Experiment: Intergroup Conflict and Cooperation* (Middletown, Conn.: Wesleyan University Press, 1988), originally published in 1961. Two in-groups, not significantly distinguishable, were formed in a boys' summer camp setting. After relationships developed within each in-group, groups were brought together under competitive conditions where one group's victory meant loss for the other. The results were frustration, hostile acts, and derogatory stereotypes against the other group. In a third stage, conflict was reduced by the introduction of "superordinate goals": goals that both groups shared and that could be achieved only through cooperation.

28. My thinking about these questions was stimulated partly by Charles Taylor's discussion of language questions in Quebec in *Multiculturalism and "The Politics of Recognition,"* ed. Amy Gutmann (Princeton: Princeton University Press, 1992). For a good discussion, see Will Kymlicka, *Liberalism, Community, and Culture* (New York: Oxford University Press, 1989), esp. chaps. 7–9.

29. So, for example, American culture is not threatened by the cultural practices of the Amish, and for that reason we may be sympathetic to Amish arguments for cultural protection. A relevant question concerns the minority culture's alternatives. The legitimacy of the argument: "This is my ... [house, land, country]; if you don't want to do things my way, you can get your own ... " depends partly on whether the person, or culture, addressed has such options. In a world where all land is spoken for, the argument possesses less force.

30. And, furthermore, as the Quebecois argue, the risk to French language and culture comes not just from Anglophone Canada but also from the behemoth of U.S. culture that threatens to swallow up North America.

11

Nationalism and the Limits of Global Humanism

STEPHEN NATHANSON

Can nationalism be good? Many people think not. They link nationalism with violence, hatred, racism, and xenophobia. These links are not just the products of overheated imaginations or paranoiac worries. They are real, and they make it easy to see why some people reject all forms of nationalism as immoral, illegitimate, and undesirable.

But what are the alternatives to a world of nations? The most obvious alternative is a unified world, one in which human beings transcend national differences and organize themselves on the basis of their shared humanity with all people. This is the ideal of global humanists.

It is easy to see why humane people would find the global humanist perspective more attractive than nationalism. For globalists, the violence, hatred, and destruction that nationalism spawns can be avoided only by doing away with nationalism itself. In the ideal world of the global humanist, no attention would be paid to the differences between people that nationalists treat as having ultimate significance.

For all of its appeal, the global humanist position has its own difficulties. I shall try to show in this essay that there are strong arguments for the legitimacy of some nationalist claims. Global humanists will have difficulty avoiding the force of these arguments because they appeal to precisely the values that global humanists claim to respect. This is not to say that all forms of nationalism are legitimate, but if some forms are, then any form of global humanism that denies this will itself be badly flawed.

I believe that if we evaluate the competing ideals of nationalism and global humanism and seek to formulate reasonable forms of these ideals, we arrive at something like a convergence of the two. Nationalism, to be morally acceptable, must conform to universal moral standards of the sort that global humanists have championed. Global humanism, however, if is to be reasonable and morally acceptable must recognize the moral legitimacy and even the positive value of certain forms of nationalism.[1]

Nations and Nationalisms

Like others who enter this area, I need to give some account of what I mean by the terms "nation" and "nationalism." These definitional questions are themselves hotly debated. I will answer them in a way that is brief and sufficiently clear to permit discussion, while recognizing that noted scholars would reject the account that I give.[2]

First, what is a nation? The best answer to this question, I think, is that of Eric Hobsbawm, who defines a nation as "any sufficiently large body of people whose members regard themselves as members of a 'nation.'"[3] This answer may be rejected on the grounds that it is either empty or paradoxical. Both of these charges emerge because the definition appears to generate an infinite regress. If we say that "a nation is a group of people who believe they are a nation," we seem to be led to the further elaboration that "a nation is a group of people who believe that they are a group of people who believe they are a group of people. . . . " Further attempts to eliminate the word "nation" from the definition fail, as it reappears each time we substitute for the word "nation" in our definition.[4]

The solution to the problem is to recognize that members of nations do not see themselves as united by their common belief. They always cite some specific things that unite them—a common culture, for example, or common ancestors, a common history, shared political institutions, or attachment to a particular territory. None of these particular features actually defines nationhood, however. While each of them may be sufficient to ground a sense of nationhood, none is absolutely necessary.

Different people believe that their claims to be a nation are rooted in different sorts of facts. As theorists, we can look at all of these claims and see that the essential thread uniting them is simply the *belief* about group membership and not the specific basis on which this or that group rests that belief. Hobsbawm's paradoxical definition brings out this fact.

What about nationalism? How shall we understand it? One of the contested issues here is whether nationalism essentially involves the goal of a separate territory and political sovereignty for one's national group. I think that while a territory and a state have been the typical goals of nationalists, neither is absolutely essential to a nationalist ideal. My view is that the essence of nationalism is the goal of national flourishing. However we conceive of the national group, nationalists are people who identify with their national group and want it to flourish.

There are good historical reasons why national flourishing has generally seemed to require a state and a territory. Nonetheless, circumstances change, and people may be able to construct other institutional frameworks that permit national groups to flourish without a territory or state. If this occurs, there is no reason why nationalists could not pursue these alternative institutions as their goal instead of seeking a separate territory. We could acknowledge this as a significant development or shift in the nature of nationalism while recognizing the features it has in common with older, territory-based conceptions of nationalism.[5]

It is important not to lose sight of the fact that established states can be nationalistic. Nationalism is not limited to those who lack a state or whose national group is endangered or oppressed. Many people who are patriotic do not think of themselves as nationalists, but "patriotism" is simply another name for nationalism. As such, it inspires in people a partiality or special concern for their own nation and motivates its adherents to promote their own nation's well-being.[6]

What Is Special about National Identity?

In considering defenses of nationalism, I want to begin with the view that Judith Lichtenberg calls the "Flourishing Argument." She identifies it as "the belief that human beings need to belong to or identify with some group beyond their immediate family or, in any case, that they flourish when they do."[7] Notice that while the Flourishing Argument stresses the importance of group membership for individual flourishing, it does not refer specifically to nations. Even if we accept this principle, then people who take membership in a nation to be especially important must show why this is so. Why do people need a national group in order to flourish? Why aren't other forms of association (such as families, religious groups, professions, et cetera) sufficient for individuals to flourish?

This gap in the argument may evoke a skeptical reply from people with global humanist sympathies. They may wonder why people must identify with the national group. All of us are members of many different groups. Why is our membership in a nation of preeminent importance? What is to keep us from identifying with all humanity? After all, if we could identify with humanity as a whole, we could avoid the worst evils that nationalism has given rise to: hatred and suspicion of other nations and the violence and destruction that these attitudes provoke.

This globalist objection may be met by the claim that humanity is too large and indistinct a group for people to identify with. While this is a plausible response, it may not seem that strong. After all, many modern nations are also extremely large and are composed of people from many diverse groups. In fact, increasingly in the modern world nation-states are homes to people of disparate cultures, religions, and national origins. Identification with nation-states may seem no less artificial than identification with humanity as a whole. So one may continue to wonder why national affiliation is so special.

To put the point rhetorically: If people have to identify with some large group in order to flourish, why not identify with all humanity and avoid the many problems to which national identifications give rise? Why must human flourishing and human associations rest on the basis of membership in a national group?

Defensive Nationalism

I have a great deal of sympathy with this globalist challenge to the Flourishing Argument. Like many others, I lament the divisive and destructive tendencies of nationalism. Nonetheless, I think that this challenge to the Flourishing Argument can be met by defenders of nationalism. In meeting it, nationalists can show both that some forms of nationalism are legitimate and that any form of global humanism that does not acknowledge this is unacceptable.

The most powerful reply to global humanists comes from the view that I will call "defensive nationalism." The strength of this position is evident in the following eloquent, highly charged statement by the Israeli writer and peace activist Amos Oz, who writes:

> I think that the nation-state is a tool, an instrument, . . . but I am not enamored of this instrument. . . . I would be more than happy to live in a world composed of dozens of civilizations, each developing . . . without any one emerging as a nation-state: no flag, no emblem, no passport, no anthem. No nothing. Only spiritual civilizations tied somehow to their lands, without the tools of statehood and without the instruments of war.
>
> But the Jewish people has already staged a long-running one-man show of that sort. The international audience sometimes applauded, sometimes threw stones, and occasionally slaughtered the actor. No one joined us; no one copied the model the Jews were forced to sustain for two thousand years. . . . For me this drama ended with the murder of Europe's Jews by Hitler. And I am forced to take it upon myself to play the "game of nations," with all the tools of statehood. . . . To play the game with an emblem, and a flag, and a passport and an army, and even war, provided that such war is an absolute existential necessity. I accept those rules of the game because existence without the tools of statehood is a matter of mortal danger, but I accept them only up to a point. To take pride in these tools of statehood? To worship these toys? To crow about them? Not I. . . . Nationalism itself is, in my eyes, the curse of mankind.[8]

What Oz presents here, with considerable reluctance, is the case for a negative or defensive nationalism. Although he regards nationalism as a curse, he nonetheless believes that a national group can justify its claims to a state and a territory because the alternative for members of that group is exposure to the risk of destruction by other groups.

I do not think that there is any plausible rebuttal to this argument. When the very existence of a group is threatened by others and when possession of a territory of its own would enable it to defend itself, then the threatened group has a strong, presumptive moral claim to a territory of its own.

I do not see how global humanists could possibly reject this argument. If they do reject the legitimacy of defensive nationalism, they are in the awkward position of beginning with a humane desire to respect all people equally and ending with the rather callous view that some people should simply permit themselves to be slaughtered or deprived of basic rights. Reasonable global humanists must concede, I think, that in some circumstances it is morally permissible for people to form national states.

On Having a National Identity

The argument for defensive nationalism is valuable for a second reason. It suggests an answer to the objection that national identity is arbitrary, that there is no more reason to identify oneself with a national group than there is to identify oneself simply as a human being.

Why do people identify with a particular nation? One reason is because other people may force them to take national identity seriously. While I might think of myself as a global humanist who wishes to ignore national, cultural, racial, or ethnic differences, others in my society may not permit me to do so. They may label me as a member of a particular group and, based on my label, subject me to various forms of negative treatment. In this situation, my identification with a particular group is forged and strengthened because important aspects of my life are made to depend on my being a member of it.

Having identified me in a certain way, others may make it difficult or impossible for me to flourish, and my ability to flourish (or even to survive) may come to depend on how effectively the group that I am identified with can deal with this situation. This in turn provides me with powerful, personal incentives to act on behalf of this group and to be more concerned about its well-being than I am about the well-being of other groups.[9]

Of course, this is not the only way that people acquire a sense of national identity, but it does serve to reveal the artificial quality of the question of why we should identify with our national group rather than with all humanity. Many people have no real choice about this because the decision is made for them by others. One's identity as a member of particular group is formed and given central importance by the fact that other people ascribe this identity and base important decisions about how to treat people on it.[10]

In other cases, of course, a national (cultural, ethnic, or political) identity is regarded positively by the person who bears it. It is not imposed by hostile others.

Nonetheless, even a positive sense of identification and the acceptance of a particular identity are not accidental occurrences. Most ethnic, religious, political, and national groups work very hard to produce a sense of group identity. They raise children to feel a sense of loyalty and kinship. They build institutions to maintain coherence among both children and adult members of the community. They develop rituals and symbols that serve to unify the group. They celebrate their histories and build monuments to the group's achievements. They also impose sanctions on those who violate the group's norms, fail to support it sufficiently, or abandon it entirely.

Globalists are right that there is nothing natural about national identity. It takes work to create these identities. In fact, however, many people and institutions are doing this work. By contrast, very few people are doing this kind of work to produce a global identity. If we compare the resources that are devoted to developing national identities to those that are devoted to developing a global, human identity, it should come as no surprise that the sense of national identity is stronger than the sense of human identity.

Flourishing

To this point, I have discussed a negative or defensive version of the Flourishing Argument. I would now like to examine a more positive version of this argument.

Before doing so, let me briefly review the defensive nationalist argument to make clear what it shows or does not show. The defensive argument shows that if people need a state to defend themselves from attack, then they have a presumptive claim to some form of national recognition. I call the claim presumptive rather than absolute because it can be undermined in some cases. For example, if a threatened group needs a territory to survive but is willing to adopt barbaric practices toward its neighbors or other inhabitants of their region, then others may have no duty to recognize this claim.[11]

With this limitation in mind, I want to return to the Flourishing Argument and examine it more carefully. As we saw earlier, this argument appeals to the idea "that human beings need to belong to or identify with some group beyond their immediate family or, in any case, that they flourish when they do." As stated, this formulation gives us a part of an argument, but it is obviously incomplete. I suggest filling it out in the following way:

1. Human beings need to identify with or belong to a national group in order to flourish.
2. Individual human beings can only flourish if their national group flourishes.
3. It is desirable for human beings to flourish.

4. Therefore, it is desirable for national groups to flourish.
5. Finally, if possessing a state, territory, or other institutional arrangements is necessary for a national group to flourish, then it is desirable that such a group possess a state, territory, or other suitable institutional arrangement.

One virtue of this formulation is that it permits some stretching of the notion of flourishing so that it can include necessary conditions of cultural flourishing like physical survival. It thus permits us to see the link between the positive and negative versions of the Flourishing Argument. What I called the case for defensive nationalism is the negative version. It interprets premise 2 as a claim about physical survival. Humans can't flourish if the groups that they belong to are victims of attack and have no way to defend themselves.

What about the positive version of this argument, which rests on the claim that individuals can only develop in valuable ways if they are members of national communities? As a universal claim, this is clearly mistaken. Not everybody has this sort of strong identification, and people may have other identifications or activities that enable them to flourish.

Still, some activities do require a culture or a community of like-valued people, and for some people, these activities may constitute what they see as the most important parts of their lives. If there are enough such people, then the existence of a minority of loners will not upset the argument. So the Flourishing Argument need not rest on a universal psychological claim in order to be persuasive. If large numbers of people can only flourish under certain circumstances and if their flourishing is a good, then the existence of those circumstances is also a good.

One might object that these people are simply mistaken. They may think that they can only flourish if they have a nation of their own, but this is false. Even without a nation, many of them would be able to live meaningful lives. The felt need for a national state of their own rests on a delusion. There is much more to life than membership in a national group.

This objection is far from conclusive. While some may be skeptical that people need a nation in order to flourish, many people find such arguments to be plausible. Indeed, the claim that people need a community in order to live meaningfully is probably the most attractive part of communitarian philosophies.[12]

Even if one is unmoved by these claims, it is important to see that they can have a self-fulfilling quality. Suppose I believe that I need a certain kind of community in order to flourish. If I do not have such a community and believe that this lack deprives me of the opportunity to possess what is most meaningful to me, the mere fact that I have this belief may contribute to my failure to flourish. Believing that I need a community that I cannot have, I may become despondent, feel that my life is empty, et cetera. So, in this case, my belief that flourishing requires a community is itself a factor in bringing it about that I cannot flourish in the absence of a community. If I did not have this belief, perhaps I would find other ways to develop myself or attain satisfaction.

Likewise, consider people who believe that a community is necessary for flourishing and have such a community. Believing that their own life fulfillment is tied up with the community and its degree of success, these people find that the health of the community is a component of the good life for them. They take pride in their community's achievements, support it, and engage in activities that contribute to its well-being. The success of the community is at the same time these people's own personal success. In some cases, then, if the well-being of one's community is thought to be a central aspect of a one's own life, the degree to which one finds personal fulfillment will parallel the degree to which the community flourishes.

It would be presumptuous for global humanists to tell people that their personal flourishing does not require the flourishing of their national community. Perhaps globalists could try to show this on a case-by-case basis, pointing out to people that they have many interests that are independent of their national community and that they can flourish in their individual pursuits even if their nation does not flourish. But there is no reason to believe this of everyone, and as I have argued, the possible self-fulfilling nature of these beliefs may make it difficult to refute them.

Nationalists can further strengthen this argument by invoking the value of self-determination. If groups of people believe that they can achieve flourishing lives only by joining together in some kind of collective, then perhaps there is some legitimacy in their efforts to join together, even if global humanists are correct that this group effort is not necessary for these people to flourish. Even if we disagree with people about the conditions that are necessary for their flourishing, we may be forced to acknowledge their appeal to the value of self-determination. If we have a commitment to respect people, this requires us to take seriously what they themselves think are the necessary conditions of their own flourishing.

This is not to say people's own beliefs about what they should have are always decisive. There may be reasons to oppose the realization of nationalist goals. Nonetheless, these arguments establish a strong presumption in favor of the view that nationalist aims and the attempt to realize them can be morally legitimate.

Nationalism within the Limits of Morality

To this point, I have tried to show that national flourishing can be a legitimate aim. Nationalists may be justified in wanting a territory and a state for their people if those conditions are necessary for them to survive and/or flourish. If this is true and if we understand global humanism as requiring the complete rejection of national aspirations, then global humanism is an inadequate ideal. Sometimes we ought to recognize and support nationalist claims.

Still, not every nationalist claim is legitimate. So it is important to see if we can provide criteria that mark the boundaries between morally acceptable and morally unacceptable forms of nationalism. I will try to do this by describing two forms of nationalism, one that I will call "extreme" and the other "moderate." While the kinds of nationalism I describe are ideal types, my hope is that they highlight some of the features we need to consider in evaluating the different actual nationalisms that confront us in the world.

As forms of nationalism, both of these conceptions involve a special commitment to the well-being of a particular nation. People who are nationalists must identify with their own nation, care about it more than about others, and be willing to do things to promote its own well-being that they would not do for other nations.

Beyond this, however, forms of nationalism may differ in significant ways. Extreme nationalists believe that the well-being of their nation is the most significant of all values and that nothing takes precedence over its pursuit. They seek to dominate other nations, believe that their own nation is superior to others, and think that any action that promotes their own nation's interests is justified. This is the nationalism that is suggested by slogans like "Deutschland über alles" and "my country, right or wrong."

Moderate nationalists believe that advancing the well-being of their nation is very important, but they recognize two things that extreme nationalists do not acknowledge. These are, first, that morality imposes constraints on the pursuit of all human goals and thus prohibits certain means of advancing the national well-being; and, second, that people who are not members of the nation are objects of moral worth, with legitimate interests and rights of their own.

What kinds of constraints do moderate nationalists recognize? They acknowledge that except in special circumstances it is wrong to kill, injure, or otherwise cause serious harm to people who are not members of their group, even if doing so advances the interests of their own nation. Although moderate nationalists believe in their own nation's right to self-defense, they do not believe that it has a right to initiate violence, including aggressive war, against others. Moreover, while they recognize that their own interests may conflict with the interests of other nations, they are committed to trying to resolve such conflicts without violence if that is possible. They do not seek or welcome the ill-being of other groups, nor are they totally indifferent to other groups' fate. While moderate nationalists may feel no duty to promote the well-being of other nations under ordinary circumstances, they do recognize a duty to do so in cases where other nations are in extreme distress and their own nation is well-off.

Moderate nationalists, then, recognize a primary duty to their own nation. Nonetheless, they recognize both negative duties (to refrain from harming) toward members of other nations and positive duties (to assist in times of distress) toward others.[13] My claim is that once we distinguish moderate nationalism from extreme nationalism, we can see why global humanists are right to reject extreme nationalism as an inherently immoral ideal. At the same time, we can see that moderate nationalism differs from extreme nationalism in just the ways that shield it from the moral criticisms justifiably aimed at extreme nationalism. While global humanists have a right to dream of a world without nations, there is no basis for them to criticize the moderate nationalist view as morally wrong or illegitimate.

The Convergence Thesis

I began by arguing that an evaluation of nationalism and global humanism would lead to the conclusion that the two must converge in order to be morally acceptable.

Nationalism, I have just argued, can only be legitimate in its moderate form, a form that combines commitment to a particular nation with a recognition of duties to treat all people decently. Without this universalist component, nationalism is no more than a ruthless, fanatical form of group egoism. With it, nationalism is a morally legitimate pursuit of group goals and group well-being.

Global humanism may seem so noble an ideal that it needs no justification. Nonetheless, if global humanism is understood in such a way that it necessarily requires the rejection of all nationalist claims, then global humanists will be committed to opposing the efforts of groups to obtain a state, even if the lack of a state will lead to slaughter and the destruction of particular cultures. This extreme form of global humanism is humanistic in name only.

In order to avoid this callous result, global humanists must both recognize that national institutions can sometimes be valuable and acknowledge the claims of national groups when they are legitimate. Once they have done this, then there is no principled moral difference between the amended "moderate" globalist point of view and the moderate nationalist point of view.

A Final Objection

Before concluding, I want to mention an objection to the defense of moderate nationalism that I have offered. Someone might object that moderate nationalism, whatever its possible virtues, is merely a philosophical abstraction, while the real nationalisms that plague the world have all the vile features that global humanists deplore. From this perspective, a defense of moderate nationalism can only confuse the issues, lending legitimacy to movements that partly share its name but completely lack its admirable qualities.

There are a number of problems with this objection. First, it presupposes a rigid form of essentialism. It supposes that every feature of a phenomenon is part of its essence, while I have argued that although nationalism has an essence, this essence is compatible with a range of other nonessential features, such as the acceptance or rejection of duties toward outsiders. Even if it is true that most nationalisms have rejected moral constraints on efforts to promote the national good, it does not follow that nationalisms must continue to do so. Likewise, even if nationalists have until now all campaigned for their own territory, it does not follow that they must continue to do so. As I noted earlier, if other arrangements can be provided that make possible national flourishing, then nationalists can accept these other arrangements.

The purpose of defending moderate nationalism is twofold. The first is to separate out the elements of existing nationalisms so that we can distinguish the aspects that possess moral legitimacy from those that do not. The second is to use this analysis to encourage the development of forms of nationalism that lack the features that have made nationalism a breeding ground of hatred, violence, and war.

Nationalism, after all, is an idea, and if we can reconceive nationalism in ways that will make it more humane and pacific, then we may sow the mental seeds that can actually make the world a safer, more peaceful place. It would be foolish to think that philosophical arguments alone can produce such changes, but it would be equally foolish to deny that ideas can make a difference. Reconceiving our goals and ideals is a first step toward changing how we act in the world.

NOTES

The original version of this essay was a response to a paper by Judith Lichtenburg. I am much indebted to her interesting discussion of these issues, as well as to comments by Jeff McMahan.

1. For a fuller development of my own views, see *Patriotism, Morality, and Peace* (Lanham, Md.: Rowman and Littlefield, 1993).

2. For an excellent discussion of these definitional issues, see Anthony Smith, *Theories of Nationalism* (London: Duckworth, 1983).

3. Eric Hobsbawm, *Nations and Nationalism since 1780: Programme, Myth, Reality*, 2d ed. (Cambridge: Cambridge University Press, 1990), p. 9.

4. I owe this objection to Jeff McMahan.

5. On this, see Yael Tamir, *Liberal Nationalism* (Princeton: Princeton University Press, 1993).

6. For a contrary view, see Walker Connor, *Ethnonationalism* (Princeton: Princeton University Press, 1994).

7. See chapter 10.

8. Amos Oz, *In the Land of Israel* (New York: Vintage, 1983), pp. 130–31.

9. For an account that stresses the connections between group identities and self-

interest, see Dov Ronen, *The Quest for Self-Determination* (New Haven, Conn.: Yale University Press, 1979).

10. The same points apply to racial identity. Even if there is no biological basis for racial groupings, the fact that people believe in races has important social and personal consequences.

11. For an excellent discussion of these sorts of issues, see Allen Buchanan, *Secession: The Morality of Political Divorce from Fort Sumter to Lithuania and Quebec* (Boulder, Colo.: Westview, 1991).

12. For a sampling of communitarian claims, see S. Avineri and A. de-Shalit, eds., *Communitarianism and Individualism* (Oxford: Oxford University Press, 1992).

13. I discuss these issues more fully in *Patriotism, Morality, and Peace* and in "Nationalism, Patriotism, and Toleration," in *Synthesis Philosophica* (international ed. of *Filozofska Istrazivanja*), 9 (1994): 135–52.

III

NATIONALISM, LIBERALISM, AND THE STATE

12

Liberalism, Nationalism, and Egalitarianism

SAMUEL SCHEFFLER

Liberalism in one form or another is the dominant position in contemporary political philosophy. Despite this, or perhaps because of it, liberalism continues to attract criticism of many different kinds. Some critics believe that liberalism underestimates the human and political significance that attaches to membership in a nation or in a cultural or communal group, and that it therefore misjudges the significance of the national and cultural diversity that is a feature of so many modern societies. These critics view liberalism as insufficiently particularist in its orientation. At the same time, there are other critics who believe that liberalism as standardly formulated places too little emphasis on questions of global or international political morality, and that it focuses too much of its attention on the individual society, which is assumed to be organized as an independent country or state, and which is treated as a self-sufficient cooperative enterprise. These critics view liberalism as insufficiently globalist in its orientation.

The philosophical disagreements among liberals and their globalist and particularist critics range over many issues. One of these issues, and the one that I wish to address in this essay, concerns the question of responsibility or, more precisely, the question of how various kinds of social ties affect the responsibilities that people have to each other. Disagreements about this issue may be thought of as disagreements about the boundaries of our responsibilities. Particularist critics charge that by focusing on the individual society, which it takes to be organized as a political unit, liberalism neglects the special responsibilities that arise from membership in a nation or community, where nations and communities are defined in cultural rather than political terms. Globalist critics, on the other hand, charge that liberalism overemphasizes the individual's responsibilities to his *own* society, and underestimates the extent of his duties to people in other societies. Although globalists allow that there may be practical or instrumental reasons why one should take special responsibility for the members of one's own society, they insist that it is a mistake to exaggerate the extent of this responsibility or to treat it as a matter of fundamental principle. Thus, whereas particularists criticize liberals for neglecting the responsibilities associated with membership in a national or communal group, globalists argue that liberals' emphasis on the individual society is itself too particularistic.

The political importance of these disagreements is clear. Both particularist and globalist ideas have become increasingly influential in contemporary politics. Particularist ideas are reflected not only in the recent resurgence of nationalism as a political force but also in the rise of the idea of multiculturalism, in the emergence of communitarianism as a nascent political movement, and in the tendency toward ethnic or communal fragmentation and conflict in many parts of the world. Globalist ideas are reflected in the various steps toward greater economic, technological, and political integration that have been trumpeted with such fanfare in recent years. One of the most important tasks for contemporary liberal theory is to address the twin challenges posed by particularist and globalist thinking.[1]

As I have said, I will be concerned in this essay with questions about the boundaries of our responsibilities. I will argue that the particularist and globalist criticisms of liberalism point to two different tensions within liberal thought: first, a tension between an explicit voluntarism and an implicit nationalism and, second, a tension between a commitment to moral egalitarianism and a commitment to some form of particularism about political responsibility. In the final section of the essay, I will assess the significance for liberalism these two tensions.

The disagreements about responsibility that I have mentioned are closely related to some central debates within normative ethics. Commonsense moral thought recognizes a variety of responsibilities that we have toward each of our fellow human beings: to avoid various forms of mistreatment, for example, and also to provide limited forms of assistance in various contexts. However, commonsense moral thought also holds that we have special duties or responsibilities to people with whom we have had certain significant sorts of interactions or to whom we stand in certain significant sorts of relations. On the face of it, there appear to be several different classes of these special duties: for example, *contractual duties,* or duties arising out of promises, contracts, and agreements; *reparative duties,* or duties to people one has wronged or harmed or mistreated; *duties of gratitude,* or duties to one's benefactors; and *associative duties,* or duties that the members of significant social groups and the participants in close personal relationships have to each other.

Associative duties, which are especially important for our purposes, seem to occupy a central position in commonsense moral thought. It is normally taken for granted that one has special responsibilities to one's associates—that is, to one's family and friends and to the members of other significant groups to which one belongs. The precise content of these duties or responsibilities is often unclear and can vary from case to case, depending on the nature of the social tie giving rise to the duty. Very generally, however, associative duties require us to give the interests of our associates priority of various kinds over the interests of other people. Sometimes this will mean incurring greater costs for the sake of our associates than we would be expected to incur for the sake of others, and sometimes it will mean assigning the interests of our associates precedence over the interests of others in cases of conflict.[2] Although there is only a partial consensus about which types of groups and relationships give rise to such duties, most people take it for granted that they have at least some responsibilities of this sort. Thus, insofar as the particularist criticism of liberalism amounts to the claim that we have associative duties to the members of national or communal groups to which we belong, it invokes a normative category that represents an important dimension of commonsense moral thought.

Despite their commonsense moral credentials, however, associative duties are philosophically controversial. One important source of controversy is an objection that we may call *the voluntarist objection*. This objection does not deny that we often have special duties to people who are related to us in certain ways and to the members of various groups with which we are affiliated. However, it insists that the mere existence of such a relation or the mere fact of membership in such a group is not by itself sufficient to give rise to special duties. Instead, the voluntarist argues, any special responsibilities that we may have to our associates must arise from our own voluntary acts. Different voluntarists disagree about which voluntary acts are duty-generating. Some require that we explicitly accept the responsibilities in question. Others require only that we voluntarily enter into the putatively duty-generating group or relationship. Still others think that our voluntary acceptance of the benefits of participation in such a group or relationship suffices. What all voluntarists agree on, however, is the idea that *some* voluntary act is necessary. One cannot simply find that one has special duties to one's associates without having done anything at all to acquire those duties. Thus voluntarists typically take the view that associative duties are genuine duties only insofar as they can be assimilated to contractual duties broadly construed or to voluntarily incurred duties of other kinds. What voluntarists deny, in other words, is that associative duties constitute an independent class of duties, which can be incurred simply by virtue of participation in relationships of certain sorts of by virtue of membership in groups of certain sorts.[3]

The voluntarist objection to unassimilated associative duties is, as it were, an objection on behalf of the individuals who are supposed to be bound by such duties. Associative duties constitute assignments of responsibility that are potentially quite burdensome for those who bear them, and the voluntarist objection reflects a sense that such responsibilities cannot be imposed on people without their consent or, at any rate, without their suitably voluntary performance of some act about which they have a genuine choice. On the face of it, this objection seems a natural outgrowth of a more general concern with the freedom and autonomy of the individual agent. As such, of course, it resonates with central values of liberalism, and, indeed, one standard liberal objection to nationalism and communitarianism simply recapitulates the voluntarist objection to unassimilated associative duties. To the liberal, the idea that one's responsibilities may be determined by social ties over which one has no control is regressive and atavistic; it is a hallmark of systems of social caste and hierarchy, and it represents an unacceptable constraint on the freedom of the individual. Moreover, insofar as it invites the thought that one's privileges may also be determined by social ties over which one has no control, it seems to many liberals to pave the way for the most invidious forms of discrimination and differential treatment. Thus, to many liberals, the repudiation of this idea represents the triumph of freedom over constraint: the liberation of the individual chooser from the stultifying and divisive claims of blood and historical inheritance. Accordingly, liberal theories tend officially to disavow associative duties. Insofar as such theories are concerned with the responsibilities of individual citizens, the responsibilities in question are usually categorized as "political obligations," which are conceived of as consensually generated obligations to uphold the laws and institutions of one's society.

Most of us who have grown up in liberal societies have internalized liberal values to a considerable extent and have a strong allegiance to them. Yet as we have seen, the idea of associative duties also has deep roots within commonsense moral thought. Thus there is a tension within the commonsense morality of our culture: a tension between a powerful strand of voluntaristic conviction and a continuing commitment to the moral relevance of various types of interpersonal bonds whose susceptibility to voluntaristic assimilation is, at the very least, open to question.

The existence of this tension is not, perhaps, very surprising. What may be more surprising is that this same tension is also reflected within liberalism itself, and that many liberal theories that explicitly reject associative duties seem tacitly to rely on them, or at least to incorporate elements that serve to mimic such duties in important respects. To see this, we may begin by reminding ourselves of a point upon which globalists insist—namely, that despite being subject to particularist criticism, liberalism itself has an important particularist dimension. Clearly, for example, liberal accounts of political obligation have a particularist character, inasmuch as such obligations are not supposed to be owed to the world at large or to other people in general. Instead, political obligations are thought of as special obligations that are owed either to the other members of one's own society or to its political officials or institutions, who are in turn conceived of as specially responsible for protecting and promoting the interests of the members of that society.

Thus, whether or not political obligations are thought of as owed directly to one's fellow citizens, they are, in any case, special obligations whose ultimate beneficiaries are one's fellow citizens.

Of course, the mere fact that liberal political obligations are particularistic in this way does not call into question their voluntarist basis. However, there are other particularist features of liberalism whose compatibility with voluntarist ideas is more doubtful. When liberals address questions of justice, for example, it is "social justice" with which they are typically concerned—that is, the justice of a single society or its major institutions. Even more striking is the liberal view of membership or of how one comes to acquire citizenship in the liberal state. Although a thoroughgoing voluntarism would presumably dictate that liberal citizenship should be purely a matter of individual choice, and although that idea is enshrined in the liberal tradition via the myth of the social contract, liberal theorists have, in general, had little to say about how membership is determined, and actual liberal societies attach far more weight to birth than to choice in assigning citizenship and its associated privileges and obligations. In addition, although liberal theorists focus explicitly on the question of how the political institutions of an individual society are to be justified, they also tend, either explicitly or implicitly, to assume that each society will be organized not merely as a state but as a "nation-state." This means that the citizens of each state are thought of as constituting a national group with a common culture. Thus, for example, John Rawls, the most prominent contemporary liberal theorist, takes the boundaries of a "well-ordered society" to coincide with those of "a self-contained national community."[4] Rawls also says that he is concerned with the problem of justice for a society "conceived as a more or less self-sufficient scheme of social cooperation and as possessing a more or less complete culture."[5]

The net result of this cluster of positions and practices is to call into question the liberal rejection of associative duties, for although liberalism officially eschews such duties, the citizens of the liberal state are standardly represented, both in theory and in practice, as constituting a national group whose members have particularistic responsibilities toward each other, either directly or as a result of their duties to shared political institutions. Moreover, liberal citizens are commonly seen as passing these responsibilities on to their children, along with the various perquisites of membership, as a matter of birthright. Thus, as Yael Tamir has emphasized,[6] there is a tension within the liberal position between an explicit voluntarism and an implicit nationalism—a largely unacknowledged tendency to invest national ties with a kind of moral and political significance that cannot be accounted for in purely voluntaristic terms.

In recent years, some liberal theorists have begun to distance themselves from the traditional liberal reliance on a thoroughgoing voluntaristic notion of political obligation. Some of these theorists, such as Ronald Dworkin and Yael Tamir, have actually suggested that political obligations should be reconstrued as associative duties.[7] In so doing, these theorists have renounced or substantially modified the voluntaristic objection to such duties. Other liberal theorists, such as John Rawls and Jeremy Waldron, have appealed instead to a "natural duty of justice" to account for the political responsibilities of the individual citizen.[8] As Rawls characterizes it, "[t]his duty requires us to support and comply with just institutions that exist and apply to us."[9] The natural duty of justice is said to be ascribable to all individuals and not to depend on their consent or any other voluntary act.

A. John Simmons has argued that the appeal to a natural duty of justice cannot serve the purposes of liberal theory because it cannot explain why a citizen has a special responsibility to the institutions of his particular society—as opposed to a general responsibility to support just institutions everywhere.[10] More precisely, Simmons claims that this "particularity requirement" cannot be satisfied by the appeal to a natural duty of justice unless the natural duty of justice turns out to be indistinguishable from voluntaristic political obligation. Of course, the natural duty as Rawls characterizes it is formally compatible with the particularity requirement, for it says that we are bound only to those just institutions that "apply to us." However, Simmons asks how this notion of "application" is to be understood. Only if it is a morally significant notion will the fact that a just institution applies to us be capable of explaining why we have special responsibilities toward that institution that we do not have toward other just institutions. There are, Simmons suggests, two broadly different ways of understanding the notion of application. In one sense, an institution might be said to apply to me just by virtue of "my birth and growth in a territory within which the institution's rules are enforced."[11] However, Simmons argues that application in this sense is not a morally significant notion because "my birth is not an act I perform, or something for which I am responsible."[12] In another sense, an institution may be said to apply to me by virtue of my having "*done* things"[13] that tie me to it, such as consenting to be governed by its rules or accepting benefits from it. Simmons argues that "[o]nly in cases of application in [this] 'strong' sense, those that involve an individual's consent, say, or his *acceptance* of significant benefits, does 'application' begin to look morally important."[14] Obviously, however, consent and the acceptance of benefits are just the sorts of acts to which voluntaristic accounts of political obligation appeal. Thus, Simmons concludes, the only way in which the natural duty of justice can satisfy the particularity requirement is by relying on a notion of application that renders this supposed natural duty indistinguishable from voluntaristically generated political obligation.

On one level, Simmons's argument seems to beg the question, for he appears simply to assume that only something that one has done could give one a morally significant tie to a particular institution. This is itself a voluntaristic assumption, which guarantees that the appeal to natural duty will seem untenable except insofar as it fails to offer any real alternative to voluntarist political obligation. It seems open to a defender of natural duty to reject this assumption and argue that there are certain relations between individuals and just institutions that can be morally significant even if they don't arise from anything that the individuals have done. For example, it might be said that citizenship is such a relationship and that the fact that one is a citizen of a just society can give one a special responsibility to support the institutions of that society even if one became a citizen at birth and not as a result of anything that one did.

Note, however, that such an argument would have one effect that seems at variance with the intentions of those who appeal to a natural duty to support just institutions, which is that it would make this duty seem more like an associative duty. For, whereas the ground of the natural duty seemed initially to lie in the justice of the just institution, this argument suggests that the individual's relation to the institution also plays a crucial role in generating the duty. And, of course, the notion that participation in certain sorts of relationships can give rise to special responsibilities is what lies behind the idea of associative duties. Admittedly, associative duties as I have characterized them are owed to specific individuals, whereas Rawls says that natural duties are owed "to persons generally,"[15] so that, even on the interpretation we are considering, a difference between the two types of duty would remain. Nevertheless, the two would also have an important feature in common, and one that would make it more difficult for liberals who appeal to natural duty to deny the possibility of unassimilated associative duties. Indeed, one moral of Simmons's argument, it seems to me, is that the voluntarist objection to associative duties can also be directed against the natural duty to support just institutions if the natural duty is defended in the way that I have suggested.

Thus the effect of such a defense is, for better or worse, to push the "particularized" natural duty of justice in the direction of an associative duty. However, the preceding remarks also raise an additional question about the internal coherence of the natural duty so interpreted. According to that interpretation, the duty appears to be the product of two factors that tend in different directions. The first factor is justice itself, whose tendency is to suggest a nonparticularized duty to support just institutions generally. The second factor, which is the particularizing factor, is the individual's relationship to a specific set of institutions. What may seem unclear, however, is why this second, particularizing tendency should take precedence over the putatively universal claims of justice. In other words, if justice really does generate nonparticularized reasons, how does the scope of those reasons get reduced by the individual's relation to a particular set of institutions? Rather than meshing smoothly to generate a single, particularized duty, the two factors may seem to represent conflicting values that cannot easily be harmonized. Thus the natural duty of justice may look like an unstable attempt to integrate opposing moral values, and as such it may seem an unattractive alternative to voluntaristic political obligation.[16]

However, I want to argue that the apparent instability of the natural duty to support just institutions is symptomatic of a broader problem that afflicts any form of liberalism that seeks to reconcile egalitarian values with a particularistic account of our political responsibilities. By a particularistic account of our political responsibilities I mean any account that claims we have fundamentally different responsibilities to the citizens or institutions of our own society than we have to the rest of the world. If I am correct, the problem of reconciling such an account with egalitarian values marks a second important tension within liberal theory.

One way to bring this second tension into focus is by taking note of a second objection to associative duties, an objection that is likely to be offered not by liberals, but by globalists. The voluntarist objection, as we saw, is an objection on behalf of those individuals who are supposed to be bound by associative duties. By contrast, this second objection, which I will call *the distributive objection*, is an objection on behalf of those who are not participants in the groups and relationships that are said to give rise to such duties.[17] And whereas the voluntarist objection claims that associative duties, unless incurred by virtue of some voluntary act, place unreasonable burdens on the participants in the relevant groups and relationships, the distributive objection claims that such duties provide the participants with benefits that may be unreasonable. The distributive objection may be developed as follows.

Associative duties require individuals to give priority of various kinds to the interests of their associates. These requirements, however, work to the disadvantage of other people. Suppose, for example, that there are three individuals, A, B, and C, none of whom has any special tie or relationship to any of the others. Each has only general duties toward the others, which is to say that each's duties toward the others are distributed equally. Indeed, a perfectly egalitarian distribution of duty obtains among the three individuals, since none of the three has any special claim on the services of any of the others. Now, however, suppose that A and B become members of some group of a kind that is ordinarily thought to give rise to associative duties. And suppose that C is not a member of this group, which we may call The In-Group. If, as a result of their membership in The In-Group, A and B come to have associative duties to each other, then the egalitarian distribution of duty that previously prevailed no longer obtains. Instead, A and B are now required to give each other's interests priority over the interests of C in a wide range of contexts. Thus each of them now has stronger claims on the other than C has on either of them. This means that for each of them, C's interests have been demoted in relative importance. Indeed, C's claims on each of them may now be weaker, not only than his claims on them were before, and not only than their claims on each other are now, but also than their claims on him are now. For, we may suppose, C has no associates to whose interests he is required to give priority over the interests of A and

B. Thus the reduction in the strength of his claims on A and B may not be matched by a comparable reduction in the strength of their claims on him; the reduction of strength may be, in this way, asymmetrical. In any case, the overall distribution of duty that now prevails seems both inegalitarian and decidedly unfavorable to C.

But, the distributive objection asks, why should the fact that A and B have become members of The In-Group have these effects? Why should their membership in The In-Group work to C's disadvantage in this way? We may suppose that both A and B attach considerable significance to their membership, that both experience their participation in The In-Group as very rewarding, and, indeed, that each of them sees membership in The In-Group as an important aspect of his identity. None of these suppositions seems capable of explaining why their membership should, as a matter of morality, work to C's disadvantage in the way that it does if it generates associative duties. Indeed, the distributive objection continues, far from explaining this, these suppositions seem rather to make the need for such an explanation more acute. For if A and B derive great value from their membership in The In-Group, then they already have an advantage that C lacks. The effect of associative duties is to build a second advantage on top of this first one. If, in other words, A and B have associative duties to each other, then, in addition to enjoying the rewards of group membership, which C lacks, A and B also get the benefit of having stronger claims on each other's services than C has. Why should this be? Why should the fact that A and B are in a position to enjoy the first sort of advantage give rise to a moral requirement that they should also get the second and that C, who has already lost out with respect to the former, should now lose out with respect to the latter?

For the purposes of this discussion, two features of the distributive objection are especially noteworthy. First, the objection as we have formulated it can be directed not only against the defender of the unassimilated associative duties but also against the voluntarist who seeks to assimilate associative duties to contractual duties. In other words, even if associative duties are thought of as voluntaristically generated, they appear still be to open to challenge on distributive grounds. For example, even if the duties of A and B are said to arise from their voluntary acceptance of the rewards of In-Group membership, the distributive objection will still deny that morality requires the very individuals who have secured those rewards to have their good fortune compounded through a favorable redistribution of duty, while C, who never acquired the original rewards, is further disfavored by that same redistribution. Or, more accurately perhaps, the distributive objection will deny that morality requires this unless C himself had an opportunity to secure the rewards of membership in The In-Group and voluntarily declined to do so. In the absence of such an opportunity, the claim that the duties of A and B arise from their own voluntary acts seems unlikely to defuse the distributive objection.

Second, the distributive objection is strongly egalitarian in spirit. As the example we have been considering makes clear, the objection is sensitive to the way in which an assignment of associative duties may build on and reinforce already-existing inequalities in the distribution of social resources—that is, in the distribution of humanly rewarding interpersonal relationships. In addition, however, the objection is also sensitive to the way in which such an assignment may serve to reinforce inequalities in the distribution of resources of other kinds. Thus, for example, if A and B are much wealthier than C, either because this has always been so or because membership in The In-Group has conferred wealth upon them, the idea that morality requires them also to receive the advantage of having increased claims to each other's services will, according to the distributive objection, be all the more clearly open to question. And this will remain so even if C and other people of modest means join together to establish a duty-generating group of their own. For proponents of the distributive objection will still charge that by requiring those who are wealthier to give each other's interests priority over the interests of those who are poorer associative duties unjustifiably reinforce the inequality in resources between the two groups. In short, the distributive objection sees associative duties as providing additional advantages to people who have already benefited from participation in rewarding groups and relationships and views this as unjustifiable whenever the provision of these additional advantages works to the detriment of people who are needier, whether they are needier because they are not themselves participants in rewarding groups and relationships or because they have significantly fewer resources of other kinds.

If we return now to the discussion of liberalism, we can see that the distributive objection may be directed by globalists against those versions of liberal theory that postulate the existence either of associative duties or of voluntaristic political obligations. For, at the political level, the distributive objection challenges the idea that the members of an individual society have special duties to each other that they do not have to other people, and as we have seen, it does not matter, for the purposes of this objection, whether the duties in question are construed voluntaristically or not. Either way, these supposed duties are seen as providing an unjustifiable mandate for the members of affluent societies to lavish resources on each other while largely ignoring the suffering and deprivation of people in much poorer societies. However widespread this pattern of behavior may, in fact, be and however natural it may seem, the idea that such conduct is not merely morally permissible but morally required strikes proponents of the distributive objection as a transparently self-serving conceit.

The fact that the distributive objection is liable to be directed both against versions of liberalism that rely on associative duties and against versions that rely on voluntaristic political obligations suggests that the tension internal to the "particularized" natural duty of justice is symptomatic of a much broader tension within liberal theory. Recall that the particularized natural duty seemed like a possibly unstable attempt to integrate a universalistic notion of justice with a particularistic conception of our political responsibilities. The distributive objection suggests that a similar problem faces liberal theories that rely on associative duties or voluntaristic political obligations. These theories, too, offer particularized conceptions of political responsibility, and as the distributive objection shows, these theories, too, are subject to challenge from the standpoint of a universalistic, egalitarian set of values.

Now it may be argued that the distributive objection represents an external challenge to these theories; it does not show that they are characterized by any internal tension. By contrast, it may be said, the difficulty with the particularized natural duty of justice was not that it was subject to external challenge but rather that the two elements that were supposed to generate it seemed in conflict with each other. Thus, it may be argued, those versions of liberalism that rely on the natural duty of justice are problematic in a way that the other versions are not. This is misleading, however, for the distributive objection implicitly appeals to an egalitarian premise upon which virtually all contemporary liberal theories insist—namely, that all persons have equal moral worth and that no person's interests are of greater intrinsic moral importance than any other person's. The distributive objection claims that associative duties, whether interpreted voluntaristically or not, are incompatible with a recognition of the equal moral importance of each person's interests. Whether or not this objection is correct, it counts as an internal objection to those versions of liberalism that rely on such duties, for it argues from a premise that is an important tenet of liberalism itself. Understood in this way, the objection points to a tension between moral egalitarianism and a particularistic understanding of our political responsibilities that is present in virtually all contemporary versions of liberalism and is the same tension that is reflected in the particularized natural duty of justice. It is true that the particularized natural duty is itself supposed to be the product of universalistic and particularistic considerations, so that the tension between those considerations is internal not merely to theories that rely on the natural duty but also to that duty itself. Although the same cannot be said about theories that rely on associative duties or voluntaristic political obligations, this does not mean that the tension within those theories is any shallower or less problematic, only that it is less conspicuous.

I said at the outset of this essay that the particularist and globalist criticisms of liberalism point to two different tensions within liberal thought. The particularist criticism, as we have now seen, points to a tension between an explicit voluntarism and an implicit nationalism that is characteristic of much of liberal theory and practice. The globalist criticism points to a tension between a commitment to moral egalitarianism and a commitment to particularism about political responsibility that is also quite typical of contemporary liberal thought. Significantly, the way that we identified these two tensions was by attending to two different objections that have been leveled against associative duties—the duties to which nationalist and other particularist critics of liberalism appeal. The voluntarist objection, as we saw, is one that is typically offered by liberals themselves, although the inability of those same liberals to avoid relying on something like associative duties at certain points in their own accounts was revelatory of the first tension within liberalism. The distributive objection, meanwhile, is one that is typically offered by globalists, and since it can be directed against associative duties whether or not those duties are construed in voluntaristic terms, it presents a challenge both to liberals and to their particularist critics. This objection reveals a tension within liberal theory because it appeals to a premise on which liberals themselves insist. The role of these two objections to associative duties in revealing the tensions within liberal thought suggests that both tensions stem from a kind of liberal ambivalence about the moral and political significance of people's social affiliations and allegiances. There is ambivalence, reflected in the first tension, about whether and in what way these affiliations and allegiances must be voluntary in order to have such significance, and there is ambivalence, reflected in the second tension, about how a recognition of their significance can be reconciled and integrated with a commitment to the equal worth of persons.

It may seem clear that the existence of these tensions constitutes a flaw in liberal theory. Yet up to a certain point, at least, it can also be viewed as a virtue inasmuch as the tensions within liberal theory bespeak a sensitivity to three important values whose joint accommodation is genuinely problematic. Along with the familiar liberal value of autonomy, there is the value of moral equality, as expressed in the idea that all people are of equal worth and that their interests are of equal importance, and the value of loyalty, as expressed in the idea that particular interpersonal relations and social ties are a source of special normative considerations.[18] The tensions within liberal theory, I am suggesting, reflect its sensitivity to these three different values, all of which matter to us, but which are also genuinely in tension with each other. This suggestion may be challenged, of course, and in a number of different ways. First, it may be doubted whether all three of these values really do matter to us. Second, it may be doubted whether liberalism really is sensitive to all of them. Third, it may be doubted whether the values really are in tension with each other.

I will say nothing about the first of these challenges. However, I do want to take up one version of the second challenge and one version of the third. The second challenge denies that liberalism is, in fact, sensitive to all three of the values I have mentioned. The version of this challenge that I will consider is implicit in an influential argument by Alasdair MacIntyre.[19] MacIntyre draws a contrast between "liberal morality" and "the morality of patriotism." Liberal morality, he says, is "a morality of universal, impersonal and impartial principles"; the morality of patriotism, by contrast, is "a morality of particularist ties and solidarities."[20] These two moralities, he says, are "deeply"[21] and "systematically"[22] incompatible. In other words, what I have represented as a tension within liberal theory MacIntyre represents as a contrast between two distinct and incompatible moral outlooks. MacIntyre says that there are different versions of liberal morality, including Kantian, utilitarian, and contractarian versions, but that all of these versions have a common core that renders them incompatible with the morality of patriotism. For example, MacIntyre argues, if each of two communities needs the use of the same natural resource in order to survive and flourish, then "the standpoint of impersonal morality requires an allocation of goods such that each individual person counts for one and no more than one, while the patriotic standpoint requires that I strive to further the interests of my community and you strive to further those of yours."[23] In effect, MacIntyre's argument is that a moral outlook is sensitive to the value of loyalty only if it holds that individuals have special duties to give priority to the interests of their own communities; that liberalism rejects such duties because of its commitment to moral egalitarianism; and, hence, that liberalism is insensitive to the value of loyalty.

However, this argument is unpersuasive because it fails to acknowledge or engage the particularist dimension of liberalism, especially liberal particularism about political responsibility. More generally, it overlooks the fact that most liberals who endorse the idea of moral equality, as a claim about the equal worth or value of persons, nevertheless deny that this idea fully determines the content of the principles governing the conduct of individual agents. Notwithstanding MacIntyre's claims about the common core of "liberal morality," this is a familiar point of disagreement between utilitarians and other consequentialists, on the one hand, and various nonconsequentialists, including Kantians and contractarians, on the other. Consequentialists argue that the right act in any given situation is the one that will produce the best overall outcome, as judged from an impersonal standpoint that gives equal weight to the interests of everyone. By contrast, however, most liberals accept what are sometimes called "agent-relative" principles, which make the rightness of acts at least partly independent of considerations of overall value.[24] Those liberals who accept agent-relative principles do not deny that people are of equal value or importance. However, they do believe that facts that have special significance for an individual agent can sometimes have special weight in determining what that agent may permissibly do, despite the fact that the agent is no more valuable or important than anyone else.[25] This general conviction has been explicitly applied to the case of associative duties by Tamir, who denies that such duties are "grounded in the idea that what is mine is more valuable than what is yours."[26] She adds: "When I claim that charity begins at home I do not intend to imply that the poor of my town are better but merely that . . . I have a greater obligation toward them than to strangers because they are members of *my* community. . . . [Such] claims do not . . . imply an objective hierarchy among different forms of life."[27] Not all liberals accept associative duties, of course, but the vast majority accept some kind of particularism about responsibility, and they would surely agree with Tamir that such particularism is not excluded by a commitment to the equal worth of persons.

These observations, however, invite a version of the third challenge. For they seem to suggest that there may be, in the end, no tension at all between moral egalitarianism and particularism about responsibility and hence, presumably, no tension between the underlying values of moral equality and of loyalty. This is not so, however. It is one thing to point out that most liberals do, in fact, accept both moral egalitarianism and a significantly particularistic account of responsibility, but it is another thing actually to demonstrate the compatibility of these two features of liberal thought. And many liberals, it seems to me, underestimate the difficulty of doing this. Tamir's defense of associative duties is a case in point. Along with other contemporary liberal writers, such as Will Kymlicka, Neil MacCormick, and Joseph Raz,[28] as well as earlier liberal thinkers like John Dewey,[29] she makes a strong case for the importance in people's lives of group affiliations of one sort or another. However, we must remember that associative duties do not merely permit the assignment of priority to the interests of one's associates; they require it. And as the distributive objection reminds us, it is not obvious how the importance to a person of his group affiliations translates into a requirement that he favor the members of his group. Tamir says that associative duties are "not grounded on consent, reciprocity, or gratitude, but rather on a feeling of belonging and connectedness."[30] However, the step from such a feeling to a requirement that one favor the interests of those to whom one feels connected remains problematic. In order to reconcile associative duties and moral egalitarianism, we need an answer to the following question: If all people are of equal value and importance, then what is it about my relation to my associates that makes it not merely permissible but obligatory for me to give their interests priority over the interests of other people? Many attempts at reconciliation fail to confront this question squarely and instead move back and forth between claims about the duty to give priority to one's associates and claims about the permissibility of doing so. It remains to be seen whether the question can be given a satisfactory answer. Certainly the fact that I feel connected to my associates seems, on the face of it, like a more promising ground for a permission to favor them than for a requirement to do so.[31]

Moreover, even if the question could be given a satisfactory answer, that would not mean that there was no longer any tension between the underlying values of loyalty and moral equality. On the contrary, there are at least two types of tension between those values that would not be eliminated by a satisfactory justification of associative duties. First, the values are *mutually constraining* in the sense that each, if accepted, places limits on the ways in which the other may legitimately be realized or advanced. Second, the values are *practically competitive* in the sense that institutions and practices that serve to recognize or foster one of them sometimes undermine or erode the realization of the other. If the distributive objection can be given a satisfactory answer, then we may conclude that associative duties help to define the relation of mutual constraint between the two values. We may not, however, conclude that the values are no longer in tension.

In summary, we have taken note of two tensions within liberal theory: the tension between an explicit voluntarism and an implicit nationalism and the tension between a commitment to moral egalitarianism and a commitment to particularism about political responsibility. These theoretical tensions reflect ambivalence about the moral and political significance of people's social affiliations and allegiances: about the extent to which and the respects in which the affiliations must be voluntary in order to have such significance and about how a recognition of their significance can be integrated with a commitment to the equal worth of persons. This very ambivalence, I have argued, indicates that liberalism is sensitive to three different values: the values of autonomy, loyalty, and moral equality. If these values are themselves in tension with one another, then theoretical tensions like the ones within liberalism may be the inevitable result of trying to accommodate within normative political thought all of the values we wish to have realized in our social world. Unless we are prepared to deny the significance of one or more of those values, our political outlook may never be entirely free of such tensions. This is, on the one hand, no cause for despair; neither tensions among our values nor tensions within our political outlook need be unlivable. More important, perhaps, it is no cause for complacency; it does not mean that liberals can simply ignore globalist and particularist criticism. While the fact that our values are in tension means that there will inevitably be tensions within any political outlook that seeks to accommodate those values, it does not mean that all forms of accommodation are equally satisfactory. Thus the inevitability of such tensions does not tell us that their manifestation within liberal theory is unproblematic. What it does suggest, I think, is that insofar as their manifestation within liberal theory *is* problematic, the problem is not that liberalism is threatened with the kind of theoretical incoherence that might disqualify it as an acceptable system of thought but that liberalism may not yet have found the most satisfactory way of accommodating an unruly set of values, none of which we are willing simply to abandon.

This characterization of the problem is significant. It is sometimes said that liberal societies are heirs to a heterogeneous set of values of varying historical provenance, only some of which are distinctively liberal in character. In consequence, it is suggested, such societies display an incoherent attachment to inconsistent moral outlooks. MacIntyre himself makes this suggestion.[32] But modern societies are hardly the first societies to build on diverse historical antecedents, nor need a mixed historical pedigree lead to incoherence. Liberalism is a living tradition of thought and practice, and the values it seeks to accommodate are the values that now make sense to people inside that tradition. The challenge for liberals is to see what kind of mutual accommodation among those values is possible.

This is not, in my view, a purely theoretical problem, or rather, it is not a problem that admits of a purely theoretical solution. For although liberal theorists do aim to produce an accommodation at the level of normative political thought, much of the point of this enterprise would be lost if the accommodation stood no significant chance of being socially instantiated. This means that the success of the liberal project—like most projects in normative political theory—is hostage to actual patterns of historical change that alter the empirical conditions within which social institutions must operate. If, for example, during a certain period of time, liberal theorists take it for granted that most societies have reasonably homogeneous populations, and if, subsequently, economic and technological changes produce a level of mobility and migration that renders that assumption empirically untenable, then a scheme of normative thought that once seemed adequate for many purposes may no longer seem adequate. In general, an institutional configuration that represents a reasonable way of balancing a diverse group of values under one set of conditions may cease to do so under other conditions. And a practice or assumption that does not offend against a given value in some circumstances may do it considerable violence in others. Our own circumstances, at present, include a very rapid rate of change in many important areas of human life. Under these conditions, it becomes even more difficult than it would otherwise be to identify feasible social and political arrangements that can do an adequate job of accommodating all of the values that liberals prize, and there is no guarantee that attempts to produce such an accommodation will meet with success.

At the same time, however, we need not assume in advance that such an accommodation is impossible. Nor need we defer to those critics who see any attempt to arrive at a reasoned accommodation among liberal values as just another vestige of a discredited Enlightenment enterprise.[33] Some writers give the impression that unless we accept an excessively ambitious conception of reason or an implausibly reductionist conception of value we must regard every choice involving diverse considerations as a tragic dilemma that admits of no rational resolution. But most of us do not think this way about the choices that we face in our daily lives, and there is no more reason why it should be true at the level of political theory. Indeed, although tragedy abounds in our world, one of the most striking things about the heterogeneity of human ends is the extent of our success in dealing with it. It remains to be seen how well liberalism can adapt to the conditions of the modern—or postmodern—world. However, the task for liberal practical reason remains what it has always been: to determine the extent to which the diverse values that liberals care about can be jointly accommodated within the constraints fixed by the prevailing historical circumstances.

NOTES

An earlier version of this paper was presented as the 1994–95 John Dewey Memorial Lecture at the University of Vermont, and I benefited from the helpful discussion on that occasion. I am also indebted to Michael Green, Christopher Kutz, and Jeff McMahan for valuable comments, criticisms, and suggestions.

1. For pertinent discussion, see the debate between Martha Nussbaum and twenty-nine commentators on the subject of "Patriotism or Cosmopolitanism?," *Boston Review* 19 (October/November 1994): 3–34.

2. For more detailed discussion of the content of associative duties, see section 3 of my "Families, Nations, and Strangers," Lindley Lecture, University of Kansas, 1995.

3. For additional discussion of the voluntarist objection, see ibid., secs. 3, 4.

4. John Rawls, *A Theory of Justice* (Cambridge, Mass.: Harvard University Press, 1971), p. 457.

5. John Rawls, *Political Liberalism* (New York: Columbia University Press, 1993), p. 272n.

6. See Yael Tamir, *Liberal Nationalism* (Princeton: Princeton University Press, 1993), esp. chap. 6. In the last three paragraphs, I have relied heavily on Tamir's discussion.

7. See Ronald Dworkin, *Law's Empire* (Cambridge, Mass.: Harvard University Press, 1986), pp. 195–216; Tamir, *Liberal Nationalism*, chaps. 5, 6.

8. See Rawls, *A Theory of Justice*, secs. 18–19, 51–52; Jeremy Waldron, "Special Ties and Natural Duties," *Philosophy and Public Affairs* 22 (1993): 3–30.

9. Rawls, *A Theory of Justice*, p. 115.

10. A. John Simmons, *Moral Principles and Political Obligations* (Princeton: Princeton University Press, 1979), chap. 6.

11. Ibid., pp. 149–50.

12. Ibid., p. 150.

13. Ibid.

14. Ibid., pp. 150–51.

15. Rawls, *A Theory of Justice*, p. 115.

16. In defending the natural duty of justice against Simmons's criticism, Jeremy Waldron argues that such duties can be particularized because principles of justice can be limited in their application and because a person can have a special duty to an institution that administers such a "range-limited" principle. This may be so if the person is an "insider" with respect to that institution—that is, "if it is part of the point of that institution to do justice to some claim of his among all the claims with which it deals" ("Special Ties and Natural Duties," p. 16). However, Waldron also suggests that range limitations are justified only on a "provisional" or "pro tem" basis (p. 15). If those who are not insiders with respect to a given range-limited principle interfere with the administration of such a principle because they wish to promote a principle of wider application, such as "a principle of global redistribution," there may be "no moral basis for condemning" this interference (p. 17n). But then, on Waldron's interpretation, the natural duty of justice hardly seems to represent a stable way of integrating universalist and particularist considerations for it presents no fundamental barrier to a thoroughgoing globalism.

17. My discussion of the distributive objection incorporates portions of section 3 of "Families, Nations, and Strangers," and there is additional discussion of the objection in that paper. I have also discussed some related issues in "Individual Responsibility in a Global Age," *Social Philosophy and Policy* 12 (1995): 219–36.

18. For a recent book-length discussion of loyalty, see George Fletcher, *Loyalty* (New York: Oxford University Press, 1993).

19. See Alasdair MacIntyre, "Is Patriotism a Virtue?," Lindley Lecture, University of Kansas, 1984.

20. Ibid., p. 19.

21. Ibid., p. 18.

22. Ibid., p. 5.

23. Ibid., p. 6.

24. As this suggests, the relation between liberalism and consequentialism is in some ways a problematic one. I have examined the contrast between consequentialism and agent-relative morality in *The Rejection of Consequentialism*, rev. ed. (Oxford: Clarendon, 1994).

25. I have discussed this point at greater length in *Human Morality* (New York: Oxford University Press, 1992), chap. 6.

26. Tamir, *Liberal Nationalism*, p. 100.

27. Ibid., pp. 100–101.

28. See Will Kymlicka, *Liberalism, Community, and Culture* (Oxford: Clarendon, 1989); Neil MacCormick, "Nation and Nationalism," in *Legal Right and Social Democracy: Essays in Legal and Social Philosophy* (Oxford: Clarendon, 1982), pp. 247–64; Joseph Raz and Avishai Margalit, "National Self-Determination," and Joseph Raz, "Multiculturalism: A Liberal Perspective," in Raz's *Ethics in the Public Domain* (Oxford: Clarendon, 1994), pp. 110–30, 155–76. See also Avishai Margalit and Moshe Halbertal, "Liberalism and the Right to Culture," *Social Research* 61 (1994): 491–510. It is significant, I think, that all of these writers are concerned primarily with the question of how liberalism can accommodate the claims of communities to recognition, legal protection, and self-determination. They have little or nothing to say about the duties of community members to each other.

29. See John Dewey, *The Public and Its Problems* (New York: Henry Holt, 1927), pp. 143–84, 211–19.

30. Tamir, *Liberal Nationalism*, p. 137.

31. For discussion of an argument that seeks first to establish the permissibility of favoring one's associates and then to move from this permission to associative duties, see my "Families, Nations, and Strangers," sec. 4.

32. MacIntyre, "Is Patriotism a Virtue?," pp. 19–20.

33. See, for example, John Gray, "Agonistic Liberalism," *Social Philosophy and Policy* 12 (1995): 111–35.

13

Context, Continuity, and Fairness

ARTHUR RIPSTEIN

Defenders of nationalism have claimed at least three advantages to cultural membership. The first two are goods for individuals. First, membership in a secure culture provides a sufficiently familiar moral space within which people can develop a rich and varied range of conceptions of the good. Second, it offers support for or confirmation of certain views of the good by placing them in a larger history. The third advantage is a good for societies: cultural membership is sometimes said to make justice possible by making citizens see the sacrifices demanded by a state as expressions of who they are rather than arbitrary burdens.

My interest is in the third role claimed for membership. To explore its significance, I distinguish it from the other two. Once the three supposed advantages of cultural membership are properly distinguished, there is little left to the idea that nations are especially well suited to being units of political sovereignty or that cultures, as such, have a right to political self-determination.

This essay begins with a brief discussion of the conditions under which a culture can provide a secure context of choice and a sense of continuity with the past. I argue that a culture's ability to provide an individual with either of these goods depends entirely on that individual's own attitude toward that culture. I then go on to consider the argument that cultural membership is necessary in order to make the sacrifices demanded by justice coherent. I distinguish between and reject three different versions of the argument. The first claims that national membership is particularly well suited to motivating sacrifices. I suggest that this argument rests on dubious empirical assumptions about the readiness to make different sorts of sacrifices. The second version claims that demands of justice only arise between people who share other things. I reject it because different things must be shared to make justice possible. The third version claims that fairness requires assessing people in light of their own fundamental commitments, many of which are culturally based. Against it I argue that the very things that make cultural membership appropriate as a source of context and continuity make it an inappropriate basis for underwriting those sacrifices.

Before turning to the three roles of membership, I begin with what I hope are some fairly banal historical and sociological observations about nationalism in an attempt to make it clear which phenomena concern me. "Nation" does not cover all state activities or all cultural affiliations. Even a cursory reading of the last two centuries of history reveals that national identity is not always identified with any one language, religion, level of economic development, or history. Benedict Anderson suggests that nations are "imagined communities" because the members may have little contact with each other, but the community exists in their image of it. In calling nations imagined Anderson does not mean to suggest that the imagining is either aesthetic or sentimental. It is political, as the image is the product of conflict and struggle. Almost any community of any size exists largely in the imaginations of its members, who seldom, if ever, meet. But nations are imagined by the few for the many.[1] In doing this, national leaders come close to the task that Rousseau assigns to the legislator: that of coming up with traditions through which people can recognize each other as fellow citizens (though nation builders may lack the unity of purpose one associates with a Rousseauian legislator).[2] Their ability to provide their members with a sense of community depends at least as much on fabricating a common history as on discovering one. Anderson's studies of Southeast Asian nationalism show how nations could be forged out of diverse cultural and linguistic groups, groups that were brought together largely by the contingencies of battles and treaties between colonial powers.[3] Other nations emerged through developments in bureaucracy and record keeping; much of the imagining of a common heritage (or even a common language) was done by what Eric Hobsbawm calls "the lesser examination passing classes."[4] For my purposes, what is most important about nations is that they aim to be both cultural and political at once.

Context

Cultural membership enables individuals to find themselves in a sufficiently familiar moral space so that they can develop, revise, and pursue their own conceptions of the good. Having others around who have made what they will of similar cultural possibilities, individuals find themselves both with a broader range of viable options and amid others whose lives and choices affirm the value of their own.

The notion of a context of choice may seem to suggest that a secure culture is needed simply as a precondition for forming a conception of the good but becomes less important once one has reached the age of reason. But developing a conception of the good is not a stage of development in the way that developing a distinctive accent or even a first language might be thought to be. Instead, developing a conception of the good is a process, which goes on throughout life, of deciding what matters most of the possibilities that are available. Thus it requires a rich store of alternatives that are familiar enough to present real options. When a culture is in danger of disappearing, its members may no longer be able to pursue a conception of the good they have already developed. More significant, they are unable to continue to develop it. But of course not every case of a disappearing culture fits this model. If a culture disappears because its members find some other, surrounding culture more appealing, they are not left without a context of choice. Instead, they slowly find themselves with a new one.

In many cases, the advantages of cultural membership come without any cost. Many cultures are sufficiently secure to provide it to their members while engaging in the myriad business of everyday life. English, for example, is a fundamental cultural resource to those who speak it, but because its use is so widespread, it is available for free to almost anyone who might want it. In societies that are culturally homogeneous or largely so, state efforts to support and reinforce that homogeneity surely enrich the context of choice for some individuals. The French ministry of culture contributes to maintaining a way of life, though perhaps less so than the agricultural subsidies that sustain the French farmers. At the same time, the absence of those policies would not deprive ordinary people of their context of choice—it would, in normal circumstances, change in different ways and perhaps more quickly. Further, the same kinds of protection and sustenance are possible in units much smaller (or larger) than the nation. Other cultural resources may be just as vital to particular people's lives but be much harder to come by. Members of cultures that are endangered may be entitled to special protection so that they get something that others are able to take for granted.[5] In this, cultural protections differ little from redistribution of income to those who have less for various morally arbitrary reasons.[6] Something like this idea underlies Will Kymlicka's arguments for special rights for minority cultures and has just about the right reach for a liberal principle: everyone is entitled to some primary good; those who find themselves with less than an equal share for morally arbitrary reasons are entitled to be brought up to the level of others. But the good in question is not a way of life or success in pursuing it.

In defending protections for context, we need not suppose that everyone is entitled to sufficient resources to guarantee success in pursuit of their chosen life.

Protecting a context does not require ensuring that people will succeed in preserving their own particular visions of their culture. It requires only that diverse cultural resources be available. Subsequent generations require the same diversity of cultural resources but not the identical culture. As a result, those who make preserving some vision of the culture the object of their choices are not entitled to succeed.

Continuity and Survival

Nation and culture are often central to the stories that people tell of themselves and the way they locate themselves in a longer time horizon. Those stories also enable them to see certain things as mattering. By placing their lives and choices in a longer perspective, people are able to find greater significance in them. Viewed in the abstract, such an attachment to the past can be made to seem puzzling. But in concrete cases, many people feel a profound desire to remain true to the ways of their ancestors or at least to be true to some vision of them.

The desire for continuity is best thought of as a special case of a more general human tendency to find oneself in some larger context. Just as people seek connection with the past, so they try to model their lives on the lives of others they admire, from the past or the present, from cultural tradition or contemporary life.[7] Just as I can find worth in my projects by looking back for centuries, I also can do so by discovering a connection with others I admire. But to do either I needn't choose a single set of identifications for all of my projects and commitments. Instead, I choose my projects and connections to others together. At the same time, others sharing various roles and projects often demand particular identifications.

The attempt to maintain continuity with the past sometimes leads to charges of betrayal by others claiming connection with the same past. But cultural membership is only one of many sources of identity that lead to such charges. What needs to be protected is the individual's source of identity, not the views of other members of some group about how well one is living those roles. The person who identifies with some rock musician or other figure from popular culture does not need to measure up to standards set by the musician's official fan club. To fulfill a desire for continuity, it is important that individuals be able to find themselves in relation to what has gone before, not that they succeed by anyone else's measure of their success.

Although a concern for continuity with the past may lead parents to raise their own children in particular ways, it does not entitle these parents (or the state acting for them) to dictate the terms on which their grandchildren shall be raised.

While continuity is both a backward-looking interest and a forward-looking one, only its backward-looking aspects are entitled to political protection. Any way of protecting backward-looking interests is bound to have consequences for forward-looking ones, but the rationale for protection must always look backward. One of the most important ways of keeping connected with one's past is raising one's children in keeping with that past. If such attempts are successful, the result will be cultural survival. Yet the rationale is not survival, any more than the rationale for tax deductions for religious charities is to keep religions alive. Instead, each allows people to connect themselves with the things they find most meaningful in their lives. The rationale for protecting their culture is the same even if parents fail to pass this culture on to their children. Although policies that enable people to pass on their culture are not mandatory, given the sort of good that continuity is, if the state acts to protect it for some, it must, on grounds of fairness, act to protect it for others also.[8]

A state policy of protecting a thin sense of continuity with the past has three virtues. First, it leaves people space within which to find continuity with some imagined past and enables the state to officially endorse their doing so without in any way preventing them from radically reinterpreting or even rejecting their past. Second, in a multicultural society (as most of the world's states now are), it holds out the possibility of teaching people to value difference and diversity. This not only gives people more pasts with which to connect themselves and a richer context within which to find themselves but also provides a model for greater tolerance and civility at an individual level. Third, it enables people from diverse cultures to be integrated into the larger society without giving up their sense of continuity with their past.

Continuity differs from what I have called context because it fills a different need. Both are required to enable people to find value in their choices. But context creates the range of possible choices, while continuity makes it possible to find value in them. Even if the context is rich enough for me to choose to live a particular way, if the surrounding culture constantly tells me that I have chosen badly, I may have a hard time finding value in my conception of the good. Yet I may be so rooted in my culture that I cannot give it up. In such circumstances, the effect of such messages may be to disparage my sense of self-worth rather than to provide me with alternatives. Conversely, someone might have a tremendous sense of continuity with the past, recognized (perhaps condescendingly) by others, yet have no real context of choice left.

Although what I have called context and continuity are distinct, it is essential to see that they matter in the same way—to those currently alive who wish to make use of a culture. They do not provide a rationale for the state acting to ensure the future survival of a culture or any particular interpretation of it. This isn't to say that parents should be denied the wherewithal to pass traditions on to their children but simply that the state should not discriminate against those who choose not to pass these traditions on or who reject the ways of their ancestors. Although most people find value in relation to some understanding of the past, no particular understanding of the past has a claim on those who reject it. Continuity is important to a person's ability to find value in the choices he or she has made. When choices conflict with the past, the past loses its claim because a culture can only provide a sense of continuity if its members see themselves as such.

Imagination and Sacrifice

I have so far pointed to two ways in which cultural membership is important to an individual's ability to be a member of a political society. I now want to suggest that whatever does the job of providing context and continuity is unsuitable to underwrite a liberal commitment to fairness. Although we come to political life thick with particularity, not all of those aspects matter, and not all that matter, matter in the same way. That I have some cultural attachments or other surely matters in political life, but which particular ones I have should not matter.

The idea that a commitment to fairness needs something like culture to underwrite it comes in at least three versions. The first is an empirical claim about motivation. The second is a conceptual claim about the conditions under which justice makes sense. The third is a claim about the nature of fairness. I examine them in turn.

Membership and Motivation

Cultural membership is sometimes offered as the solution to a problem about motivation. It is often suggested that without some further reason for citizens to care about the demands fairness makes on them, a liberal society will tend to disintegrate. In recent years, community has become increasingly popular as a candidate for the solution to this purported problem. Thus Charles Taylor suggests that community provides an alternative to the unrealistic liberal alternatives of either "moral high-mindedness or narrow self-interest."[9] Instead, people will willingly make sacrifices for those with whom they share common projects.

The search for some way to motivate sacrifices seems to suppose that the demands of justice must somehow stand over against the individual's other motives or the settled mores of the culture. Once we accept this premise, it is hard to see how anything could qualify as a solution. Anything that could do the job would have to be both sufficiently robust on its own to motivate sacrifices and flexible enough to motivate the particular demands that liberalism hopes to make. It is not surprising that the standard examples of shared goals sufficient to motivate sacrifices have little to do with politics. Michael Sandel's example is mutual concern felt by members of a family; Charles Taylor's is a group of music lovers who bring the symphony orchestra to their suburb. These examples aren't just difficult to generalize.[10] They face a more serious problem. Why would sharing a goal lead the members of a group to make sacrifices in the interest of fairness among their members? Yet those are the sacrifices that liberalism demands and is putatively unable to motivate.

Yael Tamir has offered a version of this argument that offers nationality in place of other forms of community.[11] Tamir talks less about motivating sacrifices than about making sense of political obligation. By viewing political obligations as a species of more general forms of associative obligations, Tamir hopes to use nationalism to make sense of the normative claim of a state as of a piece with the role of "social and political institutions as representing a particular culture and as carriers of the national identity."[12] The argument is interesting both because it is offered as an interpretation of liberalism and because nationality often means roughly the same thing to large groups of people. Historically it has served to motivate major sacrifices. Tamir gives the striking example of people learning, and in part making up, a new language—an enormous sacrifice when one is trying to find the right words.[13]

Inspiring though these sacrifices may be, I doubt that they can solve the supposed problem with liberalism. Liberalism doesn't need a moral psychology to explain why people will or should find it reasonable to make sacrifices for national self-determination; it needs an account of why people should make sacrifices in the interest of fairness. Even if we all share a commitment to our independence or the preservation of our language, will that lead the fortunate among us to make sacrifices for the sake of the less fortunate? Perhaps it will, insofar as doing so will promote our national aspirations—the fortunate might willingly contribute to educating less fortunate children in the ways of "our" culture. But it isn't clear that this would lead to economic redistribution or equality of opportunity unless either was perceived as aiding national goals. It is striking how one form of sacrifice—military service—does seem to derive considerable force from the idea of nation. Fighting to get rid of foreign domination requires a sharp sense of who "we" are and who "they" are. But however important these features of nationalism are for understanding political history and sociology, their relation to the more ordinary demands of fairness is far from obvious.[14]

In questioning the relevance of nation to the demands of justice, I don't mean to deny that people who share a language and culture will usually have an easier time with the administrative demands of running a state than those who don't. Nor do I mean to deny that (for example) people will usually have a harder time honoring the demands of fairness when interacting with others with whom they share a history of enmity. Such factors are plainly relevant to determining the viability of various political units.[15] Goodwill and ease make any form of cooperation run more smoothly. For that matter, there is a clear meaning of the word "culture" in which different societies have different political cultures, and nothing I have said should be taken to suggest that political cultures are irrelevant to the readiness to make sacrifices for the sake of justice. But political culture is not the same as the sort of thing that ordinarily provides context and continuity. I mean only to question the claim that readiness to make one sort of sacrifice tells us very much about readiness to make others.

Partiality

A variant of the motivational argument claims that community membership makes partiality toward its other members morally acceptable or even required. According to this reading, sacrifices—of whatever sort—for the sake of the other members of the community make moral as well as psychological sense in a way that the same sacrifices for outsiders purportedly don't. Thus Michael Walzer tells us that "distributive justice presupposes a bounded world within which distributions take place: a group of people committed to dividing, exchanging, and sharing social goods, first of all among themselves."[16] This version of the argument may seem especially compelling when it comes to economic redistribution. Some might suppose that the demands of economic redistribution are only real, or especially pressing, within the boundaries of a state.[17] According to this view, perhaps shared culture explains or justifies this sort of partiality.[18]

There are serious problems with the significance of state boundaries to obligations of political morality. Yet it is difficult to see how cultural identification could solve them. If cultural membership is construed just as a matter of subjective attachment, redistributive obligations would cease if people cease to feel strongly about their conationals. As such, the supposed rationale for partiality collapses into the motivational argument we have just considered. But if membership is thought of as unchosen, perhaps on the model of the biological family, the choice of culture as the basis of that obligation becomes obscure—even if we put to one side worries about the political processes that define it. Everyone associates with many different people on many different terms. Why not focus on geographical proximity or economic integration instead? Or, more significant, on obligations more directly connected to the justice of institutions? The idea that some obligations are unchosen but particular has considerable plausibility,[19] but the content of those obligations is tied to the particular roles that generate them. It is far more difficult to see how sharing some feature with others could form the basis of an open-ended obligation to be partial to them. Here, too, we confront a shadow version of the motivational argument, with all of its problems. If cultural membership generates obligations, they are related to cultural membership, not to distributive fairness. One might more plausibly suppose that there are greater obligations to sustain just institutions or to work to create such institutions in settings in which they are feasible. By focusing on institutions, we might make some sense of the idea of partiality within them and thus of the liberal tendency to focus on the state as the locus of questions of justice.[20] We can even put this point in terms of culture, if by that we mean political culture, so long as we do not confuse it with culture in the thicker sense that provides context and continuity.

The Demands of Fairness

In this section I look more carefully at the ways in which a liberal state makes demands of its members in the interest of fairness. Many of the most pressing questions about fairness come out of the context within which a decision must be (implicitly) made about who should bear various misfortunes.[21] All societies have practices that determine whose bad luck various things are. Consider some answers implicit in contemporary practices. I don't endorse all of these but mention them to bring out the things those practices take for granted. Some misfortunes are thought to lie where they fall: if I slip while getting out of the shower, that's (typically) just my problem. Other sorts of misfortune turn out to belong to someone other than the person they happened to: if you are careless and I am injured as a result, the misfortune is yours, and so you have to repair my losses. Still other types of misfortune are thought of as held in common: if I become seriously ill (anywhere but in the United States), the medical costs of my loss are borne by all.

In order to decide which sorts of bad luck fall into which category, a liberal community needs views about a wide variety of questions, including questions about the importance of various kinds of activities and the nature of various kinds of losses. In each case, the community must have a view about how much people can expect of each other. If I'm harmed because you get the job I want, that's just my problem; if I'm careful and you're injured, that's just your problem (unless I'm doing something like using explosives or keeping wild animals). If you're careless and I'm injured, that's your problem, unless I did something to expose myself to danger. But it depends on how I exposed myself. Some things that might have so exposed me, like going out at all even though I know I have an eggshell skull, don't make me bear the risk. Again, normally if I'm injured, I have a duty to mitigate the damages, but if my religious beliefs prevent me from doing so, that's your problem, not mine. In order to resolve any of these questions fairly, we need some understanding of how various goods matter and why. This isn't to say that we must decide which things we want to promote and set up an incentive structure accordingly. Instead, we think of certain kinds of activities—walking down the street or practicing one's religion—as the kind of things that people have an important interest in making up their own minds about.[22] We cannot decide which activities matter and how by considering how strongly people feel about them. Different people feel different ways. Instead, we need to figure out how to allocate them fairly. To do so, we need some view about how important various activities and various sorts of injuries are.

In similar ways, we need some way of determining which losses are thought of as held in common. Earthquake victims may get compensation, but those who were not fortunate enough to have anything to lose in the earthquake may get nothing. Background misfortunes and sudden losses are often treated differently. Whether or not this is fair depends in part on how unfair the background misfortunes themselves are. Like questions about how bad luck is to be borne between particular people, these questions turn on views about the importance of various activities and the seriousness of particular losses. Protecting cultural membership, as a source both of context and of continuity, can be understood in this light as a decision to treat the misfortune of having an endangered culture as something to be held in common.

Examples like these show ways in which good and bad fortune are "distributed" by any political order and the ways in which that distribution imposes costs on various people. A liberal state needs to answer such questions in order to know which "sacrifices" to demand of whom. The only setting in which it can coherently make such demands is a special sort of community. This is not a point about the psychology of sacrifice. The liberal commitment to treating people as equals means that everyone is held to the same standards or presumed to have an interest in a reasonable share of the same thing, regardless of individual departures from them. You may not care about religious freedom; I may need to concentrate much harder on driving carefully than you do. Fairness requires both that we be treated equally (which requires a common currency of equality) and that all be able in some sense to share the perspective from which such decisions are made, even if their individual concerns depart from the public perspective. As a result, that measure cannot depend on the fact that any particular person understands him- or herself in a particular way or in terms of a particular culture. Of course, any such measure will overlap the views of some more than the views of others. But that is an unavoidable feature of any impersonal measure, not a sign of unfairness.[23] Those who hold different views are not entitled to opt out. Any such perspective cannot make one person's rejection of it the measure of another's liberty or security.

In calling these things "decisions" and talking about "sharing a perspective," I'm oversimplifying. For one thing, the decisions are seldom made explicitly and the perspective is even less frequently explicitly adopted. And there are better and worse ways of dealing with various misfortunes, which concepts of fairness go some way toward addressing. If fairness requires that people bear the costs their activities impose upon others, then distributive shares must themselves be fair in order to avoid endlessly remeasuring (and reproducing) past inequalities. Conversely, the value of distributive shares depends in part on the ways in which particular misfortunes are allocated. But views about the importance of various goods are needed to give content to ideas of fairness. For present purposes, the point is that any state requires some sacrifices of its members, at least against some alternative benchmark that they can imagine. Whether those sacrifices make sense depends on the members' ability to see these sacrifices as fair in light of views about the importance of various goods. In order to make demands at all, liberalism needs a content through which to express its egalitarian aspirations. It doesn't just need to motivate people to make sacrifices; it needs some currency in which to measure costs across persons in order for talk about sacrifices being required by fairness to make any sense at all.

It's important to recognize that the demands made when bad luck is held in common are not necessarily greater than those made when it turns out to be the bad luck of someone in particular. There is no natural baseline against which such demands can be measured in the abstract. Just because I injured myself rather than being injured by somebody else, or you were careful and I got hurt anyway, or I was momentarily distracted and you got hurt, I may end up very badly off. Were various misfortunes treated differently, I might have avoided those burdens. These, too, are among the "burdens" that any state places on its members. Of course, one might be fortunate enough to go through life escaping such demands, and they aren't faced day in and day out in the way that the demands of redistribution are by those who might be materially better off without them. Still, although adjudicative demands may not involve a large-scale principle of sharing, they involve no less by way of demands.

The shared perspective from which misfortunes are distributed provides the sort of community that is prerequisite for fairness. If we share such a perspective, the claims that the state makes against us will seem reasonable. Ways of allocating misfortune provide a thin form of community in that its members will identify with their fellow citizens and perhaps locate its practices within a longer time horizon. Indeed, some measure of such attachments is probably required if the demands of justice are not experienced as utterly foreign and arbitrary. But such a civic culture is different from the sort of substantive historical culture that provides a thick context of choice or continuity with one's ancestors.

I will use a fine-grained example of a Canadian criminal case to illustrate this point. Detailed cases often show what is really at stake in profound disagreements. Large portions of criminal law are so obvious to everyone, apart from any other views they might have, that the other commitments on which it rests are easy to overlook. When we look at the ways in which conduct that is otherwise wrongful can be excused, some of those presuppositions begin to emerge. And while criminal law isn't obviously about deciding whose bad luck things are, it is part of a more general account of how much we can reasonably demand of each other, and it must often come to terms with incidents that nobody wanted to happen. One place where this is particularly apparent is in the defense of provocation, which reduces a homicide from murder to manslaughter. The law of provocation doesn't just ask whether or not someone lost his or her temper but whether a reasonable person would have lost his or her temper in the same circumstances. In so asking, it is apportioning punishment to the amount of self-control people can expect of each other. The point of imposing a standard of reasonableness is that the fact that someone may have perceived something as an insult doesn't automatically excuse it.

Consider the case of *Regina v. Ly*.[24] Ly, a Vietnamese immigrant to Canada, killed his girlfriend when she arrived home late. He offered the defense of provocation, claiming that he took her late arrival as evidence of infidelity. Ly and other members of Vancouver's Vietnamese community testified that in their culture infidelity is a grievous insult to a man's pride and should serve to excuse his loss of self-control. Ly's argument was that in deciding whether or not a reasonable person would have been provoked in like circumstances, the individual's culture should be taken into account.

In cases of provocation, the law always presumes that the victim somehow did not deserve to die. The law asks whether or not a reasonable person would have lost self-control and whether the accused did, in fact, lose self-control.[25] Ly's defense turned on the claim that since he was a member of a group that was more likely to lose self-control in such circumstances, less self-control should be required of him. If the aim of the law were to punish only people who didn't lose self-control, we could see the force of Ly's claim. But if that were the law's aim, then Ly's cultural affiliation would be beside the point because it at best provides evidence of whether or not he lost self-control and thus of whether he was subjectively guilty.

The court rejected the argument on the grounds that the law must protect people equally from each other and cannot make allowances for a person's culture any more than it can for a person's unusually short temper or deeply felt belief that he or she had been insulted, whatever the source of the belief. It especially cannot make allowances for a man losing his temper because he regards a woman as his property, however deeply ingrained such a view may be in some culture.

Ly illustrates two points of interest to a theory of liberal community. The first is that when we are faced with a dispute of this sort, a person's culture is the wrong place to look. We need to appeal to something else to do the sorting, so that the mere fact that there is an inherited culture is itself not supplying the content to the required political values. Political values provide an index of fairness between people, so the mere fact that someone feels strongly about something does not give that thing a claim against others. Fairness cannot be dictated by what an individual person or his or her culture of origin thinks fair. In rejecting Ly's claim that his culture should be taken into account, the court noted that if the provocation had taken the form of a racial slur, Ly's culture would be relevant. That is, culture matters in some ways—everyone has a legitimate, though not unlimited, interest in being free of racial invectives. The interest isn't unlimited because it provides only a limited excuse when it leads to the death of another. Being free of racial invective is a candidate for a legally protected interest in a way that one's general interest in acting in keeping with one's culture is not.[26]

Contrast this with the other two roles of cultural membership we've considered. When culture is thought of either as a context of choice or as a way of locating oneself in a longer history, the mere fact that some person finds him- or herself with that culture gives it whatever role it has within that person's life.[27] I may come to reject the culture that provided me with the resources to even think about rejecting it, but its ability to provide me with a context of choice depends on my having once identified with it. By contrast, subjective identification with culture cannot be the basis for fixing the limits of the responsibilities of one person to others.[28]

The second point is that the example is in no way idiosyncratic of the fact that Ly was Vietnamese or a member of a cultural minority. In numerous English cases, for example, men entered similar defenses (often successfully) without explicitly mentioning their culture because they could take it for granted. In those cases, culture was used to resolve issues, with results that were no more acceptable than in *Ly*.

The example may seem heavy-handed. Why condemn all cultures just because some have unpalatable aspects? But the point goes deeper. Caring deeply about something is necessary to provide both a context of choice and a time horizon, and when the right sort of thing is the object of that attachment, it is sufficient to provide both. In deciding what is fair between parties, in contrast, the mere fact that someone cares is not sufficient to decide what is fair because there is always a question about whether it is fair to others to ask that they bear the costs of that person's subjective commitment. The question arises in exactly the same way whether it is one person or the entire society that will otherwise bear the costs. The only way to answer is with an index of primary goods—a catalog of which interests count as fundamental in measuring costs across persons. Cultural identification, both as a context of choice and as a time horizon, belongs in the index of goods through which we determine how much we can reasonably ask of each other. But it is a part of that index, one important good among many, not the basis for making the list as a whole. Holding Ly to the same standards of self-control to which we hold others deprives him of neither a time horizon nor a context of choice. Although saying that the state's interest in preserving life must take priority over a culture's understanding of itself may be interpreted by some members of the culture as a rejection of that culture's worth,[29] the importance of that sort of recognition is only one good among many. Because fairness depends on measuring costs across persons, allowing each person to dictate the terms by which the costs of his or her choices to others are measured is not a coherent element of it. In the same way, an individual cannot be allowed to use the standards of his or her culture to measure his or her responsibilities to others. From the point of view of fairness, cultural membership is one interest among others that must be fairly protected for all, not utilized as the basis for evaluating in each case what someone owes to others.

The index of primary goods in light of which such decisions are made should be thought of as neither expressing the views of a particular culture nor somehow transcending all culture. A political culture that decides where bad luck is to fall can be conceptually independent of the culture that provides context and continuity. Of course its content will be causally dependent on the cultures of the people making it up (in both senses). But nothing will derive its claim to importance from the fact that it is part of the culture. The political culture is an attempt to be fair and thus can't allow any inherited culture as such to be the measure of anyone's liberty or security.

Consider another example to see how cultural attachments might be more appropriately accommodated. One summer afternoon, Ruth Friedman and Jack Katz were on their way down a ski lift in the Catskills. The attendants turned off the lift and went home for the day, stranding Friedman and Katz. Hours passed, and the sun began to set. Friedman, an Orthodox Jew, became increasingly concerned because she believed that she was forbidden to be alone with a man other than a family member after dark. She jumped from the ski lift, injuring herself, and successfully sued the State of New York, the operator of the lift.[30] Needless to say, the court did not find for Friedman on the grounds that jumping from ski lifts is the sort of activity that is always acceptable. Instead, it held that it is reasonable to give priority to one's religious beliefs rather than to mitigating damages brought about by another's wrongdoing. The principle has its limits because a court would probably have been less ready to allow Friedman to avoid liability had her religious beliefs resulted in the injury of another.

Notice that this view of the importance of religion doesn't depend on a shared religion. In fact, most religions presumably wouldn't think of their practices in terms of their costs to others. The determination of when religion is and isn't a justification for various things is for political purposes only. It also doesn't depend for its rationale on the fact that liberal cultures have a history of religious freedom. Although historical experience has shaped what we find plausible, no appeal to a particular tradition provides a unique rationale for looking at religion this way. Instead, one can endorse the view of the role of religion coming from any number of different religious or nonreligious traditions. In much the same way, one can recognize the importance of culture (or any of the other goods) coming from a wide variety of cultures. Coming from different cultures may even mean recognizing it for different reasons, in what John Rawls characterizes as an overlapping consensus.[31] Although inherited cultures may lead some people to affirm such a view (and the fact that the state leaves room for the affirmation of particular cultural practices may lead to greater allegiance to it), established nationality may or may not do the job. At least as important, the overlapping view of justice may inform the historical interpretation people make of their particular cultures.

Conclusion

A liberal community makes fairness its central political value, through which views about various goods are expressed. But fairness is a good for politics rather than for all of life; when we locate its centrality within political life, the role of the state is as an agency of fairness. But the state is the expression not of what really matters but of what is fair. Liberalism's liberating insight is that "who we really are" is of limited importance to questions of the legitimate use of state coercion. Politics at its best should make it possible for institutions to be fair toward people who may disagree about what matters most in life. As a result, political membership must be understood in terms of fairness rather than in terms of history or culture. This needn't stand in the way of people acting to preserve their cultures (even with state aid in certain circumstances), but we may at least hope that it precludes denying rights of citizenship on the basis of culture or history.[32]

NOTES

I am grateful to Jean Baillargeon, Jules Coleman, Robert Howse, Richard Katskee, Jeff McMahan, Chris Morris, Dan Ortiz, Denise Reaume, Amelie Rorty, and Benjamin Zipursky for helpful comments and advice. Earlier versions of this essay were presented at the American Philosophical Association Pacific Division meetings in Los Angeles, April 1994, and to the Social Sciences and Humanities Research Council of Canada Research Network on Multiculturalism in Toronto, March 1995.

1. Benedict Anderson, *Imagined Communities: Reflections on the Origin and Spread of Nationalism* (London: Verso, 1991). Anderson supposes that being imagined is a feature of most communities, not just nations.

2. Jean-Jacques Rousseau, *Du contrat social* (Paris: Gallimard Editions Pléiade, 1964), bk. 2, chap. 7.

3. Anderson, *Imagined Communities*.

4. Eric Hobsbawm, *Nations and Nationalism since 1780: Programme, Myth, Reality* (Cambridge: Cambridge University Press, 1989), p. 118.

5. How often does this happen? Kymlicka's example of Canada's aboriginal peoples may be misleading because the history of racism, discrimination, and unsuccessful attempts at forced assimilation against them pretty much precludes their using mainstream Canadian culture as an alternative context. For examples, see Geoffrey York, *The Dispossessed: Life and Death in Native Canada* (London: Vintage, 1990). In other cases, a surrounding culture might provide a context of choice over a period of several generations.

6. Often the only way to protect a culture is to transfer material resources to members of the culture so that they don't exhaust their other resources in attempting to protect their culture. See Will Kymlicka, *Liberalism, Community, and Culture* (Oxford: Oxford University Press, 1989), esp. chap. 9.

7. For a discussion of this point, see Amelie Rorty and David Wong, "Aspects of Identity

and Agency," in *Identity, Character and Morality*, ed. A. Rorty and O. Flanagan (Cambridge, Mass.: MIT Press, 1990), p. 23.

8. I postpone to another occasion the question of policies appropriate to doing so.

9. Charles Taylor, "Cross Purposes," in *Liberalism and the Moral Life*, ed. Nancy Rosenblum (Cambridge, Mass.: Harvard University Press, 1989).

10. Sandel's more recent suggestion is easier to generalize but seeks to build community out of overlapping goals rather than use community to motivate them. President Clinton is reported to have taken notes furiously when Sandel suggested that an emphasis on making the streets safe from crime might bring Americans together as a community (Sidney Blumenthal, "The Education of a President," *New Yorker*, January 24, 1994, p. 41).

11. Yael Tamir, *Liberal Nationalism* (Princeton: Princeton University Press, 1993), p. 105.

12. Ibid., p. 74.

13. Ibid., p. 88.

14. Questions about how much sacrifice can be called forth by various affiliations and memberships turn on empirical issues about which philosophers are notoriously lacking in expertise. The psychology of perceived gains and losses is itself at best poorly understood. To mention one example, most people apparently regard a tax refund as some sort of windfall, even though in economic terms the refund plainly represents a recovery from a loss. One's sense of what sort of person one is plainly figures in such evaluations—many people would pay someone else to have some domestic chore done but would not consider doing the same chore for someone else, even for a larger sum of money, because they don't wish to think of themselves as the sort of person who would do such things for money. Such examples make me wary of speculating about what will be perceived as a loss and what as a gain and of what sacrifices are seen as legitimate in light of particular memberships. People are plainly willing to give things up if the demands seem fair, but just what makes things seem fair is murky at best.

15. See the discussion of these issues in Will Kymlicka, *Multicultural Citizenship* (Oxford: Oxford University Press, 1995).

16. Michael Walzer, "Members and Strangers," in *Spheres of Justice* (New York: Basic Books, 1983), chap. 1.

17. This seems to be close to Tamir's position (*Liberal Nationalism*, p. 139).

18. This question is explored in Jeff McMahan, "The Limits of National Partiality," paper presented at the Conference on the Ethics of Nationalism, University of Illinois at Urbana-Champaign, April 1994.

19. See the excellent discussions of this point by Michael Hardimon, "Role Obligations," *Journal of Philosophy* 91, no. 7 (July 1994): 337.

20. These remarks are by their very nature tentative, as I am not firmly convinced that there is sense to be made in this area. Compare Ronald Dworkin's claim that a liberal can be integrated into his or her community in the sense that how well or badly his or her life goes will in part depend on the justice of the community. Dworkin points out that an "integrated" community is constituted by the attitudes and practices that create the community as a collective agent. As such, the communal concerns with which people properly identify are those tied to those attitudes and practices rather than those that extend amorphously to all members. Although Dworkin doesn't focus on culture, his argument points to the same conclusion as mine: institutions organized around justice make the sacrifices demanded by

justice a plausible object of affiliation; other institutions do not. See "Liberal Community," in *Communitarianism and Individualism*, ed. S. Aveneri and A. de-Shalit (Oxford: Oxford University Press, 1992).

21. I develop this idea in "Equality, Luck, and Responsibility," *Philosophy and Public Affairs* 23, no. 1 (1994): 3–23, and Arthur Ripstein and Jules Coleman, "Misfortune and Mischief," *McGill Law Journal* 41, no. 1: 91–130.

22. That is, we treat them somewhat like the way John Rawls advocates treating "primary goods," although the index of such goods may be indefinitely long. See *A Theory of Justice* (Cambridge, Mass.: Harvard University Press, 1990).

23. Some readers of earlier versions of this essay have suggested that those whose views did not prevail in determining what costs were important and which should be borne by whom were being treated unfairly. Such an objection misunderstands the role of interpersonal measures in making fairness possible. Complaining that such treatment is unfair is no different from complaining that those whose views about fairness do not prevail are being treated unfairly. The latter complaint slides directly into incoherence for modifying practices so as to treat those people fairly would require treating still others unfairly. A view of fairness that allows one person's view to determine the legitimate claims of others is no view of fairness at all.

24. *Regina v. Ly*, 33 C.C.C. (3d) 31 (1987).

25. The details of provocation vary in different common-law jurisdictions. For example, English law asks whether a reasonable person who lost self-control would have done the act in question. For discussion, see Jeremy Horder, *Provocation and Responsibility* (Oxford: Clarendon, 1992).

26. So, too, is being able to participate in consensual activities that would otherwise be classified as minor assaults. See the discussion of *Regina v. Abesanya* in Bhikhu Parekh, "British Citizenship and Cultural Difference," in *Citizenship*, ed. Geoff Andrews (London: Lawrence and Wishart, 1991). Abesanya was a Nigerian mother who cut the cheeks of her nine- and fourteen-year-old sons in a ceremony. Abesanya was granted an absolute discharge in part because the children had been willing parties and in part because the ceremony was unlikely to leave permanent marks. Cultural sensitivity allowed the court to treat what at first appeared as a brutal practice no differently than it would treat ear piercing.

27. Although such communities typically need to be imagined together to be imagined at all, the individual's use of that culture depends on his or her taking it seriously.

28. A similar point is made by Samuel Scheffler in his discussion of what he calls "the distributive objection" to associative obligations. Scheffler raises this as one objection to all associative obligations. I am making the more limited point that associative obligations can only be given a political role in circumstances in which all can be supposed to benefit from parallel obligations. See Scheffler, "Families, Nations, and Strangers," Lindley Lecture, University of Kansas, 1994.

29. This theme is developed in Note, "The Cultural Defense in Criminal Law," *Harvard Law Review* 99 (1986): 1293.

30. Friedman almost certainly had her Jewish law wrong, as all rules contain exceptions to allow for protection against serious danger. However, the court accepted the testimony of her expert witness, a rabbi who had known her since childhood. *Friedman v. New York*, 282

N.Y.S. 2d 858, 862 (1967), cited in Guido Calabresi, *Ideals, Beliefs, Attitudes, and the Law* (Syracuse: Syracuse University Press, 1986).

31. John Rawls, *Political Liberalism* (New York: Columbia University Press, 1992), p. 133.

32. If fairness is a central value, self-rule must always be secondary. I conclude this overly abstract and academic discussion with a more concrete example to make this point. In debates over the last two failed Canadian constitutional accords, a central question was whether self-government for minority groups should be subject to the "notwithstanding" clause of the *Charter of Rights and Freedoms*, which allows governments to override Supreme Court rulings that legislation violates the charter. Part of the issue was fueled by distrust on both sides. But even if we suppose that the "notwithstanding" clause would never be used in a way that violated fundamental rights and thus that the issue would make little practical difference, there was a deep symbolic question as well. Is self-rule subject to the demands of equality, or does equality get its claim from being chosen by a self-ruling people? This very same question arises about cultural belonging. It carries the weight it does because of fairness, not vice versa.

14

Pro Patria Mori!
Death and the State

YAEL TAMIR

> Fortunate indeed are they who draw for their lot a death so glorious as that which has caused your mourning, and to whom life has been so exactly measured as to terminate in the happiness in which it has been passed.
> —Pericles, in Thucydides, *History of the Peloponnesian War*

The awareness of death, says Heidegger, confers upon human beings a sense of their individuality: "Dying is one thing no one can do for you; each of us must die alone."[1] Yet death—the commemoration and veneration of the dead, the fear of death—plays a major role in political life; it is used to strengthen communality, to build a collective identity, and to define communal obligations. The central role that the tomb of the unknown soldier plays in national ceremonies can serve to illustrate this phenomenon. By its very nature, this tomb is meant not to commemorate a particular person but to promote an *ideal* of a soldier, *our* soldier as, although his personal identity is unknown, his communal identity is certain; he is a fellow citizen. And as he has performed the ultimate act of sacrifice, he has become the perfect fellow citizen. All his flaws are forgiven, as his "good action has blotted out the bad, and his merit as a citizen more than outweighed his demerits as an individual."[2]

The glory of the fallen is closely intertwined with the glory of the state—the fact that exemplary individuals willingly give up their lives for the state is purported to prove that the state is worthy of such an offering, while the merits of the state make the sacrifice of the fallen worthwhile. The fact that citizens care about

their state and are motivated to defend it is taken as a manifestation of its legitimacy, as evidence that citizens see the state as their own, cherish its existence, and
support its government. This is especially true for democratic states, whose legitimacy is grounded in consent. It is therefore in the interest of such states to demonstrate that individuals are ready to risk their lives in defense of their state and that
they are ready to do so for the right reasons—namely, out of identification, pride,
love, and support for their country.[3]

Yet the readiness to risk one's life for one's state clashes with the most powerful
individual interest—self-preservation. Why would anyone be willing to make
such an offering? This is the essence of the question Einstein poses to Freud in
their famous exchange of open letters.[4] In his answer Freud makes reference to the
duality of the human psyche, which is motivated by erotic instincts that seek to
"preserve and unite" on the one hand and by destructive instincts that seek to "kill
and destroy" on the other. This duality, he argues, is reflected in the political
sphere. Political life thus embodies an aspiration to promote identification and
love, alongside a permission to foster hatred and aggressiveness. The subjects of
these feelings are the members of two different groups: members of in-group or
"us" and members of other groups or "the enemy."[5] The dual nature of political life
suggests that the hope that human aggressiveness will wither away is no more than
an illusion. Even those who, like the Russian communists, aspire to eliminate bel-
ligerency, Freud sarcastically observes, are "armed to day with the most scrupulous
care and not the least important of the methods by which they keep their supporters together is hatred of everyone beyond their frontiers."[6]

Nationalism carries well this dual message of love and hostility. This is why it
has been such an effective ally for a wide range of political ideologies. Its services
are especially necessary at times of war, when internal devotion and external ani-
mosity must be intensified and when the cost of such attitudes—namely, massive,
brutal, daily death—is incurred.

War is bound to sweep away the conventional treatment of death, Freud argues.
At bottom "no one believes in his own death, or to put the same thing in another
way, in the unconscious every one of us is convinced of his immortality." Yet at
times of war death can no longer be denied; "we are forced to believe in him."[7]
When death becomes "believable," it is much harder to repress the fear of death.
Under such bleak circumstances one would expect that it would be much harder
to convince individuals to risk their lives for the state, yet this is not necessarily the
case. Quite often war incites rather than discourages the readiness of individuals to
risk their lives in defending the state. Many different reasons could explain this
phenomenon. War may evoke feelings of fear, revenge, humiliation; it can highlight the importance of a cause or a set of values one finds just and worthy of defense; and it can grant those who enjoy taking risks or acting recklessly and vio-
lently permission to behave in these ways. These feelings and attitudes could be

harnessed by the state and used to enhance the readiness to fight. The state can also adopt a different strategy; it can attempt to confront the most painful aspect of war—death—and ameliorate the natural fear of it. This essay is an attempt to look at this latter strategy; hence it looks at the strategies states adopt in those cases in which the presence of death is evident, when the state is involved in actual fighting that demands many young lives. This—apart from my own personal background—is the reason why Israeli examples play such a major role in the argument.

At such moments of crisis, states searching for an ideology that enables them to justify their demand that their citizens risk their lives in their defense will find support in nationalism. Using a nationalist discourse, states restructure the image of both the political community and the conflict itself. Thus, creating a frame in which the difficult question of how an individual should act in relation to a certain conflict "is simplified and reinterpreted in terms of emotional ties and moral obligations to family and community. . . . Cognitively, it focuses individuals' attention on a small subset of all the consequences of the choice to sacrifice for the nation or not, and thus makes the choice set simpler, while also biasing it towards the nation."[8] This restructuring of the citizen's choices is indispensable for states that foster a contractual ethos as they lack the ideological foundations necessary to incite in individuals a readiness to risk their lives for the state and is much less essential for states whose constitutive set of values provides a justification for self-sacrifice. Ironically then, an appeal to national feelings and ideology is much more necessary and effective in the case of liberal democracies.

While it is commonly claimed that nations need states to secure their existence, the argument developed here suggests that the reverse is also true. Nationalism should therefore be seen not as the pathology infecting modern liberal states but as an answer to their legitimate needs of self-defense or, to put it in even more dramatic terms, as a remedy to their malaise—namely, the atomism, neurosis, and alienation that inflict liberal states and may leave them defenseless.[9]

In the Name of the Fatherland; in the Name of God

Before I turn to develop this argument, let me take a short interlude and explore two alternative conceptions of the state that could justify self-sacrifice without making any reference to nationalism. According to the organic view of the state, both the life and the welfare of individuals are wholly contingent on the existence and well-being of the political whole. If individuals are viewed as parts of a whole and lifeless without it, it would seem natural to say, as does Pope Pius II, that "for the benefit of the whole body a foot or a hand, which in the state are the citizens, must be amputated, since the prince himself, who is the head of the mystical body of the state, is held to sacrifice his life whenever the commonwealth would demand it."[10]

According to this description, acts performed with the welfare of the state in mind are motivated by an instinct for self-preservation. The readiness to defend the state even at the price of one's life is thus seen as no different from the readiness to raise one's arm in order to protect oneself at the risk of severe injury or even amputation. The question of why individuals would risk their lives for the state therefore receives a clear answer.

The marriage between the state and religious ideals provides an even more convincing answer to this question. If the state is endowed with a religious content, then dying in its protection could be portrayed not only as a holy obligation but also as a desirable end, as it would allow a person to enter into the *patria eterna*, into a better, heavenly world. For their self-sacrifice in the service of Christ, the fallen receive "the martyr's crown in the life hereafter."[11] The words of a Crusader's song reflect this belief:

> He that embarks to the Holy Land,
> He that dies in this campaign,
> Shall enter into heaven's bliss
> And with the saints there shall he dwell.[12]

Those who die in war thus leave this world only to become citizens of the heavenly kingdom.

According to Islam, death in a jihad (a holy war against infidels) ensures passage through the heavenly gates. During the Iran-Iraq war, both sides sent young children onto the battlefield with a key to heaven tied to a ribbon around their neck. Hizzballa warriors are promised a place in heaven for making suicide attacks, and Palestinians killed during the Intifada (Palestinian uprising) are regarded as *shahids* (martyrs). After a deadly suicide bus bombing, Hamas, the Muslim militant group that launched the attack, threatened to unleash more violence. When the late Israeli prime minister Yitzhak Rabin ordered that Hamas's top military leaders be killed on sight, the organization vowed to retaliate for Rabin's hard-line stance. Rabin must be shown, a press release stated, "that Hamas loves death more than Rabin and his soldiers love life."[13]

The religious dimension of politics turns the death in war of a brother, husband, or friend into a gain that outweighs the personal loss. "Don't come to express your condolences; come to congratulate me," said the father of the youngest victim at the Hebron massacre. "I have become the father of a *shahid*."

As these examples clearly demonstrate, when a state or a political movement is seen as a carrier of religious ideals, these ideals can endow individuals with the motivation not only to risk their lives for the state but also to die in its name.[14]

Beyond Contractarianism

Rational individuals could well enter a contract that reduces their risks—namely, a contract that, without granting absolute security, offers better terms than the state of nature. Yet according to Hobbes, it would be perfectly rational and legitimate for such individuals, when found in a life-threatening situation—soldiers fighting a national war, police officers trying to enforce law and order, firefighters combating a fire—to try their best to save their own skin, leaving their fellow citizens unprotected. This would be true even if individuals had willingly entered a contract committing them to some communal obligations, including the obligation to fight and die for the protection of their community. "A man who risks his life for the state accepts the insecurity which it was the only end of his political obedience to avoid."[15] This is especially true for a young man asked to serve in a wartime army. In such cases "the personal threat becomes so obvious that even a cognitively lazy follower of rules of thumb will notice that supporting the group is not in his self-interest."[16]

When facing death, Hobbes argues, individuals are justified in seeking to ensure their own self-preservation rather than abiding by the contract. True, their defection may destabilize the contract and even rescind it altogether, bringing them back to the state of nature. Nevertheless, no matter how threatening the state of nature might be, it is likely to be less threatening than the risk of immediate death. According to this analysis, the higher the risks faced by the state and the greater its defense requirements, the lower the readiness of its citizens to rally to its defense.

The threat of death seems to invalidate a contract whose main aim is the preservation of life. Death is, therefore, the "contradiction of politics."[17] In its presence, each person is left alone. But if a Hobbesian contract is necessarily abrogated in the face of external threats or internal disorder, leaving each individual to face the risks of nature alone, what might be its justification?[18]

Other contractarian approaches seem to lead to a similar deadlock. If individuals enter political agreements in order to protect their interests, life, rights, property, or well-being, agreeing to expose themselves to the dangers of death would be ridiculous, as "the means, death, would forthwith annul the end, property and enjoyment."[19] They would therefore be justified in taking any possible means in order to avoid risking their lives (though they could have good reasons to support the state's existence by a variety of "non-life-threatening actions").

Liberal morality offers no coherent guideline on such questions as "to fight or not to fight," argues Annette Baier. Liberal morality can only say "the choice is yours" and hope "that enough will choose to be self-sacrificial life providers and self-sacrificial death dealers to suit the purpose of the rest."[20] The catch, however, is that individuals reared within a liberal contractarian tradition, especially a Hobbesian one, are likely to have acquired the kind of atomistic identity that precludes the possibility of becoming self-sacrificial life providers. Liberal states thus run the risk of not having enough, or even any, individuals who will voluntarily choose to risk their lives in defense of the state. Such states must therefore stand defenseless or cultivate in their citizens an identity inconsistent with their political ethos.[21]

The Usefulness of Nationalism

History shows that faced with a choice between inconsistency and insecurity, liberal states have opted to foster an identity more communal in nature than their professed political ethos might have implied. They attempt to offer their citizens a stable and continuous national identity, thus imbuing the social contract with a new meaning—portraying it not only as a means to protect individual interests but also as a means to meet the need for roots, for stability, for a place in a continuum that links the past with the future.

National ceremonies, memorial days, the veneration of fallen soldiers, and the geographic and symbolic centrality of the Place de la Republique in Paris, Trafalgar Square in London, Arlington National Cemetery in Virginia, Piazza Venezia in Rome, and Mount Herzl in Jerusalem all convey the same message: the state is not merely a voluntary association but a community of fate.

But why would the insertion of nationalistic ideals and images influence the citizens' preferences and choices?[22] The answer has to do with the ability of the nationalist way of thinking to transform the self-image of individuals by portraying their personal welfare as closely tied to the existence and prosperity of their national community, as well as to its ability to contextualize human actions, making them part of a continuous creative effort whereby the national community is made and remade. By so doing, nationalism imparts special significance to even the most mundane actions and endows individual lives with meaning. It is in this sense that nationalism bestows extra merit on social, cultural, or political acts and provides individuals with additional channels for self-fulfillment that make their lives more rewarding.

Defending the continuity of their national community can thus be seen by individuals as a ground project, an endeavor on which the successful pursuit of all other significant projects is dependent. Ground projects are of the kind of projects for which it is worth fighting and risking one's life. There is no contradiction, claims Bernard Williams, in the idea of death for the sake of a ground project— "quite the reverse, since if death really is necessary for the project, then to live would be to live with it unsatisfied, something which, if it is really [a person's] ground project, he has no reason to do."[23] If a person's ground project is to live a meaningful life and if membership in a particular national-cultural community is a necessary, though by no means sufficient, condition to living such a life, a person may have a reason to risk his or her life in order to ensure the continuity and growth of his or her nation. But would not this argument lead to the paradox mentioned above? If one's purpose is to lead a worthwhile life, death would certainly thwart this goal.

One way to confront this issue is to proclaim a close link between the readiness to die for a cause and the belief that one's life is meaningful. According to Williams, the readiness to die for specific projects reaffirms the self-image of the person not as someone to whom all projects are equally external or contingent but as someone who has some constitutive commitments that make his or her life meaningful. The process is one of active equilibrium; identity generates obligations and obligations define identity. This interplay between identity and obligation is of a special importance for liberal agents whose ends and commitments are elective. By expressing readiness to risk their lives in the pursuit of some of their projects, liberal agents draw a distinction between contingent and constitutive projects, between projects that are theirs and projects that define their identity.

Ground projects need not be collective or, if they are, need not have the state, or the nation, as their object. States, however, are obviously interested in their citizens adopting collective ground projects in which the state plays a central role and will therefore devote considerable effort to cultivating a preference for such projects. As will be demonstrated in the following sections, nationalistic language and symbols are extremely useful for the purpose of endowing the state with a collective mission—that of protecting the continuity and prosperity of the nation.

The importance of endowing the state with a national task that creates a link between the present generation, its ancestors, and future generations cannot be overstated; it helps individuals conquer the fear of death by promising them an opportunity to enter the sphere of the eternal.[24] Hence even states whose main molding power is ideological adopt the genealogical and exclusivist language and symbols typical of nationalism. This is well expressed by Edmund Burke's words: "It has been the uniform policy of our constitution to claim and assert our liberties, as an ensiled inheritance derived to us from our forefathers, and to be transmitted to our posterity."[25]

Yet individuals who adopt a national project may still prefer that others defend their nation-state for them. Freeriding is especially tempting as the existence of a state is a collective good whose benefits individuals would enjoy even if they did not personally contribute to its defense. Commemoration rites and national ceremonies are meant to solve this collective action problem—namely, to convince individuals that they ought to *commit themselves* to protecting their state with their lives. In venerating and remembering the fallen, the state conveys to its citizens the following message: in committing yourself to the welfare, endurance, security, and prosperity of your state, a commitment that may force you to face danger and risk death, you will secure substantial gains; refraining from such a commitment will, on the other hand, entail social costs.

Tilting the Balance: How to Counter the Fear of Death

The attempt to convince individuals that they should risk their lives for the state runs counter to one of the most powerful human fears—the fear of death. One might attempt to counter this fear by following Epicurus's line of argument: "Make yourself familiar with the belief that death is nothing to us, since everything good and bad lies in sensation, and death is to deprive us of sensation. So that most fearful of all bad things, death, is nothing to us, since when we are, death is not, and when death is present, then we are not."[26] Based on the Epicurean argument, Walter Glannon suggests an analysis that shows the fear of death to be irrational:

1. The state of being dead is not (good or) bad for the one who is dead.
2. If something is not bad when it is present, however, there are no rational grounds for fearing its future presence at a previous time.
3. Therefore, it is irrational for a person to fear his future state of being dead.[27]

If we accept Epicurus's argument, we ought not fear death itself, and yet we may still be anxious about the implications of that future state of affairs for our present life. Four kinds of implications suggest themselves. The first relates to our fear of the moment of death itself: What will it feel like? Will it be painful? Will I suffer? The second reflects the difficulties involved in accepting mortality, the incidental and nonessential nature of human existence, the fact that the world will go on existing without us. The third is closely related to the second and has to do with the implications of our mortality for the meaning of our life, as the fact that our existence is contingent and finite may cast doubts on the relevance and meaningfulness of our being here at all. The fourth has to do with our concern for our loved ones who might be left unsupported and unprotected.

The following sections explore some of the strategies by which states attempt to contend with these fears.[28] These strategies demand a shift in the self-image of the state and its political discourse, adding the national perspective with its promise for continuity and fraternity between generations to the liberal democratic one.

Glorifying Death

In an attempt to counter the fear of the moment of death itself, memorial rites and patriotic literature portray the deaths of patriots as peaceful and gentle, playing down any bloody or gory features. This becomes evident if we think of a following comparison of two scenes of death. The first appears in "The Silver Platter," a nationalistic poem that for many Israelis has an equal status to the Yizkor, the memorial prayer of traditional Jewish liturgy. The heart of the poem is a scene in which a young man and woman, holding hands, weary of toil and battle, quietly step forward to face the nation: "We are the silver platter / On which the Jewish state has been given you," they say, and "enveloped in shadow at the people's feet they fell."[29] The death of the young couple seems pure, sublime, even appealing. Although they have just emerged from a long and bitter national struggle, they are neither wounded nor mutilated; their appearance bears no traces of their suffering. "Silently the two approached / And stood there unmoving. / There was no saying whether they were alive or shot."[30] Death is implied but never mentioned.

This scene of death calls to mind the death of another young couple, whose story ends with these famous words:

> A glooming peace this morning with it brings;
> The sun for sorrow will not show his head:
> Go hence, to have more talk of these sad things;
> Some shall be pardoned, and some punished:
> For never was a story of more woe
> Than this of Juliet and her Romeo.

The deaths of Romeo and Juliet seem much less graceful and inviting than those of the young couple in "The Silver Platter." Romeo's and Juliet's deaths are portrayed realistically, as bloody and painful. The sight of Juliet's tormented body causes her father to moan:

> O heaven!—O wife, look how our daughter bleeds!
> This dagger hath mista'en,—for, lo his house
> is empty on the back of Montague,—
> And is mis-sheathed in my daughter's bosom![31]

While in *Romeo and Juliet* the ugliness of death is contrasted with the splendors of love, in "The Silver Platter" the glory of death is contrasted with the ugliness of war.

According to George Mosse, a change in the attitude toward death in war took place during the eighteenth century: "The image of [death as] the grim reaper was replaced by the image of death as eternal sleep."[32] This shift is well expressed in Wilfred Owen's poem "Asleep," written on November 14, 1917:

> Under his helmet, up against his pack,
> After the many days of work and waking,
> Sleep took him by the brow and laid him back.
> And in the Happy no-time of his sleeping,
> Death took him by the heart.[33]

As these brief examples suggest, nationalist discourse attempts to portray the moment of death as instantaneous, gracious, and painless rather than as brutal and painful.

Moreover, nationalist literature ties death to hope and a promise for a better future, rather than to despair and destitution. Unlike Romeo and Juliet, whose deaths are motivated by despair, the youths portrayed in "The Silver Platter" are motivated by their hope that their deaths will help to achieve a nationalistic aim, the establishment of a Jewish state, which they considered worth dying for. This explains why death in *Romeo and Juliet* is the end of the story while death in "The Silver Platter" is but a beginning. "The rest," we are promised, "will be told in the annals of Israel."

Promising Redemption from Personal Oblivion

The second kind of fear touches upon the human desire not to be forgotten. It is hard for people to accept that their lives will end leaving no impression, that they will wither without a trace. A man, Milan Kundera writes, "knows that he is mortal, but he takes it for granted that his nation possesses a kind of eternal life."[34] In these words Kundera captures the message that national myths convey: nations are immortal; they transcend contingency. Nationalism thus shifts finite human experience from the sphere of the mundane and contingent to the realm of the eternal.

National monuments, memorial services, funerals, and rites of commemoration constitute *les lieux de memoire*, the domains of collective memory. In performing them, the nation asserts that as long as it will endure, it will show gratitude to all who struggle and sacrifice their lives for its survival. It will turn them into heroes, perhaps even canonize them. The military cemeteries, the memorial days, are all ways of living up to this solemn oath: the fallen shall not be forgotten; they will go on living in the memory of the nation. We live because of them, and in living we save their memory and imbue their death with meaning.

On the verge of their almost certain death in battle, King Henry promises his men immortality, a chance to attain glory by entering the national pantheon:

> This story shall the good man teach his son
> And Crispin Crispian shall ne'er go by,
> From this day to the ending of the world,
> But we in it shall be remembered;
> We few, we happy few, we band of brothers.[35]

This promise is meaningful because King Henry and his men are convinced that England will go on until "the ending of the world," for if it does not, the memory of this glorious battle, and with it the promise of immortality, might wane. Members of other nations may also remember the war; for example, many of us remember the war in Marathon even though we are not Greek. But only members of the nation take a vow to remember and feel they have a moral obligation to do so.

The fallen are seen as part of the nation's chain of being, regenerating time and again with each new generation. The most striking metaphorical expression of this continuity can be found in the identification of fallen soldiers with nature. As the poet compares the rhythm of the nation to that of nature, the fallen are portrayed as "an integral part of the changing seasons, from the death of winter to the resurrection of the spring."[36] Like the drought of summer, the death of soldiers is seen as another stage of being in the life of the nation. Wilfred Owen's words, once again, provide a vivid representation of this tendency:

> Yet his thin and sodden head
> Confuses more and more with the low mould,
> His hair being one with the grey grass
> And finished fields of autumns that are old.[37]

Death in war is thus portrayed as an integral part of the national chain of being, which embodies endless regenerations. In Chaim Guri's poem, well known to all Israelis, the dead promise to return as red poppies:

> We shall raise, to break through again as then,
> and come to life again.
> We shall stride, terrible, large, as we race to the rescue,
> for it all within us still lives and floods our veins, and burns.[38]

Poppies are a symbol of renewal; in Britain they are used as a symbol of commemoration, and in Hebrew they were given an indicative name: "the blood of the Macabees." The identification of fallen soldiers with nature is represented in the heroes' grove in Germany, in the French *jardin funebre*, in the Italian Parco della Rimembranza, as well as in many forests in Israel where the names of the fallen are affixed to trees.

The notion of continuity and regeneration embodied in nationalism is of particular importance in a secular era, in which identification with the nation is "the surest way to surmount the finality of death and ensure a measure of personal immortality."[39] This is the most valuable reward for death in the service of the nation.

The Meaning of Life

Rites of commemoration attempt to break the link between the length and meaningfulness of one's life. They express a belief that one's ability to live a meaningful life depends not only on the way one lives but also on the way one finds his or her death.

This is not such an unusual claim; we can easily imagine a person who has lived a shorter but more meaningful life than another who lived longer. When comparing the misfortune entailed by the death of two individuals—Gerry, who lived to his biological limit, and Joe, who died relatively young—Jeff McMahan argues that "the explanation of why there is less reason to grieve for Gerry is simply that he has had a fair share of life. Relative to reasonable expectations, he had a rich and full life."[40] It thus seems that regrets over a person's death correspond to an estimate of the value of his or her life.

Why does Keats's death at twenty-four seem tragic while Tolstoy's death at eighty-two does not? Probably because we assume that had Keats lived to be eighty-two he would have continued writing. Yet as he had defined himself as a person for whom writing was a necessary and sufficient condition for living a meaningful life, it would seem reasonable to assume that if he had to choose between being creative only until the age of twenty-four and living on to be eighty-two, or being creative only until the age of thirty-four and dying at thirty-five, he would have chosen the latter.

The relations between longevity and meaningfulness might even be inverse if the fullness and richness of one's life are closely related to the way one finds his or her death—for example, if one's life is richer and more meaningful because one has volunteered to defend one's state. Indeed, one of the strategies used to encourage soldiers to commit themselves to fight for their country is to present this commitment as an act that will make their lives more meaningful, allow them to "be all that they can be," to develop their abilities to the fullest. Military life is therefore portrayed as "exemplifying courage, strength, hardness, control over passions, and the ability to protect the moral fabric of society by living a so-called manly life."[41] The test of manliness becomes a challenge best met by war. Combat soldiers are thus seen not only as the best citizens but also as the finest people. The meaning and worthiness of their lives are defined by their readiness to face death.

Money, Status, and Sex

Once the state has established the moral worthiness of those who are ready to risk their lives in its defense, it can offer them a series of benefits, ranging from material goods, social status, and mobility to sexual rewards, to more abstract awards such as glory, respect, and public idolization. Most of these benefits are differential; the highest go to those who join the combat units. Once individuals are convinced to join such units, the army invests great effort in building up an esprit de corps that will pressure soldiers, when the time comes, to join the actual fighting. Wartime experiences are thus depicted as embodying a moral opportunity as they allow individuals not only to develop their own character but also to express true equality and camaraderie, and experience the brotherhood of warriors.

Some rewards, however, are more concrete. For many years there was a saying in Israel: "Pilots are the best men, and the best [girls] are for the pilots." Although crude, this phrase accurately describes the terms of the sexual exchange available to those who volunteer for the most risky and prestigious units. Similar transactions are offered in other societies, too, in the shape of romantic Hollywood melodramas like *An Officer and a Gentleman*, the sexy photographs that soldiers' wives send their husbands at the front, or the license to rape the enemy's women—all varieties of sexual rewards granted to those who risk their lives for the state.

Soldiers are also rewarded with material benefits. In Israel, for instance, soldiers are entitled to financial help and to preferential treatment from university acceptance boards and job placement centers. Retired military officers are propelled to the top of the political, economic, and administrative hierarchy and enjoy wide support from "old boy" networks. In other countries where military service is voluntary, it is advocated as a major vehicle of mobilization. Army service is presented as a means to acquire education and a reliable job and even to see the world. In any case, the state tends to emphasize the economic benefits and social advantages while minimizing the dangers involved.

The reverse side of the benefits awarded for participation are the costs incurred for refusing to fight, ranging from social exclusion to the restriction of working opportunities and career development. Pericles's words again successfully capture the essence of such an exchange: "And surely, to a man of spirit, the degradation of cowardice must be immeasurably more grievous than the unfelt death which strikes him in the midst of his strength and patriotism!"[42]

When enlisting, many people probably hope that they will never need to face danger and that, if they do, the state will fulfill its promise to do its best to lessen the risks involved, come to their rescue, never leave them behind if wounded, and make an exchange for them if they are ever captured by the enemy. Committing oneself to defend the state in a distant and uncertain future in exchange for actual and immediate benefits may then seem a calculated risk.

NOTES

1. Martin Heidegger, in R. Olson, "Death," *The Encyclopedia of Philosophy*, ed. P. Edwards (New York: McMillan, 1967), p. 309.

2. Pericles, in Thucydides, *The History of the Peloponnesian War* (Encyclopedia Britannica, 1952), p. 398.

3. Hence individuals who fight for the state but are motivated by a desire to ensure certain rewards for themselves, such as members of the Foreign Legion and other mercenaries, are not considered patriots, and their action cannot serve to support the legitimacy of the state.

4. The interchange was arranged by the International Institute of Intellectual Cooperation under the auspices of the League of Nations and was first published simultaneously in German, French, and English in Paris in 1933.

5. Thucydides, *History of the Peloponnesian War*, p. 398.

6. S. Freud, "Reflection upon War and Death," in *Character and Culture* (Collier, 1963), p. 114.

7. Ibid., pp. 122, 124.

8. P. C. Stern, "Why Do People Scarify for Their Nations?," *Political Psychology* 16, no. 2 (1995): 232.

9. I explain this point in greater detail in my book *Liberal Nationalism* (Princeton: Princeton University Press, 1993), chap. 6.

10. H. Kantorowicz, "Pro Patria Mori in Medieval Political Thought," *American Historical Review* 56 (1950): 490.

11. Ibid.

12. Ibid., p. 481.

13. Jerusalem, Associated Press, October 24, 1994.

14. In some cases, not only the state but also the nation will be endowed with religious ends, and therefore the distinction between religious and nationalistic arguments will be obscured.

15. M. Walzer, *Obligations: Essays on Disobedience, War, and Citizenship* (Cambridge, Mass.: Harvard University Press, 1970), p. 82.

16. Stern, "Why Do People Scarify for Their Nations?," p. 234.

17. Walzer, *Obligations*, p. 82.

18. Ibid., p. 86. Moreover, a contract that forces individuals to surrender all their authority in return for only partial security might not be attractive. If all that the contract can offer is a new spread of risks, exchanging permanent fears and threats for periods of extensive protection alternating with periods of substantial risk, then the price of subscribing to absolute authority might be considered far too high.

19. Georg Wilhelm Friedrich Hegel, quoted in ibid., p. 89.

20. Annette Baier, cited in R. Rorty, "Why Can't a Man Be More like a Woman, and Other Problems in Moral Philosophy," *London Review of Books*, February 24, 1994.

21. Contractual states that are defenseless are unable to fulfill the role that justifies their creation. Losing their main source of justification implies not only that these states cannot call upon their members to protect them with their lives but also that they do not deserve such protection.

22. I have provided a much more detailed answer to this question in *Liberal Nationalism*, chap. 2.

23. B. Williams, *Moral Luck* (Cambridge: Cambridge University Press, 1981), p. 13.

24. See my discussion of these issues in "The Enigma of Nationalism," *World Politics* 47, no. 3 (1995), and in "Reconstructing the Landscape of Imagination," in *National Rights and International Obligations*, ed. S. Cancy, D. George, and P. Jones (Boulder, Colo.: Westview, 1996), pp. 85–102.

25. Edmund Burke, in J. Waldron, *Nonsense on Stilts* (London: Methuen, 1987), p. 118.

26. Epicurus, in *The Extant Remains*, ed. C. Bailey (Oxford: Oxford University Press, 1926), p. 85.

27. W. Glannon, "Epicureanism and Death," *Monist* 76 (1993): 224.

28. One may rightly comment that if Epicurus's argument is rejected—namely, if people fear the state of being dead rather than being concerned about the implication of future death for their present lives—the task of the state becomes much more difficult. Presumably the reason states embark upon a project that fits Epicurus's argument is neither because they have considered the validity of his argument nor because they have been convinced by it but because its consequences are easier to confront.

29. "The Silver Platter," Natan Altermann:

> And the land was silent. The incarnate sun
> Flickered languidly

Above the smoldering borders.
And a nation stood—cloven hearted but breathing . . .
To receive the Miracle.
The one miracle and only . . .
The nation made ready for the pomp. It rose to the crescent moon.
And stood there, at pre-dawn garbed in festive and fear—then out they came
A boy and a girl
Pacing slowly towards the nation.
In workaday garb and bandoleer, and heavy-shod,
Up the path they came
Silently forward.
They did not change their dress, and had not yet washed away
The marks of the arduous day and night of fire-line.
Tired, oh so tired, forsworn of rest,
And oozing sap of young Hebrewness—
Silently the two approached
And stood there unmoving.
There was no saying whether they were alive or shot.
Then the nation, tear-rinsed and spellbound, asked,
Saying: Who are you? And the two soughed
Their reply: We are the silver platter
On which the Jewish state has been given you.
They spoke. Then enveloped in shadow at the people's feet they fell.
The rest will be told in the annals of Israel.

30. Ibid.

31. W. Shakespeare, *Romeo and Juliet*, in *The Complete Works* (New York: Oxford University Press, 1959), p. 164.

32. George L. Mosse, *Fallen Soldiers: Reshaping the Memory of the World Wars* (Oxford: Oxford University Press, 1950), p. 39. This change in the perception of death transformed the Christian cemetery into a peaceful wooded landscape of groves and meadows.

33. Wilfred Owen, "Asleep," in *The Collected Works of Wilfred Owen*, p. 57.

34. M. Kundera, *The Book of Laughter and Forgetting* (Middlesex, Eng.: Penguin, 1980), p. 229.

35. W. Shakespeare, *Henry V* in *The Complete Works*, p. 491. Although this text was written in a prenational era, it has repeatedly been used in later periods to evoke national feelings and commitments.

36. Mosse, *Fallen Soldiers*, p. 44.

37. Owen, "Asleep."

38. H. Guri, "Here Our Bodies Are Casted."

39. A. D. Smith, *National Identity* (Reno: University of Nevada Press, 1991), p. 160.

40. J. McMahan, "Death and the Value of Life," *Ethics* 99 (1988): 51.

41. Mosse, *Fallen Soldiers*, p. 27. This discussion can explain some of the major sources for the marginalization of women in modern politics.

42. Pericles, in Thucydides, *History of the Peloponnesian War*, p. 398.

IV

TOLERATION AMONG
NATIONAL GROUPS

15

The Politics of Difference
Statehood and Toleration in a Multicultural World

MICHAEL WALZER

I will begin, like a good professor, by making a couple of distinctions. I am not going to focus in this essay (except at the very end) on the toleration of eccentric or dissident individuals in civil society or even in the state. Individual rights may well lie at the root of every sort of toleration, but I am interested in those rights primarily when they are exercised in common (in the course of voluntary association or religious worship or cultural expression) or when they are claimed by groups on behalf of their members. Eccentric individuals, solitary in their differences, are fairly easy to tolerate, and at the same time social repugnance for and resistance to eccentricity, while certainly unattractive, are not terribly dangerous. The stakes are much higher when we turn to eccentric and dissident groups.

I am also not going to focus here on the political toleration of oppositional movements and parties. These are competitors for political power, necessary in democratic regimes, which quite literally require that there be alternative leaders (with alternative programs), even if they never actually win an election. They are fellow participants, like the members of the opposing team in a basketball game, without whom there couldn't be a game and who therefore have a right to score baskets and win if they can. Problems arise only in the case of people who want to disrupt the game while still claiming the rights of players and the protection of the rules. These problems are often hard, but they don't have much to do with the toleration of difference, which is intrinsic to democratic politics, but rather they have to do with the toleration of disruption (or the risk of disruption)—another matter entirely.

My concern here is with toleration when the differences at stake are cultural, religious, way-of-life differences—when the others are not fellow participants and there is no common game and no intrinsic need for difference. Even a liberal society doesn't require a multiplicity of ethnic groups or religious communities; nor do any of the groups require any or all of the others. The groups will often be competitive with one another, seeking converts or supporters among uncommitted or loosely committed individuals, but their primary aim is to sustain a way of life among their own members, reproducing their culture or faith in successive generations. They are in the first instance inwardly focused, which is exactly what political parties cannot be. At the same time, they require some kind of extended social space (outside the household) for the sake of assembly, worship, argument, celebration, mutual aid, schooling, and so on.

Now, what does it mean to tolerate groups of this sort? Understood as an attitude or state of mind (from which characteristic practices follow), toleration describes a number of possibilities. The first of these, which reflects the origins of religious toleration in the sixteenth and seventeenth centuries, is simply a resigned acceptance of difference for the sake of peace. People kill one another for years and years, and then, mercifully, exhaustion sets in, and we call this toleration. But we can trace a continuum of more substantive acceptances. A second possible attitude is passive, relaxed, benignly indifferent: "It takes all kinds to make a world." A third expresses openness to the others, curiosity, respect, and a willingness to listen and learn. And furthest along the continuum is the enthusiastic endorsement of difference: an aesthetic endorsement if difference is taken to represent in cultural form the largeness and diversity of God's creation or of the natural world or a functional endorsement if difference is viewed as a necessary condition of human flourishing, offering to individual men and women the choices that make their autonomy meaningful.

But perhaps this last attitude falls outside my subject; how can I be said to tolerate what I, in fact, endorse? If I want the others to be *here*, in this society, among us, then I don't tolerate otherness; I support it. I don't, however, necessarily support this or that version of otherness; I might well prefer another other, culturally or religiously closer to my own practices and beliefs (or, perhaps, more distant, exotic, posing no competitive threat). So it seems right to say that though I support the idea of difference, I tolerate the instantiated differences. And there will always be people, in any democratic society and however well entrenched the commitment to pluralism is, for whom some particular difference—this or that form of worship, family arrangement, dietary rule, or dress code—is very hard to tolerate. I shall say of all people who actually accept differences of this sort, without regard to their standing on the continuum of resignation, indifference, curiosity, and enthusiasm, that they possess the virtue of tolerance.

Similarly, I shall treat all of the social arrangements through which we incorporate difference, coexist with it, allow it a share of social space, as the institutionalized forms of this same virtue. Historically, there have been four different sorts of arrangements that make for toleration, four models of a tolerant society. I want now to describe these briefly and roughly and then to say something about the self-understanding of the men and women who make them work today (insofar as they actually work—toleration is always a precarious achievement). What exactly do we do when we tolerate difference?

The oldest arrangements are those of the great multinational empires— beginning, for our purposes, with Persia and Rome. Here the various groups are constituted as autonomous communities, political/legal as well as cultural/religious in character, ruling themselves across a considerable range of their activities. The groups have no choice but to coexist with one another, for their interactions are governed by imperial bureaucrats in accordance with an imperial code, like the Roman *jus gentium*, designed to maintain some minimal fairness, as fairness is understood in the imperial center. Ordinarily, however, the bureaucrats don't interfere in the internal life of the autonomous communities for the sake of fairness or anything else—so long as taxes are paid and peace maintained. Hence they can be said to tolerate the different ways of life, and the imperial regime can be called a regime of toleration, whether or not the members of the different communities are tolerant of one another. Under imperial rule, they willy-nilly manifest tolerance in their everyday interactions, and some of them perhaps learn to accept difference, standing somewhere on the continuum that I have described. But the survival of the different communities doesn't depend on this acceptance. It depends only on bureaucratic toleration, sustained, mostly, for the sake of peace (though individual bureaucrats have been variously motivated, a few of them famously curious about difference or even enthusiastic in its defense).

This is probably the most successful way of incorporating difference and facilitating (requiring is more accurate) peaceful coexistence. But it isn't, or at least it never has been, a democratic way. Whatever the character of the different "autonomies," the incorporating regime is autocratic. I don't want to idealize this autocracy; it can be brutally repressive, for the sake of maintaining its conquests, as the history of Assyria and Israel, Rome and Carthage, Spain and the Aztecs, and Russia and the Tatars amply demonstrates. But settled imperial rule is often tolerant—and tolerant precisely because it is everywhere autocratic, which is to say not bound by the interests or prejudices of any of the conquered groups, equally distant from all of them. Roman proconsuls in Egypt and British regents in India ruled more evenhandedly than any local prince or tyrant was likely to do, more evenhandedly than local majorities today are likely to do.

Imperial autonomy tends to lock individuals into their communities and therefore into a singular ethnic or religious identity. It tolerates groups and their authority structures and customary practices, not (except in a few cosmopolitan centers and capital cities) free-floating men and women. Lonely dissidents or heretics, cultural vagabonds, and intermarried couples and their children will flee to the imperial capital, which is likely to become as a result a fairly tolerant place (think of Rome, Baghdad, and Vienna)—and the only place where social space is measured to an individual fit. Everyone else will live in homogeneous neighborhoods or districts, tolerated there but not likely to be welcome or even safe across whatever line separates them from the others; they can mix comfortably only in neutral space—the market, say, or the imperial courts and prisons. Still, they live, most of the time, in peace alongside one another, respectful of cultural as well as geographic boundaries.

Today all of this is gone (the Soviet Union was the last of the empires): the autonomous institutions, the carefully preserved boundaries, the ethnically marked identity cards, the far-flung bureaucracies. Autonomy did not mean much at the end (which is one reason, perhaps, for imperial decline); its scope was greatly reduced by the impact of modern ideas about sovereignty and by totalizing ideologies uncongenial to the accommodation of difference. But ethnic and religious differences survived, and wherever they were territorially based, local agencies, more or less representative, retained some minimal functions and some symbolic authority. These they were able to convert very quickly once the empires fell into a kind of state machinery, driven by nationalist ideology, aiming at sovereign power. With sovereignty, of course, comes membership in international society, the most tolerant of all societies but until very recently not so easy to get into. I shall not consider international society at any length in this essay, but it is important to recognize that this is where and how most groups would prefer to be tolerated: as nation-states (or religious republics) with governments, armies, and borders coexisting with other nation-states in mutual respect or at least under the rule of a common (even if rarely enforced) set of laws.

Before I consider the nation-state as a possibly tolerant society, I want to turn briefly to a morally similar but not politically more likely heir to the multinational empire—the consociational or bi- or tri-national state. Examples like Belgium, Switzerland, Cyprus, Lebanon, and the stillborn Bosnia suggest the range of possibility here and also the imminence of disaster. Consociationalism is a heroic program since it aims to maintain imperial coexistence without the imperial bureaucrats and without the distance that made those bureaucrats more or less impartial rulers. Now the different groups are not tolerated by a single transcendent power; they have to tolerate one another and work out among themselves the terms of their coexistence.

This isn't impossible. Success is most likely where there are only two groups roughly equal in either size or political power—and where the equality is stable over time. Then the proportionate allocation of resources and offices in the civil service is relatively easy, and neither group need fear the dominance of the other. Each pursues its own customs, perhaps even enforces its own customary law, undisturbed. It's the fear of disturbance—even more, of domination by the other group—that breaks up consociations. Mutual toleration depends on trust not so much in each other's goodwill as in the institutional arrangements that guard against the effects of ill will. I can't live tolerantly alongside a dangerous other. What is the danger that I fear? It is that the consociation will collapse into an ordinary nation-state where I will be a member of the minority, seeking to be tolerated by my former associates, who no longer require my toleration.

Most of the states that make up international society are nation-states. To call them that doesn't mean that they have nationally (or ethnically or religiously) homogeneous populations. Homogeneity is rare, if not nonexistent, in the world today. It means only that a single dominant group organizes the common life in a way that reflects its own history and culture and, if things go as intended, carries the history forward and sustains the culture. It is these intentions that determine the character of public education, the symbols and ceremonies of public life, the state calendar, and the holidays it enjoins. Among histories and cultures, the nation-state is not neutral; its state apparatus is an engine for national reproduction. At the same time, nonetheless, it can, as liberal and democratic nation-states commonly do, tolerate minorities. This toleration takes different forms, though it rarely reaches the full autonomy of the old empires. Regional autonomy is especially unlikely, for then members of the dominant nation living in the region would be subjected to "alien" rule in their own country.

Toleration in nation-states is commonly focused not on groups but on members of groups, minorities, generally conceived stereotypically, qua members, and allowed (or expected) to form voluntary associations, organizations for mutual aid, private schools, cultural societies, publishing houses, and so on. They are not allowed to sustain a corporate existence or exercise legal jurisdiction over their fellows. Minority religion, culture, and history are matters for what might be called the private collective—about which the public collective, the nation-state, is always suspicious. Any claim to act out minority culture in public is likely to produce anxiety among the majority (hence the controversy in France over the wearing of Muslim headdress in state schools). In principle, there is no coercion of individuals, but pressure to assimilate to the dominant nation, at least with regard to public practices, has been fairly common and, until recent times, fairly successful. When nineteenth-century German Jews described themselves as German in the street, Jewish at home, they were aspiring to a nation-state norm that made privacy a condition of toleration.

The politics of language is one key area where this norm is both enforced and challenged. The majority insists that all minorities learn and use the language of the dominant nation, at least in their public transactions. Minorities, if they are strong enough, and especially if they are territorially based, will seek the legitimization of their own languages in schools, state documents, public signage, and so on. Sometimes one of the minority languages is recognized as a second official language; more often, the dominant nation watches its own language being transformed by minority use (which is also, I suppose, a test of toleration).

There is less room for difference in nation-states than in multinational empires or consociations. Since in nation-states the tolerated members of the minority group are also citizens, with rights and obligations, the practices of the group are more likely than in multinational empires to be subject to majority scrutiny. Nonetheless, a variety of differences, especially religious differences, have been successfully sustained in liberal and democratic nation-states. Minorities often, in fact, do fairly well in sustaining a common culture precisely because they are under pressure from the national majority. Individuals may drift away, pass themselves off as members of the majority, or slowly assimilate to majority lifestyles. But for most people these self-transformations are too difficult or too humiliating; they cling to their own identities and to similarly identified men and women.

National minorities are the groups most likely to find themselves at risk. If they are territorially concentrated, they will be suspected, perhaps rightly, of hoping for a state of their own or for incorporation into a neighboring state where their ethnic relatives hold sovereign power. In time of war (whether they are territorially concentrated or not), their loyalty to the nation-state will readily be called into doubt—even against all available evidence, as in the case of anti-Nazi German refugees in France during the first months of World War II. Once again, toleration fails when minorities look, or when nationalist demagogues can make them look, dangerous. The fate of Japanese-Americans a few years later makes the same point —their fellow Americans imitating, as it were, conventional nation-statehood. In fact, the Japanese were not, and are not, a national minority in the United States, at least not in the usual sense. Where is the majority nation? American majorities are temporary in character, differently constituted for different purposes and occasions, whereas a crucial feature of the nation-state is its permanent majority. Toleration in nation-states has only one source, moves or doesn't move in only one direction. The case of the United States suggests a very different set of arrangements.

The fourth model of coexistence and possible toleration is the immigrant society. Now the members of the different groups leave their territorial base, their homeland, behind them, come individually or in families, one by one, to a new land, and then disperse across it. They cluster for comfort only in relatively small numbers, always intermixed with other, similar groups in cities, states, and regions. Hence no sort of territorial autonomy is possible. (Quebec is the crucial exception here—and another exception must be made for conquered native peoples; I will focus primarily on the immigrants.) If ethnic and religious groups are to sustain themselves, they must do so as voluntary associations—which means that they are more at risk from the indifference of their own members than from the intolerance of the others. The state, once it is pried loose from the grip of the first immigrants (who imagined in every case that they were forming a nation-state of their own), is committed to none of the groups that make it up. It is, in the current phrase, neutral among them, tolerant of all of them, autonomous in its purposes.

The state claims exclusive jurisdictional rights, regarding all of its citizens as individuals rather than as members of groups. Hence the objects of toleration, strictly speaking, are individual choices and performances: acts of adhesion, participation in rituals of membership and worship, enactments of cultural difference, and so on. Individual men and women are encouraged to tolerate one another as individuals, difference being understood in each case as a personalized (rather than stereotypical) version of group culture—which also means that the members of each group, if they are to display the virtue of tolerance, must accept each other's different versions. Everyone has to tolerate everyone else. No group is allowed to organize itself coercively, to seize control of public space, or to monopolize public resources. In principle, the public schools teach the history and "civics" of the state, which is conceived to have no national but only a political identity. The history and culture of the different groups are either not taught at all or taught, as in the United States in recent times (and in some places), in equal doses, "multiculturally." Similarly, the state provides no help to any group or is equally supportive of all of them—encouraging, for example, a kind of general religiosity, as in subway and bus advertisements of the 1950s that urged Americans to "attend the church of your choice."

As this last maxim suggests, neutrality is always a matter of degree. Some groups are, in fact, favored over others—in this case, groups with "churches." But the others are still tolerated; nor is church attendance or any other culturally specific practice turned into a condition of citizenship. It is relatively easy, then, and not at all humiliating to escape one's own group and take on the reigning political identity ("American"). But many people in an immigrant society prefer a hyphenated or dual identity, differentiated along cultural/political lines as in, say, Italian-American. The hyphen joining the two symbolizes the acceptance of "Italianness" by other Americans, the recognition that "American" is a political identity without strong or specific cultural claims. The consequence, of course, is that "Italian" represents a cultural identity without political claims. That is the only form in which Italianness is tolerated, and then it must sustain itself, if it can or as long as it can, privately, through the voluntary efforts and contributions of committed Italians. And this is the case, in principle, with every cultural and religious group, not only with minorities (but, again, there is no permanent majority).

Whether groups can sustain themselves under these conditions—without autonomy, without access to state power or official recognition, without a territorial base or the fixed opposition of a permanent majority—is a question still to be answered. Religious communities, of both sectarian and "churchly" sorts, have not done badly in the United States up until now. But one reason for their relative success, it might be thought, is the considerable intolerance that many of them have, in fact, encountered—which often has, as I have already suggested, group-sustaining effects. The form of toleration characteristic of immigrant societies is still emergent, not yet fully realized. We might think of it—the toleration of individual choices and personalized versions of culture and religion—as the maximal (or the most intensive) kind of toleration. And, again, it is still radically unclear whether the long-term effect of this maximalism will be the fostering or the dissolving of group life.

The fear that soon the only objects of toleration will be eccentric individuals leads some groups (or their most committed members) to seek positive support from the state—in the form, say, of quota systems or subsidies. Given the logic of multiculturalism, however, state support must be provided equally to every social group. Since quotas and subsidies cannot be provided equally on that scale, hard choices would have to be made if policies like these were ever adopted. Toleration is, at least potentially, infinite in its extent, but the state can underwrite group life only within some set of political and financial limits.

Let me summarize the argument so far by considering these four regimes first in terms of the power relations they involve and then in terms of the range of (morally problematic) practices they tolerate. It is often said that toleration is necessarily a relationship of inequality, where the tolerated groups or individuals are cast in an inferior position. Therefore, we should aim at something better, beyond toleration, like mutual respect. Once we have mapped out the four regimes, however, the story looks more complicated; mutual respect is one of the forms toleration can take—the most attractive form, perhaps, but not necessarily the most stable.

In multinational empires, power rests with the central bureaucrats. All of the incorporated groups are encouraged to regard themselves as equally powerless, hence incapable of coercing or persecuting their neighbors. Any local attempt at coercion will produce an appeal to the center. So Greeks and Turks, for example, lived peacefully side by side under Ottoman rule. Were they mutually respectful? Some of them probably were; some were not. But the character of their relationship did not depend on their mutual respect; it depended on their mutual subjection. Consocation, by contrast, requires mutual respect at least among the leaders of the different groups, for the groups must not only coexist but negotiate among themselves the terms of their coexistence. Cyprus, before its partition into Greek and Turkish states, represents a failed example.

In nation-states, power rests with the majority nation, which uses the state, as we have seen, for its own purposes. This is no necessary bar to mutuality among individuals, which is, in fact, likely to flourish in democratic states. But minority groups are unequal by virtue of their numbers and will be democratically over-ruled on most matters of public culture. The case is similar early on in the history of immigrant societies, when the first immigrants aspire to nation-statehood. Successive waves of immigration produce what is, in principle again, a neutral state, the democratic version of imperial bureaucracy. But this state addresses itself to individuals rather than to groups and thus creates an open society in which everyone is required to tolerate everyone else. The much-heralded move "beyond toleration" is, presumably, now possible. As I have argued, however, it remains unclear how much of group difference will remain to be respected once this move is made.

Toleration is no doubt widest in the case not considered here: international society, where no one is authorized to decide whether or not to tolerate this or that group or practice. International law legitimates "humanitarian intervention" by any capable state in cases of massacre, radical persecution, or mass deportation. Hence we can say, I suppose, that these practices, in principle at least, are not tolerated, and whenever there is an actual intervention (relatively rare in the history of states), we can say that they are, in fact, not tolerated. But in general the agents of international society—political leaders and diplomats—and perhaps also the people they claim to represent are remarkably tolerant of what goes on across their borders. They are resigned, indifferent, curious, or enthusiastic (it hardly matters) and thus disinclined to interfere. It may also be the case, of course, that they are hostile to their neighbors' culture and customs but, given the conditions of international society, are unprepared to pay the costs of interference. Or, though culturally intolerant, they may accept the logic of sovereignty, which decrees a kind of institutional toleration.

Among the political regimes with which I am directly concerned, the multinational empire comes closest to accepting a similar logic. Each autonomous community has its own legal system, and until its members interact with the members of other communities—in commerce, for example—it is likely to be allowed to enforce its own shared understandings of lawful behavior. Strange commercial customs won't be tolerated in the common markets, but there will not be much interference in the work of local courts dealing, say, with domestic affairs.

Consider the extraordinary reluctance with which the British finally, in 1829, banned suttee (the self-immolation of a Hindu widow on her husband's funeral pyre) in their Indian states. For many years first the East India Company and then the British government tolerated the practice because of what a twentieth-century historian calls their "declared intention of respecting both Hindu and Muslim beliefs and allowing the free exercise of religious rights." Even Muslim rulers, who had, according to this same historian, no respect whatsoever for Hindu beliefs, made only sporadic and halfhearted efforts to suppress the practice. Imperial toleration extends, then, as far as suttee, which—given British accounts of what the practice actually involved—is pretty far.

It is at least conceivable that consociational arrangements might produce a similar toleration if the power of the joined communities was in near-balance and the leaders of one of them were strongly committed to this or that customary practice. A nation-state, however, in which power is by definition unbalanced, would not tolerate customs like suttee among a national or religious minority. Nor is toleration at that reach likely in an immigrant society, where each of the groups is a minority relative to all the others. The case of the Mormons in the United States suggests that deviant practices won't be tolerated even when they are wholly internal, involving "only" domestic life. In these last two cases, the state grants equal citizenship to all of its members and enforces a single law. There are no communal courts; the whole country is one jurisdiction within which state officials are bound, say, to stop a suttee in progress in exactly the same way that they are bound to stop a suicide attempt if they possibly can. And if the suttee is coercively assisted, as it often was, in fact, they have to treat the coercion as murder; there are no religious or cultural excuses.

In other sorts of cases in which the moral values of the larger community—the national majority or the coalition of minorities—are not so directly challenged, religious or cultural excuses may be accepted and nonstandard, even illegal practices tolerated. This is the case with narrowly constituted or sectarian minorities like the American Amish or the Hasidim, to whom state authorities are sometimes ready to offer (or the courts to mediate) one or another compromise arrangement. But similar concessions won't be offered to larger, more powerful groups—and even the standing compromises can always be challenged by any sect member who claims his or her citizen rights. Imagine that an arrangement is worked out allowing Muslim girls in French public schools to wear their customary headdress. (What stands in the way of any such arrangement is the fact that the Muslims in France are not a narrowly constituted minority, but let's leave that aside for the sake of the example.) This would be a compromise with the *laiciste* traditions of French education, which would continue, however, to govern the school calendar and curriculum. At some point let's say a number of Muslim girls claim they are being coerced by their families to wear the headdress and that the compromise arrangement facilitates this coercion. Then, perhaps, the compromise would have to be renegotiated. In the nation-state and in the immigrant society, though not in the multinational empire, the right to be protected against coercion of this kind would take precedence over the values of the minority religion or culture.

I have talked about some of the limits of toleration, but I haven't said anything yet about regimes of intolerance, which is what many empires and nation-states actually are. These sometimes succeed in obliterating difference but sometimes (when they stop short of genocide and mass deportation or "ethnic cleansing") serve, in fact, to reinforce it. They mark off the members of minority groups, persecute them because of their membership, compel them to rely on one another, and forge intense solidarities. Nonetheless, neither the leaders of such groups nor their most committed members would choose a regime of intolerance. Given the opportunity, they usually seek some form of individual or collective toleration: assimilation into the body of citizens or recognition of their standing in domestic or international society, with this or that degree of self-rule—autonomy, consociation, or sovereign statehood.

We might think of these two as the central projects of modern democratic politics. They are standardly conceived in mutually exclusive terms; either individuals or groups will be liberated from persecution and invisibility—and individuals only insofar as they abandon their groups. Thus Jean-Paul Sartre's description of the prototypical democrat's view of the Jewish question: "He wants to separate the Jew from his religion, from his family, from his ethnic community, in order to plunge him into the democratic crucible whence he will emerge naked and alone, an individual and solitary particle like all the other particles." (This project can obviously be described in a more positive way; since it is not my subject here, I don't need to say anything more about it.) The alternative is to provide the group as a whole with a voice, a place, and a politics of its own. For many people on the political left, this was once thought to require a struggle for inclusion, on the model of the working-class and socialist movements, storming and breaching the walls of the bourgeois city. But the groups with which I am concerned here require a struggle for boundaries.

The crucial slogan of this struggle is "self-determination," which implies the need for a piece of territory or, at least, a set of independent institutions—hence decentralization, devolution, autonomy, partition, sovereignty. Getting the boundaries right, not only in geographic but also in functional terms, is enormously difficult, but it is necessary if the different groups are to exercise significant control over their own lives and to do so with some security.

The work goes on today, adapting the old imperial arrangements, extending the modern international system, proliferating nation-states, self-governing regions, local authorities, and so on. Note what is being recognized and tolerated here: always groups and their members, men and women with singular or primary identities, ethnic or religious in character. The work obviously depends upon the mobilization of these people, but it is only their leaders who are actually engaged with one another, across boundaries, one-on-one (except when the engagement is military in nature). Autonomy confirms the authority of traditional elites; consociation is a kind of power-sharing arrangement among those same elites; nation-states interact through their diplomatic corps and political leaderships. For the mass of group members, toleration is maintained by separation on the assumption that these people understand themselves *as members* and want to associate mostly with one another. Like a character from Robert Frost's "Mending Wall," they believe that "good fences make good neighbors."

The last of my toleration models, however, suggests a different pattern and, perhaps, a postmodern project. In immigrant societies (and also now in nation-states under immigrant pressure), people experience what we might think of as a life without boundaries and without secure or singular identities. Difference is, as it were, dispersed, so that it is encountered everywhere, every day. Individuals mix but don't necessarily assimilate to a common identity. The hold of groups on their members is looser than it has ever been, though it is by no means broken entirely. And the result is a constant commingling of ambiguously identified individuals, intermarriage among them, and hence a literal multiculturalism, instantiated not only in the society as a whole but also in each and every family, even in each and every individual. Now tolerance begins at home, where we often have to make ethnic, religious, and cultural peace with our spouses, in-laws, and children—and with our own hyphenated or divided selves. Religious fundamentalism must be understood in part as a rejection of any such peace, an attack on ambiguity.

The Bulgarian-French writer Julia Kristeva has been the most important theoretical defender of this postmodern project, urging us to recognize a world of strangers and acknowledge the stranger in ourselves. In addition to a psychological argument, which I must pass by here, she restates a very old moral argument, whose first version is the biblical injunction: do not oppress the stranger, for you were strangers in the land of Egypt. Kristeva changes the verb tense and the geography for the sake of a contemporary reiteration: do not oppress the stranger, for *you* are strangers in *this* very land. Surely it is easier to tolerate otherness if we acknowledge the other in ourselves. I doubt, however, that this acknowledgment is sufficient by itself or in a merely moral form. We don't live in the world of strangers all of the time; nor do we encounter each other's strangeness only one-on-one but also, still, collectively, in situations where morality must be seconded by politics.

It is not the case that the postmodern project simply supersedes modernism, as in some grand metanarrative of historical stages. The one is superimposed on the other, without in any way obliterating it. There are still boundaries, but they are blurred by all of the crossings. We still know ourselves to be this or that, but the knowledge is uncertain for we are also this *and* that. Strong identity groups exist and assert themselves politically, but the allegiance of their members is measured by degrees, along a broad continuum, with greater and greater numbers clustered at the further end (which is why the militants at the near end are so strident these days).

This dualism of the modern and the postmodern requires that difference be doubly accommodated, first in its singular individual and collective versions and then in its pluralist, dispersed, and divided versions (or the other way around; I am not committed to a sequential argument, though the order as I have just stated it is the more likely). We need to be tolerated and protected as citizens and members and also as strangers. Self-determination has to be both political and personal—the two are related, but they are not the same. The old understanding of difference, which tied individuals to their autonomous or sovereign groups, will be resisted by dissident and ambivalent individuals. But any new understanding focused solely on the dissidents will be resisted by men and women struggling to enact, elaborate, revise, and pass on a common religious or cultural tradition. So difference must be twice tolerated, with whatever mix—it doesn't have to be the same mix in both cases—of resignation, indifference, curiosity, and enthusiasm.

Even those of us who are enthusiasts are bound to come up against differences, cultural and personal, that give us trouble. We don't want to tolerate hatred and cruelty; nor does our respect for difference extend to oppressive practices within groups (which were commonly tolerated by imperial bureaucrats). The more closely we live together, the more the limits of toleration become everyday issues. And closeness is one of the aims of the postmodern project. So the solid lines on the old cultural and political maps are turned into dotted lines, but coexistence along and across those lines is still a problem.

16

National Identity and Respect among Nations

ROBERT McKIM

Identifying with Your Nation

The Nation

It is useful to distinguish two aspects of our concept of a nation, each of which seems to dominate in different contexts, although neither of which is ever entirely absent. First, there is a cultural aspect. A nation is a group that shares characteristics such as a way of life, language, and religion. In general, the characteristics I have in mind are roughly those that are distinctive of what Avishai Margalit and Joseph Raz call an "encompassing group."[1] Associated with each such group are various forms of life, types of activity, occupations, pursuits, and relationships. Such groups typically have their distinctive cuisines, architectural styles, literary and artistic traditions, music, customs, dress, ceremonies, holidays, et cetera. The tastes, values, moral code, and options of individuals growing up within the group are affected by its culture to a significant degree. The members of such a group enjoy an ease of association and feel at home with each other, are linked by bonds of fellow feeling, and share an understanding of much of their experience just as they share much of their outlook on life and on a broad array of issues. Part of what makes such a cultural group exist typically is the fact that the people who constitute it have a sense that they are a distinct group.

There is a second and quite distinct aspect to our concept of a nation. A cultural group is a nation only if it has what we might think of as a political dimension, and this dimension normally must be present across time, probably across a number of generations. A sufficient condition of a cultural group having such a political aspect is that it has its own state. It is in this particular case—when a cultural group has its own state—that it seems especially appropriate to talk of "nation building"; to build the nation appears to be to work toward improving the state in cases in which this involves the cultivation of a culture or perhaps, in an extended sense, the creation of such a culture in a context in which it is understood that doing so will improve or strengthen the state.

However, the political dimension in question may just be a matter of there being an aspiration to have a state; this may merely be part of the political agenda within a cultural group. Or it may merely be that significant factions within such a group wish to achieve a state for the group, so this is a matter of serious discussion. Indeed, the political dimension may just be a matter of there being an aspiration on the part of a cultural group to have a particular political arrangement (other than its own state) that will give expression to the aspirations of the group. There are good reasons for cultural groups to have a political dimension. They are more likely to thrive and less likely to be at the mercy of outsiders if what is distinctive about them is reflected in their political arrangements.

The fact that a nation has a political dimension seems to be connected to and to partially explain the fact that it is natural to think of nations as having a right to self-determination. This sort of group has a vision of its project as a group, and in particular its political destiny, such that there is something that would *count* as its having achieved self-determination.

So nationhood has both a cultural dimension and a political dimension. It seems that if the political dimension is completely absent, we would not normally talk of there being a nation. Thus the Amish in the United States, the Chinese in Malaysia, and evangelical Protestants in Ireland are all well-defined cultural groups, but none of them counts as a nation; the reason, I think, is that they lack a well-defined political agenda of the right sort. In this they differ from, say, the Quebecois in Canada, the Kurds in Iraq, Iran, and Turkey, and the French, each of which is a cultural group that either has a political aspiration of this sort or has its own state and hence is considered to be a nation. Irish nationalists and Irish unionists are also groups that ought to be classified as nations, given the analysis I have just suggested.

Identifying Oneself with One's Nation

For some people the fact that they are, for example, Irish or American or French figures prominently in their conception of themselves. But many people consider the fact that they are members of their nation to be rather unimportant. Perhaps they prefer to adopt a cosmopolitan perspective on themselves and on their relation to others, thinking of themselves as "citizens of the world." Or perhaps they give little thought to such matters, so that neither the awareness that they are part of a nation, the thought that they belong to some transnational group, nor indeed the thought that they are "citizens of the world" figures prominently in their thinking.

I want to distinguish some different ways of identifying oneself with one's nation. Weak identification involves a mere awareness that one is a member of one's nation; one sees oneself as Irish, for example, just in that one sees that one *is* Irish or just in that one counts oneself as Irish. Strong identification with one's nation, on the other hand, involves the following eight dimensions. First, it involves loyalty to the nation, including support for the national political aspiration, if there is such a well-defined aspiration. Second, the trappings of one's culture—the forms of life, pursuits, traditions, customs, and so forth that are characteristic of one's national culture—are dominant in one's life, and one thinks of them as the trappings of one's nation and embraces them as such. Third, the strong sort of identification involves holding certain beliefs, including the belief that the way of life of the nation is the best way of life, at least for this nation, as well as the belief that it is important that the nation should flourish. Typically there also are beliefs about the nation's past, about its destiny, about what should be aimed for in its future, and about the national heroes and villains. Fourth, strong identification involves having certain hopes, such as the hope that the nation will continue to flourish and will achieve its destiny. Fifth, there are also various commitments, such as a commitment to contributing to the nation's achievement of its destiny. Sixth, various feelings are involved, too, such as joy or pride in the successes of the nation, embarrassment or shame at its failures, and anticipation upon contemplating how it might flourish in the future. Seventh, one thinks of oneself as a member of the group of people who make up the nation and who share the relevant loyalties, aspirations, commitments, and so forth; this is the group to which you would point if you were asked who "your people" are. Eighth, the thought that one belongs to one's nation, that one is Irish or American or Kurdish, for instance, is central to one's conception of oneself, as distinct from being incidental or peripheral. Finally, there are numerous connections between these various aspects; thus the relevant beliefs include the belief that the hopes and commitments of our group are the right ones, at least for our group. So strong identification is a multifaceted affair. When I discuss identification in what follows, it is usually strong identification that I have in mind. The weak and strong sorts of identification are of course end points on a continuum between which there are numerous intermediate forms of identification. For example, one intermediate type of identification would combine a strong sense of belonging to the national culture with indifference to the national political agenda.

Even when one identifies strongly with one's nation, clearly this is almost always only one of several competing sources of identity. Other obvious sources of identity include, for example, one's association with groups as various as one's family, friends, neighbours, coreligionists, and those who share one's economic interests. And of course there are ways of thinking of oneself that have little to do with any of one's associations with others; thus one might think of oneself as a person who is concerned about justice or about pursuing the truth.

A full account of when and to what degree it is permissible (or obligatory or admirable) to identify oneself strongly with one's nation is likely to be complex and multidimensional. It depends, for example, on the character, projects, and practices of one's nation. It also probably depends on considerations such as the following: whether one's nation is under threat and needs its members to show their solidarity with it; if there *is* a threat, whether the threat has been brought on the nation by its own wrongdoing and whether the members of the nation are able to opt out of membership in the nation if they so wish. There is a lot to take into account. I will restrict discussion in what follows to cases in which the character, projects, practices, and circumstances of one's nation are all such that there is a prima facie case for thinking that it is permissible to identify oneself strongly with the nation. So we are dealing with a nation that at least meets some minimal standard of acceptability or decency. Being minimally decent involves, among other things, having institutions and practices that are not cruel or barbaric; such a nation scores reasonably well in terms of fairness and generosity toward its members. Moreover, it does not aspire to achieve unreasonable or outlandish political objectives, and a case with some force can be made for its achieving what it aspires to achieve. Whatever aims such a nation is pursuing are in turn bolstered by its conception of its history, distinctiveness, destiny, and so forth. Although this is not, strictly speaking, necessary, such a nation probably has a conception of its history (which may be spelled out in myths, stories, verse, or song, as well as through what is taught in the formal educational process) that captures accurately central aspects of its past as well as its aspirations for its future. That is, its conception of its past is not based on fabrication and confabulation, whatever embellishments may have been added to it.[2] But this is just a sketch of a theory of what it is for a nation to be decent. Rather than attempt to provide a fuller theory of this sort, I make the reasonable assumption that some such theory can be provided and limit discussion to nations that meet the standards specified by that theory. My concern will be with certain cases in which there is reason to weaken one's sense of identification with such a nation.

I take it for granted that people often have self-interested reasons to identify themselves with their nation. Thus, doing so may provide them with a healthy sense of participation in enduring traditions that they believe to be worthwhile. The sense of cultural belonging that is involved may afford them valuable opportunities for self-fulfillment that would otherwise be unavailable to them, perhaps providing them with a language that they need to define and pursue their conception of the good.[3] I also take it for granted that nationalism can involve tolerance and respect both toward members of one's nation and toward others. My aim is to examine some features of nationalism of that sort.

Narrowing the Scope of the Discussion

I will make some suggestions about the extent to which one ought to identify oneself with one's nation and about the attitude one ought to take to other nations. To make this a manageable topic and to get at the types of cases that interest me most, I will narrow the discussion to cases that satisfy the following four conditions:

1. Two nations have, and understand themselves to have, incompatible objectives, share the same territory or occupy contiguous territories, and interact extensively. Most likely such nations are in competition in a number of areas, such as in economic, cultural, or territorial matters. The political aspiration of each nation has a bearing on the other nation in that each wants something that bears directly on the future of the other. So there is much that divides them and their members. They have disagreements or differences in all, or most, of the areas that bear on what it is to identify oneself with one's nation. These competing nations are also members of a larger and more comprehensive group, one that has each of them as part of *its* history. The history of each, therefore, is part of a larger historical tapestry, the full account of which will also make reference to the history of its opponent and to the ongoing competition and interaction between the two groups.

I also restrict discussion to cases in which each of the competing nations satisfies the following three conditions. (Unlike the first condition, which can be satisfied only by two or more nations, the next three conditions may be satisfied by individual nations.)

2. As already indicated, the nations involved are minimally decent; strong identification with them is therefore permissible unless there is reason to think otherwise.

3. Each nation has enjoyed a long history, and many people who are intelligent, sensible, reflective, wise, and generally fair-minded have identified themselves with it and continue to do so. Let's say that many people who have integrity have identified themselves with such a nation. This integrity incorporates aspects of different types. For example, reflectiveness is an intellectual virtue, whereas general fair-mindedness is a moral virtue. Intelligence, on the other hand, being largely beyond one's control, has a different status, and including it under the umbrella of integrity stretches normal usage a little. When a nation has, and has had, many members who have integrity, it is likely that it satisfies the conditions (conditions that have to do with its character, projects, practices, and so forth) such that it is prima facie permissible to identify oneself with it. For the fact that people of integrity identify with a nation suggests that it is worthy of identification. Also, the

fact that certain beliefs—in particular beliefs whose acceptance is partially constitutive of identification with one's nation—are held by people with integrity increases the probability that those beliefs are true; the assumption is that people
with integrity are less likely to be careless in the acquisition and maintenance of
their beliefs just as, in turn, they are less likely to be careless in the formation of
their allegiances.

4. A reasonable and impartial outsider can see the point of the aspirations of
each of the nations involved; such a person could be persuaded by the correctness
of much of the story that the nation tells of its past, and of what is distinctive of it,
and could feel the appeal of its sense of what matters about its future.

A nation that satisfies these last three conditions meets a high standard. Let's say
that it is an "impressive" nation. Impressive nations deserve a hearing. They have
stood the test of history and have elicited long-term loyalty from people of integrity. The loyalty such nations elicit is not just a function of the heat of a conflict
of the moment or of carelessly formed allegiances.

The third and fourth conditions are significant partly because by showing that
these conditions are met in the case of a nation we provide reason to believe that
the crucial second condition is satisfied. In addition, a recognition that there are
people of integrity on the other side will make it more difficult for the caricatures
that are used to belittle or discredit the other side and are often the stock-in-trade
of groups that are engaged in a struggle with each other to do their mischief. Also,
the facts about who has supported a cause may serve as an indicator of whether it
is worthy of support, for in deciding what causes are worthy of support, as in deciding what beliefs to hold, a natural, sensible, and perhaps unavoidable procedure
is to rely on people who seem reliable. Of course neither the third nor the fourth
condition is an altogether reliable indicator that the important second condition
has been met, since insiders can be blind to the flaws of their nation and outsiders
can be duped into giving support when it is undeserved. Still, these third and
fourth conditions serve as reasonably reliable indicators. As mentioned, showing
that they are met may have persuasive value; and they also serve to illuminate what
is typically involved in the second condition being met.

Let's refer to situations in which the four conditions are satisfied as "contested
situations." In a contested situation, people of integrity have identified with each
nation over long periods of time. In such a situation, it is also considered axiomatic by each side, or at any rate by many people on each side, that many of the
views, hopes, commitments, longings, et cetera, that are definitive of the other
side lack validity. I want to consider the extent to which one ought to identify
with one's nation and the attitude one should take to the competing nation in
such situations.

There are some features of nations in contested situations that it is useful to
make explicit here. A nation in such a situation has, by definition, a well-defined
political agenda. Hence there is a political agenda with which it is possible for the

members of the nation to identify. And since I am limiting the discussion to nations in contested situations, in what follows I can ignore the fact that nations often lack a well-defined political agenda, so that strong identification as I have defined it is not even on the cards for the members of such nations. Members of nations in contested situations are also likely to have a well-developed sense of national identity for they are in conditions in which their nationality and definition of themselves as different from their opponents matter. Thus when they participate in the forms of life, traditions, pursuits, and customs that are characteristic of their nation, they are likely to think of themselves as doing so *as* members of their nation. In general, the strong sort of identification, with the explicit sense of belonging that it involves and the attendant feelings, hopes, commitments, and so forth, is to be expected in such situations. In other (uncontested) situations, there may not be a well-defined political agenda and the sense of national identification is likely to be present in a more implicit or dispositional way.

As I proceed, I will attempt to illuminate my suggestions about how members of nations in contested situations should react by considering their implications in the case of Ireland and especially for the extent to which it is morally acceptable to identify oneself with either of the two main political groups on the island of Ireland—namely, Irish nationalists and Northern Irish unionists—although my concern is also with theoretical issues that admit of application in other contexts. (I choose the Irish case partly because of my personal experience and background, having grown up as a member of a minority Protestant [Methodist] community in the Irish Republic.)

A brief word or two on the main competing groups in the Irish situation.[4] Central to the aspirations of the Northern Irish unionists, the majority of whom are Protestants, is the ideal of preserving what unionists conceive of as their distinctive way of life. They feel that in the event of unity with the rest of Ireland they would be an outnumbered and beleaguered minority and their culture, identity, religion, and, in effect, what makes them who they are would be submerged. At least as important to them is the aspiration signified by the term "unionism": the desire for the six counties that constitute Northern Ireland to continue to be united with the rest of the United Kingdom. Unionists generally feel British, think of themselves as British, and want to remain British. Why, they ask, should they be forced into unity with the Irish Republic, which they regard as a foreign state, and with the people of the Irish Republic, with whom they feel that they have a lot less in common than they have with the people of Great Britain?

Unionists typically do not think of themselves as a nation. Consider these remarks from the unionist economist Patrick J. Roche: "The entire mode of nationalist argument lacks authority for unionists. Unionists are not part of an Irish nation but neither do they perceive themselves to be a distinct nation. Unionists have a localized territorial identity ('Ulstermen') but their political perception is of belonging to a British nation constituted by a shared allegiance to the state."[5] However, when the term "nation" is understood as in the first section of this chapter, the unionists should be classified as a nation. They have this status in virtue of their culture, religious orientation, lifestyle, general outlook, history, conception of their history, and political aspirations. To think of them in this way is not to deny or even de-emphasize their conception of themselves as British, which would be repugnant to most of them; it is simply to classify them as a national group that is currently within the United Kingdom.

Central to the aspirations of Irish nationalists, the vast majority of whom are Catholics, is the wish for Northern Ireland to be part of an expanded Irish state, the island of Ireland to be unified politically, and the British to leave Northern Ireland. Irish nationalism is motivated to a considerable degree by a sense of grievance, a sense of having been treated unjustly by the British, as well as by unionists since the partition of the island. To some extent Irish nationalism traditionally has conceived of unionists as not really belonging on the island and as being a relic of colonial occupation. Irish nationalists also generally believe that a single state for the people of the island is the natural and appropriate political arrangement and have generally argued that the group that should make decisions about the future of Northern Ireland is the population of the island of Ireland as a whole, in which, of course, the unionists would be outvoted many times over. Here, for instance, is a typical statement of this view from the Irish artist Robert Ballagh: "[The plain answer to the] question as to whether the decision about the future of . . . 'Northern Ireland' *ought* to be left to the people there . . . is 'no.' 'Northern Ireland' was and is a glorified gerrymander whereby six Irish counties were partitioned from the rest because they were the largest area that the unionists could dominate. The truly democratic demand is for majority rule in Ireland, albeit on the basis of devolution and non-discrimination, and [for] Britain to accept that and to start a process of disengagement to help realize it."[6]

It seems clear that the four conditions are satisfied in the Irish case. Thus, for example, the aspirations of the two groups are incompatible; if either achieves its political objectives, the other will thereby be prevented from doing so. Each group has aspirations, projects, practices, and so forth, that are at least minimally decent. In the case of each nation, a case of some force can be made for its achievement of what it aspires to achieve. It is reasonable to think that each has a right to self-determination.[7] Each has many people with integrity, and each has an account of its history and destiny that could convince an impartial outsider. However, I shall assume rather than try to show that the four conditions are satisfied in the Irish case, although I hope at least to weaken resistance to the view that this is so.

Attitudes to the Other Nation

Tolerance and Respect

I begin with some comments on the sort of attitude to the practices, interests, style of life, beliefs, institutions, pastimes, symbols, and so forth, of the other community, and indeed to them as a group and as individuals, that is appropriate in contested situations. A distinction between tolerance and respect is useful in this context. My suggestion is that in such situations respect is the far better attitude than tolerance, although tolerance obviously is better than intolerance.

What is it for the A's to tolerate the B's? In the view of the A's, at any rate, there must be something wrong with the B's, ranging from their being morally repugnant to their being merely mildly distasteful or unpleasant. If there is indifference to, or acceptance of, the behavior of the B's, or of the B's themselves, then there is nothing to tolerate; in that case, one of the necessary conditions for tolerance is not met. Tolerance involves living with something, accepting it, enduring it, putting up with it, and refraining from reacting negatively to it in spite of the fact that there is something wrong with it or that it is not as one would wish it to be.

Respect involves a more positive attitude to its object. While tolerating or putting up with something always involves an element of reluctance, respect involves an appreciation of the other nation/tradition/group to some extent for its own sake; it sees the other group as worthy of preservation and of exploration. While tolerance is likely to be accompanied by a mere willingness not to attack its object, respect is likely to be accompanied by a willingness to protect and preserve the group toward which it is directed.

Respect also involves an element of humility; it involves a recognition that our group may need to learn from its competitor and that the other culture has its own appeal and its own virtues. It sees the other side as a repository of valuable resources of, for example, the literary or linguistic sort or with respect to the dispositions, attitudes, ethic, or styles of life that it encourages. Hence there is a case for paying attention to what the other side may have to offer us. We may need to study our own culture and our own institutions and practices and see if they can be improved in the light of the alternative. So respect has a self-critical dimension.

To have respect is also, in effect, to acknowledge that you can see how a reasonable person would belong to the other group. And the fact that a group includes reasonable people among its prominent members recommends it to us. Being one of them is not outrageous or foolish. Respect permits it rather to be seen as perfectly reasonable. Another part of the respect in question is a matter of appreciating others as responsible acquirers and holders of beliefs. Respect for them as acquirers of beliefs puts a certain amount of pressure on the assumption that we are right and they are wrong; it suggests that their beliefs in an area in which we disagree are at least very worthy of attention.

We can locate the sort of respect under discussion at a certain point on a spectrum, at one end of which is the view that our group and its aims, projects, traditions, and so forth, matter, while the other group and all that is distinctive of it do not matter, the views of its members are not to be taken seriously, and their causes do not constitute a challenge to ours. At the other extreme is the view that both groups are on a par and are to be taken with equal seriousness; roughly they are equally worthwhile, neither has anything terribly wrong with it, and either is worthy of allegiance. Respect tends toward the latter end of this spectrum.

One reason for advocating respect toward other nations is provided by the thought that while tolerance will help you to get along with each other to some extent, it will often make for unstable relations. If you are merely tolerating others, this is likely to become clear; a comment here, a raised eyebrow there, a rerouted march yonder will give the game away about what you really think of the other group. And, at least in modern democratic states, that may have destabilizing consequences. Respect, on the other hand, will have stabilizing effects. (No doubt this and other benefits of respect require for their full achievement reciprocation from the other side, but unilateral steps can contribute to bringing about such effects.)

However, the consideration that is especially relevant in contested situations appeals to principle rather than to pragmatism. In such contexts it is not enough for one group to put up with or endure the other nation and its beliefs and practices; this is a too begrudging and insufficiently generous attitude. There has to be something deeply wrong with others for it to be appropriate to settle for mere tolerance of them. When both groups are impressive, each needs to go further than that.[8]

Another argument for respect is to be found in this area, which I will present with reference to the Irish case. If one were to identify oneself with, say, the cause of Northern Irish unionists in such a way that one failed to respect the ideals and aspirations of Irish nationalists, one would not be able to understand properly what makes the nationalists tick; one could not feel what they feel and would be blind to their ideals. The same point applies of course to identification with the Irish nationalist cause; a whole set of worthwhile concerns, admirable dispositions, and valuable cultural resources would in that case not be appreciated.

The practical implications of a respectful approach should not be underestimated. For example, it would rule out the contemptuous, and harmful, attitude of many unionists to the Irish language, and, in general, to Irish culture.[9] As you would expect in a contested situation, this failure to respect is well matched by attitudes on the other side in the Irish case. Thus the prominent Irish journalist and author Tim Pat Coogan writes—and here I move from a cultural to a political illustration—that "[the] essence of unionism is based on supremacy: 'what we have we hold'. . . . Unionism is aimed at 'keeping the foot on the neck' of the nationalist."[10] But this is just to confuse some pathological features of unionism with its main aspirations. (In contested situations, it is likely that neither nation is free of pathological features.) Again—and this is another political example—there is the nationalist assumption, which is sometimes apparent, that the unionists will eventually come to their senses and realize that they really are Irish and that their sense of themselves as British was illusory.

Identifying with Your Nation in Contested Situations

The Case for Reduced Identification

I suggest that in a contested situation the extent to which one identifies with one's nation should be diminished and that one should also identify to some extent with the more comprehensive group that includes one's own nation and the opposing nation; one should to some extent cast one's lot with that larger unit, expanding the group of people whom you think of as "your people." It is strong identification with one's nation that is inappropriate in contested situations. Obviously, you have every right to count yourself as Irish or Palestinian or Quebecois, if that is what you are. But the rules governing strong identification in contested situations are different. Both the cultural and the political aspects of nationhood are relevant to why this is so.

First, consider the cultural aspect. An appreciation, and even an appropriation, of some of the cultural resources associated with the other nation may be possible while one strongly identifies with one's own nation. However, to view the other nation as a rich source of cultural resources is to diminish your sense of it as alien; it is to see its resources as something that it is good for your group to have available and to open yourself to embracing much of what makes members of the other nation who they are. The relevant resources in question include, for example, those of the literary, artistic, linguistic, and recreational sorts; they also include the customs and traditions of members of the other nation, the distinctive insights and types of awareness that their particular historical experience has enabled them to develop, and, in general, much that is characteristic of them and of their way of life. To look at the other nation in this way is to be on the way to thinking of oneself as a member of a larger group that includes both nations and that would make available a richer set of cultural possibilities than is made available by either nation.

In a contested situation, the political aspirations of members of the other group also ought to be seen as reasonable; their aims ought to be taken seriously, and it ought to be seen to be desirable that those aims should be reflected to some significant degree in policies and institutions. If your nation recognizes that this is so, this in effect limits its pursuit of its own political aspirations and moves the nation in the direction of seeing itself as part of a larger group that takes seriously the political aspirations of both nations.

The presence of competing national groups that are impressive is also significant in another way. Each such nation probably has well-established lines of thought that support its distinctive institutions, practices, and political aspirations. Since the practices, political aspirations, and so forth, are those of an impressive nation, we can assume that there is a good deal to be said for the lines of thought in question. There may be some way to combine some of these lines of thought and the values that underpin them—that is, there may be some way to accommodate some of the considerations advanced by each side or more of them than either side alone can accommodate. This thought provides another reason to adopt a perspective from which the appeal of both sides may be appreciated and taken to heart.

My suggestion, then, is that members of a nation ought to respond in certain ways to the fact that the nation is in a contested situation. In particular, in such situations there is reason both to have a diminished sense of identity with one's own nation and to identify to some extent with the larger group that includes both nations. This is so in spite of the fact that in such situations one's own nation satisfies a high standard. But so does the competing nation, and this has important implications.

We might think of this point in a quite different way—namely, that a nation in a contested situation is deserving of strong identification only if its ethos is such that it gives expression to and encourages the suggested responses. To the extent that a nation reacts appropriately to the fact that it is in a contested situation— which will involve promoting an attitude of respect for the other culture, making room for its members to adopt a sort of pan-national identity, and so forth—one may strongly identify with it. And to the extent that it fails to do so, it is less worthy of identification.

The effects of reducing one's sense of identification with one's own nation would be felt across all or most of the eight dimensions of what it is to identify strongly with one's nation. For example, it involves diminished support for the political aspiration of one's nation and a diminished sense of oneself as a member of it; and while one may still participate wholeheartedly in various national traditions and practices, one does so in a different mode—the traditions and practices in question will be seen as more optional and as existing alongside alternatives that are equally worthwhile. On the other hand, the identification of oneself with the larger group that is discussed in this section is identification of one of the intermediate sorts rather than either weak or strong identification. It is not strong identification partly because of the incompleteness of the idea of the larger group in question; thus, by definition, that larger group lacks a well-defined political agenda.

If a sense of belonging to the more comprehensive group were to become widespread, that larger group might in due course develop its own character. What form it would take would emerge only through time and experience, and it probably would to some extent need to be constructed. The larger group might come to focus more on the shared history of the two nations. Even the struggles and conflicts between the two communities might be regarded as matters of shared experience through which both communities have come. In the Irish case, there might emerge a new perspective that would focus on the sense of being an island people who are at the edge of Europe or of being less secular than most of the rest of Europe.[11] It would be hard to predict in advance what form a new common story might take. One of the great virtues of respect as an attitude to the other nation is that it will help to make possible a search for common ground.

To identify with one's own nation in a contested situation and to fail to identify to some extent with the larger pan-national group that includes both nations are to go wrong in a certain respect. It is useful to distinguish this particular way of going wrong from another—namely, having an insufficiently comprehensive or insufficiently inclusive conception of what it takes to belong in a certain state or in a certain territory. Consider, for instance, a conception of what it is to be Malaysian that excludes the Malaysian Chinese or Malaysian Indians or gives them second-class status or a conception of what it is to be an American that excludes atheists, for instance. Or consider the fact that when Ian Paisley talks of "the people of Ulster" he forgets, or at least fails to treat with the same seriousness, the presence of the nationalist community and its aspirations. Indeed it is striking that his conception of what it is to belong in Ulster suffers from much the same defect as a nationalist conception of the Irish people that ignores the unionists. (Often someone who trots out the relevant exclusivist notion of what it takes to belong will say that what he or she has in mind is what it takes to be a real Malaysian or a real American or a real Irishman; could it be that the excluded unfortunates are not even real?) The problem in each of these cases is that the notion of what it is to belong in a state or in a territory is framed in such a way that it is implied that a certain group does not belong even though it both belongs and has every right to do so. The mistake, and it is as much a factual one as a normative one, is to think of a certain group, such as one's own nation, as *constituting* the larger group or as the really important part, or the defining part, of the larger group. Clearly the cure for this particular ailment is to have a more inclusive conception of what is required for belonging in the relevant group.

This mistake is made in contested and uncontested situations alike, but it takes a particular form in contested situations, and it does so in virtue of the political aspect of nationhood. To identify oneself with one's nation is to support and foster its political aspiration; such an aspiration, if it is to be worthy of support, has to meet certain conditions. In particular, the idea of the nation involved must find the right sort of place in its political vision for everyone who belongs in the territory with which it concerns itself. If it fails to do so, it is less worthy of our loyalty, and whatever loyalty we have to it should be tempered by an awareness of this flaw. Thus in the case of Irish nationalists, since their aspiration is to have a single state that includes all of the people on the island of Ireland, this consideration requires that the interests and aspirations of the unionists be given weight and be taken seriously. And the implications of this point in the case of the Northern Irish unionists pertain to their attitude to the residents of the body of territory to which their political aspiration applies—namely, the entire population of Northern Ireland—and require that the interests and aspirations of the nationalist community in Northern Ireland be given weight and be taken seriously.

Conclusion

In the Irish case, strong identification with either nationalism or unionism is unsatisfactory. Neither side is worthy of strong identification because both are impressive nations. Those who endorse either the nationalist or the unionist cause need to incorporate an awareness of the legitimacy of the cause of the other side. A mature political outlook, in this as in other contested situations, requires that people on either side be curious about and take a healthy interest in the other nation, that they explore what is attractive about it, and that they recognize the value of richer and more complex allegiances that go beyond traditional loyalties. It requires that the members of each nation be outwardly focused to some extent, take a generous attitude to the other nation, and think of themselves to some extent as fellow members of the larger group that includes both nations. What I am describing is, in fact, something that is very difficult to achieve; it requires the substitution of one framework for another, a move away from the familiar and comfortable, and a changed conception of oneself and of others. It is especially difficult to make these changes in contested situations, for such situations probably encourage obliviousness and even hostility to what may be valuable on the other side. (Perhaps the very facts that one's own nation is impressive and that people of integrity have been and are among its supporters encourage this obliviousness.) Nevertheless, it is worthwhile to appeal to an impressive nation and to its members on such matters of principle; it is reasonable to expect its members to understand the point of the appeal and to be capable of responding in the right way. I consider the fairness of my suggestions to be apparent from the fact that they are roughly equally demanding in the case of each nation.

Three issues merit further discussion. First, if one identifies with two groups—one's own nation and the more comprehensive group that also includes the competing nation—how much weight should these different sources of identity have? This remains a gray area. Much also could be said about various loose forms of connection with one's own group that involve continued identification with it even while the appeal of the alternative is taken to heart.

Second, the interconnected set of suggestions I discuss is particularly relevant in contested situations. That is, the case for my various suggestions is strongest when there has been extensive interaction, there is a well-defined larger group, and other conditions that characterize contested situations are met. But the proposed principles also apply, if to a lesser extent, in some cases that do not satisfy the four conditions. Thus they apply to some extent even in the case of some national groups that deal with each other from a distance and do not share a territory or neighboring territories. They also apply to some extent when it is unclear or controversial whether there is a well-defined larger group that consists of both nations in a situation that is otherwise contested. Furthermore, the proposed principles apply whether or not either nation has its own state, and they apply irrespective of whether one group is a minority relative to the other.

Third, it seems that many of the benefits of a culture are available only if there is wholehearted identification with it. Cultures that provide rich and interesting possibilities for people to understand themselves and their experience seem to work best if they are well defined and vigorously embraced. (There may also be something to the idea that it is qua vigorous and thriving cultures that they are worth preserving.) Hence the case for identification with one's own cultural group cannot so easily be expanded into a case for identity with a more comprehensive and less homogeneous group. The larger group does not have a capacity to play the same role. Still, whatever resulting losses there are may be mitigated in ways such as the following. Reduced identification with one's nation and all of its trappings is compatible with continued enjoyment of many of the benefits of one's national culture—that is, to some extent the benefits of cultural belonging may be left intact. Furthermore, the richer set of goods that is made available by a measure of identification with the larger group in a contested situation may help to counterbalance, and may even outweigh, what is lost.

Finally, I have no doubt that in the Irish case, as in many other contested situations, the most urgent need is for political arrangements that are acceptable to both nations. The hard job is to hammer out such arrangements. But just as in the case of interpersonal relations it is not enough to develop ways of coexisting that are tolerable for all and it also matters what attitudes we take to others, likewise in the case of relations among nations there is reason to ask what attitudes to one's own nation and to other nations are appropriate. I do not assume that changes in attitude such as those I discuss would solve the problems of Northern Ireland or of any other contested situation, but they surely would contribute to doing so.

NOTES

I am greatly indebted to David Archard, David Copp, Jeff Jordan, Jeff McMahan, Don Moulds, and Jim Wallace for comments on earlier drafts.

1. Avishai Margalit and Joseph Raz, "National Self-Determination," *Journal of Philosophy* 87, no. 9 (September 1990): 439–61. Margalit and Raz argue that when there is an encompassing group, there is a case for self-determination. Much of my account of groups of

this sort is drawn from Margalit and Raz. I have also benefited from reading chapter 17 in this volume.

2. For a balanced discussion of the role, importance, and dangers of such embellishments, see David Archard, "Myths, Lies, and Historical Truth: A Defence of Nationalism," *Political Studies* 43 (1995): 472–81.

3. Will Kymlicka makes the point well: "It's only through having a rich and secure cultural structure that people can become aware, in a vivid way, of the options available to them, and intelligently examine their value. Without such a cultural structure, children and adolescents lack adequate role-models, which leads to despondency and escapism" *Liberalism, Community, and Culture* [Oxford: Clarendon, 1989], pp. 165–66).

4. Useful sources include Kevin Boyle and Tom Hadden, *Northern Ireland: The Choice* (London: Penguin, 1994); *Nordirland in Geschichte und Gegenwart* (Northern Ireland— past and present), ed. Jürgen Elvert (Stuttgart: Franz Steiner, 1994); Padraig O'Malley, *The Uncivil War: Ireland Today* (Boston: Houghton Mifflin, 1983); and *Northern Ireland: The Background to the Conflict*, ed. John Darby (Syracuse: Syracuse University Press, 1983). The deepest and most insightful analysis I have found is provided by John McGarry and Brendan O'Leary in *Explaining Northern Ireland* (Oxford: Blackwell, 1995).

5. Patrick J. Roche, "Nationalism and British Policy in Northern Ireland," unpublished paper, p. 3. On this, see also D. George Boyce, *Nationalism in Ireland*, 2d ed. (London: Routledge, 1991), p. 364.

6. Robert Ballagh, *Irish Times*, letters page, August 7, 1992.

7. I argue for this in "Ireland: The Case for Impartiality," in *Resolving Regional Conflict*, ed. Roger E. Kanet (Urbana: University of Illinois Press, 1997).

8. My contention is that in contested situations the dominant attitude to the other nation should be that of respect. This is compatible with merely tolerating some things about them, such as some of their traditions or practices, for example, and with believing that some of the views that define them are mistaken.

9. See, for example, McGarry and O'Leary, *Explaining Northern Ireland*, p. 221. On the other hand, consider the following as a small example of the opportunities in this area: "UUP member of Belfast City Council Dr Chris McGimpsey suggested that Irish should be taught in the North's state schools. Speaking at a seminar on the language in Gweedore, Co. Donegal, Dr McGimpsey said that he felt this was the best way to change attitudes among unionists, who currently saw the use of the language as a threat" (*Irish Emigrant*, no. 453 (October 9, 1995).

10. Tim Pat Coogan, *Disillusioned Decades: Ireland 1966–87* (Dublin: Gill and MacMillan, 1987), pp. 195, 199. If Coogan were right and the essence of unionism were supremacy and "keeping the foot on the neck" of the nationalist, then unionism would fail the "minimal decency" test and my discussion here would not bear on it. Indeed, all of this is so if it merely is the case that supremacy is essential to unionism. There are, of course, equally unsavory representations of the nationalist agenda, and the same points apply in that case. I take it for granted that a nonpejorative and yet reasonably accurate account of the agenda of both nationalists and unionists can be provided, along the lines suggested above.

11. Clare O'Halloran, *Partition and the Limits of Irish Nationalism: An Ideology under Stress* (Atlantic Highlands, N.J.: Humanities Press International, 1987), p. 204.

V

NATIONAL SELF-DETERMINATION, SOVEREIGNTY, AND INTERVENTION

17

Democracy and Communal Self-Determination

DAVID COPP

The standard issues in political philosophy take the division of the world into political units as given. For example, the question whether there is an obligation to obey the law assumes that a state is given and asks whether there is an obligation to obey its laws. Similar things could be said about the questions: What would a just state be like, and what is the appropriate form of government? The standard issues are concerned with moral constraints on the state. I believe that there are also moral constraints on the division of the political world into states. In this essay, I want to pursue the issue of what these constraints are. I call this issue "the problem of political division." A natural model to have in mind is one in which stateless people coalesce into groups that then decide to form states. This state-of-nature model cannot deal adequately with some of the most interesting dimensions of the problem, however, which arise after a division into states already exists. In this essay, I focus on whether there are any kinds of groups that have a right to secede from the states that govern them. I believe it is useful to consider this question in the context of the larger problem of political division.

I shall approach the problem of political division by asking the following question: Which groups, in which territories, have the right to be or to constitute themselves as states? Or, as I shall say, which groups have "the right of self-determination"?[1]

I assume that justice requires states to be governed democratically, at least in many familiar circumstances. I will argue that John Stuart Mill was correct to think that a reasonable answer to the question of why justice requires democracy supports an answer to the problem of political division.[2] In particular, I will argue, it supports the proposal that, subject to qualifications that I discuss, societies with a territory and a stable desire for self-government have the right to constitute themselves as states. In short, "territorial-political" societies have this right. I will argue that in a world of pluralistic societies, the idea that "nations" and certain culturally unified groups have the right of self-determination is antidemocratic.

The Right of Self-Determination

What is a state? Roughly speaking, a state exists when a legal system is in force over the population of a territory, when a government exists with the legal power to alter the legal system, and when the government, together with other agencies over which it has legal authority, has (relatively) effective control over the territory. A state is a self-governing political unit. For example, its government is not under the authority or control of some other government, such as a remote colonial authority or an occupying power.

By the right of "self-determination," I mean the right to acquire or continue to possess the status of a state. The right of self-determination is a "cluster right"; as I will explain, it includes certain privileges and claim-rights, as well as certain moral "powers."

A full discussion of the concepts of a power, a privilege, and a claim-right is obviously beyond the scope of this essay, but I do need to explain the basics. I will follow Judith Jarvis Thomson's account; she, in turn, was following Wesley Newcomb Hohfeld.[3]

Person A has a *claim* against B that *p* if and only if B has an obligation toward A that *p*—the obligation that B discharges if and only if *p*. Person A has a *privilege* regarding B to let it be the case that p if and only if it is not the case that A has an obligation toward B that not-*p*—an obligation that A discharges if and only if not-*p*. Person A has a *power* if and only if A has the ability to alter the rights of some person by performing some (morally permitted) action. Finally, a cluster right is a complex of rights. For example, a *liberty* to do something is a cluster consisting of a privilege to do the thing plus a claim that others not interfere.

Thomson argues—correctly, I believe—that claims are not "absolute." That is, from the fact that A has a claim against B that B do alpha, it follows that B has an obligation to do alpha, but it does *not* follow that B ought *simpliciter*, or "all things considered," to do alpha; what follows is that B ought to do alpha *other things being equal*. In some cases where A has a claim against B but B does not perform, A may have a case for compensation. Thomson proposes that if person A has a claim against B that B do alpha, then if B anticipates that he will not do alpha, B ought (other things being equal) to request A to release him from the obligation, or failing that, B ought (other things being equal) to compensate A for losses he incurs as a result of B's failure to do alpha.[4]

The right to self-determination is, as I said, the right to acquire or continue to possess the status of a state. Consider, first, groups that are not states. If such a group has this right, it has two key powers: (1) the power to bring it about that it has a claim against (other) states that they not interfere with its forming a government and (2) the power to bring it about that it has a claim against these states that they deal with the government it forms in the way they are obligated to deal with the government of any state. If a group has these powers, there is something it could do that would bring about that it has the corresponding claims; I propose that a vote of the members of the group in favor of the group's forming a state would bring this about. An entity that has the right of self-determination has (3) the liberty to conduct such a vote. That is, it has a privilege to conduct such a vote and a claim against other states that they not interfere (other things being equal).

It would be peculiar to hold that a group has the right to acquire the status of a state, a right that includes the power to place other states under a duty not to interfere with its forming a government, if one supposed that these other states might nevertheless have no obligation not to interfere with the operation of the resulting government. For this reason, I think that in acquiring the status of a state, a group would acquire the right to govern itself without interference. Call this "the right to government."[5] Notice the way that this right is related to the right of self-determination. Specifically, if legitimate states have the right to government, as I believe they do, then, in addition to the powers and the liberty I have already mentioned, a group with the right of self-determination has the following power: (4) the power to bring it about that it has a claim against (other) states that they not interfere with its governing itself.

Turn now to existing states, but restrict attention to legitimate ones. Existing states do not have powers (1), (2), and (4), for there is nothing an existing state can do to *bring it about* that it has the relevant claims; it already has these claims. But a state does have (1') the power to abandon its status as a state, to release some other state from the obligation not to interfere with its governing itself. For example, it might choose to unify with the other state. Its right to government gives it (2') the liberty to conduct a plebiscite about such matters. Moreover, an existing state has the following "immunity": (3') no other state has the power to extinguish its rights, especially its right to government.

In the case of an entity that is not a state, the right of self-determination consists of certain powers and related liberties; in the case of a state, the right consists of a different power and a related liberty plus an immunity. What unifies these cases? A group that is not a state has the right just in case, essentially, it has the power to bring it about that it has the right to government, and it has the liberty to conduct a plebiscite about acquiring this right. A state has the right just in case it has an immunity to having its right to government extinguished by the action of any other state, but it has the power to extinguish its own right to government by conducting a plebiscite—and it has the liberty to conduct such a plebiscite. To summarize, an entity has the right of self-determination just in case it has moral control over whether it acquires or continues to have the right to government. Control over the right to government is what unifies the cases.[6]

The right of self-determination is not absolute; there may be circumstances in which it is not permissible to exercise this right. First, there can be circumstances in which it is permissible, all things considered, to interfere with a society's becoming a state or continuing to be a state. Such interference may be necessary to minimize a risk to international peace and security, or it may be required in justice. The society may have unjustly seized its territory from another group, for example, or its political and economic system may be seriously unjust. The Confederate States sought to sustain slavery, for example. Second, there can be circumstances in which it would not be morally permissible, all things considered, for a society to exercise its right to self-determination. It may be wrong for a society to secede from a state if the remaining parts of the original state would be so fragmented that they could not form themselves into a viable state or even into a group of viable states. David Gauthier argues that secession is not justified if it would involve a violation of "the requirement that one not better oneself by worsening another."[7] It may be wrong to exercise the right to self-determination because of the requirements of global distributive justice; Kai Nielsen suggests that the only way to achieve the rough equality in everyone's life prospects that justice requires may be to create a global state.[8]

In some cases where a society's right to self-determination is abridged or a society refrains from exercising its right for moral reasons, compensation may be due.[9] As compensation, for example, the society might be given a form of limited subordinate self-government within the state of which it is a part. There can also be circumstances where a society would owe compensation to groups that would otherwise be harmed by its choice to constitute a state. A seceding society may have to compensate the remainder of the original state for investments that the original state made in the society's territory.[10]

I will not attempt to address in a systematic way issues about the circumstances in which it is permissible to abridge the self-determination right of some group or impermissible for the group to exercise it or in which compensation is required by one party or another. The issue I want to address is the logically prior issue of whether there is, in fact, a moral right to self-determination. If there is, which entities possess it? I will ignore issues about international law. For all that I say, it is possible that international law should recognize only the self-determination rights of existing states.

Secession and Existing States

Let us assume that legitimate states have the right to government, the right not to be interfered with in governing themselves. Given this assumption, we can argue that they have the right of self-determination. First, it would be peculiar to allow that a state has the right to government while denying that it has the power to abandon the right. It is arguable that a person cannot abandon his or her right to not be interfered with, but a state's right to government is not as fundamental morally as a person's right to noninterference. If a plebiscite of the citizens is in favor of abandoning the status of a state, there seems to be no reason to deny moral effect to the vote. Hence if a state has the right to government, it also has the power to abandon the right. Second, having the right to government, a state has the right not to be interfered with if it decides to conduct a plebiscite about abandoning this right. Third, it would be peculiar to hold that state A has the right not to be interfered with in governing itself but to think that some other state B has the power to extinguish this right. If B could extinguish A's right that B not interfere, A's right against B would be empty. It would not constrain B's interference in a significant way. Hence if a state has the right to government, it is plausible that it has an immunity against having its right extinguished by a (permissible) action of some other state.[11] Putting all of this together, we have an argument from the claim that legitimate states have the right to government to the conclusion that they have the right of self-determination. In any event, I will assume that legitimate states have the right of self-determination.

The thesis that legitimate states are the *only* entities with a right of self-determination seems quite implausible. Consider the right of secession. This would be the right of self-determination in a case where it is possessed by a part of an existing state, for it would be the right of a part of an existing state to exit from that state and form a new state; it would be a cluster right containing the same liberties and powers as are included in the right of self-determination. Therefore, the thesis that existing legitimate states are the only entities with a right of self-determination implies that there is no right of secession. This seems quite implausible, however, especially since secession may be a minority group's best way to resist injustice on the part of the state in which it finds itself.

The most interesting argument against a right of secession turns on the claim, which is emphasized by Allen Buchanan, that a right to secede requires a valid claim to territory.[12] Any legitimate state has a claim over its territory, for a state's right to government is its right not to be interfered with in governing its territory. Since the secession of a part of the state would involve an interference with the state's governing its territory, it may appear that secession is precluded by the rights of a legitimate state.

My reply, in brief, is that the right to government gives a state a claim against other states that they not interfere with its governing its territory. But it does not give a state a claim against populations *internal* to it that *they* not interfere with its governing them in their territory. Hence it does not give a state a claim that rules out the right of secession.

In this context, we should ignore claims to territory that depend on a state's having a special relationship to its territory, such as a historical, religious, or mythological relationship. I do not deny that some such claims have moral weight, but not every state has a special claim to its territory, and special claims can cut both ways; states could have them, but so could secessionist groups. Moreover, special claims could compete with the right of secession without precluding it. The question we need to ask is whether legitimate states necessarily have a claim over their territories of a kind that precludes the right of secession. I see no reason to believe this. The territory of a state is the area in which its legal system is in force and over which it has (relatively) effective control; a state has the right that outsiders not interfere with its governing this territory. I see no reason to think anything more need be involved. If not, then the rights that legitimate states have over their territory in virtue of their rights to government and self-determination do not preclude the right of secession. Rather, if a part of an existing state has a right to secede, it has a right over the territory in which it lives that is of the same nature as the right of the state over the territory; in particular, it has a liberty to conduct a plebiscite regarding the establishment of a state in that territory and a power to acquire the right to government over the territory.

My position may appear to allow for conflict between an existing legitimate state's right to govern the population of its territory and a secessionist group's right to form a new state in a part of that territory. But this is no objection, for it is possible for rights to conflict. More important, a state's rights of government and of self-determination do not, in fact, give it a right that conflicts with the right of a part of its territory to secede. I will explain this at the end of this essay.

Allen Buchanan thinks the right to secede is restricted to cases involving injustice or malfeasance on the part of the state. The state may have treated a secessionist group unjustly in some way, for example, or a group may need to secede to preserve its culture or to protect its members from abuse within the state.[13] In cases of these kinds, Buchanan holds, the injustice or malfeasance justifies the group in abridging the state's right of self-determination. The interesting question, however, is whether there is a more basic right of secession, a right that is not derived from the right to avoid or combat injustice or malfeasance.

Consider a case that does not involve secession. Suppose, for example, that empire A breaks up into a number of provinces and that another imperialistic empire, B, is considering whether to occupy and annex the provinces. Other things being equal, B's annexing a province would surely have the same moral character regardless of whether it took place just slightly before or just slightly after the province managed to constitute itself as a state. Therefore, if a province would have the right of self-determination once it managed to constitute itself as a state, which I am assuming it would, then it would have the right of self-determination just before it managed to constitute itself as a state. B's annexing a province would violate the province's right of self-determination regardless of its timing. The provinces have a right of self-determination even if they are not yet states.

The key question is whether the provinces had the right of self-determination prior to the breakup of the empire. We have seen that a plausible account of why existing states have the right to self-determination would also support the proposition that the provinces in my example have the right to self-determination after the breakup of the empire, regardless of whether they are yet states. Given this, I believe a plausible account would support the proposition that they had the right all along, regardless of whether they were subject to injustice or malfeasance on the part of the empire. I do not see how arguments based on democratic considerations, the interests of people in associating with whomever they choose, or the value of a culture could show that the provinces after the breakup of the empire have the right of self-determination without showing equally well on the same basis that the provinces before the breakup of the empire have the right of self-determination. And if they have the right of self-determination, they have the right of secession.

In the following sections, I will consider arguments both that "cultural groups" and that "nations" have the right of self-determination. Ultimately, as I said, I will attempt to show that the values underpinning democracy support the idea that "territorial-political" societies have the right. In this section, I have tried to make a case that existing legitimate states have the right to self-determination. I used the example of the provinces to argue that if existing states have that right, then certain entities that are not states also have that right. And I argued that an entity may have a right of secession even in cases not involving injustice or malfeasance.

Culture, Self-Respect, and Encompassing Groups

A variety of arguments have been offered, from claims about the value of culture, or about the role of culture in constituting our "identity," to the conclusion that groups characterized by a distinctive culture have a right to self-determination. Let me call groups of this kind "cultural groups"; a cultural group is a group that exists over several generations, that has a distinctive culture, and that, at any time in its history, consists of all and only the people who "have" the culture at that time.[14] Avishai Margalit and Joseph Raz use the term "encompassing group." An encompassing group is a cultural group with a "common character and a common culture," a culture that is "pervasive" in that it encompasses "many, varied and important aspects of life"; the members of such groups are "marked by" the "character" of the group's culture.[15]

The arguments I want to consider make use of the following cluster of ideas.

First, membership in a cultural group is needed in order for a person to come to have values and a sense of what is important in life; the culture of a person's community is the source of his or her ideas about value and importance. Second, because of this, membership in a cultural group is a precondition for self-respect, for the sense that one's life is worthwhile.[16] Third, also because of this, membership in a cultural group is a precondition for autonomy, for the ability to make "meaningful choices."[17] Finally, membership in a cultural group is needed in order for one to have a sense of belonging and a sense of who one is—a sense of "identity." People "pigeonhole" themselves and are "pigeonholed" by others on the basis of their membership in such a group.[18]

There is truth in these claims, although they need further development. It is not clear what is meant by a "culture," for example, and the term "identity" is especially slippery in this context. I believe I can ignore these problems, however, for the arguments I want to consider turn on the nature of the connection between self-respect and the status of our cultural community, and I think the idea of self-respect is clear enough for my purposes. I will consider two arguments: an "expressivist" argument that was discussed by Charles Taylor and an "instrumental" argument that was proposed by Margalit and Raz.

The distinctive premise in the expressivist argument is that in treating a community as sovereign, the international community thereby expresses a kind of respect. If our community were held in disrespect, this might undermine our confidence in the values we have learned from our community's culture, and in turn this might undermine our self-respect by undermining our confidence in the value of the life we have chosen. In this way, our self-respect depends on the respect accorded to our community. To achieve statehood is to achieve a status that can bring respect to the community. Moreover, it is to achieve a status that essentially involves international recognition, which itself expresses respect. Since we have a right that others not interfere with our securing the conditions of our own self-respect, we have a right that others not interfere with our community's achieving statehood.[19]

Taylor himself rejects this argument, for he points out that a community can gain respect by making achievements of a variety of kinds that do not require statehood. Moreover, he says, lack of respect for our community need not undermine our self-respect since there are other "poles of identification" that can be more important than identification with the community.[20]

Margalit and Raz offer an instrumental argument. They point out that in certain circumstances political sovereignty may contribute to the prosperity and self-respect of an encompassing group. And because of the connection between our identity and self-respect and our membership in an encompassing group, the prosperity and self-respect of the encompassing group to which we belong are vital to our welfare. Hence it can be vital to our welfare that our encompassing group be self-determining. Moreover, given the importance of the self-respect and prosperity of such a group to the well-being of its members, it is "reasonable to let the encompassing group that forms a substantial majority in a territory have the right to determine whether that territory shall form an independent state." That is, Margalit and Raz conclude, such groups have a right of self-determination.[21]

According to Margalit and Raz, if an encompassing group forms a substantial majority in a territory, then it is the group that has the right of self-determination; *it* has "the right to determine whether that territory shall form an independent state," not the overall population of the territory. Its members are entitled to decide whether a state shall be formed in the territory. Nonmembers are disenfranchised in the process by which the decision about statehood is made even if they reside permanently in the territory and are members of the overall society. Margalit and Raz's position therefore runs contrary to democratic and egalitarian considerations.

To be sure, according to their position, the right of self-determination belongs only to groups that form a substantial majority in a territory, and the exercise of the right requires that the "overwhelming majority" of the group desire that there be a state for the group.[22] In such circumstances, if everyone voted his or her desire, a democratic plebiscite would favor sovereignty even if those who did not belong to the majority group were permitted to vote. Yet this is no defense against the objection that the scheme is unjust. We do not think that the justice of depriving a person of the vote is settled by showing that, in the circumstances, the person could not have changed the result of an election.[23]

One reason for favoring democracy, I believe, is that it treats citizens with equal respect by giving them equal authority over key political decisions. It seems to me that a system that disenfranchised members of a society on the issue of political sovereignty, on the ground that they do not belong to the majority group in the society, would indicate precisely the kind of disrespect for them that democratic decision procedures are intended to foreclose. It is likely, for example, that the Québecois—the members of the French-speaking community in Québec—qualify as an encompassing group. They are also a substantial majority of the population of Québec. According to Margalit and Raz, then, the Québecois have the right to decide the political future of Québec. But we surely would not find it acceptable to disenfrachise the remaining parts of the population in a plebiscite on sovereignty. To deprive them of the vote would be to fail to accord them equal respect.

It may seem that Margalit and Raz could easily amend their scheme to allow all the people in a territory to vote on the issue of sovereignty, especially given that the right of self-determination is not absolute. They could argue that although a majority encompassing group has the right of self-determination, the need to show equal respect supports extending the right to vote in a plebiscite on sovereignty to the entire population of the group's territory. To me, however, this move seems equivalent to giving up the idea that the right of self-determination belongs to encompassing groups as such. For, in the amended scheme, people who are *not* members of an encompassing group have the same authority over a decision about self-determination as people who *are* members of the group.

Moreover, it seems to me, Margalit and Raz's argument does not support the idea that encompassing groups have the right rather than the entire populations of the relevant territories. Their argument turns on the importance of sovereignty to the welfare of the members of a majority encompassing group. But the entire population of the territory of an encompassing group is also a group whose members' welfare will be affected by the creation of a sovereign state in the territory. The creation of a state would affect the welfare of members of the minority as well as the welfare of members of the majority; sovereignty for Québec would affect the welfare of an Anglophone as much as the welfare of a Québecois. Hence, by parity of reasoning, Margalit and Raz's argument supports the idea that the entire population of the territory of a majority encompassing group has the right of self-determination.

We now have to face the question: Why limit the right of self-determination to the populations of territories in which some encompassing group is the substantial majority?[24] Many societies are culturally pluralistic; they include members of several different encompassing groups, and in many cases, no encompassing group is a substantial majority in any (continuous) part of the society's territory.

For example, Canadian society is pluralistic in the sense that it includes members of several encompassing groups without (I believe) being itself an encompassing group. Suppose, however, that the Canadians want to be self-determining because they know that this is the only way they can ensure that the freshwater of the northern part of North America is not piped into the American desert, thereby destroying the lakes and rivers in Canada. Culture does not enter into the content of this reasoning, and the reasoning may turn on environmental concerns rather than concerns about the welfare of Canadians. Yet it would be antidemocratic to hold, as do Margalit and Raz, that this reasoning cannot legitimate the self-determination of Canada, no matter what proportion of Canadians vote this way.[25]

Basically the same considerations that Margalit and Raz believe to support the right of self-determination of (majority) encompassing groups would show that the populations of pluralistic societies have the right. Just as the welfare of members of an encompassing group can depend on the group's prosperity, so the welfare of the members of a pluralistic society can depend on its prosperity. It may seem that people's welfare depends more centrally on the prosperity of their encompassing group than it could on the prosperity of a pluralistic society because their "identity" is derived from their encompassing group rather than their society. Yet the multicultural nature of a pluralistic society can be important to a person's "identity" in much the same way that the culture of his or her encompassing group can be. If our society is pluralistic, we can see alternate ways of life being lived out and come to accept some of the values of other encompassing groups within the society. We can be supported in our unwillingness to conform to the culture of our group by the existence of other cultural groups within the society as a whole.[26] I conclude, then, that Margalit and Raz's argument for according the right of self-determination to majority encompassing groups, once it is amended to support according the right to the entire populations of the territories of majority encompassing groups, also supports holding that the right belongs to the populations of pluralistic societies.

The argument still turns at least in part on the ideas that connect our welfare to our culture, given that the lasting instantiation of a culture by a society may depend on the society's becoming a state. Yet there are other properties of societies, the lasting instantiation of which can similarly require that a society be a state, and which can be similarly important to our welfare. If Margalit and Raz are on the right track in their argument, then the importance of these properties to our welfare may also ground the right of self-determination. If these societal properties are important to our welfare, it is not clear why they must be connected to our sense of "identity" in order to ground the right to self-determination.

We are left, then, with a scheme that is quite different from the one favored by Margalit and Raz. Encompassing groups do not have the right of self-determination; rather, societies have the right whether or not they are culturally pluralistic. And the basis of the right is the fact that the welfare of the members of a society may be enhanced if it is or becomes a state.

There is a fundamental problem with Margalit and Raz's scheme that I have not yet addressed. In particular, the fact that the welfare of the members of a society would be enhanced if the society were to constitute a state does not mean that the society has the right to constitute a state. It does not mean, for example, that the society has the moral power to obligate existing states not to interfere with its constituting itself as a state. I have no right to many of the things that would enhance my welfare, such as your bank account. Will Kymlicka makes a case that there can be circumstances in which special political arrangements for a group would be crucial to restoring the damaged self-esteem and self-respect of the group's members.[27] These considerations suggest a justification for creating institutions that allow oppressed or demoralized communities some form of self-rule, at least in some circumstances, but they do not show that such communities have the cluster of moral liberties and powers that constitute the right to self-determination. Margalit and Raz may be able to show that it would be a good thing in certain circumstances for a society to constitute a state, but this is not yet to say that the society has the moral right that is at issue in this essay.

Nations

"Nations" have a political character; they are political groups. In particular, I will argue, they are characterized by a stable desire that the group constitute a state. If I am correct, this fact contributes to the plausibility of the idea that nations have the right of self-determination. Nevertheless, the idea that nations have the right suffers from problems similar to the problems that afflict the idea that cultural groups have the right. Most important, a nation is almost always a proper part of the society that lives in a territory. In such cases, it would be antidemocratic to accord the right of self-determination to the nation rather than to the entire society.

In the relevant sense of the term, a nation is not necessarily organized into a state, nor is a state necessarily the political organ of a nation. Think of the Ukrainian nation, which only recently formed a state, and the Austro-Hungarian Empire, which comprised several nations. Consider the Scottish nation.

Nations are similar to cultural groups and encompassing groups in some respects. They are large groups, on the scale of the population of a state, they exist over several generations, and they are sometimes said to be characterized by a shared language and culture. Taylor describes nations as groups that speak the same language and share "a common history," where these shared features are "subjectively reflected in a people's identifications."[28] However, it is not necessary that a nation have a single language and culture. The Swiss may well be a nation. In addition, some cultural groups and encompassing groups are not nations. The Protestants of Northern Ireland appear to qualify as an encompassing group, for example,[29] but I would not count them as a nation because even though they have political aspirations, they do not aspire to constitute a state.

Elsewhere I proposed a threefold account of the idea of a nation.[30] A group that exists over several generations is a nation only if the following conditions are satisfied.

First, the group has a history and a set of traditions, and its members identify with these and are accepted as members by others who so identify.[31] Identifying is a matter of having appropriate feelings, such as pride, shame, and resentment. So we can say that a group of people identify with a given tradition and history if and only if they have appropriate feelings with respect to some of the events, and the same events in that tradition and history, or would do so if they were equally well informed about the tradition and history. And we can say that someone accepts a person as a member of such a group if he or she is disposed to regard accomplishments or failures of that person as part of the tradition and as objects of the appropriate feelings.[32]

Second, there is a widespread and stable aspiration or desire among the members of a nation that the group be a state. This is the sense in which nations are "political" groups, in my view, rather than merely ethnic or cultural groups. The people in a nation have sentiments that make the formation of a state always a "live issue," a "serious possibility," or something that naturally is given consideration from time to time. I describe the sentiment that conationals have, the sentiment that makes the formation of a state a real issue for them, as the "desire" that their group be a state.

It is, unfortunately, easy to misunderstand what I am saying. I am obviously using the word "desire" in a broad sense to speak of a general pro-attitude. I am not saying that the members of a nation desire, *all things considered*, that the group be a state. They may prefer in the end to be part of a federation with some other nation, perhaps for security reasons. Hence I am not claiming that the members of any nation would vote for sovereignty in a referendum. Votes in a referendum would be affected by a variety of factors, not simply by the desire that the nation be a state. Also, I am not saying that the members of a nation have a nationalistic desire to promote the interests of their group over the interests of any other. I am simply saying that there is, among the members of a nation, a widespread desire to associate in a state with people who identify with the same tradition and history. This desire needn't be especially intense and it may not override all other considerations, but it must be stable in a way that means it is more than merely a temporary whim.[33]

This factor explains why we would likely view the Québecois as constituting a nation, but we might be unclear whether the Welsh constitute a nation. The Québecois have a history of having a widespread desire to be a state, but even if there is a desire among the Welsh to preserve elements of their culture, it is doubtful that there is a desire for statehood, except among a small minority.

Third, a nation has a territory within which a state could feasibly be formed for exactly its members, or at least for the bulk of its members, allowing for cases where members are absent and nonmembers are present in the territory. It either occupies this territory or has the right to occupy the territory in virtue of historical or other considerations, even if it does not now occupy it.

I will explain these ideas more fully in the next section. For now I should say that the existence of a border across the territory of a group does not mean that the territory is not one in which a state could feasibly be formed for the group. For instance, the territory of the Basques is divided between France and Spain, but this does not mean that the Basques are not a nation. However, religious or ethnic groups can intermingle in a geographical area over which none has a special right, and they can intermingle in a way that makes it unfeasible to form a state for any of the groups. India may have been an example of this prior to partition. I think the Hindus and the Muslims did not constitute nations, not even if they were separate societies and not even if each desired to constitute a state, because the groups did not have their own territories.[34]

It is common and plausible to think that nations have the right of self-determination.[35] But I think that a group's being a nation is neither necessary nor sufficient for it to have the right of self-determination. A multinational society may surely have the right of self-determination, and if so, then nationhood is not necessary for possession of the right. Identification with a common history and tradition does not seem necessary to have the right of self-determination. The interesting question is whether nationhood is sufficient for possession of the right.

Notice that the population of a nation might be a proper part of the society living in a territory; its members might intermingle with nonmembers in the same territory in the way that the Québecois share a territory with the non-French-speaking people of Québec. A member of the local society who is a permanent resident of the nation's territory might be excluded from the nation, in the sense that his or her accomplishments or failures would not widely be viewed as part of the relevant tradition, as objects of the relevant emotions. In such cases, it would be contrary to democratic considerations to assign the right of self-determination to the nation rather than to the society that contains it. If a nation has the right, then there is something *it* can do that would give *it* a claim not to be interfered with in governing its territory. If a decision about sovereignty is to be taken by a democratic vote of the members of the group with the right, then to assign the right to the nation would be to disenfranchise any members of the society who are not members of the nation. The objection here is similar to the objection to Margalit and Raz's idea that the right of self-determination belongs to a majority encompassing group rather than to the entire population of the group's territory. For reasons of democracy, then, it seems that the right properly belongs to the entire society of a territory rather than to a nation in cases where the nation is not the entire society.

The reason it seems plausible to suppose that nations have the right of self-determination is that they are political groups in the sense I explained and they are territorial. Yet considerations about democracy suggest that if the right belongs to any groups, it belongs to groups that are complete societies. I will now try to combine these ideas.

Democracy and Self-Determination

My view is that all and only societies that are relevantly "territorial" and "political" have the right of self-determination. I shall argue that considerations about democracy support this view. I begin by introducing the concept of a society. I then use considerations about democracy in arguing that only societies have the right of self-determination. After explaining what I mean by a "territorial" and "political" society, I argue that only territorial and political societies have the right of self-determination. I conclude by arguing that this position is compatible with the guiding idea of democracy.

A full account of what societies are would be beyond the scope of this essay.[36] The general idea can be explained quickly, however. A society is quite a large group, comparable in size to the population of a state; it has a multigenerational history; it is characterized by a network of social relationships and by norms of co-operation and coordination that are salient to its members; it is comprehensive of the entire population of permanent residents of a relevant territory, with the exception of recent arrivals who may not yet fit into the group's network of social relationships—they may not yet have friends or acquaintances in the group, for example.

It seems reasonable to say that a group would have to be a society in order to have the right of self-determination. A group's having the right of self-determination means, of course, that it has a right to form or sustain a state for its members. Now, first, to have this right, a group would have to be multigenerational in nature and at least have the potential to exist several generations into the future. The governmental structure of a state can take generations to build. The creation of institutions that would transform a population into a state requires significant effort over a significant stretch of time. This is especially true of democratic structures, for the successful functioning of a democracy requires a widespread pattern of loyalty, a widespread commitment to democratic norms of behavior, a widespread willingness to abide by these norms voluntarily, and a widespread belief about the appropriateness of each citizen having equal authority over political decisions. Second, a group with the right of self-determination would have to share some significant norms of cooperation and coordination. If it seeks to constitute a state, its shared norms will be crucial to securing its members' cooperation in building and sustaining the institutions needed to create a state. Third, such a group would have to be largely comprehensive of the people with whom its members interact on a daily basis in a variety of significant social relationships. The reason for this is that the boundaries of a state can become difficult to cross. The permeability of the boundaries is not something that will be entirely in the control of the group if it constitutes a state. Finally, for the same reason, the group would have to be characterized by a network of a variety of significant social relationships, including, for example, relationships of friendship. Societies have all of these characteristics.

The populations of states also have these characteristics, of course, and the population of permanent residents of a state is a society, or it would be if it were not for immigration and emigration.[37] Hence, to simplify, let me stipulate that the population of a state, including immigrants and excluding emigrants, counts as a society for present purposes.

I now want to argue that my proposal that the right of self-determination is possessed only by societies is supported by considerations about democracy. It would obviously be beyond the scope of this essay to provide a fully articulated theory of democracy. All that I need to do, however, is show that the guiding idea of democracy supports my proposal. If it does, then since this guiding idea would have to be justified by any adequate theory of democracy, it follows that any adequate theory of democracy would support my proposal.

Democrats hold that a state ought to be governed in accord with a constitution that shares authority over political decisions equally among its citizens. Some citizens might come to have special authority by being elected to office, by being appointed to an office by someone previously elected to office, or as a result of some other decision made according to the constitution. But in advance of such decisions, authority over political decisions is divided equally among the (competent adult) citizens. This is the core of the democratic response to the question of how states ought to be governed; it is the guiding idea. An adequate theory of democracy would justify this idea on the basis of underlying principles that support democracy.

One such principle is a requirement of equality, the proposition that people must be shown equal respect. Combined with the proposition that showing equal respect in political matters requires giving people equal authority over political decisions, this principle supports the guiding idea of democracy. It is an unjust lack of regard for a person to fail to give him or her authority over decisions that affect only his or her own life; it is similarly an unjust lack of regard to fail to give this person equal authority with other members of his or her society over political decisions regarding that society. I will assume this principle is correct for present purposes.

The population of a state is a society. But some societies are not states even though they occupy or have the right to occupy territories within which states could feasibly be formed for them. If the members of such a society have a stable desire for statehood, it would show a lack of respect for them and for their judgment if they were not given the authority to make a decision about statehood. Democracy requires that the members of the society be given equal authority over the decision.

Societies are groups of an appropriate kind to form states—at least they are if they have a territory. No lack of respect is shown to a person if he or she is denied equal authority with the other members of some *other* kind of group to decide whether *it* should become a state. Hence I believe it is not possible to make a sensible case on democratic grounds that groups that are not societies have the right of self-determination. I have already considered cultural groups and nations and argued that democratic considerations speak against the idea that groups of these kinds have the right. And these are the most plausible candidates.[38]

The argument so far suggests that in order to have a right of self-determination an entity must be a society. I now want to argue in addition that it must occupy or have the right to occupy a territory within which a state could feasibly be formed for it. Furthermore, if it does not already constitute a state, its members must have a stable desire for statehood. As I say, the society must be both "territorial" and "political." Let me now attempt to explain and defend these restrictions.

The governmental structure of a state can take generations to build. Because of this, a society has no right to secede from an existing state, and to create a new state for itself, unless there is a stable and widespread desire for statehood among its members. In our world, every group is part of some state or other. To form a state for a group that does not already constitute a state is to break up an existing state. It would be implausible to think that a group has the right to do this on a merely temporary whim or momentary desire.

In some cases, cultural affinities or traditional affiliations of the kind we discussed before may explain why the desire to constitute a state is stable and widespread in a group. In other cases, shared political goals may explain it. Recall the example of the Canadians and the freshwater. The key point, however, is that the desire exist and be nontemporary.

To focus ideas, consider a hypothetical society that has been incorporated into a larger state much as the Welsh have been incorporated into the United Kingdom. Assume that there is not a stable and widespread desire among the members of the society that it secede and form a new state. Its members are disenchanted with the current political situation, but their disenchantment does not reflect a stable and widespread desire for statehood. I propose that there would be no injustice if the existing state acted to restrain the society from seceding. Moreover, this proposal seems consonant with the principles underlying democracy. The existing state would run afoul of democratic considerations if it prohibited the members of the society from voting in ordinary elections. But it would not run afoul of democratic considerations or show disrespect to the members of the society if it refused to permit a plebiscite on secession for the reason that there is no lasting widespread interest in secession but only a temporary one. This reason would acknowledge the importance of the views of the members of the society. Recall that a secessionist society can come to have a stable widespread interest in secession if its members acquire a stable desire for statehood. A change of desire by the members of the society would give it the right to secede.

I agree of course that in a controversy about secession it would not be ideal if the existing state decided to prohibit, or ignore the result of, a secessionist plebiscite simply on its own. Perhaps an international judicial body ought ideally to have the authority to adjudicate such matters, but I need to set aside issues about international law.

My conclusion is that a society has the right of self-determination only if either it constitutes a state or there is a stable and widespread desire among its members that it constitute a state. I will say that only "political" societies have a right of self-determination.

Finally, let me explain the idea of a territory. Every state has a territory in which its legal system is in force and over which it has (relatively) effective control. Moreover, a legitimate state has the right to government, which gives it a claim against other states that they not interfere with its governing its territory. It follows that the right of self-determination belongs only to groups that have the right or have the power to acquire the right to govern and control a territory. Such groups must be "territorial" in a sense I will now explain.

As I will use the term in what follows, a "territory" is a region of land or a sum of regions of land within which people can (in principle) move about, meet with other people, form significant social relationships, and otherwise live their lives; a territory is a region within which a state could feasibly be formed. So understood, a territory need not be very large and it need not be geographically continuous, but it must consist of regions that are geographically continuous.

As I use the terms, the territory "of a society" is a territory such that virtually all of the members of the society reside permanently within it and virtually all of the permanent residents of the territory are members of the society.[39] A region of France is not a part of the territory of the Basque society in the relevant sense unless virtually all of the people living permanently in it are members of the Basque society. This turns on whether they are integrated into the social network characteristic of Basque society. Similarly, the Basque region is not a part of the French society's territory unless the Basques are also members of French society.

The example of the Basques living in France shows that societies may overlap, for I assume the Basques are members of French society as well as members of Basque society. Of course, it is not necessarily the case that when members of one society live permanently within the territory of another they are also members of that other society. But it is normally the case that they are, for in the ordinary course of events, those who come to reside permanently in the territory of a society eventually become members, just as those who leave for extended periods of time eventually cease to be members. This is explained by the fact that societies are characterized by what I call a "social network." People come to associate with members of the society in which they live, to find their friends in that society, their mates, and their coworkers, and their children find their friends there, and their mates, and so on. So the immigrants come to be part of the social network of the society in which they live, which means they come to be members of the society. We can think of this as a kind of adoption process. Given this, the permanent residents of the territory of a society either are or, in the ordinary course of events, will come to be members of the society.

There may be no definite point at which a new arrival in the territory of a society becomes a permanent resident, and there may also be no definite point at which he or she becomes a member of the society. Rather, the immigrant forms various intentions about future residence, and a gradual process of adoption takes place. I want to be strict about these matters for purposes of this theory but without doing violence to the idea of a society. I will stipulate that once the territory of a society is identified on the basis of the account I have given so far, any permanent resident of the territory is to be counted as a member of the society during the period of his or her permanent residency.

The reason for this stipulation is that if societies have the right of self-determination, then, on democratic principles, any decision about sovereignty would be taken by a democratic vote of the members of the society. In view of the vague criteria for membership in a society, a democrat would view all of the permanent residents of the territory of a society as members for the purpose of deciding voting rights. Permanent residents of the territory are affected in all of the ways that (other) members of the society are affected by an assignment of the society to a state. Temporary residents are not going to be affected in the way they would be if they were members who were part of the social network that characterizes the society or if they resided permanently in the society's territory. They are not shown any lack of respect if they are denied the vote in a plebiscite on statehood.[40]

Given my stipulation about membership, if a society has a territory, then its members include all of the permanent residents of its territory. The population of a state counts as a society for present purposes, as I explained before, and the territory of the state counts as the territory of that society. Hence if a geographical region counts as a society's "territory" for these purposes, then if the society does not already constitute a state, a state could be formed for the society in that territory without requiring the displacement of any population of permanent residents.

Territories can be disputed among different groups on the basis of historical or other claims. A society may acquire a territory in a morally unacceptable manner, by conquest and then purging nonmembers, for example, and it is plausible to think that in some such cases the society from which the territory was acquired would continue to have the right to live in the territory. I want my account to acknowledge the possibility that this is so. Hence by a "territorial society" I will mean a society that either has a territory in the sense I have been explaining or has the right to occupy a given territory by virtue of historical or other considerations, even if it does not now occupy that territory.

I said before that the right of self-determination belongs only to groups that have a right to control and govern a territory. This is trivially true, given that the right of self-determination implies the right to form a state that will control and govern a territory. But I want to insist that the right of self-determination belongs only to societies that are "territorial" in the sense I have just defined.

This position is consonant with the guiding idea of democracy. If a society does not occupy a territory, then there is no territory in which a state could be formed for its members, except by moving populations around in order to create space for the society. The creation of a state for the society would require more than simply the formation of a government and the noninterference of others. For this reason, the decision whether to form a state for the society could not be viewed as simply the business of the society, and it is therefore compatible with democratic considerations to give other groups some authority over the decision unless there is a territory it has a historical right to occupy. Unless there is a territory the society has a special moral right to occupy, a society that does not have a territory does not have the right to self-determination, for it does not have the power to constitute itself as a state by any action of its own.

Consider a society that is territorial and political. Since it is territorial, it can feasibly be organized into a state, and since it is political, it is consonant with the guiding idea of democracy to hold that all and only the members of the society should have equal authority over any decision about the assignment of the society to a state. Assuming that underlying democratic principles are correct, this means the society has a claim that it not be interfered with in holding a plebiscite on forming a state, and further, given a majority vote in favor of the society's forming a state, it has a claim against all other states that they not interfere with its forming a government or with its governing its territory. Given the underlying principles of democracy, the society has the right of self-determination.

My account allows self-determination rights to conflict. For example, in a case where one society wrongfully exiled another society from its territory, my account implies that both the society occupying the territory and the society wrongfully displaced from it may have the right to constitute states in that territory. However, the right to self-determination is defeasible. A society may be wrong to exercise the right in a territory it wrongfully acquired.

I want to conclude by considering what my account would imply about the case of Québec if a majority of Québec society were to vote to secede from Canada. Canada's maintaining its unity would abridge Québec's right to secede, but it may seem that it is also true that Québec's seceding would abridge Canada's right to govern itself. But Canada's political rights do not entail the right to maintain its unity by preventing Québec from seceding. The right of self-determination includes an immunity against having the right of government extinguished by any other state and includes the liberty to give up the right of government, but it does not include the right to prevent secession. The right of government is a claim against other states that they not interfere with the state's governing itself. But it does not give a state a claim against its *citizens* that *they* not interfere. On the contrary, the guiding idea of democracy is that a state's institutions should be set up in a way that gives its citizens equal authority to "interfere." And if I am correct, it implies that a territorial and political society within an existing state has the right to secede. Secession from a state is not "interference" of a kind that abridges the state's right to government or its right to self-determination.

This way of looking at sectional conflict is in accord with the guiding idea of democracy. Canada has no business deciding Québec's future, assuming Québec has a serious desire for statehood. It is no disrespect to non-Québeckers to deny them authority in a decision as to whether Québec forms an independent state. But it would be an injustice to Québeckers to give non-Québeckers authority in a decision as to Québec independence or to deny authority to Québeckers. I say "Québeckers" rather than "Québecois" for in my view, as in the view of the independence movement in Québec, it is the members of the society in Québec, regardless of their language and culture, who have authority over the issue of self-determination for Québec. The right of self-determination is possessed by the entire society, not by the French-speaking nation that forms a part of the society.

The problem of division is a neglected problem in the background of political philosophy. It is the problem of determining what moral constraints there are on the division of the social world into political units. I have tried to make plausible that certain groups have a right to self-determination and that this right is grounded in the same considerations that ground democracy. My arguments are, unfortunately, sketchy, due at least in part to the fact that the grounding of democracy is not entirely clear to me. Nevertheless, if I am correct, the right of self-determination is not grounded in a group's cultural or national characteristics. Rather, if a group is a territorial and political society, it has a right of self-determination grounded in the democratic rights of its members.

NOTES

Early versions of this essay were presented in 1994 to the Economy, Justice, and Society Program at the University of California, Davis, and to the Pacific Division of the American Philosophical Association. I am indebted to a number of people for valuable suggestions and comments. Christopher Morris urged me to think again about self-determination and thoroughly reviewed several drafts of this essay. Will Kymlicka urged me to integrate my thinking about societies with my thinking about self-determination. Harry Brighouse, Arthur Ripstein, and Yael Tamir provided helpful comments and criticisms. I am especially grateful to Jeff McMahan and Robert McKim for extensive written criticisms and suggestions.

1. Compare Pierre Trudeau's question: "Essentially, the question to which I would seek an answer is: what section of the world's population occupying what segment of the world's surface should fall under the authority of a given state?" Pierre Trudeau, "Federalism, Nationalism, and Reason," in *Federalism and the French Canadians* (New York: St. Martin's Press, 1968), p. 182.

2. See John Stuart Mill, "Considerations on Representative Government," in *On Liberty, the Subjection of Women, Etc.*, ed. M. G. Fawcett (London, 1924), p. 381.

3. See Judith Jarvis Thomson, *The Realm of Rights* (Cambridge, Mass.: Harvard University Press, 1990), chap. one; and Wesley Newcomb Hohfeld, *Fundamental Legal Conceptions*, ed. Walter Wheeler Cook (New Haven, Conn.: Yale University Press, 1919).

4. Thomson, *The Realm of Rights*, chap. 3.

5. Rawls calls this right "the principle of self-determination." See John Rawls, *A Theory of Justice* (Cambridge, Mass.: Harvard University Press, 1971), p. 378.

6. If a state extinguishes its right to government in favor of government by some other state, it can impose conditions, such as that it be given a limited form of subordinate self-government within that other state. Hence, presumably, anything with the right of self-determination also has some powers and liberties regarding the choice of a limited or subordinate form of self-government within some other state, assuming (the rest of) the state is willing. I will not be concerned with such limited forms of self-government.

7. David Gauthier, "Breaking Up: An Essay on Secession," *Canadian Journal of Philosophy* 24 (1994): 363–68.

8. Kai Nielsen, "World Government, Security, and Global Justice," in *Problems of International Justice*, ed. Steven Luper-Foy (Boulder, Colo. : Westview, 1988). See also Thomas Pogge, "Cosmopolitanism and Sovereignty," *Ethics* 103 (1992): 48–75.

9. Christopher Wellman says that in some cases the secession of a group may leave the "remainder state" in a condition it has a right not to experience. He thinks that if this is so, then the group has no right to secede. In my view, the group would still have the right to secede, but it might be wrong to exercise the right or wrong to exercise it without compensating the remainder state. See Christopher Wellman, "A Defense of Secession and Political Self-Determination," *Philosophy and Public Affairs* 24 (1995): 160–64.

10. Allen Buchanan discusses compensation in "Toward a Theory of Secession," *Ethics* 101 (1991): 339–42. Also, see Allen Buchanan, *Secession: The Morality of Political Divorce from Fort Sumter to Lithuania and Quebec* (Boulder, Colo.: Westview, 1991).

11. There are circumstances in which another state would be morally justified in interfering with A's governing itself even though A still has the right not to be interfered with. It is important not to confuse the issue of whether the right to government is absolute with the distinct issue of whether other states have the power to extinguish the right.

12. Buchanan, "Toward a Theory of Secession," p. 328. Buchanan cites two articles by Lea A. Brilmayer: "Secession and Self-Determination: A Territorialist Reinterpretation," *Yale Journal of International Law* 19 (1991): 177–202, and "Consent, Contract, and Territory," *Minnesota Law Review* 39 (1990): 1–35.

13. Buchanan, "Toward a Theory of Secession," pp. 329–32, and *Secession*, pp. 152–53.

14. I owe the term "cultural group" to Will Kymlicka. See Will Kymlicka, *Liberalism, Community, and Culture* (Oxford: Clarendon, 1991), esp. pp. 166–67.

15. See Avishai Margalit and Joseph Raz, "National Self-Determination," *Journal of Philosophy* 87 (1990): 439–61. The notion of an encompassing group is introduced on pp. 443–47. The quoted remarks are on pp. 443–44.

16. These ideas are developed in Charles Taylor, "Why Do Nations Have to Become States?," in *Philosophers Look at Canadian Confederation*, ed. Stanley G. French (Montreal: Canadian Philosophical Association, 1979), pp. 19–35, esp. pp. 22–24. Also see Kymlicka, *Liberalism, Community, and Culture*, pp. 166–67, 172, 175–77.

17. This is proposed in Kymlicka, *Liberalism, Community, and Culture*, pp. 166–67, 172. See also Yael Tamir, *Liberal Nationalism* (Princeton: Princeton University Press, 1993), and "Liberal Nationalism," *Report from the Institute for Philosophy and Public Policy* 13 (1993): 1–7.

18. This idea is developed in Margalit and Raz, "National Self-Determination," esp. pp. 446, 449–50. It is defended by Kymlicka (*Liberalism, Community, and Culture*, pp. 175–76).

19. Taylor, "Why Do Nations Have to Become States?," pp. 26–31.

20. Ibid., p. 32.

21. Margalit and Raz, "National Self-Determination," pp. 450–51, 454–57. The quoted passage is on p. 457.

22. Ibid., pp. 458, 459. Moreover, certain conditions must be met if a group's decision in favor of statehood is to be "morally binding." These restrictions do not affect my argument, however, since they have no bearing on whether members of minorities take part in the decision about statehood (ibid., pp. 459–60).

23. Margalit and Raz point out that we permit the use of different decision procedures

for dealing with different kinds of social or political problems. But this merely clarifies the nature of the issue; it does not help to settle it (ibid., p. 456).

24. Margalit and Raz identify encompassing groups by what they say to be the "characteristics which are relevant to the justification of the right." They add that if these characteristics "do not apply to peoples or nations, we shall have shown that the right to self-determination is misconceived" (ibid., p. 443). Their idea appears to be that if nations are not encompassing groups, then nations do not have the right. They seem to hold, then, that only (majority) encompassing groups have the right of self-determination. See ibid., p. 458.

25. Margalit and Raz say that "the right [to self-determination] is conditional on its being exercised . . . to secure conditions necessary for the prosperity and self-respect of the group" (ibid., pp. 459–60). Note that I am not saying that the right of self-determination can legitimize hoarding resources; there are moral limits on what a state can rightfully do.

26. Kymlicka (*Liberalism, Community, and Culture*) stresses some of these ideas.

27. Ibid., esp. chaps. 9, 10.

28. Taylor, "Why Do Nations Have to Become States?," p. 33. Benn and Peters would add that the members of a nation must think of their group as a nation. But this is circular; if we do not understand what nations are, we do not understand what the members are supposed to think. See S. I. Benn and R. S. Peters, *The Principles of Political Thought* (New York: Free Press, 1965), p. 294.

29. See Margalit and Raz, "National Self-Determination," p. 447.

30. David Copp, "Do Nations Have the Right of Self-Determination?" in French, *Philosophers Look at Canadian Confederation*, pp. 71–95.

31. Ibid., p. 73. The basic idea is suggested in A. I. Benn, "Nationalism," in *The Encyclopedia of Philosophy*, vol. 5, ed. Paul Edwards (New York: Macmillan, 1967), pp. 442–45. See also Mill, "Considerations on Representative Government," chap. 16. Tamir points out that a nation's history and tradition can be "invented" (*Liberal Nationalism*, pp. 64, p. 173, n. 25).

32. In personal communication, Harry Brighouse pointed out that because of political disagreements, some members of a nation may take pride in events that other members view as shameful. The members of a nation may not all identify in the same way with the group's history.

33. I was helped in these paragraphs by Harry Brighouse, Robert McKim, Jeff McMahan, and Christopher Morris.

34. Each of the three factors comes in degrees. Since we nevertheless tend to think of groups as either being nations or not, we must suppose we have intuitive thresholds for the factors. A nation has each of the three characteristics to a relatively high degree.

35. Yael Tamir argues that nations have the right of self-determination, but for her, this does not mean that they have the right to constitute states. She says the right can be satisfied by a variety of political arrangements short of statehood (*Liberal Nationalism*, p. 75).

36. For a fuller account, see David Copp, "The Concept of a Society," *Dialogue* 31 (1992): 183–212.

37. This does not follow logically from the definition of a society, but it is true in fact. I explain this in ibid.

38. Christopher Wellman defends the view that the right to self-determination in "the territory it occupies" belongs to "any group able and willing to perform the functions required of a liberal political state." He adds the proviso that this right is "not valid" if exercise

of it would "leave the remainder state in a condition that it has a right not to experience." See Wellman, "A Defense of Secession and Political Self-Determination," p. 164. I have already discussed Wellman's proviso (in note 9). The main part of his proposal is similar to mine. However, first, a group may satisfy Wellman's criterion even if it is not a society. It may not be the entire population of permanent residents of the territory. Suppose an aggressive tribe has occupied a territory of which it is a minority of the permanent residents and suppose it is able and willing to perform the functions of a liberal state. For reasons I gave in discussing encompassing groups, I think it would be undemocratic to say that this group, as opposed to the population as a whole, has the right of self-determination in the territory. Second, a territorial society that desires to constitute a state may not be a liberal society, so it may not aspire to creating a liberal state. Wellman's view does not give this society the right to self-determination, which is contrary to what democracy implies.

39. A "permanent" resident is one who lives in the territory and has no definite intention to cease to live there.

40. The restriction that only members of the society have authority over the exercise of the right is analogous to a citizenship requirement on the right to vote.

18

Self-Determination, Secession, and the Rule of Law

ALLEN BUCHANAN

The Age of Secession

Future historians may call our era "the age of secession." It may become "the age of *wars* of secession." Even for those who view the modern nation-state as a necessary evil at best, the prospect that the state system may be shattered provokes deep anxieties.

The risks of uncontrolled state breaking are great, as cataclysmic events in the former Yugoslavia and elsewhere illustrate. There are, in fact, several distinct risks. First, given that virtually all states are grimly determined to cling to all of the territory they claim as their own, attempts at secession are likely to be strongly resisted, often with deadly force. Second, secession may lead to the persecution of minorities. Even in those rare cases when the initial separation itself has been peaceful, the newly independent state sometimes violates the rights of minorities within its borders (as in Armenia, for example). In addition, successful secession by most members of a minority may result in greater vulnerability to persecution for those members of that minority group who remain within the original state.

Third, there is the danger that secessionist conflicts will spread beyond the borders of the states within which they originate, engulfing an entire region or, as in the case of the Serbian secessionism in 1914, the entire world. To paraphrase Winston Churchill, secessionist movements tend to produce more violence than they can consume domestically.

Irredentist secession is especially dangerous in this regard. A state that covets part of its neighbor's territory can support, stimulate, or even simulate secessionist movements by its conationals who are "languishing under alien rule" across the border. Unjust annexation may then masquerade under the apparently legitimate banners of self-determination and minority rights. For examples, one need not go as far back as Hitler's annexation of the Sudetenland; the irredentist secessionist movements in Kosovo, the Crimea, and Translyvania pose similar risks.

In some instances, a state's fear of losing territory by irredentist secession may lead it to deny more moderate claims for self-determination for the minority in question, and this refusal may then fuel the demand for total independence and stimulate support for it from the neighboring state with which the minority wishes to merge. Thus fear of irredentist secession can turn out to be a self-fulfilling prophecy. Fearing that acceding to Kosovon demands for less extreme forms of autonomy (regional self-government) will be followed eventually by demands for independence and ultimate merger with Albania, Serbia may resist, and Serbia's denial of autonomy for Kosovo may provoke intervention by Albania, with the ultimate aim of annexing Kosovo. The same scenario may lead to Russian intervention in the Crimea (or Hungarian intervention in Transylvania).

Fourth, the prospect of secession, as Abraham Lincoln feared, can undermine democracy.[1] A territorially concentrated dissident minority can sometimes use the threat of secession as a bargaining tool to thwart majority rule. Where the majority regards secession by a minority as unacceptable, the threat of secession can function as a minority veto on majority decisions. A minority's credible threat to "exit"—taking a part of the state's territory with them—can be a form of "voice" that drowns out the proclaimed will of the majority. In South Africa, the threat of Zulu secession (more so than that of white separatism) poses a serious impediment to the establishment of democratic institutions.

Fifth, even if secession does not meet bloody resistance, result in new persecutions of minorities, spread conflict across borders, provide a cover for unjust annexation, or serve as a strategic threat to undermine majority rule, the economic costs of secession, to the primary parties and to others as well, may be quite serious. The costs of renegotiating treaties, of agreeing upon borders and upon the division of the national debt, the disruption of economic activity, the loss of economies of scale, the impairment of arrangements for national defense and security, as well as the possible erection of barriers within what had been open internal markets, all may prove significant. Moreover, in the rush of enthusiasm for independence, the magnitude of these costs may be seriously underestimated.

Even for those willing and able to evaluate them dispassionately, accurate estimates of transition costs may be hard to come by because much will depend upon whether negotiations between the primary parties are extended or stymied by strategic behavior and upon how other states respond to the behavior of each of the primary parties. Given the current lack of a coherent international practice regarding secession, the latter may be as hard to predict as the former. For all of these reasons, secession is everyone's concern, both from the standpoint of a prudent self-interest in international stability and from the perspective of humanitarian considerations, including, first and foremost, the protection of human rights. A proper concern about uncontrolled state breaking is rooted not in any belief that states as such are sacrosanct or even valuable but in regard for the human losses that can occur when states fragment.

Although contested secessions carry these grave risks, there can also be substantial benefits from state breaking: a minority may escape oppression (as in the secession of East Pakistan to become Bangladesh), or those whose territory was unjustly taken may recover it (as with the Baltic Republics). Accordingly, a reasonable approach to creating an international legal order for contested secession must reflect an appreciation of the possible benefits as well as the risks. For this reason, the approach presented below does not attempt to prohibit all cases of contested secession but seeks to develop a principled account of when it should be regarded as legitimate and when it should not.

The Need for Coherent International Principles and Procedures concerning Secession

What is needed is a coherent set of principles to distinguish legitimate from illegitimate secession and to channel and control secessionist movements, along with a set of international institutions to secure compliance with these principles. The problems of secession cannot be dealt with in isolation, however. They must be treated as an integral part of a more complex international institutional response to a wider range of problems of self-determination. In the remainder of this essay, I will concentrate on the task of beginning to develop appropriate principles for an institutionalized international response to secession crises, but I will do so by first locating this project within the larger endeavor of bringing self-determination under the rudiments of the rule of international law.

The focus will be on principles, though with an unblinking recognition that principles are at most only half of the story. Appropriate institutions for implementing principles are also necessary. It is worth noting, however, that effective implementation of principles may require structural changes in existing institutions of international law (for example, enlarging the membership of the Security Council of the United Nations to include representatives from Japan, Germany, and the Southern Hemisphere or expanding the functions of the World Court of Justice to include adjudication of disputes over secession). A basic assumption of this essay is that significant progressive institutional change must be motivated in part by a growing consensus on principles and that the latter can be facilitated by articulating principles more clearly and defending them by moral arguments that have wide appeal in their own right and that also build on central principles of international law as it now exists.

The approach pursued here does not rest on the erroneous assumption that international law is created by the fiats of some central international legislature (suitably advised by political philosophers). The processes by which international law is actually made are complex. The base of acceptance of an initially vague moral-political norm (such as the principle of self-determination) is gradually broadened, while the contours of the norm are sharpened by applications to cases. Conventions or resolutions signed by the more progressive members of international or regional organizations and alliances gradually receive broader support as the list of signatories increases. And, of course, at all times the distribution of power shapes or at least constrains the direction and speed of the process. Nevertheless, there is a role for what might be called moral target setting, so long as targets are set with an eye to the nature of the actual processes by which they might be attained.

I should emphasize from the outset that my proposals focus upon cases of contested secession because it is in these that the risks cataloged above are likely to be greatest. (The greater the risk, the stronger the case for subjecting the secessionist efforts to the rule of international law.) What I have to say will not apply to cases of political divorce by mutual consent, as in the case of the dissolution of Czechoslovakia.[2] Similarly, if Quebec secedes from Canada, it is unlikely that Canada will attempt to preserve the federal union by force. The general presumption in such cases is that the decision to secede and the decision to accept secession are the business of the parties involved and that they are to be permitted to work out the terms of secession together (though third-party mediation should be available if requested). Only if the political divorce by mutual consent is likely to result in violations of individual or minority rights (on either side of the new border) does the question of unrequested international supervision or intervention even arise. More specifically, if both parties consent, then issues that arise in the case of contested secession—in particular, whether injustices perpetrated by the state against those seeking to secede ground a right to secede—are simply irrelevant.[3]

I should also like to stress that the principles I propose are intended to guide truly international institutional responses to secession. They are not proposed as principles upon which it would be appropriate for individual states to act unilaterally. The requirement that the invocation of these principles is to be limited to collective, institutional responses to secession crises lessens considerably the risk of abuse, partiality, and precipitous intervention.

Criteria for Evaluating Principles

In the next section I present and defend one particular approach to a principled response to secessionist crises in international law. Before I do so, however, it is crucial to clarify the criteria for evaluating such proposals.

The first thing to observe is that the appropriate standard of evaluation is not the utopian requirement that a proposal be able to solve all possible secessionist problems satisfactorily. Nor is it reasonable to expect that proposed principles be implementable immediately, given institutional resources as they are at this moment. Most important, the evaluation of proposals must be essentially comparative. The proper question to ask is not, "Will this approach deal effectively with all the problems?" but rather, "Can the proposal be reasonably expected to provide more satisfactory outcomes than both rival proposals and the status quo (in which there is virtually no coherent international legal response to secession)?"

Second, a proposal for beginning the task of bringing secession crises under the rule of international law must be both morally progressive and at the same time at least minimally realistic. A morally progressive proposal is one that, if successfully implemented, would better serve basic values, preeminent among which is the protection of human rights, than the status quo. A proposal satisfies the minimal requirement of realism if it has a significant prospect of being adopted in the foreseeable future through the processes by which international law actually is made.

Third, as was already indicated, the principles advocated should be morally accessible to a broad international audience (not requiring, for example, acceptance of a particular religious ethics). Fourth, the principles should build upon, or at least not contradict, the more morally acceptable, deeply entrenched principles of existing international law.

Fifth, and finally, a proposal, at least when implemented under reasonably favorable circumstances, should not produce perverse incentives. In other words, a general recognition that the principles in question are rules of international law should not stimulate states or groups of citizens or international agencies to engage in behavior that violates morally sound political principles or other acceptable rules of international law. For example, an international legal principle concerning secession whose acceptance encouraged groups to engage in ethnic cleansing would not be acceptable.

Although these requirements for principles are relatively commonsensical and unexceptionable, their cumulative impact is to impose significant constraints on what would count as an acceptable international law of secession. As we shall see, these requirements are satisfied better by some proposals than by others. Indeed, I shall argue that the proposal I am forwarding in this essay does a better job of satisfying them than what I take to be its chief rival, which I will consider in due course.

A Proposal for Bringing Secession Crises under the Rule of International Law

The first step in the larger strategy is to distinguish clearly between secession and the many other, less radical forms self-determination may take. Much mischief can be avoided if two essential points become the focus of an international consensus, formalized by treaties or conventions, if possible. The first is that not every demand for self-determination is or should be a demand for complete independence (sovereign statehood). The second is that recognizing some particular right or rights of self-determination (such as the right to be a distinct unit in a federation) does not carry the presumption that the group in question has the unlimited right to choose which forms of self-determination it will exercise, including the most radical form—namely, secession.[4] Indeed, it is probably best to dispense with the notion of a right to self-determination (as if there were a single, generic right) and replace it with more precise reference to various particular rights of self-determination.

The reasons supporting each of these two principles will become clearer later, when we consider the nature of the right to secede. For now it can be said that there are two main considerations that speak in favor of them. First, once the distinction between secession and other forms of self-determination is grasped, it becomes clear that a group may have a legitimate interest in self-determination without having a right to secede. (Roughly, a group has a legitimate interest in self-determination if there are considerations that ground a presumption that some particular right or rights of self-determination ought to be recognized for it.) Second, as I have already argued, due to the grave risks of uncontrolled secession, the international community has a legitimate interest in bringing secession under the rule of law, and once the legitimacy of this interest is recognized, the assumption that the choice of the secession option should be left to the discretion of the group seeking self-determination is no longer plausible.

The second step toward bringing the right of self-determination under the rule of law is to articulate a range of possible forms of self-determination short of full sovereignty and to make it clear that in many cases the legitimate interest that a group has in self-determination will be better served by achieving some combination of these more moderate forms rather than by seeking to secede. For example, for a number of weighty practical reasons, it would be neither feasible nor, even if feasible, desirable for many indigenous groups to achieve independent statehood. For one thing, it is often the case that the colonial exploitation whose remediation calls for rights of self-determination has also deprived the peoples in question of the natural resources and human capital required for succeeding as a sovereign state in an increasingly demanding global economy.[5]

The forms of self-determination short of secession are diverse. They include but are not limited to minority cultural rights—the rights of peoples to wear their distinctive cultural dress, to practice their own cultural rituals, and to be called by their own names, as well as the right to support for preserving minority languages. Of increasing importance are various rights not just of self-administration but also of self-government, including, at least in the case of indigenous peoples, collective rights to regulate the use of land and the development of natural resources.[6]

A complex array of rights of cantons, states, provinces, and autonomous regions under the various types of federations also fall under the broad heading of rights of self-determination. In principle, these federative rights include everything from special rights of representation that give disproportional weight to minorities through bicameral legislative schemes (with representation in one house not based on population); to supermajority requirements for presidential elections, for constitutional amendments, or for some or all categories of federal legislation; to the more extreme rights of nullification and veto.

The distinction between a right of nullification and a right to veto is important. The right of nullification is the right of a group to render void some or all national or federal legislation within that group's territory only. John C. Calhoun argued at length but unsuccessfully for recognition of a constitutional right of nullification for the southern United States.

The closest existing approximation of a right of nullification (as a constitutional right) of which I am aware exists in Canada. Each Canadian province, by an act of its legislature, can in effect void the application of even fundamental constitutional rights within the jurisdiction of that province.

In contrast, the right to veto is the right of a group (for example, a legislature of a territorial unit within a federation) to block a proposed federal law from being enacted at all and hence from being valid in any jurisdiction within the federal union. As unlimited rights applicable to all types of legislation in a federal system, both the right of group veto and the right of nullification would not be practicable under most circumstances. As limited rights applying only to certain categories of legislation, they may be more attractive.

The third step in the overall strategy is to build international consensus on the principle that there is a strong presumption that secession (except where it occurs by mutual voluntary consent) is generally to be regarded as a last resort—that in general less extreme forms of self-determination are to be tried first.[7] Such a principle is easily supported by appeal to one of the most basic pillars of international law: respect for the territorial integrity of existing states.

The chief justification for the principle of territorial integrity is to protect the self-determination of political communities by safeguarding their control over the territories they occupy. If the citizens of an existing political community agree to divide into two independent and fully sovereign political communities, then this justification and hence the principle itself are inapplicable. For this reason, I will understand the principle of the territorial integrity of existing states to ground a presumption against secession only in cases in which the dissolution of the political community is contested, and again I am concerned only with cases of contested secession in this essay.

Despite secession's attraction as a formal legal principle for the international order, a sober appreciation of the risks of secession cataloged above provides solid support for adopting the presumption against secession (in contested cases) as a principle of international political ethics. Accepting this principle means explicitly rejecting what is sometimes called the Nationalist Principle, according to which "every nation (or nationality or people) has the right to its own state."

A justifiable fear of the consequences of international acceptance of the Nationalist Principle has done much to fuel a wholesale resistance to all demands for self-determination. Given the mingling of nations, ethnic groups, and peoples (however defined) throughout most of the modern world (and the fact that virtually no existing states are truly monoethnic or mononational), widespread application of the Nationalist Principle is a recipe for genocide, forced removals, or unworkable patchworks of microstates (in many cases no larger than neighborhoods).[8] Once secession is clearly distinguished from other forms of self-determination and the Nationalist Principle is resolutely rejected, the way is clear for a more rational and flexible evaluation of demands for self-determination. Then the demand for self-determination need not be seen as a threat to the very existence of the state.

The fourth and most difficult element in the strategy for bringing the right of self-determination under the rule of international law is to develop ethically sound and politically feasible principles for responding to those self-determination movements that aspire to full sovereignty—and with the violent reactions they are likely to provoke. This fourth task is divisible into distinct components. The first, and in some ways the most urgent, is the development of principles and procedures for guiding the process of secession, for determining how the right to secede, once it is acknowledged, is to be exercised. Included here is a complex set of problems falling under the heading of the just terms of secession. These include procedures designed to achieve (1) an equitable settling of boundaries; (2) a fair division of the national debt; (3) the continuation, renegotiation, or dissolution of treaties with third parties; (4) adjudication of claims for compensation for private property lost or devalued as a result of changes in property rights systems; (5) measures to avoid disruptions of national defense and security; and, above all, (6) credible guarantees of the rights of minorities in both the seceding area and in the remainder state.

In the case of item 5, particular states or alliances could provide continuity in national defense and security by entering into agreements to protect the secessionist state and/or the remainder state. In the first four cases, the best to be hoped for may be the establishment, under international supervision and with participation by neutral third-party states or international agencies, of fair processes for resolving the issues in question. The issues here often do not admit of any uniquely correct solution, and when this is the case, heavy reliance must be placed upon the virtues of procedural justice. These include impartial adjudication by disinterested third parties, the opportunity for the primary parties to receive a fair hearing for their interests, accurate fact-finding by credible authorities, and full disclosure of the bases upon which rulings are ultimately made.

The debacle in former Yugoslavia highlights the importance of the sixth item.

Credible guarantees of the rights of minorities within the seceding area should be achieved before the seceding group is accorded status as an independent sovereign state under international law and should be a nonnegotiable condition of such recognition. If guarantees are to be credible, explicit provisions will have to be made for monitoring their implementation. In addition, some international legal organ, such as the World Court of Justice, will have to be identified as having the authority to evaluate the results of monitoring and to issue rulings as to whether implementation is sufficient.[9]

Just as important, international conventions or treaties are needed to specify substantial sanctions to be applied to any individual state or alliance that recognizes the legitimacy of a seceding group before such guarantees of the rights of minorities are provided. If such provisions had been in place at the time of Croatia's bid for independence, Germany might have had a sufficient incentive to refrain from recognizing it as a legitimate state, and the Croatian government, being eager for recognition of its sovereignty, especially by Germany, might have had more of an incentive to take effective measures for protecting the rights of Serbs within the new Republic of Croatia. As it was, there was no authoritative condemnation of Germany's actions by a recognized organ of international law, and no international conventions existed at the time to provide a coherent, principled basis for such condemnation, much less for the imposition of sanctions in consequence of it.

It would be naive to assume that if Croatia had given credible guarantees of the rights of the Serbian minority there would have been no armed conflict in the Balkans. For one thing, there is some evidence that Serbian expansionist moves were already under way at the time of the Croatian secession. However, it is reasonable to suppose that if such guarantees had been provided and their implementation had been monitored and facilitated by appropriate international agencies, Serbia would have been deprived of a justification for its expansionist policy and it would have been somewhat easier for the international community or at least the Western European powers and the United States to pursue more effectively a coherent and morally justifiable policy toward the conflict.

Second, and perhaps even more challenging, is the specification of conditions under which a group ought to be recognized as having a prima facie right to secede. To say that a group has a prima facie right to secede is to say that it has a right to secede subject to the condition that the just terms of secession are met. A group would then be said to have the right to secede (*simpliciter* rather than prima facie) if its case satisfied the primary justifying grounds for seceding and the just terms of secession were being observed in the process of its seceding.

Given this distinction between the prima facie right to secede and the just terms of secession, legitimate secession would then be a two-stage process, regulated by international legal institutions. In the first stage a group of secessionists would make a case that they have a prima facie right to secede by demonstrating that the primary justifying grounds for secession applied in their situation. If they succeeded in making this case, an authoritative international body (such as the World Court of Justice or, perhaps, the Committee of Twenty-four of the UN General Assembly) would make a ruling to that effect, signaling that the process of determining and implementing just terms of secession could begin.

From the standpoint of developing principles for secession under the rule of international law, then, the second major task is to articulate and gain consensus on the primary justifying grounds for secession—the conditions under which a group may be said to have a right to secede, assuming that the just terms of secession will be observed in the exercise of the right (fair procedures for dividing the national debt will be followed, credible guarantees of the rights of minorities will be offered, et cetera).

In a recent book on the morality of secession, I rejected the idea that anything so general and open-ended as a right of self-determination (of all "peoples" or "nationalities") could serve as a primary justifying ground for secession. I argued instead that there is a limited set of special conditions under which a group can be said to have a right to secede.[10]

The approach I began to develop there construes the right to secede as a remedial right. More precisely, the right to secede is seen as a remedy of last resort for serious injustices, not as a general right of groups or even of certain kinds of groups ("nations," "peoples," et cetera, as such). Chief among the grievances I identify as providing primary justifying grounds for secession are these: (1) persistent and serious violations of individual human rights and (2) past unredressed unjust seizure of territory. If a state persists in serious violations of the human rights of a minority within its borders, it is permissible for that group to attempt to establish its own state as a sanctuary from persecution if no other recourse is available. Or if, as in the case of the Baltic Republics, a sovereign state was unjustly annexed, secession can be viewed as a legitimate rectification of that injustice.

A third and more controversial primary justifying ground for secession is discriminatory redistribution (or, as it is sometimes called, internal colonialism or regional exploitation). Discriminatory redistribution occurs wherever the state implements taxation schemes, property rights systems, regulatory policies, or economic development programs that systematically work to the disadvantage of some groups while benefiting others in morally arbitrary ways. More simply, discriminatory redistribution occurs when a group is subjected to unequal economic treatment without sound justification for this inequality. Examples would include the state imposing higher taxes on one group while spending less on it or placing special economic restrictions on one region without just cause.[11] In most, if not all, cases of secessionist movements of which there is any record, the charge of discriminatory redistribution has been at the forefront of the grievances cited to justify separation.

Historical and contemporary instances of the charge of discriminatory redistribution as a justification for secession are plentiful. The following are only a few examples. American southerners complained that federal tariff laws were discriminatory, serving to foster the growth of industries in the North at the expense of the import-dependent southern agricultural economy. Basque secessionists and the Northern League of Italy claim that their regions make disproportionately large contributions to the coffers of their respective states. (As the Basque protest song puts it: "The cow of the state has its mouth in the Basque country, but its udder is elsewhere.") Biafrans, whose secession was bloodily suppressed, complained that while their region contained only 22 percent of the total population of Nigeria, it contributed over 38 percent of the country's total revenue.[12]

None of these three justifications for recognizing a prima facie right to secede is without problems, and none can be plausibly maintained without qualification. The first is the least problematic in principle, unless, of course, there are intractable disputes about what the list of human rights includes. While there certainly are disagreements about what qualifies as a human right (especially regarding some of the more generous alleged economic rights), there nevertheless are clear and unproblematic cases of violations of indisputable human rights. For example, if Iraq perpetrates clearly genocidal policies against its Kurdish minority and the Kurds' best prospect for self-defense is to establish their own state and defend its borders, then it is hard to see how the Kurds' moral right to secede could be denied. The basic idea here is that the right of self-defense against basic human rights violations preempts or voids whatever legitimate title the state had to the territory in question.

The case of secession to rectify a past unjust seizure of territory may seem the least controversial because secession in this instance is simply a matter of taking back what was unjustly taken. Nevertheless, thorny problems lurk here as well. The most serious is what I have elsewhere dubbed "the moral statute of limitations problem." Just how far back may we or must we go in determining the rightful owners of a territory and how clear must the title be?

Given that virtually every state in existence originally acquired all or some of its territory by theft, genocide, or fraud (or acquired it from those who gained it by such methods), this is no minor issue. Nevertheless, there are situations in which this justification for a right to secede is compelling. The case of the Baltic Republics is perhaps the most obvious instance. The Soviet annexation was recent, well documented, and clearly unjust, and the Republics' claims to territory were at least as valid as those of most, if not all, states that are now recognized as sovereign under international law.

In such cases, the most difficult problem seems to lie not with whether there is a right to secede but rather with determining the just terms of secession. In particular, there is the problem of providing adequate protections for the rights of the large Russian minorities in the two of the newly independent Baltic states (Estonia and especially Latvia, in which 48 percent of the population is Russian). To say that the Russians who now exist there have no rights because they were colonists sent in after an unjust annexation ignores the fact that most of them were not even alive at the time of annexation.

My purpose here, however, is not to focus on these or other problems concerning the first two justifications for recognition of a right to secede or on the just terms of the exercise of the right as justified in these ways. Instead, I want to concentrate on what some might initially regard as a fatal difficulty with the proposal to recognize the third justification, discriminatory redistribution, as a primary justifying ground for secession in international law.

The Problem with Discriminatory Redistribution as a Justifying Ground for Secession

To my knowledge, none of the other contemporary writers who have offered accounts of the right to secede has considered discriminatory redistribution as a justification.[13] This is puzzling for two reasons. The first, which has already been mentioned, is that to ignore discriminatory redistribution is to neglect what is probably the most common grievance secessionists raise. (At the very least, we are owed an explanation of why this pervasive grievance can never serve as a justifying ground for secession.) The second is that discriminatory redistribution was universally, if only implicitly, recognized as *a* major justification, if not *the* major justification, for the legitimacy of that wave of secessionist movements that has received the widest and firmest support from international legal doctrine and institutional practice so far: cases in which peoples severed colonial territory from colonial empires, cast off the yoke of colonialism, and established their own independent states. Although it is true that colonialism almost always involved violations of basic individual human rights as well, a significant part of the evil of colonialism, and one important strand of justification for anticolonial wars of independence, was the economic exploitation of colonial peoples by the metropolitan states. But if discriminatory redistribution can justify secession from an imperial state that happens to lie across the sea (as in the case of Belgium or France and their African colonies or, for that matter, as in the case of the thirteen American colonies and Britain), why does it not justify secession from an empire (such as the Soviet Union) whose subject peoples happen to occupy the same landmass as their exploiters?

What might account for the absence of discriminatory redistribution in considerations of the primary justifying grounds for secession? The most obvious explanation is that to determine whether economic arrangements constitute discriminatory redistribution (exploitation) against a group within the state requires reference to a substantive standard of distributive justice. However, the prospects for achieving international consensus on such a standard are doubtful. Accordingly, any proposal that the justifying grounds for secession should include the grievance of discriminatory redistribution is impractical. Obtaining international consensus on basic human rights, such as the right not to be tortured or imprisoned without trial, has been a long and arduous journey. Attempting to forge an international consensus on distributive justice would be futile and utopian. For this reason, then, some may be reluctant to take seriously any proposal that the international community should recognize discriminatory redistribution as a primary justifying ground for secession.[14]

This objection has some merit. However, I do not think it is decisive. It is an exaggeration to say that discriminatory redistribution as a primary justifying ground is impractical in the absence of an international consensus on a substantive standard of distributive justice if a substantive standard is taken to be something approaching comprehensive theory of distributive justice. Often something much less ambitious may suffice. All that is needed for this proposed general justifying ground to serve a valuable function is a broad consensus that certain states of affairs are unjust, and this may be possible without anyone, much less everyone, agreeing on a comprehensive theory of justice.

In other words, even if there is a significant range of distributive arrangements about which there is intractable disagreement as to whether they are just, there may well be a substantial area of agreement as to when serious distributive injustices are occurring. And as was noted earlier, the needed agreement in judgments about the injustice of a range of distributive arrangements in a number of countries did, in fact, exist in the case of the condemnation of colonialism. Similarly, it can be argued that the international community's acceptance of the secession of East Pakistan (Bangladesh) was based at least to some extent on the recognition that Pakistan's economic policies were highly discriminatory toward that region, as the secessionists charged.

This is not to deny, of course, that disagreements over what counts as discriminatory redistribution would not in some cases lead to a lack of consensus on the legitimacy of a bid for secession. (I take up the question of how international law should respond to such an eventuality later.) The point is that it should not be assumed, however, either that there are no clear cases of discriminatory redistribution or that all disagreements about whether discriminatory redistribution is occurring will remain intractable forever. It was only after a long and difficult process, after all, that the broad international consensus on the most basic (and now least controversial) human rights took shape.[15]

Why Not a More Liberal Right to Secede?

A natural objection to the international legal right to secede advocated in this essay is that it is too restrictive. By requiring that secessionists bear a burden of argument to show that they are victims of one or more of the injustices described in the three general justifying grounds, that approach creates a strong presumption against secession (in contested cases). One might well ask, however, at least from the standpoint of liberal philosophy broadly construed, why the burden should not lie with the state to show why a particular group, if it so desires, should not be able to have a sovereign state of its own. In other words, at least from the perspective of a political philosophy that honors the autonomy and liberty of individuals, respects their right to freedom of association, and sets great store by the notion of government by consent and the ideal of democratic self-government, is there not a strong presumption in favor of secession, at least in the case of territorially concentrated groups a substantial majority of whom wish to form their own state?

There are two variants of this objection. One attempts to ground a less restrictive international legal right to secede on a consent theory of political obligation, the other on a right to democratic government (understood roughly as majority rule). Each will be considered in turn because each raises its own distinctive issues. However, what the consent view and the democratic government view have in common is that they purport to show that any group that wishes to establish an independent state on the territory it happens to occupy may do so even if it is not the victim of any injustice.[16]

A consent theory of political obligation holds that consent, either tacit or express, is a necessary condition for political obligation. A consent theory of secession is the view that because citizens are obligated to obey the state only if they consent to it, the only way to assure that citizens do consent is to allow them to "exit" the realm of state control if they so choose. But since exiting by emigrating will always mean entering into the territory of another state and therefore tacitly consenting to its authority, and since in many, if not most, cases the options for finding a more satisfactory state are extremely limited or nonexistent, those who do not consent to state authority should be able to form their own state through consent with other like-minded individuals.[17]

There are a number of powerful arguments for rejecting a consent theory of political obligation and hence for rejecting any theory of justified secession based on it. Here I will only mention briefly what I take to be the most serious problems with a consent theory of secession specifically. First, as Lea A. Brilmayer has argued, consent theory as such seems to be silent on the issue of claims to territory or, if it speaks, to beg the question.[18] It is one thing to say that individuals are obligated to a political entity only if they consent to it and another to say that by consenting to form a state they thereby come to have rightful title to the land they happen to occupy, even though that territory is claimed by others. In other words, consent seems at best to be able to establish bonds among individuals or to subject individuals to the authority of other individuals. How such voluntarily created relationships among individuals are supposed to generate a claim to the territory on the part of the individuals so related remains a mystery. If, on the other hand, the consent theorist simply assumes that by living in a particular territory a group of people comes to have a claim to it if the group desires to exercise sovereignty over it, then he or she begs the question. If the territory in question is unclaimed by others—if the convenient colonialist fiction of *terra nulles* is a fact in this case—then the mere presence of the group in the area, along with its desire to exercise control over it, might do something to generate an entitlement to it. But in the case of secession, others do claim the territory as their own.

Similarly, a commitment to the liberal individual right of free association is incapable of grounding a right to secede. The right of individuals to associate with one another cannot itself explain why associated individuals have a right to territory claimed by others simply by virtue of their association with one another.

A second problem with consent theory, as a theory of justified secession, is that it seems to face this dilemma: Either it takes its own preoccupation with consent seriously, allowing any group (or individual!) that desires to secede from any larger group to do so, and so on indefinitely, or it places a limit on fragmentation by allowing a majority in a certain area to prevent a minority from seceding, thereby repudiating the requirement of consent on the basis of which it is supposed to tell us when secession is justified. In other words, if consent really means consent, then in principle any group, no matter how small (or, indeed, any individual), that wishes to form its own state has a right to do so, in which case the alleged theory of secession is, in fact, a license for anarchy. Instead of "every man's home his castle," we have "every man's yard his sovereign territory." If, in contrast, the will of the majority is allowed to override the will of those who do not consent to the existing state, then this is an admission that political obligation does not require consent, and the basis of the theory of secession, the consent theory of political obligation, is abandoned.

The proposal for a more permissive international legal right to secede based on the right to democratic government fares no better.[19] The most obvious objection to any attempt to ground the right to secede on the right of individuals to democratic government is that the latter right is generally understood to be a right to be governed democratically within the boundaries of some state or other, not a right to determine by majority rule the boundaries of the state. In other words, argument would be needed but to my knowledge has not been supplied to show why the same considerations that support the former right also require recognition of the latter.

That the latter right is, in fact, not only stronger than the former but morally dubious as well becomes clear once we notice its implications. To recognize the right of a majority in a territory to secede when it votes to do so is nothing short of empowering the majority to determine unilaterally the nationality of others (the minority not voting in favor of secession), thus depriving them of their citizenship in the country in which they have always lived, transforming them into citizens of another state (or resident aliens in it), even when neither they nor their state is guilty of any injustice whatsoever, either toward the secessionists or toward anybody else.

A second difficulty is that if a democratic right to secede were recognized in international law, this would create extremely perverse and destructive incentives, both for groups seeking independence and for the state itself. If it were known and accepted that any substantial majority located in a certain territory could simply vote to sever that territory from the state and establish its own state, then groups seeking to form their own state would have an incentive to move en masse to a particular region in hopes of becoming a majority there and seceding. This would give a new and, I think, rather sinister meaning to the slogan "voting with your feet." More important, if this democratic right of secession were recognized in international law, every state would have strong incentives either to restrict immigration so as to avoid groups coming into the state only to vote to fragment it when they achieve a majority in a certain region or to restrict the mobility of citizens (or citizens in certain minority groups) within the state to prevent them from concentrating in a region and voting to make it an independent state.

More specifically, acceptance of the majority rule proposal for an international legal right to secede would give states a strong incentive to refuse to consider any form of territorially based federalism, at least under conditions where populations in federal units might someday come to have majorities that would vote to secede. Thus the paradoxical and unfortunate result of recognizing the more liberal right to secede advanced by the right to democratic rule approach is to foreclose as a practical option the more limited rights to self-determination that federal schemes offer.

A less obvious difficulty with both the consent and democratic theories of the right to secede is that they legitimize the secession of the rich from the poor, thus threatening to undercut the functioning of the state as an instrument of distributive justice. They would allow the citizens of a richer region to secede (if a majority within it so chose) simply to make themselves even better off by divesting themselves of the burden of sharing part of their wealth with their less fortunate countrymen. (There are, in fact, several recent instances of secessionist movements that might be said to fit this description—for example, the secession of Slovenia from Yugoslavia and the separatist movement in Northern Italy, as well as the earlier case of the secession of Katanga Province from the Congo.) At least for those who, unlike the most extreme libertarians, believe that the state should engage in some redistribution of wealth from the better-off to the worse-off, this is a troubling prospect.

There is yet another, even more compelling reason for rejecting both consent and democratic theories of the right to secession in international law. As noted earlier, what these theories have in common is the proposal that international law should recognize that any territorially concentrated group has the right to secede, even if the group is not the victim of any injustices (violations of human rights, past unjust seizure of territory, discriminatory redistribution, et cetera). Both views therefore constitute nothing short of a frontal assault on what is surely the most firmly entrenched principle of international law: a strong presumption in favor of the territorial sovereignty of existing states. Indeed, what is remarkable about the proposed consent and democratic theories of the international legal right to secede is that they go even further, rejecting the more qualified, more morally persuasive, and only recently emerging principle that the presumption in favor of the territorial integrity of existing states is restricted to states that are not persistent and massive violators of human rights. (As evidence that this more qualified principle of territorial integrity is gaining ground in international law, one might cite the international community's refusal to recognize South Africa under apartheid as a sovereign state, the United Nations supported invasion of Iraq in response to Iraq's invasion of Kuwait, and the United Nations' "no fly zone" in Northern Iraq, which infringes Iraq's borders to protect the human rights of the Kurds.) The consent and democratic theories deny the right to territorial sovereignty not just of states as such but even of states that respect human rights.

Furthermore, by rejecting even the qualified principle of the territorial integrity of existing states, both the consent theory and the democratic theory of the right to secede in international law expose themselves to the charge that they fail to meet even the most minimal realist condition. Given that it is existing states that, for the most part, determine what becomes international law, an approach to the problem of bringing secessionist crises under the rule of international law that begins with a rejection of even a qualified principle of the territorial integrity of existing states is probably doomed to failure. Even if the consent or democratic theorist qualifies his or her position by advancing only the claim that a group has a prima facie right to secede if it so chooses, independently of having suffered any injustice, it seems extremely unlikely that this approach, as threatening as it is to the most deeply entrenched principle of international law and to the legitimacy of existing states, will bear much practical fruit.

A distinct advantage of the more restrictive approach I have advocated in this essay is that it does not present a direct challenge to the territorial integrity of existing states. Or, to be more precise, the challenge it presents is neither so new nor so radical as that posed by consent and democratic theories. The "grievance theory" or "remedial right" theory of secession under international law that I advocate defends existing states from involuntary fragmentation except in cases in which secessionists can make a case that separation is the remedy of last resort for serious injustices. In that sense, it presents no more (and no less) of a threat to territorial sovereignty than the doctrine of human rights.

Nor does the approach advocated here suffer from the problem of perverse incentives that afflicts both the consent and democratic right to secede positions. If accepted as a matter of international law, the grievance or remedial theory approach would not encourage groups to migrate for strategic reasons or states to bar them from concentrating as a counterstrategy. Nor would it provide states with incentives to reject proposals for achieving more limited forms of self-determination through federal systems out of fear that federal units eventually would claim a right to split off whenever a majority in them favored secession. So from the standpoint of what I have referred to as the minimal realist condition and from that of facilitating, rather than hindering, free mobility both within and across borders, as well as allowing less extreme forms of self-determination such as federalism, the grievance theory approach is seen to be superior to those that advocate a much less restrictive right to secede.

Finally, the approach advocated here seems to score at least as well on the other desiderata as the consent and democratic theories. It appeals to widely accepted moral principles—the importance of respecting human rights, the right to recover what is unjustly taken, and the right of a group to escape from a state in which it is systematically exploited. Also, if implemented, this view promises significant moral gains over the status quo in which uncontrolled secession movements frequently result in massive violations of human rights and severe disruptions of economic well-being.

In contrast, while the consent and democratic theories of the international legal right to secede appeal to principles of consent-based obligation and the right to democratic government that have broad appeal, they fail to link their proposals regarding secession to those principles in a plausible justification for the latter. In the case of the consent theory, whatever appeal the idea that political obligation is based on consent enjoys does not explain how consent generates an entitlement to a portion of the state's territory. In the case of the democratic theory of secession, the connection between the right to democratic government within a state and the alleged right to determine state boundaries by majority rule is similarly tenuous. Moreover, the latter right is morally dubious since it amounts to a right of a majority unilaterally to change the nationality of others against their will by making them citizens of a new state (or by making them aliens) in what had been their own country, even when neither they nor their state has committed any injustice.

All things considered, then, the remedial or grievance theory seems to score higher on the criteria for comparative evaluation than its rivals. However, even if from the standpoint of broad moral accessibility the proposals were in a dead heat, the grievance or remedial theory clearly wins on the criteria of minimal realism and avoidance of perverse incentives.

The Feasibility of Gaining Consensus on Justifying Grounds

I have argued that an effective and principled international response to crises of secession must be one component of a larger international institutional response to a wide range of problems of self-determination. International law should distinguish clearly between secession and less radical forms of self-determination, enunciate a presumption that less radical forms are to be pursued first, and unambiguously reject both the Nationalist Principle and the notion that any group with a legitimate interest in self-determination in some form or other thereby has the right to opt for the most radical form of self-determination. To handle those cases in which the secession option is pursued but in which secession is contested, two areas of international law require coherent development: principles specifying procedures for working out agreement on just terms of secession (assuming that secession is occurring or will occur) and principles specifying justifying grounds, conditions that must be met before a group is to be recognized as having a prima facie right to secede and authorized to engage in negotiations concerning the determination and implementation of just terms of secession.

I then focused on the task of developing an account of the primary justifying grounds for secession, concentrating on the third—discriminatory redistribution (or regional exploitation).[20] Next, I observed that there appears to be an obstacle to including discriminatory redistribution as an internationally recognized justifying ground for secession. The difficulty is that the consensus on a standard of distributive justice needed for making such determinations may not be available. I then argued, however, that consensus on a comprehensive theory of distributive justice is not a precondition for the usefulness of the notion of discriminatory redistribution as a primary justifying ground for secession in international law. Agreement on a significant range of real-world cases as instances of distributive injustice (regional exploitation, internal colonialism) is all that is required.

Nevertheless, at least in the approach advanced here, controversies over distributive justice may impose significant limitations on the project of bringing secession under the rule of international law. Indeed, gaining a consensus on an understanding of discriminatory redistribution as a primary justifying ground may require achieving a convergence on moral standards that is at least as daunting as the project of gaining international recognition of basic human rights norms was fifty years ago.[21]

Given that this is so, a word of caution is in order. My claim is not that the current institutional resources of the international legal order are up to the task of recognizing discriminatory redistribution as a prima facie justification for secession or even that they will be in the foreseeable future. My task in this essay is one of moral target setting, not prescribing policies for immediate implementation. Whether or not international legal institutions will develop to the point at which they could provide resources for impartially and consistently adjudicating claims of discriminatory redistribution will depend in part on whether international or at least regional institutions come to perform some of the redistributive functions that are now largely left to individual states. If the state's current virtual monopoly on redistributive functions is successfully challenged and regional or international entities come to be recognized as playing a legitimate and important role in assuring distributive justice, progress toward consensus on minimal international standards of distributive justice may be forthcoming.

Nevertheless, even if in some cases there turns out to be unresolvable disagreement about whether a state's economic arrangements constitute discriminatory redistribution, there may be a broad and more stable consensus that certain secessionist groups (such as citizens of the Baltic Republics) are justified in seceding (because they are merely taking back what was wrongly taken from them) or that other groups (such as the Kurds) who secede are legitimately defending themselves from serious violations of uncontroversial human rights.

More pessimistically, if reaching a consensus on any of these three justifying grounds for secession proves impossible (which I doubt is likely), it still would not follow that the project of endeavoring to constrain secession crises by international law is quixotic. Progress in developing principles and institutions for working out what I have called the just terms of secession can, to a large extent, proceed without waiting for a solution to the problem of specifying a complete list of the primary justifying grounds for secession.

Perhaps the most troubling cases would be of the following sort. A group tries but rejects as inadequate less radical forms of self-determination and resolutely presses for secession. Other justifying grounds (in particular, clear and persistent violations of basic human rights) do not apply, and the only possible case for secession is the charge of discriminatory redistribution or the charge of prior unjust annexation. However, there is a lack of international consensus either on the existence of discriminatory redistribution or on the validity of the group's claim to sovereignty over the territory prior to the annexation. Under such circumstances, the best policy might well be to implement the principle that intervention either in support of or against secession by any state is prohibited, and a schedule of increasingly severe sanctions is to be visited on any who intervene. However, once an appropriate international agency determines that separation is inevitable or highly likely, the state and the secessionists are required to participate in an internationally supervised process for ensuring just terms of secession. Further, if either party refuses to participate in this process, it should be subject to sanctions.

Above all, it should be kept in mind that providing a comprehensive blueprint for resolving all possible secessionist conflicts is almost certainly not a realistic goal. The aim, rather, is to begin to develop principles and institutions for constraining and containing attempts at state breaking within the rudiments of the rule of international law while at the same time providing protection and support for those who have a legitimate interest in forming their own state in order to avoid serious injustices. The sole object of the present essay has been to stimulate discussion that may contribute to this vital endeavor.

NOTES

This essay builds upon some of the argument in my article "Theories of Secession," *Philosophy & Public Affairs* 26, no. 1 (1997): 31–61. The latter focuses on a more systematic analysis of types of theories of secession, develops the criteria for assessing them in more detail, and contrasts institutional and noninstitutional forms of ethical reasoning about secession.

1. I offer an analysis of Lincoln's views and some proposals for procedural mechanisms to reduce the danger of strategic bargaining with the threat of secession while still making room for legitimate cases of secession. See Allen Buchanan, *Secession: The Morality of Political Divorce from Fort Sumter to Lithuania and Quebec* (Boulder, Colo.: Westview, 1991), pp. 98–100.

2. That the partition of Czechosolovakia was peaceful is beyond doubt. Whether there was adequate consent is less clear. There was no referendum on partition, and there are some indications that if there had been one, a majority would not have voted for the creation of separate Czech and Slovak states.

3. My discussion here simplifies by sidestepping the fact that a secession may be uncontested even though it does not occur with the (voluntary) consent of both parties. For example, the citizens and government of what will become the remainder state may not contest a group's secession because they feel they would be beaten if they attempted to resist it by force and because they do not believe that any third party would help them to resist the secession.

4. Because self-determination can take many forms, it is probably less confusing to speak of *rights* of self-determination rather than of *the right* of self-determination. A number of different considerations support the conclusion that a group has a sufficiently weighty legitimate interest in some form or forms of self-determination to justify the recognition of a particular institutional (legal) right of self-determination or cluster of such rights. See Allen Buchanan, "Liberalism and Group Rights," in *In Harm's Way*, ed. Jules L. Coleman and Allen Buchanan (Cambridge: Cambridge University Press, 1994), pp. 1–15, for a discussion of broadly liberal justifications for various types of rights of self-determination for groups.

5. For a discussion of the interest of indigenous peoples in self-determination, see Hurst Hannum, *Autonomy, Sovereignty, and Self-Determination: The Accommodation of Conflicting Rights* (Philadelphia: University of Pennsylvania Press, 1990), pp. 27–49. See also Allen Buchanan, "The Right to Self-Determination: Analytical and Moral Foundations," *Arizona Journal of International and Comparative Law* 8 (1990): 41–50.

For one of a number of instances in which political leaders of indigenous groups clearly distinguish between secession and less extreme forms of self-determination, clearly rejecting the former and seeking the latter, see Chief Ted Moses, ambassador to the United Nations, Grand Council of the Crees (of Northern Quebec), "The Crees, Self-Determination, Secession, and the Territorial Integrity of Quebec," paper presented at the Conference on Nationalism and Self-Determination in Multicultural Societies at McMaster University, Hamilton, Ontario, May 3, 1994.

6. For an analysis of the ambiguities of the now-popular phrase "collective land rights" and a discussion of the different forms collective control over land may take, along with the relationship between such collective rights and individual rights, see Allen Buchanan, "The

Role of Collective Land Rights in a Theory of Indigenous Peoples' Rights," *Transnational Law and Contemporary Problems* 3, no. 1 (Spring 1993): 90–108.

7. One qualification of this generalization is in order. In cases in which the group wishing to secede is simply striving to regain its own formerly sovereign territory from a state that unjustly annexed it, it may be inappropriate to require that the group first try other, less radical forms of self-determination.

8. This objection to the Nationalist Principle is elaborated and references to others who have raised it are provided in Buchanan, *Secession*, pp. 49–51.

9. The establishment of protections for minority rights must be viewed diachronically, not as a once-and-for-all affair. In other words, monitoring of the implementation of protections for minority rights, if it is to be effective, must take place over an extended period of time. In this sense, international recognition of the sovereignty of a new state that had begun to implement institutional arrangements for the protection of minority rights would have to be regarded as provisional or probationary. There is, of course, no uniquely correct interval for the probationary period in all cases. What would count as a reasonable period would vary depending upon the circumstances of the particular case and even then would be to some extent a matter of convention rather than substantive principle.

10. Buchanan, *Secession*, esp. pp. 27–80, 151–62.

11. Another important issue, which I do not take up in this essay but do discuss to some extent in ibid., is that of how to determine which sorts of groups are candidates for the right to secede. My view is that the correct answer to this question is to be found in the conception of the right to secede as a remedial right. Roughly, the idea is that what makes a group a candidate for being recognized as having a right to secede is the fact that it is a victim of the sorts of injustices for which secession is the remedy (of last resort). In other words, what I call the primary justifying grounds for secession supply criteria for determining whether a given group has the (prima facie) right to secede. This position is to be understood as subject to an important proviso, however: the group in question (on the territory they seek to sever from the state) must have a reasonable prospect of being able to form a state that will successfully discharge the basic legitimating functions of a state—the protection of basic individual rights and the provision of national security—and to maintain an economy capable of providing subsistence and at least minimal economic well-being for its citizens. This proviso has two advantages. First, it places a limit on fragmentation since not every group can support a state that satisfies these legitimating functions and the criterion of economic viability. Second, the proviso reflects a proper concern for the freedom and welfare of those who will be affected by the decision to secede but will have no voice in that decision— namely, the dependents, including children, and later descendants of those who choose to secede.

Another important issue that I do not take up here but do discuss in ibid. is the question of authentic voice. What is to count as an adequate expression of the will of a group to secede? See ibid., pp. 139–42, for the beginning of an account.

12. This paragraph is adapted from ibid., p. 41. The verse from the Basque protest song is quoted by Donald Horowitz in his deservedly influential book *Ethnic Groups in Conflict* (Berkeley: University of California Press, 1985), p. 250.

13. See, for example, John Dugard, "Secession: Is the Case of Yugoslavia a Precedent for Africa?," *RADIC* 5 (1992): 163–75; Ved P. Nanda, "Self-Determination under International Law: Validity of Claims to Secede," *Case W. Res. J. Int'l L.* 13 (1981): 256–89; and Lea A. Bril-

mayer, "Secession and Self-Determination: A Territorialist Interpretation," *Yale Journal of International Law* 16, no. 1 (January 1991): 177–202.

14. It is important to understand that merely showing that there is a net wealth flow from one region of the country to the rest, as Calhoun purported do in the case of the American South, does not itself establish that there is discriminatory redistribution. According to any conception of distributive justice that requires or permits redistribution from the better-off to the worse-off (within the country), such a net wealth flow may occur if the better-off happen to be concentrated in one region.

15. It might be argued that the problem of gaining consensus on standards of distributive justice (or even agreement as to when serious injustices are occurring) can simply be sidestepped by employing a different conception of the justification for secession. The idea would be that secession is only justified against illegitimate states and that having representative government is both necessary and sufficient for a state to be legitimate. I consider and raise serious objections to this view in "Democratization, Secession, and the Rule of International Law," unpublished paper.

16. The more plausible versions of these theories of the international legal right to secede would include other conditions—in particular, a guarantee of the rights of minorities in the seceding area. Since this condition is common to the consent and majority rule view and the rival position I am advocating, I will make no further mention of it here.

17. Harry Beran, *A Consent Theory of Political Obligation* (New York: Croom Helm, 1987), pp. 37–42.

18. Lea A. Brilmayer, "Secession and Self-Determination: A Territorialist Reinterpretation," *Yale Journal of International Law* 16, no. 1 (January 1991): 186–87, and "Consent, Contract, and Territory," *Minnesota Law Review* 74, no. 1 (October 1989): 6–10.

19. For a clear presentation of this approach, see David Copp, "Do Nations Have a Right of Self-Determination?," in *Philosophers Look at Canadian Federation*, ed. Stanley G. French (Montreal: Canadian Philosophical Association, 1979), pp. 71–95, "Democracy and National Self-Determination," paper presented to the annual meeting of the Pacific Division of the American Philosophical Association, Chicago, March 1994, and comments on an earlier draft of the present essay presented at the conference on The Ethics of Nationalism at the University of Illinois at Urbana-Champaign, April 1994. It is only in the latter that Copp explicitly endorses what I have called the plebiscite or majoritarian theory as a proposal for institutions of international law. In a perceptive dissertation titled "Political Self-Determination" (University of Arizona, 1994), Christopher (Kit) Wellman develops in more detail a view similar to Copp's. However, Wellman, unlike Copp, does not address directly the question of this essay—namely, what the content of an international legal right to secede should be.

21. Buchanan, *Secession*, pp. 38–45.

22. For a more extended discussion of the problems of recognizing discriminatory redistribution as a prima facie justification for secession under international law, see my "Democratization, Secession, and the Rule of International Law." There I argue that for the present it is probably unrealistic to expect international legal institutions to be able to adjudicate a wide range of claims of discriminatory redistribution. I also suggest that the competence to do so may emerge if international institutions continue to take on an increasingly significant role in ensuring distributive justice. See also Allen Buchanan, "Federalism, Secession, and the Morality of Inclusion," *Arizona Law Review* 37, no. 1 (1995): 53–64 (special issue in honor of Joel Feinberg).

19

The Case for Linguistic Self-Defense

GEORGE FLETCHER

A near-majority of Quebec residents want to secede from Canada, in part because they think that the French language will thereby become more secure against the pervasive threat of English culture. This motive for secession puzzles many American intellectuals. It seems petty and irrational to break up a country for the sake of an incremental advantage to a language. We smile as well at the efforts of the French in France to outlaw the onslaught of English culture. What is the point of trying to banish universal words like "cheeseburger"? After all, Americans are willing to adopt expressions like "c'est la vie" and "gemütlich" when they are useful. Why can't everyone be as flexible as we are?

But perhaps Americans do not understand the attachment felt by many people to their native languages. The movement to entrench English against the supposed threat of Spanish in the United States has a distinctly right-wing, almost xenophobic cast. Also, many Anglophone Canadian intellectuals, including distinguished thinkers like Will Kymlicka and Steven Pinker, undervalue the distinctive place of language in defining culture. Kymlicka seems to think that if the Francophone and Anglophone Canadians share the same attitudes on the issues of the time, then the cultures are the same; that these views are expressed in different languages is of minimal relevance.[1] Pinker argues that because we all think in a prelinguistic medium called Mentalese and because all languages share the same deep grammatical structure, the mode of linguistic expression is arbitrary.[2] His book ends in the fantasy that someday we will recognize that everyone in the world indeed speaks the same universal language. Perhaps because of the worldwide utility of

English, Anglophone intellectuals are inclined to see language as a transparent medium of expression, about as relevant to habits of thought as the choice of a word-processing program.

In this essay, I defend the contrary position. I argue that each language distinguishes a living culture and that precisely for this reason every group of native speakers has an inherent right to defend its language against influences that threaten to eradicate or displace it. It does not follow from this claim that the Quebeckers should secede. They might be able to take adequate measures to protect their language within a federal union with the Anglophone provinces. But if my argument is sound, it might yield some understanding for those who think that defending their language is a proper basis for political action.

For the time being, I refer to this right to defend one's language against eradication as linguistic self-defense. The kinds of defensive measures I have in mind are those that governments frequently have imposed on their citizens. They range from selecting a particular language as the compulsory language of instruction in the schools, to insisting upon the use of particular languages in governmental offices, to prohibiting the use of alternative languages in public advertising. There are serious problems, as in all cases of self-defense, in deciding how severe the measures may be and how much cost they may impose on those who prefer an alternative language.

To make the case for the propriety of at least some of these measures of linguistic self-defense, I must argue for three basic propositions: (1) that language is sufficiently important to trigger a right of defensive political action; (2) that linguistic self-defense is not subject to moral criticism as intolerance or xenophobia; and (3) that self-defense is the correct figure of speech for describing the right I seek to delineate. I begin with the critical claim that languages are worth defending because of their role in constituting cultures.

The Centrality of Language in Culture

Assuming That Each Language Constitutes a Culture

The conventional understanding of self-defense in international law is that nations have a right to defend their territory and national integrity against physical invasion. People invest meaning in their national territory, I take it, because a specific territory provides the stage for the unfolding of the national narrative. These narratives are based on an amalgam of musical and artistic culture and a specific form of government. Those who conquer the territory change the narrative by substituting one government for another and eventually one culture for another. What makes territory worth fighting for, therefore, is the culture, the way of life, and the government that define the identity and the history of the inhabitants.

Some people might respond to this argument with the following objection: it is not the culture or anything like it that one seeks to defend by repelling aggressors; it is the actual space that is at stake. Jews defend Jerusalem for the sake of its stones. Muslims claim the Dome of the Rock because of their attachment to a specific mound of earth. This is true, but it is the respective cultures of the Jews and Muslims that charge these sites with meaning. People may fight for specific places but only because their cultures invest these physical spaces with compelling significance. In the end they fight to protect their physical space but only because this space as mediated by their culture, shapes their sense of identity.

Now I want to assume for a moment that language and culture are inseparable. I know that I must give an argument for this position, but let us take it to be true for the sake of a simple thought experiment. Let us suppose that during World War II the Germans abandoned their efforts to conquer England by invasion and instead devised a mode of linguistic subterfuge. They concocted a way to substitute the use of German for English on radio, in motion pictures, and in the internal mechanisms of Linotype machines. The upshot of the latter was that even if the typesetter typed in English, all newspapers and textbooks came out printed in German. Further, the Germans used electronic means to rig the telephones so that if you spoke English at one end, it would come out German at the other end. In order to communicate with each other on the airwaves, in print, or by telephone, English-speaking people had to understand German. The Germans called this campaign of linguistic aggression "Operation Babelosa."[3]

Now if language were a neutral, invisible medium that has no bearing on culture, Operation Babelosa would hardly constitute a serious interference with English sovereignty. It would be no more a casus belli than, in our current conceptual world, disabling all word-processing programs of the enemy other than the local favorite. But if the English language is essential to the maintenance of English culture, the English legal system, and the specific traditions of the English constitution, then the imagined substitution of German for English would arguably be as serious a form of aggression as a physical invasion. The English would have as much a right to go to war for their language, I think, as they would have to fight for the flowered fields of Wiltshire or the white cliffs of Dover. They would, in brief, have a right of linguistic self-defense.

In this imaginary scenario, fighting for a language could take the form of physical violence. If the English could locate the nerve center of the German operation, I should think that they would be entitled, if no lesser means were available, to bomb it out of existence. Others acts of war would be as clearly legitimate as if the German army had occupied English territory.

If the military value of Operation Babelosa seems dubious, just imagine that in the course of two generations English-speaking became German-speaking. Would not an Austrian-style Anschluss be a more plausible aim of peaceable German politics? Whether it would or not depends, in large measure, on whether changing languages is likely to result in a change of political loyalties. I believe that it would, but that takes us back to the proposition about language and culture, for which I have yet to argue.

There is, of course, a major difference between Operation Babelosa and the kind of danger that Quebeckers are concerned about. The German scheme represents deliberate aggression. The dangers confronting the use of French come from spontaneous waves of cultural development. It just happens to be the case today that young people all over the world listen to music with American lyrics, watch American films and television programs, and eat *le fast food* at the local McDonald's.

For most people, the possibility that the nation's youth would learn English would appear to be an advantage rather than a liability. Acquiring a second language is generally not a threat to the maintenance of the first language at home. The Dutch have hardly lost any of their culture as a result of learning English, French, and German. But if the number of native speakers falls below a critical mass, the ever-present availability of a more widely used, more commercially valuable language does represent a serious threat. It is hard for Navajos to maintain their language or for Jews to cultivate Yiddish in the face of dominant languages around them. The predictions of language disappearance in the next decades are dire. Of the 6,000 extant languages, no more than 600 are thought to be likely to survive another century.

Linguistic extinction is a virtually irreversible process. The only case I know of in which nationalist urges have led to the revival of a dormant language is modern Hebrew in Israel. For practical purposes, therefore, linguistic extinction is worse than the loss of physical territory. Charles de Gaulle could return to France, but if the French language ever died out, it could never—absent extraordinary circumstances—be revived. If individuals have a right to use defensive force in response to physical aggression, then they have the right to use appropriate means to save their language from extinction.

The dangers of linguistic transformation became apparent to me a few years ago when I returned to my mother's hometown in eastern Slovakia. When my mother lived there, the town was called Nagymihaly and it was Hungarian-speaking. After World War I, Slovak was instituted as the language of instruction in the schools and as the obligatory language of commerce. Gradually, the town became Slovak-speaking. Its name became Michalovce. Nagymihaly as a cultural entity disappeared. There were serious economic consequences for the Hungarian-speaking population, and this indeed was the major reason that my mother and her family left in the 1920s and came to the United States.

When I returned a few years ago to Nagymihaly (as we in the family always called the town), I found a few older people who could still speak Hungarian. But there was no public evidence of Hungarian language or culture. There was no visible record of the town's Hungarian past, no sign of the name we had cherished in memory, no trace that the people there had once nourished loyal ties to their cultural center in Budapest.

As Nagymihaly was wiped off the map, every ethnic group in Eastern Europe fears that its cultural moorings could easily be overwhelmed by foreign influences. This is not exactly the fear of extinction, for these are languages still spoken as native tongues by millions. But none of the peoples or nations of Eastern Europe wants to take the risk that they, too, will lose cultural ground as the Turks, Germans, or Russians sweep across the landscape. My claim is that these people also have a right of linguistic self-defense. What means are appropriate for them to use, or for the Navajos to use to defend their language against extinction, remain to be considered.

Proving the Constitutive Role of Language in Culture

The entire argument up to this point depends on the assumption that language is sufficiently connected to culture to justify the inference that if you can use appropriate means to defend your culture, you may do the same to protect your language. I must now make the case for the centrality of language in constituting a culture.

One easy way to make this case would be to argue that if anything constitutes the core of a culture, it is the indigenous pattern of thinking. If language affects thought, then, by implication, language also defines the core of the culture. The problem with this tack is that the relationship between thought and language has turned out to be a tough intellectual nut to crack. The landscape is littered with broken theses. One failed attempt lies in the extreme position, recently revived by Pinker, that thought takes place in some mystical nonverbal medium.[4] If this is true, then thought functions autonomously from language, which implies that the structure of language is irrelevant to our inclinations to think one way or another.

There is just as much intellectual support for the opposite position—namely, as formulated by Benjamin Lee Whorf, that the structure of language shapes the way we think about the world. Whorf, along with Edward Sapir, hypothesized that this was the case on the basis of some exotic features of the tense structure in Hopi. In a syntax that seemed to blur noun and verb, Whorf concluded, speakers of the other language must think differently about time and human action.[5]

The correct view about thought and language, as our intuitions tell us, must lie someplace between these two extremes. Yet that middle ground is notoriously difficult to describe. As far as I know, neither linguists nor philosophers have charted a sensible middle course. The problem resembles one of the standard conundrums of legal philosophy: How much do legal rules and principles control the decisions of judges? Everyone knows that the correct answer lies someplace between "not at all" and "entirely," but no legal philosopher has even come close to formulating the right middle position. The same point holds about the middle course between

Pinker and Whorf, between the views that language has no bearing and that it has total bearing on the way we think.

Considering the intractability of the thought/language problem, it might be more productive to focus directly on the relationship between language and culture. But the omnibus term "culture" covers too much ground. My approach will be to focus on particular subcultures in which language plays an important part. At the outset, therefore, I will argue in favor of a connection between legal culture—the form of culture I know most about—and the language in which the law is written and argued. If what I have to say is true about law and language, it is a fair guess that it might also be true about poetry, humor, historical memories, and other subcultural arenas that require the use of words.

The first thing to note about law and language is the strong connection between English and the common-law system that originated in England. It is more than a coincidence that all English-speaking peoples have adopted the English common-law system and, further, that this system has not lent itself to translation into any other language of the world. English and the common law come together as a cultural package. The question we have to ponder is whether this is merely a contingent fact or whether there is some deep reason for the tight historical connection.

European legal systems do lend themselves, more or less, to translation. The French system has found adoption in many countries, notably in Latin America, to some extent in Italy, and in Romania. This is hardly a counterexample, however, for all of these national languages derive from Latin, and therefore translation from French is relatively easy. German law has had a more imperialistic career. Greeks, Japanese, and Russians all adopted some aspects of the German codes and the German conceptual system. In many cases, this was achieved simply by coining a special technical language for translating the German terms. Also, it is not clear to me that the transplanting of German legal culture in these countries has ever gone below the surface of academic legal discourse. The strong connection between law and language is not refuted by these examples.

I will try to explicate the strong connection between the English language and the common-law legal tradition by focusing on three factors. First, there are a number of terms that simply do not lend themselves to translation. It is not easy to explain the special sense that English and American lawyers invest in terms like "proximate cause," "probable cause," "quasi-contract," "privacy," "estoppel," or "felony-murder." These specific terms might not seem to pose a major impediment to translating the common law into a foreign language. After all, if necessary, one could simply adopt these terms as "loan words" in the foreign language. The Japanese now speak of "doo processu" when they discuss constitutional issues. If they wanted common-law principles, they could simply fill in the gaps in their language by importing English, and in fact they have already done this with the term "privacy."

Two other factors go to the heart of the matter. One of the most striking particularities of common-law legal discourse is its pervasive reliance on the term "reasonable." English-speaking lawyers routinely refer to reasonable time, reasonable delay, reasonable reliance, and reasonable care. In criminal law, we speak routinely of reasonable provocation, reasonable mistake, reasonable force, and reasonable risk. A good example for purposes of this study is that individuals exercising self-defense may use no more than reasonable force to protect their interests. A culture seeking to protect its language can do no more than use reasonable means to that end.

Every time the term "reasonable" comes forth, the "reasonable person" lurks nearby. This hypothetical character summons us to have faith in a community standard for judging individual behavior. This character of reason has become so dominant in our legal culture that we cannot discuss issues of responsibility and liability without first asking what a hypothetical reasonable person would do under the circumstances.

Our reliance on reasonableness distinguishes our legal discourse from legal discourse in other cultures. The fact is that French, German, and Russian lawyers argue in a different idiom. Their languages deploy a concept of reason, and their terms for "reason"—*raison, Vernunft,* and *razumnost*—readily yield corresponding adjectives. Yet these parallels to our term "reasonable" do not figure prominently in legal speech on the Continent. The French civil code uses the term *raisonnable* precisely once (art. 1112); and the French are likely to invoke the community standard of the *bon père de famille* instead of the reasonable person. Interestingly, however, Quebec lawyers, under the influence of surrounding Anglophone legal culture, do rely upon the figure of the *homme raisonnable.*

In my view, it is no accident that we pervasively rely upon the concept of reasonableness while Europeans do not. This pattern of our speech serves a purpose, perhaps many purposes. For one, the term "reasonable" functions as a placeholder for a range of values that are typically invoked to fine-tune legal rules by recognizing the peculiarities of every case. When we say that you can use only reasonable force in self-defense, we imply that a variety of individual and social considerations can enter into a judgment that the defensive force has gone too far. This generates a style of thinking that is "holistic" in nature; lawyers in the common-law tradition start with a single rule of reasonable force that signals all the variables of cost and benefit that the judge needs to know.

In contrast to a single rule based on reasonableness, European lawyers start their arguments with broad, sweeping rights. They would say, for example, that you have the right to use all the force necessary to protect your interests regardless of the costs that fall on others. But this is only the first step of a structured argument. If it appears that the defensive force imposed a disproportionate cost on others, European lawyers would apply the doctrine of *abus de droit*—the principle that defeats the exercise of absolute rights in particular situations. Not surprisingly, in view of the doctrine of reasonableness, English-speaking lawyers have no need for the doctrine of "abuse of rights."

The prominence of "reasonableness" in the thinking of Anglo-American lawyers suggests a preference for pluralism in legal thought. There are many reasonable answers to any problem. The common law does not insist upon the right answer at all times but only a reasonable or acceptable approach to the problem. Europeans, in contrast, take the notion of Right much more seriously and do claim that the law in this higher sense is single-valued.

The language of reasonableness in the common law stands in a reciprocal relationship with the way lawyers think. Lawyers approach issues like self-defense in a characteristic way, and they develop the vocabulary appropriate to their tasks. Once the language practices become common, new generations of novitiates are inducted into the established pattern of professional discourse and argument. The circle is complete—from thought to language to thought.

A slightly different mode of linguistic influence comes to light in the way Americans and other English-speaking peoples talk about fairness. We have coined the phrases "fair play" and "fair trial" and have bequeathed them to the Western world —both in law and in daily speech. Many of our neighboring cultures simply adopt the word "fair" into their vocabularies as an untranslatable American idea. Thus you can hear Germans and Israelis using the American word "fair" as though it were their own. Others like the French try in vain to translate the notion of fairness as *équitable* or *juste*, but these and other cognates in other Romance languages overlook the procedural bedrock of fair dealing.

Americans learn the notion of fair play as soon as they begin playing with other children. Enter any kindergarten and watch children playing with a single ball or Lego set. Sooner or later one of them will complain that another is not sharing, that he or she is "not fair." The charge of unfairness is a tool that children quickly learn in order to protect their interests. Not sharing is paradigmatic unfairness. So is not playing by the rules.

Understanding the idea of fair play has become a challenge to the two dozen European countries that have ratified the European Convention on Human Rights, which provides that in all criminal as well as civil cases "everyone is entitled to a fair and public hearing."[6] The requirement of a fair trial also emerges in the newly enacted Canadian Charter of Rights and Freedoms, which provides by analogy to the European charter that everyone charged with a crime is presumed innocent until proven guilty "in a fair and public hearing."[7] The translations of "fairness" as "just" or "equitable" miss the nuance that every American schoolchild learns on the playground. For philosophers, the best way to make this point is to ponder the meaning of John Rawls's classic formula "justice as fairness" in a culture that has no indigenous concept of fair play. Translating the idea as "justice as justice" or "justice as equity" obviously fails. The whole point of the original position and the veil of ignorance is that these conditions yield fair procedures in precisely the sense that exists only in English.

Surprisingly, the term "fairness" appears neither in the U.S. Constitution nor in the Bill of Rights. Though our basic document omits the word, the idea of a fair trial runs through our provisions on criminal justice and renders them coherent. The most basic idea of justice in the Constitution, due process of law, is commonly defined as fair procedure.[8] As the Supreme Court put it: "A fair trial in a fair tribunal is a basic requirement of due process."[9]

The best explanation for this faith in fairness lies in our cultural roots. To appreciate the uniqueness of English-language culture, we need only pause to reflect upon the sporting metaphors that abound in everyday speech. A fair competition is one in which the playing field is level, the dice are not loaded, and the deck is not stacked. Fairness consists in playing by evenhanded rules. Neither side hits below the belt. No one hides the ball. You don't sandbag the opposition by passing on the first round and then raising your opponent's bet. In a fair competition, both sides retain an equal chance of winning. And the winning side should gain the upper hand without cheating, without playing dirty, without hitting the other when he or she is down. These idioms pervade the English language. No other European language relies so heavily on sporting metaphors to carry on the business of the day. This is a striking feature of English and American culture. We cannot think about human relations without thinking about sports and the idiom of fair play and foul play. This is not true in French, German, Russian, Italian, or any other major language or culture of the West. This correlation provides powerful evidence of the strong link between culture and language.

These are three signs, then, that the English language is bound up with the way Anglophone lawyers think about law. Specific untranslatable terms, the romance with reasonableness, and the faith in fairness all testify to the uniqueness of English legal discourse. If Americans had to start speaking German or Spanish, their notions of law and legal principle would not survive translation. And if this is true about law in English, it is likely to be true about poetry, humor, and our historical memories.

The history of any people is tied to its language. The narrative of the people unfolds in legends, historical events, poetic renditions of key moments, slogans that never die, great oratory, and, of course, legal phrases that define a culture's sense of justice. Just as Jews living in Israel would not have the same culture if they did not hear biblical phrases coming back to them in daily interactions, our lives would be different if we did not use at least a dozen Shakespearean idioms in daily speech. To belong to any great culture is to know and to use the words that move people to tears and anger.

If one day Americans woke up and found themselves in a predominantly Spanish country, we could obviously continue our cultural lives in the new idiom. We could write laws, tell jokes, recite love poetry, and swear at each other in a new syntax. It would be difficult to deny, however, that in switching to a new language we would suffer a deep alienation from our past.

This is the case that I can offer for the proposition that language plays a major role in shaping culture. It is neither an easy nor a perfect case. The constitutive impact of language on culture might be one of those matters that is intuitively obvious but empirically elusive. But if the reader is with me on this point (or can at least suspend disbelief), I can continue to the next stage of the argument on behalf of linguistic self-defense.

Self-defense is, above all, a doctrine of survival. When organisms and cultures are threatened, they understandably seek to survive. This impulse becomes a "right" on the basis of the assumption that all nonaggressive living entities are prima facie entitled to survive. The right to survival is subject to being overridden by the rights of other organisms and cultures, and later we shall consider the roles of self-defense and necessity as principles for overcoming the prima facie right to existence. But assuming that the right is not overridden, existence implies the right to exist and this right, in turn, grounds a right of self-defense. Later we shall consider how far this right goes and which measures are permissible to protect a language against extinction. But first we should consider a serious challenge against the asserted right of linguistic self-defense—namely, that claiming this right is a species of intolerance.

Linguistic Self-Defense and Intolerance

The history of tolerance is closely connected with religious diversity, particularly among Protestants. John Locke's seventeenth-century writings convinced generations of philosophers and politicians that governmental toleration of diverse religions was a better policy than the attempt to coerce observance of a state religion.[10] In this century, policies of tolerance have come to apply as well to cultural and political activity. The expression of outrageous and obscene views invites governmental intervention, but for various reasons governments in the West now choose to stay their hand. The frontier of tolerance now lies in the field of what used to be called deviant sexual relations. Until a decade or two ago, governments routinely punished these allegedly immoral acts. Now the trend is to place the value of individual privacy ahead of controverted criteria of morality, and therefore these "deviant" sexual acts—with the exception of incest—are no longer thought to be the business of the criminal law.

Let us try to see how the principles of tolerance or toleration would extend to the use of a foreign (other than the conventional) language in public space. At a personal level, the question could come up if you encounter, say, a French tourist in a New York City department store who needs help with translation. If you speak French, do you, if you have the time, offer to help? It seems to be obvious: yes, you do. (Or if you are a clerk and you speak French, you switch to the customer's language.) The only argument against extending linguistic help would be that the Frenchman should learn English before he dare use his tourist francs in the United

States. This coercive hard-heartedness could be thought of as an extended form of self-defense. But in this case it is hard to see a significant interest at stake that would warrant a defensive response. Turning the other way when communication is possible in somebody else's language seems at least close to intolerance.

But suppose the same thing happens in a schoolroom. Children show up for school who do not speak English. You are the principal of the school. Do you seek to accommodate them by finding a teacher on the staff who speaks their language or by requesting a budgetary allocation to hire one? Now the question becomes more subtle. Prescribing the language of education is one of the ways, if not the primary way, that a culture propagates itself. Schools can accommodate children who refuse, on religious grounds, to pledge allegiance to the flag or can welcome Muslim girls who insist on wearing the chador in class. With these acts of tolerance, schools do not sacrifice their essential mission of propagating a specific culture. But when the language of instruction begins to yield to that of immigrants, the culture is put at risk—of course, not by a single child but by a million children who want to be educated in another language.

There is an important difference between the customer in the department store and children coming to school without knowing English. In the former case, one cannot hope, with one inhospitable act, to convert the Frenchman into an English speaker. But children are malleable. After six months of hearing English, they will become functionally adept in the language. With regard to the adult tourist, his speaking a foreign language is an unchallengeable aspect of his person—something like his facial features or the color of his skin. But the question whether we should impose English on children resembles the standard cases of intolerance. Forcing a change in language is something like imposing a state religion, censoring speech, or effectively prohibiting certain sexual acts. Tolerance is a virtue when change is arguably possible; the state could intervene and impose outward conformity with its demands, but for reasons of privacy and respect for persons, it chooses not to do so.

Some people might say that as much respect is due to the language of children as is due to their religion. As we let a thousand religions bloom in the United States, we should allow the same to occur in the primary languages of communication. Schoolchildren in Los Angeles speak over 400 languages at home. Why should there not be—finances permitting—400 different modes of instruction? Anything less than this degree of respect, some might say, is intolerance. And those who favor voucher plans for the future of education might think that when a group of parents gets together, the parents should be able to organize a school in any language they choose. I disagree. The position of a dominant language—like English in the United States, French in France, German in Germany—can claim for itself prerogatives that religions no longer dare assert.

The advocates of bilingual education in the United States always seek to justify their proposals on the pedagogic grounds of easing children into the use of English. Instruction in Spanish, for example, is meant simply as a transitional measure. Whether this is sound education is a matter I leave to others. My point is simply that when the representatives of a minority culture begin to demand state-funded instruction in their own language, the single unifying culture begins to fracture.

The only genuine form of multiculturalism, in my view, is linguistic multiculturalism. It is only when people speak different languages that they think of themselves as different peoples. (The case of Northern Ireland suggests that linguistic differences might not be necessary to sustain nationalist tension.) In all of the cases of state disintegration in the last decade — Yugoslavia, the Soviet Union, Czechoslovakia, and Canada (almost) — the rallying point of divergent identity has been language. True, language sometimes correlates with differences of religion and sometimes with different histories that one or both sides may recall as the history of oppression of one group by another. The point of this generalization is that if a country seeks to avoid the risk of secession, it should be wary of any practice that could lead to subcultures thinking they have the right to speak and hear their languages in the schools.

This proposition clearly holds for public schools. But what about private schools? If parents pay tuition or deploy their vouchers, should they not have the right to choose the language of instruction? Should not the Amish have the right in their parochial schools to educate their children in Pennsylvania Dutch or Hasidic Jews in Brooklyn have the right to use Yiddish in the schools? In an important decision expressing toleration of minority languages, the Supreme Court ruled in *Meyer v. Nebraska*[11] that a state could not prohibit the teaching of a foreign language in the schools — in that case, German. The ruling is certainly correct. But tolerance of teaching a language as a foreign language — a practice certainly to be encouraged — is not the same as displacing English as the language of instruction. The unity and stability of American culture presuppose that new generations of speakers grow up with a solid command of English as well as other languages that they, to their credit, can master.

What we encounter in these examples is the fine distinction between tolerance of difference and linguistic self-defense. The two concepts brush up against each other, and there might well be disagreement at the interface. Where the dominance of English in American culture is at risk, tolerance ceases to be the commanding value and the right of cultural self-defense justifies the coercive imposition of a language.

Is Promoting a Language Appropriately Described as Self-Defense?

We started with the hypothetical German campaign of cultural aggression known as Operation Babelosa and we ended up with a few schoolchildren coming to school without knowing English. Did we not lose the analogical thread along the way? Are these both appropriately described as the kind of "aggression" that properly triggers a right of self-defense? After all, it might be right to impose a single language as the medium of instruction, but it does not follow that "self-defense" is the right concept for justifying our action. Necessity or lesser evils might be the more apt construct for justifying the state's policies.

One difference between self-defense and necessity is that the former is available only to ward off aggression; necessity applies to the collision of two incompatible interests, regardless of which side is the aggressor. For example, blowing up a house to prevent the spread of a natural fire is considered, in law, a case of necessity, not of defensive action. Because self-defense applies against aggressors and necessity against natural threats like fires, the amount of force permissible in self-defense is characteristically greater than in cases of necessity. You can justify killing a rapist on grounds of self-defense, but you cannot justify it on the cost/benefit balance required under the defense of necessity (the sexual integrity of the victim being of less value than the life of the aggressor).

It is true that in most legal systems self-defense requires a sense of proportionality in gauging the permissible amount of force. But proportional force can still result in a balance lopsided in favor of the defender, provided that the balance is not too far askew (for example, killing to prevent a scratch). The important point is that necessity requires a strict balancing of costs and benefits, and therefore on grounds of necessity you cannot justify killing an aggressor to preserve the sexual integrity of another person (worth less, presumably, than life).

Because more force is permitted under the label of self-defense, theorists are constantly tempted to nudge cases from the realm of necessity into the domain of self-defense. For example, a moving (but not acting) human body or a growing fetus is not properly labeled an aggressor, but many people are tempted to fudge in these cases so that the case is considered one of self-defense and killing becomes a permissible option. This kind of ambivalence about abortion is evident in Jewish law, which originally held in the Talmud that a fetus threatening the welfare of the pregnant woman is not an aggressor (*rodef*)[12] but later, in Maimonides, supported the view that abortion is justified as akin to defending against an aggressor.[13]

In the case of the linguistic threat represented by a growing immigrant population, the threat is not purposely aggressive at the outset. Later, when the population grows to the point that demands are made to change the language of instruction in the schools, the threat does become purposeful. To return to our original example of the fear of American influence tendered by the French, neither of these categories seems to apply. The spread of the English language in popular entertainment as well as commerce is a spontaneous phenomenon. No one is directing aggression against the French, but the threat is nonetheless real. It seems that in some of these cases of linguistic politics the notion of self-defense is out of place and the more restricted principle of justification by necessity would be more appropriate.

There is, however, another important difference between self-defense and necessity that renders the notion of necessity less than fully apt for the case of linguistic conflict. The underlying principle of self-defense is the imperative of individuals and social entities to survive. The foundation of necessity is not the individual perspective but the social point of view. Individual actors, acting out of necessity, are supposed to think about the costs and benefits of their conduct for the society as whole. It is good for the society to blow up a house to prevent the spread of a fire, and that neutral Archimedean view of the action justifies the intrusion against an innocent, nonaggressive party.

In the struggle between competing languages for dominance, there is no Archimedean point for judging whether one language or another should prevail. True, there is some value in diversity, and as it is good for all to protect threatened biological species, it is good to defend some of the 5,000 or more languages that are likely to die in the next century. But it is difficult to apply this general principle to the context of specific cases of conflict. If one language were to yield to a more dynamic language in a particular region, the speakers of one language would lose and those of the other language would gain. But there is no neutral perspective for deciding which is the "better" language. For purposes of resolving linguistic conflict, therefore, the principle of necessity or lesser evils is inapt. It is better to think of the struggle to retain a language as an expression of a localized imperative to survive against an external threat. Thus it seems that the principle of self-defense provides a better framework for justifying measures of defense than does the neutral standard of necessity.

Of course, both sides can claim an imperative to survive in the same geographical space. Both the Romanians and the Hungarians can assert a claim to self-defense in the use of their languages in Transylvania. The problem of priority nags this as well as other instances of self-defense. Recall Kant's famous example of two shipwrecked sailors fighting for a sole plank. The first occupant of the plank, Kant claims, can assert a right of self-defense against a subsequent interloper.[14] The same kind of temporal claim arises in disputes about linguistic priority. The people who were there first, whose language became established first, claim the right to use their language against external threats of displacement. Quebec nationalists describe themselves appropriately not as immigrants to Canada but as original settlers. The same argument is heard from the Afrikans-speaking inhabitants of South Africa. Settlers are like the first sailor on the plank: they can defend themselves against subsequent interlopers.

In the end, for all of its limitations, the notion of linguistic self-defense is the better model for understanding the patriotic urges that express themselves in linguistic conflicts. Under the model of self-defense, the enduring problem is how far particular cultures may go to defend their languages. Two desiderata appear obvious. First, the measure taken should be effective; it should actually serve the purpose of protecting and promoting the language. Some of the measures taken by the French, such as prohibiting the use of the word "cheeseburger" on Parisian menus, are probably counterproductive for they engender ridicule without stimulating the study and use of French. Second, in keeping with the theory of self-defense, the measure taken should be reasonably necessary in the sense that it is the cheapest means available for reaching the particular goal of linguistic survival. Requiring the dominant national language as the means of instruction in the schools is an effective and probably the cheapest means available for ensuring that the younger generation master the language. Requiring the use of the language in all governmental offices is probably unnecessary and expensive. Third, the measures taken in linguistic self-defense must meet the standard of proportionality. When they go too far—when linguistic patriots refuse to speak anything else—then the costs to others become excessive and the defensive action begins to bespeak intolerance.

Assessing these issues under the label of self-defense does not solve the difficult issues at the frontier. But choosing the right descriptive concepts does help us to understand the moral claims of those locked in linguistic struggle.

NOTES

1. See generally Will Kymlicka, *Liberalism, Community, and Culture* (1989). I infer the proposition stated in the text from Kymlicka's downplaying of the role language in the determining cultural identity.

2. Steven Pinker, *The Language Instinct* (1994), pp. 55–82.

3. Hitler's plan to conquer the Soviet Union, it will be recalled, was called Operation Barbarossa.

4. Pinker, *The Language Instinct*, pp. 55–82.

5. See generally *Language, Thought, and Reality: The Selected Writings of Benjamin Lea Whorf* (Carroll ed. 1956). For a discussion of this thesis as applied to legal discourse, see George Fletcher, "The Presumption of Innocence in the Soviet Union," *UCLA Law Review* 15 (1968): 1203.

6. European Convention on Human Rights, art. 6, para. 1, sent. 1: "In the determination of his civil rights and obligations or of any criminal charge against him, everyone is entitled to a fair and public hearing within a reasonable time by an independent and impartial tribunal established by law."

7. The charter's article 11 (d) reads: "Any person charged with an offence has the right . . . (d) to be presumed innocent until proven guilty according to law in a fair and public hearing by an independent and impartial tribunal."

8. See, for example, Thomas Sargentich, "Due Process, Procedural," in *The Oxford Companion to the Supreme Court*, ed. K. Hall (1992), p. 236: "The central aim of due process doctrine is to assure fair procedure."

9. *In re Murchison*, 349 U.S. 133, 136 (1955).

10. J. Locke, *A Letter concerning Toleration*, ed. J. Horton and S. Mendus (1991).

11. *Meyer v. Nebraska*, 262 U.S. 390 (1923).

12. *Babylonian Talmud*, Tractate Sanhedrin, p. 72.

13. See generally George Fletcher, "Self-Defense as a Justification for Punishment," *Cardozo Law Review* 12 (1991): 859.

14. Immanuel Kant, *The Metaphysics of Morals*, trans. Mary Gregor (1991), pp. 60–61.

20

Eroding Sovereignty
The Advance of Principle

HENRY SHUE

> The worship of the great man, or perhaps the idea of sovereignty, paralyses the moral sense of humanity.
> —Lord Wright, "War Crimes under International Law,"
> reprinted in *History of the United Nations War Crimes Commission and the Development of the Laws of War* (1948)

Much argument about the sovereignty of states is made hopelessly simplistic by its generality. Should we recognize state sovereignty or not? Do states have too much sovereignty or just about the right amount? And so forth. In order to get a firm grasp, we must examine specific matters over which states could be permitted or denied sovereignty of specific kinds one at a time. Sovereignty is not some mystical cloud that either envelops the state entirely or dissipates completely; there are bits and pieces of asserted sovereignty. These assertions can be granted or contested one by one and accepted in this era and rejected in the next, or vice versa. Sovereignty should, I would think, be treated more like a (crazy) quilt that can be left to cover some things but pulled off of others.

Purported causal connections and alleged conceptual relations, in both directions and various mixtures, between nationalism and sovereignty abound. One incessant refrain goes as follows:

1. Every nation has a right to self-determination.
2. The best, or only, means by which any nation can protect and guarantee its right to self-determination is to control a sovereign state of its own.

In order for a nation to be genuinely self-determining, this argument goes, it needs its own sovereign state. A nationalist wants a state for (what he or she takes to be) his or her nation. Why must Croatia secede from Yugoslavia and form a separate state? Because Croatians (taken to be a nation) will not be safe under a Yugoslav state in which they are a minority; Croatians need to form a sovereign Croatian state. Why must Bosnian Serbs secede from Bosnia and join a state controlled by Serbs? Because Serbs (taken to be a nation) will not be safe under a Bosnian state in which they are a minority; Serbs need to join a sovereign Serbian state. A self-respecting nation must never settle, according to nationalists, for being a minority in a state controlled by some other nation. A sovereign state is an indispensable weapon for the protection of a nation's right to self-determination.

I consider the dominant contemporary conceptions of both the nation and the state to embody extremely dangerous myths; a state with a nationalistic basis is, I believe, doubly dangerous. Other chapters here discuss the problematic character of so-called nations, or peoples, whose integrity is claimed to ground the argument for the separate state. What I will try to establish are some limits on the state, whose sovereignty is supposed to guard the nation's alleged integrity. If I am correct about state sovereignty, nationalists—and non-nationalists—could be a little less desperate to control a state of their own.

A separate state is most desirable to a nationalist if it is a sovereign state. A sovereign state is thought to be the best, or only possible, guardian of its people. Why? As a first approximation, we can say that a sovereign state can be valuable for a people because the sovereignty of the state embodies a right to give the interests of the people represented by the state special attention. A sovereign state may grant special attention to the interests of its own people. The interesting question is: What exactly can justifiably be meant here by "special"?

Hereafter I will be discussing the acceptable attitude of a state toward everyone outside of its territory, which is roughly what is customarily called external sovereignty. Before moving to my own topic of external sovereignty, it is worth noting quickly in passing that part of what is frightening to people like me about the internal sovereignty of a state with a nationalistic grounding is its likely understanding of who "its own people" are. If the Croatian state, for instance, believes that the people to whose interests it may, and ought to, give "special" attention are exclusively the ethnic Croatians, then it is liable to be willing to drive ethnic Serbs out of their houses and off of their land in order to turn the houses and land over to ethnic Croatians, precisely as the newly rearmed Croatian army did, in fact, do in 1995 in the region of Krajina. Thus self-determination for the favored group brings denial of the self-determination of individuals of other groups. Internally, "special" attention with a nationalistic grounding seems extremely likely to lead, at best, to inequality in the self-determination of individuals, based upon which group they belong to, and often, in fact, leads to persecution and expulsion of individuals from other groups. This is a domestic application of special attention that is unacceptable. Domestic policies, however, are explored in other chapters.

What about the foreign policy of a sovereign state? The state's sovereignty entitles it to give, I initially said vaguely, "special" attention to the interests of its own people. A partial, more definite account of special attention for nationals (however they are specified domestically—and I will worry no further here about that specification), as contrasted with foreigners, that would seem sensible to many people is that a state is obligated to take positive measures to promote the interests only of its own nationals. A state is never bound to act positively to advance the interests of foreigners; for any given foreigner, the task of promoting his or her interests falls upon his or her state. Whatever else is included under the sovereignty of the state, a state is free to ignore the interests of foreigners in the precise sense that it is bound to do nothing at all to advance the interests of foreigners. Its positive goals all have inward-looking justifications.

A sharp and exclusive division of labor among states applies when they are seen as sovereign in this sense. For instance, in the case of jobs, the state is in the business of promoting jobs strictly for its own nationals; it should promote jobs for non-nationals only when, and only to the extent to which, the indirect means of producing additional jobs for foreigners is the most efficient way to produce additional jobs for citizens, as it might, in an economically interdependent world, often be. According to conceptions of sovereignty, a state may, and ought to, promote the interests of its own nationals exclusively. May it also promote the interests of its nationals without restraint?

Limiting Sovereignty Externally

Consider one familiar kind of restraint. The doctrine of just war is centuries older than the doctrine of state sovereignty.[1] A glance at the former will provide valuable perspective on the latter. When Bodin, Hobbes, and the others were first concocting their notions of state sovereignty, the case had already been made long ago that what political units (empires, city-states, nation-states, and whatnot) may rightly do is constrained by principled limits. The limits were understood to be principled in being external to the political units (city-states or whatever) and existing independently of judgments made about their meaning by the individual units limited. That is, the principles were genuine limits with an internationally shared meaning, not merely whatever the heads of the individual units limited might claim they meant, which would have made them effectively no limits at all.

If whatever I judged to be the case were the case just because I judged it to be, I could not—logically could not—be wrong; there would be no intersubjective understanding beyond my own judgment itself on the basis of which my judgment could be judged by others. The all-important feature of the criteria of just war is their analogous independence of any one state or other unit to which they applied. The criteria were part of an international—cross-unit—understanding. None of this is to deny either disagreement or disregard; of course sovereigns (and their scholars) often disagreed with each other about what the principles of just war meant, and sovereigns frequently chose to disregard what the principles plainly did mean. War crimes are not a modern invention, although we have improved the technology. The crucial point is simply that there was an international meaning— a cross-cultural understanding—to be disagreed about and to be disregarded. It is intersubjective meaning external to individual judgment that gives principles power and allows them to function as external limits on otherwise arbitrary judgment. This is true whether the "subjects" are individual persons or single states.

No one, to my knowledge, ever thought the principles of just war meant for each state whatever that state said they meant—no one thought these principles were subject to self-certifying arbitrary interpretations, criticisms of which could only be groundless. No one, that is, until Hobbes, who did try to claim that a sovereign could modify intersubjective meanings as he (subjectively) wished. Totalitarians and Madison Avenue still try to twist socially established intersubjective understandings, but this is hard even for institutions with their power because some meanings are very deeply entrenched in culture and therefore socialized into individual understandings from very early on, as language is acquired. Here Hobbes wildly underestimates the social character of language and meaning and the difficulty of deconstructing the most fundamental social constructions.

Leaving aside bizarrely asocial Hobbesian theories of meaning, we find that while it was recognized that de facto each state would decide for itself whether it had just cause to go to war, this de facto judgment was by no means self-certifyingly de jure. On the contrary, other states could decide that a first state did not have just cause for war and precisely for that very reason—that the de facto judgment of the attacker was wrong—decide that it was right to resist the attack, which was clearly understood to be a conceptually distinct judgment from whether it was in its interest to resist, especially for some third parties deciding whether to assist the victim of the attack (in the role of defender of justice de jure). The limits constituted by the principles of just war were seen to be external to the judgments of sovereigns, such that a sovereign could get them wrong. As Michael Walzer has eloquently shown, normative as well as strategic concepts, "massacre" as well as "retreat," have established meanings that cannot be changed simply by, say, issuing an announcement at a televised briefing.[2]

This quick reminder about the doctrine of just war is intended as evidence that the thought that sovereignty does not involve complete arbitrariness and that even sovereigns are subject on at least some points to principled limitation is not a new, dreamy, or academic notion. Perfectly sensible and tough-minded heads of state and commanders of military forces have for centuries acknowledged that it is not the case that indiscriminate slaughter is in the eye of the beholding sovereign. The dawn of principle in international relations was centuries ago, however cloudy some matters have subsequently become.

Like all concepts, the normative concepts in the principles of just war are in principle subject to change, and conversations are always under way about, for example, whether the city busting by Allied bombers during World War II should be taken as precedent for or as violation of the meaning of "discriminate attack." But these very conversations presuppose that international consensus is both attainable and desirable and that a consensus once reached is authoritative until changed by another consensus. Meanings change, but they do not change until *they* have changed. A social principle like the prohibition of indiscriminate attacks can of course be deconstructed and reconstructed but only socially—not by arbitrary individual assertion and not for alleged "reasons" that are not compelling for other parties to the consensus and certainly not by the unreasoning behavior of individual sovereigns, however powerful. It is the purpose of principles like these to contest and limit power, especially putatively sovereign power.

What I am calling the externality, or independence, of principle is recognized in international law in the distinction between conventional law and customary law. A convention, like a treaty, is initially binding only upon the sovereigns who choose voluntarily to become parties to it by ratifying it. Customary law, by contrast, is binding on particular sovereigns involuntarily, whether they like it or not. A principle will have become a matter of customary law only if, very roughly speaking, a large majority of sovereigns have accepted it in both theory and practice; only well-entrenched practices come to represent customary law. This is the legal analogue of coming to be the content of an intersubjective, but not necessarily unanimous, consensus. Significant portions of just-war doctrine now constitute customary international law.[3]

Whether they wish to use torture, to take a second kind of example, is simply not up to sovereign states to decide for themselves. Torture remains widespread, as everyone knows, but it is a widespread violation of customary (and conventional) law, not a widespread practice that is on its way to becoming an entrenched precedent for acceptable state conduct. In *Filártiga v. Peña-Irala*, in a domestic U.S. court, the judge ruling that torture is a violation of customary international law commented: "The torturer has become—like the pirate and slave trader before him—*hostis humani generis*, an enemy of all mankind."[4] An additional reason why torture has no prospect of being accepted as a precedent is that even those who use it in practice avoid defending it in theory. (Instead, they lie about their practice.) Yet even a sovereign willing to admit and defend this practice would have to change many other minds before anything changed in customary law. R. J. Vincent noted that some principles of human rights, such as the right not to suffer racial discrimination, have attained not only the status of customary law but also, as recognized in *Barcelona Traction* by the International Court of Justice, the status of *jus cogens*, making them peremptory as well as universal.[5]

The principles of just war, then, are a demonstration that external sovereignty can be, and in practice long has been, limited by international principles; more recently, international principles of human rights have begun to limit internal sovereignty. Naturally restraints on both kinds of sovereignty are often honored in the breach, just as much violation of domestic law occurs and goes unpunished. But we can nevertheless distinguish an unpunished breach of these international principles governing both external and internal sovereignty from a disputed interpretation because the core meanings of the fundamental principles are clear. We can even, as in the rare case of Nuremberg—and possibly the Bosnian war-crimes proceedings—enforce the limits by punishing violators.[6]

Leaving Sovereignty Unchallenged

Next I would like to examine a current instance in which so far, I think, less is happening than meets the eye. One frequently hears these days expressions of the hope that international cooperation in dealing with global environmental problems, like severe ozone depletion and rapid climate change, each of which I discuss briefly below, is already proving to be "social learning" from which more general lessons will be drawn about the value of multilateral action and coalition formation, leading in the end to some kind of decline of sovereignty. Since the hope is that we will come to agree that genuine global environmental problems are problems that we all really must face together, we will be driven by necessity to cooperate more fully than we might otherwise like. Once we have had the experience, the hope continues, we may find that we like it, or at least can tolerate it, and may then carry the new modes of cooperation into other issue areas quite unlike the environment.[7]

I think that any hope for a gradual evolution by this route away from sovereignty rests on a misunderstanding about sovereignty, but the misunderstanding is instructive. I am not convinced that international cooperation on global environmental problems will provide even small victories over sovereignty for we must not assume that cooperation is somehow a compromise of sovereignty. Sovereigns have always formed alliances, but temporary cooperation and ad hoc coalitions for specific purposes and for limited periods are scarcely harbingers of a new world order.

This is not to deny that some of the environmental dangers that we have only belatedly understood, like rapid climate change, are unique.[8] The speed of climate change is accelerated by increased emissions of gases that are produced by almost all productive human activities, the worst being the carbon dioxide from industrial production (as long as we stupidly cling to fossil fuels as our energy sources) but also the methane from rice paddies and from the digestive processes of ruminants (the famous cow-belch problem, which is no joke, as this planet hosts a lot of cows).[9] Because the economic activities of the poor, like the herding of ruminants, and even more the economic activities of the now-poor attempting to enrich themselves a bit through processes like carbon-based industrial activity, could cancel out the environmental initiatives of the rich and because enhanced global warming is the result of the atmospheric swirl of greenhouse gases (GHGs) irrespective of point of origin on the surface of the planet of any particular quantity of gas, any significant reduction in the current acceleration of warming trends would require very widespread international cooperation. China alone, simply by using its own coal for its own industrialization, can produce more carbon dioxide than all of the rest of the world's nations together can eliminate from their emissions by any methods anyone is willing to consider.[10]

One feature distinctive of the problem of rapid climate change, then, is that the rich states cannot simply buy their way out of the problem with or without the cooperation of the poor states. Every state with a large economy and every state with a large population that demands a higher standard of living will have to cooperate if global warming is to be slowed (as long as we insist on using fossil fuel for transportation and manufacturing—Saudi Arabia's oil is, along with China's coal, one of the greatest threats to human welfare). Assuming that rapid climate change is a threat to agriculture and the existing world food system, the states of the world face a common threat that can be handled only through widespread—virtually universal—cooperation. Costs will have to be borne, and sacrifices will have to be made.

Yet none of this necessarily limits state sovereignty, insofar as sovereignty consists in the exclusive promotion of the interests of a state's own nationals, which I earlier said constituted special attention. To the extent that any international cooperation is basically voluntary and each state decides for itself whether the terms on which it is asked by the others to cooperate serve the interests of its own people, sovereignty is untouched. The exclusive focus of sovereignty on promoting interests of nationals is uncontested and, so far, unqualified. If a state wishes to decide that allowing its citizens the capacity to prevent the temperature in their homes from ever rising above sixty-eight degrees even in July and August is more important than the extinction of the uncounted plant and animal species that will result from the electricity-generation emissions, that state is free, according to the usual doctrines of sovereignty, to do so. Any level of comfort that a rich state's economy allows its people to pay for goes unquestioned whatever its probable effects on planetary climate, just as the Brazilian state remains free to allow "developers" to turn the Amazon into gold mines and strawberry patches unless Brazil chooses, for reasons of the interests of Brazilians, not to do so.

As my tone already suggests, I will be trying to establish that the colossal global damage that can be done by "domestic" economic policy is a compelling reason why state sovereignty ought to be limited in this area; I spell out some of the normative case in the next section. As things are now, however, threats to the global environment are simply (mis)handled by assembling representatives of sovereign states to discuss possible multilateral treaties and protocols.[11] The states determine whether there is anything they all consider to be in their respective interests; if there is, they agree to do it and perhaps even create enforcement mechanisms and sanctions to provide assurance that the mutually advantageous agreement will be complied with.

Sometimes, in short, there are common goods that are correctly understood to be attainable only if mutual restraint is agreed to and practiced. Recognizing that common goods sometimes are attainable only through mutual restraint in *no* degree qualifies sovereignty, however; Hobbesian denizens of the state of nature recognize this much. Sometimes agreed-upon restraint is forthcoming and sometimes not. While this is practically important, it is theoretically uninteresting; sovereigns have always been considered, according to dominant conceptions of sovereignty, to be bound by their own word only as long as being bound can be made to be in their own interest.

A crucial distinction must be drawn here. It is one thing to claim, in accord with one commonsense interpretation of special attention, that a sovereign state may promote only the interests of its own nationals; call this the thesis of *exclusive promotion*.[13] It would be quite another matter to claim that a sovereign state may promote the interests of its own nationals no matter what the effects are on the interests of others; call this the thesis of *unlimited promotion*. It might well be that although a state need never make a point of advancing the interests of non-nationals, it must refrain from harming at least some interests of non-nationals however much harming the non-nationals' interests would serve to promote nationals' interests. Unlimited promotion certainly does not follow from exclusive promotion. On the contrary, exclusive promotion could turn out to be conditional upon its avoidance of certain harms—upon the prohibition of unlimited promotion.

The same distinction can be made in another way. Allowing the claim (1) that each state is free to play along or not to play along with environmental agreements entirely on the basis of its own *interests* may appear to be allowing the very different claim (2) that each state is free to play along or not to play along with environmental agreements entirely on the basis of its own *reasons*, meaning that each state is entirely its own judge of which considerations it pays attention to. But the latter would mean not simply that each state was free of any obligation to promote interests of non-nationals but that each state was entirely free to ignore the interests of non-nationals, harming them where such harm promoted the interests of its own nationals. The slide from 1 to 2 is a slide from self-centeredness to arbitrariness. For instance, Saudi Arabia, whose oil was pulled out of the fire for it in 1991 in the Gulf War by an international coalition, has done its arbitrary best since (as it did before) to spread havoc within the negotiations about global warming, because the top Saudi priority is to sustain, whatever the harm to everyone else's interests, the long-term market for fossil fuel, far and away the most significant cause

of global warming.¹³ I do not think this kind of arbitrary behavior, with its fla-
grant disregard of all interests except Saudi interests, need be accepted as a responsible exercise of sovereignty, and I will now try to explain why not.

Contesting Sovereignty "at Home"

It may be that when states are making war outside of their own territory,
they must act with some restraint, but surely, it will be said, a sovereign state operating at home may look out for the economic welfare of exclusively its own people. One of the defining purposes of the modern state is the management of the
domestic economy for the enrichment of its own constituents.¹⁴ Will not other
people's states in turn look out for them? The short answer is: no, because the interests of the other people affected may be vital, and their own states may be powerless to defend them against fatal harm initiated abroad. A longer answer follows.

It has been a decade and a half since Charles R. Beitz pointed out that the
Hobbesian picture of international relations could have been correct only if four
false propositions had all been true; one of those decisive mistaken Hobbesian assumptions is the following: "States are independent of each other in the sense that
they can order their internal (i.e., nonsecurity) affairs independently of the internal policies of other actors."¹⁵ That, for instance, even the richest and most powerful states, the Group of Seven, think they need regular meetings in order to co-
ordinate their economic policies is one of innumerable symptoms of the depths to
which the so-called domestic economic policies of the most nearly independent
states that exist can be buffeted by the so-called domestic economic policies of the
others. Much remains to be understood about the modalities of economic inter-
dependence, but its depth seems beyond question. The Hobbesian argument was
headed for a conclusion about domestic authority, but this particular erroneous
Hobbesian premise was about domestic power—about the actual extent of effective control over an "inside" that was much too sharply dichotomized from an
"outside."

That the actual control over their economic fortunes that can be successfully exercised by modern states is, in fact, limited is, of course, not at all the same thing
as their sovereignty over economic matters being limited, since sovereignty is a
matter of the proper authority to try to exert power even where the exertions may
turn out to be futile. Domestic criminal law is regularly broken, but until the violations approach the point of general disorder, only the power, not the authority,
of the state is put in question by the lawbreaking. That domestic economic policy
regularly fails is similarly no grounds for challenging the authority, as distinguished from the competence, of the state. If, as Beitz maintains, the Hobbesian
conclusion about authority rests upon this premise about domestic power that is
falsified by the penetration of the economic "inside" that comes with economic in-

terdependence, a pillar of the Hobbesian argument for sovereignty is undermined. But sovereignty itself is not undermined unless the Hobbesian case for it was the best case there was.

Unlike Beitz, I want to argue not against an argument for sovereignty but against sovereignty directly. I want to contest it, as I have already indicated, not wholesale but in specific aspects in a specific area. Namely, I shall argue that there ought to be external limits on the means by which domestic economic ends may be pursued by states, limits that ought to become binding on individual sovereigns irrespective of whether those sovereigns wish to acknowledge them, just as sovereigns are already bound by both legal rights and moral rights against the domestic use of torture whatever their own opinions on the subject of torture may be— the sovereign's own opinion about torture is of no consequence legally or morally. The same should be true of some particular means of pursuing economic ends. I take this to be a controversial thesis.

An analogy may also be drawn between my thesis and the portion of just-war doctrine traditionally called *jus in bello*, the principles governing the means, as distinguished from the ends, of warfare. While the competence of the modern state to succeed in attaining its narrow economic ends is very much in doubt, I shall not challenge, for the sake of this argument, its authority to promote exclusively the welfare of its own people, or exclusive promotion, as it was called at the end of the previous section.[16] That is, I shall try to show that even if it were the case that a sovereign government is entitled, as a matter of its proper choice of ends, to pursue actively the economic welfare only of its own people, there nevertheless ought to be limits on the means acceptable in the pursuit of that end. The formal structure of the position advanced here, then, is the same as the formal structure of *jus in bello*: even once ends are accepted, many means remain unacceptable.[17] I emphasize this analogy in order to establish that while I may be advocating a new limit on sovereignty, I am not advocating a new kind of limit. Sovereignty's coverage is simply being contested in a new area. Since long before anyone thought up the doctrine of state sovereignty, civilized people have understood that even in the pursuit of fully legitimate ends, including extreme cases like self-defense against arbitrary attack, there are some harms one may not inflict upon uninvolved parties.

A further aspect of the unoriginality of my thesis calls for emphasis. At least since Locke it has been generally acknowledged in this part of the world that the liberty to pursue one's own legitimate ends does not include or entail any liberty to inflict serious harm upon others. This is a negative requirement—no positive assistance whatsoever is mandated, and exclusive promotion is not challenged. My argument for the thesis that pursuit of the end of economic welfare for one state, like the end of defense of a state against military attack, is subject to limits upon means has the general shape of showing that the pursuit of economic goals unlimited in the ways to be specified would inflict unacceptable harms on what amount to innocent bystanders in other states.

In order to begin, then, to make this case, one needs to consider an intolerably severe harm that is inflicted across state boundaries—that is, a severe harm that is caused by economic activities within the territory controlled by one state that affects people who live on the territory of other states. Skin cancer is such a harm; no one's liberty to pursue his or her economic welfare entitles him or her to inflict skin cancer on others. So, too, is clouding of the cornea of the eye to such an extent that sight is impaired. Both these harms result from increases in ultraviolet-B (UV-B) radiation from the sun, and ultraviolet radiation is increasing sharply because of the progressive thinning of the stratospheric layer of ozone, which is the only element in the Earth's atmosphere that can block UV-B.[18] The destruction of the atmospheric ozone is caused, in turn, by the long-lived molecules of chlorofluorocarbons (CFCs) that are continuing to migrate and reside there. In spite of regular denials by ill-informed members of Congress, the mechanisms are increasingly well understood.[19] Only true kooks any longer doubt either the seriousness or the reality of the problem of ozone depletion, and international agreement to deal with it was reached in 1987 under the Montreal Protocol on Substances That Destroy the Ozone.[20] The manufacturing of CFCs is being greatly reduced, although at a pace (apparently designed to guarantee that no manufacturer actually loses any money) that is rather leisurely, given the long atmospheric-residence times of the various CFCs and the seriousness of the afflictions caused by the increased accumulations of CFCs in the upper atmosphere.

Apart from the slow pace of its implementation, the Montreal Protocol is in several respects an admirable precedent. People are doing basically the right thing, even if not at the right time; even under the terms of the Montreal Protocol some manufacturing of CFCs continues, and it will be decades before all of the existing air conditioners and refrigerators rust enough to release their CFCs for the journey to the stratosphere, where the CFCs will gobble up ozone for about another century. The question here about the international action taken to protect the ozone layer lies entirely with the interpretation of its significance. It seems evident that while on the whole the right thing is, in fact, slowly being done, there was morally no other choice. One is no more at liberty to rain malignant melanomas than nuclear missiles down from the heavens upon random people in other states. Consequently, any economic dislocations suffered by the manufacturers (and their employees, who may be as "innocent" in the relevant sense as the affected foreigners and may of course themselves develop skin cancer as well as lose their current jobs [and therewith their medical coverage for cancer treatments]) will simply have to be absorbed. Who exactly absorbs them is a matter of justice in distribution that bears looking into. Here what matters is only that it is plainly unconscionable to continue to manufacture and distribute a substance whose presence on the planet (CFCs are not a naturally occurring compound—they are an entirely human creation developed in 1930 by Thomas Midgley Jr. at General Motors Research Laboratories)[21] will cause cancer in people who are not using the substance and, in fact, never heard of it or went near it, merely on the grounds that jobs will be lost and other economic penalties will be suffered as the substance is restricted. Other jobs will have to be created (preferably, I would think, at the expense of those, like Dupont, who profited most from the substance in question, for the sake of the incentive effects of following the principle "the polluter pays," even apart from consideration of justice).

The fundamental fact here is the utter falsity of the Hobbesian assumption of internal control, as noted years ago by Charles R. Beitz. Beitz emphasized the fact that the success of "internal" economic policies is dependent upon "internal" economic policies elsewhere and upon multinational and transnational actors. The CFC case illustrates how "internal" health policies and health itself are dependent on choices among industrial technologies made on the other side of the planet by foreign states or left by those states for their firms to make as those firms wish. The national energy policies that are driving rapid global climate change are a second, more complex but fundamentally similar illustration.[22] My question about sovereignty, then, is: Is a state any freer—or indeed as free—to decide for itself whether it will cooperate with reasonable measures (that is, do its fair share) to restrict CFCs, or to slow and reduce global warming, than it is to decide for itself whether it will slaughter innocents during a war fought for a just cause? That my suggested answer is no is, I hope, no surprise.

To insist upon whatever economic policies are best for one's own economy while ignoring the distinct possibility that an indirect but predictable effect may be that children in the tropics may develop malignancies caused by excessive UV-B radiation or starve from crop failures produced by climate shifts is an assertion of arbitrary willfulness for which I can imagine no grounds. Of course one is entitled to pursue one's own economic well-being to some degree and in some ways but not at absolutely any cost to others. What is wrong (beyond criminality) with being a cocaine dealer? It is not wrong to want to do well, even perhaps very well, financially. But when it is possible to do well enough in alternative ways that are not destructive of other people's lives, even perhaps in ways that are mildly useful, it is wrong to choose to do that much damage. A state that enriches itself in utter disregard of indirect effects that make survival impossible for innocent strangers seems to me to be no different morally from a cocaine dealer. Some means of pursuing economic goals—namely, means that lead to the severe disruption of the environment within which others, too, must try to survive and prosper—should be removed from the range of options over which states have discretion.[23] We can specify a guiding principle by returning to the consideration of warfare and embracing a theoretical innovation from Michael Walzer's *Just and Unjust Wars*.

Taking Due Care

To my knowledge, Michael Walzer first introduced into the doctrine of double effect as employed in just-war doctrine an explicit requirement of "double intention," which he grounded in what he nicely called "a right that 'due care' be taken."[24] As Walzer, following Kenneth Dougherty, had spelled out the received doctrine of double effect, one of the four conditions that must be satisfied by an act that is likely to have evil consequences in order for the act nevertheless to be permissible is that "the intention of the actor is good, that is, he aims only at the acceptable effect; the evil effect is not one of his ends, nor is it a means to his ends."[25] Walzer's proposal is that this requirement be replaced by the following more demanding requirement: "the intention of the actor is good, that is, he aims narrowly at the acceptable effect; the evil effect is not one of his ends, nor is it a means to his ends, *and, aware of the evil involved, he seeks to minimize it, accepting costs to himself.*"[26]

This is a compelling and important strengthening of the condition. It moves from requiring, in addition to the intention to do the good, the mere absence of any intention to do the evil that will, in fact, also result to requiring the presence of an active intention to keep the unintended evil as restricted as possible. Consequently, Walzer requires a "double intention": an intention to do the good and an intention to hold the unintended evil to a minimum in spite of significant risks to oneself required by the second intention. Part of the beauty of Walzer's reformulation is that he ties a strong requirement of proportionality tightly together with the requirement of discrimination. One is permitted the unintended death and destruction—it may be credited as not indiscriminate—*only if* it is proportional in a more than usually demanding sense: as little as one can make it, significant costs to oneself notwithstanding. Otherwise, the doctrine of double effect enables one in practice to get away with simply waving one's hand over death and destruction that one could have avoided if one had taken more care, and perhaps had run more risk, and declaring, "I wish it had not happened." Walzer's requirement has the further virtue of naturally focusing attention on concrete measures that might be taken in order to reduce seriously unintended bad consequences and their respective risks and benefits. Then the issue becomes not an intractable one about one's intentions, hopes, and wishes but a palpable one about measures taken and measures not taken to protect the innocent: was a (very risky) ground patrol sent in to see who was actually there before the (very safe) air strikes were ordered, and so forth.

A "right that 'due care' be taken" would be a natural and helpful explication of the already-mentioned Lockean right not to be harmed; seriousness about not harming involves taking some considerable care to be sure that one does not harm or, where the harm is unavoidable in doing something that must be done, taking some care to be sure that the harm is the least that is compatible with what must be done. The most frightening thing I ever learned from talking to people in the Pentagon came from the civilian who revealed that he relied on the principle that "it is easier to get forgiveness than permission." In itself the principle is chillingly correct—it *is* much easier since the damage is then already done. But any serious conviction that others have a right not to be harmed leads one not into preparations for saying that one is sorry but into measures taken in advance to prevent the harm.

The general application to economic policy seems clear enough.[27] If one can expect soldiers fighting in a just cause to bear extra danger in order to inflict less damage, one can expect those with other worthwhile but less urgent and less dangerous pursuits to take at least as much care to minimize "collateral" damage. It may not be convenient for us to switch to electric cars whose batteries need frequent recharging (although battery technology is rapidly improving) before the cheap Saudi oil runs out. Yet if that is a good way to cut GHG emissions quickly and sharply enough to avoid shocks to the fragile agricultural systems of states where life is generally a lot less convenient than it would be for us even with electric cars, allegedly sovereign control over domestic economic and energy policy seems an extraordinarily self-indulgent excuse for totally discounting severe effects upon other human beings.

In the utter discounting of the profound human effects across political borders lies the arbitrariness of assertions of sovereignty over "domestic" economic policy. Sometimes some interests of uninvolved strangers may be discounted, and sometimes, as when they will otherwise be the unintended victims of military action, they may not be discounted. The fact that vital interests of outsiders will suffer if our economic policies ignore dangers like global warming and trivial preferences of our own for historically unprecedented levels of comfort and convenience are protected strikes me as good grounds for judging that those interests ought to take priority over these preferences. Defenders of any economic sovereignty that extends beyond exclusive promotion to unlimited promotion—that is, promotion without due care for people outside of the state's borders—need to explain the grounds for their view.

Perhaps I have overlooked some good argument to show that the vital needs of all individual human beings are best served in some cases by a division of labor under which each state completely ignores the welfare of all humans who are not its own citizens. In the instances of ozone depletion and climate change, in particular, this could not possibly be true; no state is able to protect its own people against the effects on the planetary atmosphere of the choices of other states about whether to use CFCs and to use fossil fuels. In fact, these so-called domestic economic decisions have four critical features that together add up to a compelling case for demanding that states take responsibility for *everyone affected* rather than for only those who live on their own political territory:[28]

1. The policies contribute substantially to harm to people living outside the territory of the state that controls the policies.

2. The states that govern the territories in which the people harmed live are powerless to block this harm.

3. The harm is to a vital human interest like physical integrity (a physically sound body).

4. An alternative policy is available that would not harm any vital interest of anyone inside or outside the state that controls the choice among policies.

For a state to assert a right to continue to contribute to such harm in such circumstances is by all commonsense standards wildly irresponsible and arbitrary. Any state that considers itself entitled to inflict severe harms outside its borders by some doctrine of sovereignty that slides from exclusive promotion to unlimited promotion needs to explain to those outside, in the line of fire, the grounds of its asserted entitlement to inflict severe harm.

Second only to the arbitrariness of declaring that palpable harms do not exist is the arbitrariness of declaring that in the moral calculus they do not matter. States that violate domestic human rights often make people disappear physically (through arbitrary executions). States that promote the economic interests of their own people unconstrained by due care for the fundamental interests of outsiders are attempting to make the outsiders disappear morally (through dropping out of the moral calculations).[29] Either way, making people "disappear" is unacceptable.

Why do we ask young soldiers to walk toward the snipers in the trees to check for innocent civilians also perhaps hiding nearby when we can incinerate the whole forest, snipers and civilians alike, from a safe distance with airpower?[30] Why should young soldiers risk death when old civilians will not incur discomfort in order to take care not to inflict avoidable harm upon the uninvolved? Perhaps our economic policies should be as civilized as our methods of warfare are supposed to be.[31]

NOTES

For penetrating critiques that radically reshaped my argument, I am abashedly grateful to the editors and to Gerald Dworkin and his comment on the original paper, "Ought? Replies Khan." Additional helpful suggestions were made at the workshop on this book by Belden Fields, Robert Goodin, Amy Gurowitz, and Michael Walzer.

1. See Norman Kretzmann, Anthony Kenny, and Jan Pinborg, *The Cambridge History of Later Medieval Philosophy: From the Rediscovery of Aristotle to the Disintegration of Scholasticism, 1100–1600* (Cambridge: Cambridge University Press, 1982), pp. 771–84.

2. Michael Walzer, *Just and Unjust Wars: A Moral Argument with Historical Illustrations*, 2d ed. with a new preface (New York: Basic Books, 1993), p. 14.

3. For a current overview, with emphasis on the use of airpower, see Robert K. Goldman, "The Legal Regime Governing the Conduct of Air Warfare," in *Needless Deaths in the Gulf*

War: Civilian Casualties during the Air Campaign and Violations of the Laws of War, A Middle East Watch Report (New York: Human Rights Watch, 1991), pp. 25–64.

4. Richard Pierre Claude, "The Case of Joelito Filártiga and the Clinic of Hope," *Human Rights Quarterly* 5 (1983): 291. Claude powerfully relates the dramatic story of how a Paraguayan policeman who tortured to death the son of a doctor (who ran the Clinic of Hope) came to be tried in a U.S. court, establishing an important legal precedent about the universality of the right not to be tortured (pp. 275–300). Significantly, the U.S. Department of State submitted a brief arguing that the U.S. court did indeed have jurisdiction even though the torture-death occurred in Paraguay. On the customary international law of human rights more generally, see Paul Sieghart, *The International Law of Human Rights* (Oxford: Clarendon Press, 1983); for a more introductory treatment, see Paul Sieghart, *The Lawful Rights of Mankind: An Introduction to the International Legal Code of Human Rights* (New York: Oxford University Press, 1985).

5. R. J. Vincent, *Human Rights and International Relations* (New York: Cambridge University Press, 1986), p. 46. For *Barcelona Traction*, see Louis B. Sohn and Thomas Buergenthal, eds., *International Protection of Human Rights* (Indianapolis: Bobbs-Merrill, 1973), pp. 18–19. On *jus cogens*, see Ian Brownlie, *Principles of Public International Law*, 3d ed. (Oxford: Clarendon Press, 1979), pp. 512–15, 596; and Lauri Hannikainen, *Peremptory Norms (Jus Cogens) in International Law: Historical Development, Criteria, Present Status* (Helsinki: Finnish Lawyers' Publishing Company, 1988), pp. 1–19.

6. For a penetrating, and chilling, analysis of the U.S. effort to undermine the Nuremberg precedent and maintain that national security decisions are not subject to external review in order to get off the hook for the mining of Nicaraguan harbors, see Paul W. Kahn, "From Nuremberg to the Hague: The United States Position in *Nicaragua v. United States* and the Development of International Law," *Yale Journal of International Law* 12, no. 1 (Winter 1987): 1–62.

7. For optimism about "the introduction of novel elements of *governance* into the international system," although no thesis specifically about sovereignty, see Martin List and Volker Rittberger, "Regime Theory and International Environmental Management," in *The International Politics of the Environment*, ed. Andrew Hurrell and Benedict Kingsbury (New York: Oxford University Press, 1992), pp. 108–9.

8. The fundamental studies are J. T. Houghton, L. G. Meira Filho, et al., eds., *Climate Change 1995: The Science of Climate Change*, Contribution of Working Group I to the Second Assessment Report of the Intergovernmental Panel on Climate Change (Cambridge: Cambridge University Press, 1996); Robert T. Watson, Marufu C. Zinyowera, and Richard H. Moss, eds., *Climate Change 1995: Impacts, Adaptations, and Mitigation of Climate Change*, Contribution of Working Group II to the Second Assessment Report of the Intergovernmental Panel on Climate Change (Cambridge: Cambridge University Press, 1996); and James P. Bruce, Hoesung Lee, and Erik F. Haites, eds., *Climate Change 1995: Economic and Social Dimensions of Climate Change*, Contribution of Working Group III to the Second Assessment Report of the Intergovernmental Panel on Climate Change (Cambridge: Cambridge University Press, 1996).

9. On the significance of methane, see Thomas E. Drennen, "After Rio: Measuring the Effectiveness of the International Response," *Law and Policy* 15, no. 1 (January 1993): esp. pp. 28–31; see also Thomas E. Drennen and Duane Chapman, "Negotiating a Response to Cli-

mate Change: The Role of Biological Emissions," *Contemporary Policy Issues* 10 (July 1992): 49–58.

10. See National Environmental Protection Agency of China, State Planning Commission of China, United Nations Development Programme, and World Bank, *China: Issues and Options in Greenhouse Gas Emissions Control*, Summary Report (Washington, D.C.: World Bank, 1994).

11. For a brief critique of the "treaty-and-protocol" method, see Lawrence Susskind and Connie Ozawa, "Negotiating More Effective International Agreements," in Hurrell and Kingsbury, *The International Politics of the Environment*, pp. 142–65. For a longer discussion, see Lawrence E. Susskind, *Environmental Diplomacy: Negotiating More Effective Global Agreements* (New York: Oxford University Press, 1994).

12. I am not convinced of even the thesis of exclusive promotion, which is to say that I reject conventional conceptions of state sovereignty, as I have indicated in *Basic Rights: Subsistence, Affluence, and U.S. Foreign Policy*, 2d ed. with a new afterword (Princeton: Princeton University Press, 1996), chap. 6. In the present essay, however, I am accepting state sovereignty as exclusive promotion for the sake of argument to show that unlimited promotion would still not follow.

13. See "IPCC Chairman Says 'Political Wrangling' Now Gives Way to Science and Technology," *International Environment Reporter: Current Reports* 16, no. 15 (July 28, 1993): 544. Saudi Arabia and Kuwait are the exceptions to a trend of general cooperativeness.

14. See Christian Reus-Smit, *The Moral Purpose of the State* (Princeton: Princeton University Press, forthcoming).

15. See Charles R. Beitz, *Political Theory and International Relations* (Princeton: Princeton University Press, 1979), p. 36, for all four of Hobbes's mistaken assumptions.

16. I very much challenge, on other grounds, the acceptability of assigning absolute priority to the satisfaction of superfluous preferences entertained by one's compatriots over the fulfillment of urgent needs suffered by strangers. See Shue, *Basic Rights*, esp. chaps. 5, 6. If the argument there that rights to economic subsistence are as fundamental as rights not to be tortured were accepted, it would follow straightaway that even sovereign governments are not at liberty to ignore the harm they do to noncitizens' economic welfare in their pursuit of the economic welfare of their citizens. In this essay, however, I make no appeal to the subsistence rights I defended there.

17. Michael Walzer and Jeff McMahan have each separately pointed out to me that there is no general reason not to challenge state ends by analogy with *jus ad bellum*, which restricts acceptable wars to, for instance, those with "just cause," in addition to challenging state means by analogy with *jus in bello*. I hope to explore that elsewhere.

18. A highly accessible account is in Jonathan Weiner, *The Next One Hundred Years: Shaping the Fate of Our Living Earth* (New York: Bantam, 1990), pp. 153–55. "The E.P.A. estimates that every 1 percent depletion in ozone will cause something like a 2 or 3 percent increase in UV-B and a 5 percent increase in skin cancer, including a 1 percent increase in malignant melanomas. In our lifetimes, the thinning of the ozone shield may lead to a 60 per cent rise in the incidence of skin cancers of all kinds in the United States" (p. 155). Weiner cites John S. Hoffman, ed., *Assessing the Risks of Trace Gases That Can Modify the Stratosphere* (Washington, D.C.: Office of Air and Radiation, U.S. Environmental Protection Agency, 1987); and "Skin Cancer Facts and Figures," newsletter, The Skin Cancer Foundation (May 1988).

19. See R. L. Miller, A. G. Suits, et al., "The 'Ozone Deficit' Problem: $O_2(X,v \geq 26)$ + $O(^3P)$ from 226-nm Ozone Photodissociation," *Science* 265 (September 23, 1994): 1831–38; and "Ozone Depletion: Environmentalists Say Nobel Prize Demonstrates Need for More Action," *International Environment Reporter: Current Reports* 18, no. 21 (October 18, 1995): 796.

20. Useful analysis is in Jason M. Patlis, "The Multilateral Fund of the Montreal Protocol: A Prototype for Financial Mechanisms in Protecting the Global Environment," *Cornell International Law Journal* 25 (1992): 181–230.

21. Midgley's life approaches the dimensions of a Greek tragedy. In addition to his disastrous invention of CFCs, he also conceived of adding lead to gasoline. After being paralyzed in the legs by polio, he invented, in order to move himself in and out of bed, a harness with pulleys, in which he one day became entangled and strangled to death. It is difficult now not to see his brilliantly innovative chemistry as the global analogue of his clever bed harness. See Weiner, *The Next One Hundred Years*, pp. 45–47.

22. Like the firing of an intercontinental missile and like the release of CFCs into the atmosphere, the processes that are building toward changes in surface-level temperatures around the world will cause severe harm to people far away from the territory from which any particular GHGs originate. The extent of temperature change within a state's territory will in no way correlate with the amount of GHGs released within that territory. On the all-important danger to agriculture and food, especially in the tropics, see Cynthia Rosenzweig and Martin L. Parry, "Potential Impacts of Climate Change on World Food Supply: A Summary of a Recent International Study," in *Agricultural Dimensions of Global Climate Change*, ed. Harry Kaiser and Thomas E. Drennen (Delray Beach, Fla. : St. Lucie Press, 1993), pp. 87–116; and, for fuller detail, C. M. Rosenzweig et al., *Climate Change and World Food Supply* (Oxford: Environmental Change Unit, 1993). My own attempts to contribute to analysis of the ethical issues about climate change are "The Unavoidability of Justice," in Hurrell and Kingsbury, *The International Politics of the Environment*, pp. 373–97; "Subsistence Emissions and Luxury Emissions," *Law and Policy* 15, no. 1 (January 1993): 39–59; "After You: May Action by the Rich Be Contingent upon Action by the Poor?," *Indiana Journal of Global Legal Studies* 1, no. 2 (Spring 1994): 343–66; "Avoidable Necessity: Global Warming, International Fairness, and Alternative Energy," in *Theory and Practice*, NOMOS XXXVII, ed. Ian Shapiro and Judith Wagner DeCew (New York: New York University Press, 1995), pp. 239–64; "Equity in an International Agreement on Climate Change," *Equity and Social Considerations related to Climate Change: Proceedings of IPCC Working Group III Workshop, Nairobi 1994* (Nairobi: ICIPE Science Press, 1995), pp. 385–92; and "Environmental Change and the Varieties of Justice," in *Earthly Goods: Environmental Change and Social Justice*, ed. Fen Osler Hampson and Judith Reppy (Ithaca: Cornell University Press, 1996), pp. 9–29.

23. Thomas W. Pogge has made a similar point: "If we follow Rawls's brief sketch . . . we repeat a failing that is common to all historical social-contract doctrines. In assessing the institutional structure of a society by looking merely at how it affects (distributes benefits and burdens among) *its members*, we fail to come to terms with how our society affects the lives of foreigners (and how our lives are affected by how other societies are organized)— we disregard the (negative) externalities a national social contract may impose upon those who are *not* parties to it" (Thomas W. Pogge, *Realizing Rawls* [Ithaca: Cornell University Press, 1989], p. 256 [emphasis in original]). In this essay I concentrate on a specific subset of

negative externalities, physical harms, as I did in "Exporting Hazards," in *Boundaries: National Autonomy and Its Limits*, ed. Peter G. Brown and Henry Shue, Maryland Studies in Public Philosophy (Lanham, Md. : Rowman and Littlefield, 1982), pp. 107–45. For a society to ignore the physical harms its institutions inflict, provided that the harms are suffered by foreigners, is, I shall be arguing here, a foreign policy that is barbaric.

24. Walzer, *Just and Unjust Wars*, pp. 155, 156. I very briefly discussed a more general notion that I called "a responsibility to take due care," probably unconsciously influenced by the first edition of *Just and Unjust Wars* (1977), in "Subsistence Rights: Shall We Secure These Rights?," in *How Does the Constitution Secure Rights?*, ed. Robert A. Goldwin and William A. Schambra (Washington, D.C.: American Enterprise Institute for Public Policy Research, 1985), p. 92.

25. Walzer, *Just and Unjust Wars*, p. 153.

26. Ibid., p. 155. I have italicized Walzer's addition; he also changed "only" to "narrowly" in the second clause.

27. For provocative thoughts about legal change, see Alfred C. Aman, Jr., "The Earth as Eggshell Victim: A Global Perspective on Domestic Regulation," *Yale Law Journal* 102, no. 8 (June 1993): 2107–22; and Christopher D. Stone, *The Gnat Is Older than Man: Global Environment and Human Agenda* (Princeton: Princeton University Press, 1993). Aman's title refers to the "thin skull" rule of legal liability: you take your victim as you find him. Stone's title is from lines in the Talmud noted by his father, I. F. Stone: "The world was made for man, though he was the latecomer among its creatures. . . . Let him beware of being proud, lest he invite the retort that the gnat is older than he. "

28. These conditions are jointly sufficient for responsibility. Whether any of them are individually necessary conditions is another issue.

29. Jeff McMahan has pointed out that if one pressed the analogy with just-war restrictions hard enough, the conclusion reached would be not that no harm at all (with the four features I have listed) could be inflicted but that once one had taken due care, one could inflict only *proportionate* harm (as unintended "collateral damage"). I think this can be adequately dealt with in either of two ways. First, there is no compulsion to press the analogy that hard into every twist and turn of just-war doctrines. My only essential thesis is that even in matters of such extreme significance that a state could be justified in going to war over them, the state must nevertheless constrain how it attempts to win; it is not the case that in war everything is justified. Second—and essentially equivalent in substance—even if one were somehow forced to press the analogy to the point of granting that these kinds of harm (with the four features outlined) were not totally prohibited but restricted to being proportional to the ends being pursued, it is most unlikely that the ends being pursued by normal economic policies are sufficiently momentous to make the infliction of skin cancer (through ozone destruction) or the flooding of agricultural land and homes (through sea-level rise produced by global warming) anywhere near proportional unless one discounts the welfare of the billions of noncompatriots at some outrageously implausible rate. The single greatest cause of GHGs is superfluous driving of excessively powerful automobiles with extremely inefficient internal combustion engines (namely, sport utility vehicles and light trucks) that guzzle fossil fuel. See William K. Stevens, "With Energy Tug of War, U.S. Is Missing Its Goals," *New York Times*, November 28, 1995, pp. A1, B8. This is not even economically rational—it is sheer waste—much less urgently important enough to justify

physically harming people (and causing species extinctions, as climate change surely will). Severe damage to the vital interests of billions would not conceivably be a proportionate side effect qualitatively or quantitatively to the pursuit of frivolous whims by hundreds of millions. See Shue, "Subsistence Emissions and Luxury Emissions. "

30. See Walzer, *Just and Unjust Wars*, pp. 154–55, 188–96.

31. A more moderate conception of state sovereignty also has implications for military intervention, as I have tried to show in "Let Whatever Is Smoldering Erupt?: Conditional Sovereignty, Reviewable Intervention, and Rwanda 1994," in *Between Sovereignty and Global Governance: The State, Civil Society, and the United Nations*, ed. Chris Reus-Smit, Anthony Jervis, and Albert Paolini (New York: St. Martin's Press, forthcoming).

Index